Full Moon O Sagashite

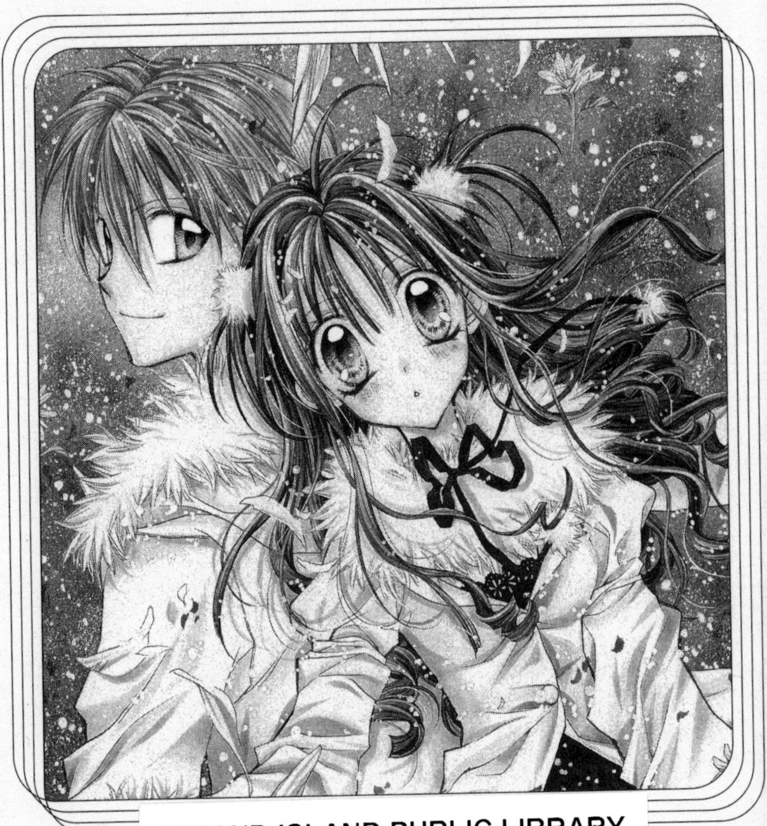

Story & Art by Arina Tanemura

Table of Contents

Chapter 28 – Full Moon o Sagashite ———————— 4

Chapter 29 – If My Wishes Will Never Come True, I Will... – 51

Final Chapter – To My One and Only Eichi ———————— 85

Bonus Story – A Rose on Monday ———————— 127

Bonus Manga – Totsugeki! Dokodoko ★ Final ———————— 131

Taiwan Autograph Session Report ———————— 135

Full Moon o Sagashite Super Dictionary ———————— 140

Penchi de Shakin ★ Special ———————— 154

Assistants' Comments ———————— 157

Kokoro Liner Notes ———————— 171

CHARACTER INTRODUCTIONS

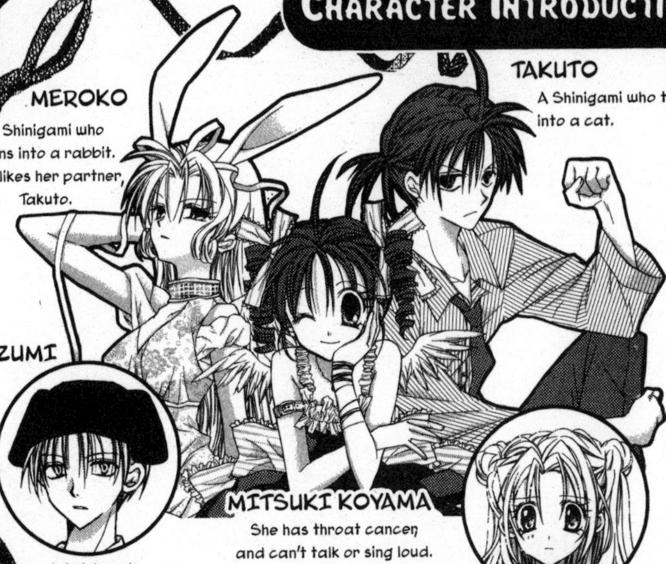

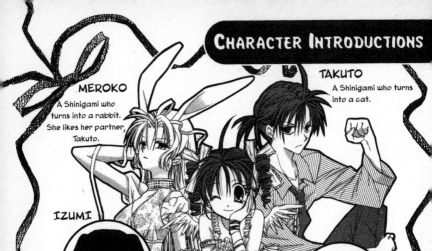

MEROKO
A Shinigami who turns into a rabbit. She likes her partner, Takuto.

TAKUTO
A Shinigami who turns into a cat.

IZUMI
A Shinigami. Meroko used to like him before, and now he likes her.

MITSUKI KOYAMA
She has throat cancer and can't talk or sing loud. She's not good at competing or quarreling.

MITSUKI KOYAMA
Mitsuki's alter ego, the singer "Fullmoon."

Full Moon o Sagashite

Mitsuki is 12. She loves Eichi, who's studying in the U.S., and she dreams of fulfilling her promise to him by becoming a singer. But Mitsuki has sarcoma, a form of cancer in her throat. Dr. Wakaoji wants her to have an operation, but Mitsuki refuses because it would destroy her singing voice. One day, two Shinigami appear, Takuto and Meroko, and transform her into a healthy sixteen-year-old. Because of the transformation, Mitsuki is able to make her debut as "Fullmoon."

As Takuto watches over Mitsuki during her successful singing career, he begins to fall in love with her. Meroko, who is in love with Takuto, asks her former partner, Izumi, to prevent the two from getting any clos However, when Meroko and Izumi come in contact with Mitsuki's pure heart, they change their attitude towa her, and now they watch over Mitsuki too.

The Shinigamiiz discover that Eichi died in an airplane crash and that Mitsuki had known all along. When Mitsuki learns that the Shinigamiiz know the truth about Eichi, she disappears. Takuto finds Mitsuki and tells her that he loves her, but Mitsuki still loves Eichi. The only thing left for her is to keep singing.

But on the day she was going to meet Takuto for a date, Mitsuki sees Takuto together with his ex-girlfriend, Hikari. She chases the two, but falls unconscious. She is taken to a hospital, and must decide whether she'll go through with the operation. The operation holds no guarantee of savin her life, and even if it is a success, she will not be able to sing again. Mitsuki feels Takuto's love in the way he cheers her up, and she decides to go through with the operation. Takuto and Meroko go to the Underworld to save Mitsuki's life. Meanwhile, Mitsuki is trapped by Jonathan Sheldan, Head of the Shinigami Pediatrics Ward...

STORY THUS FAR

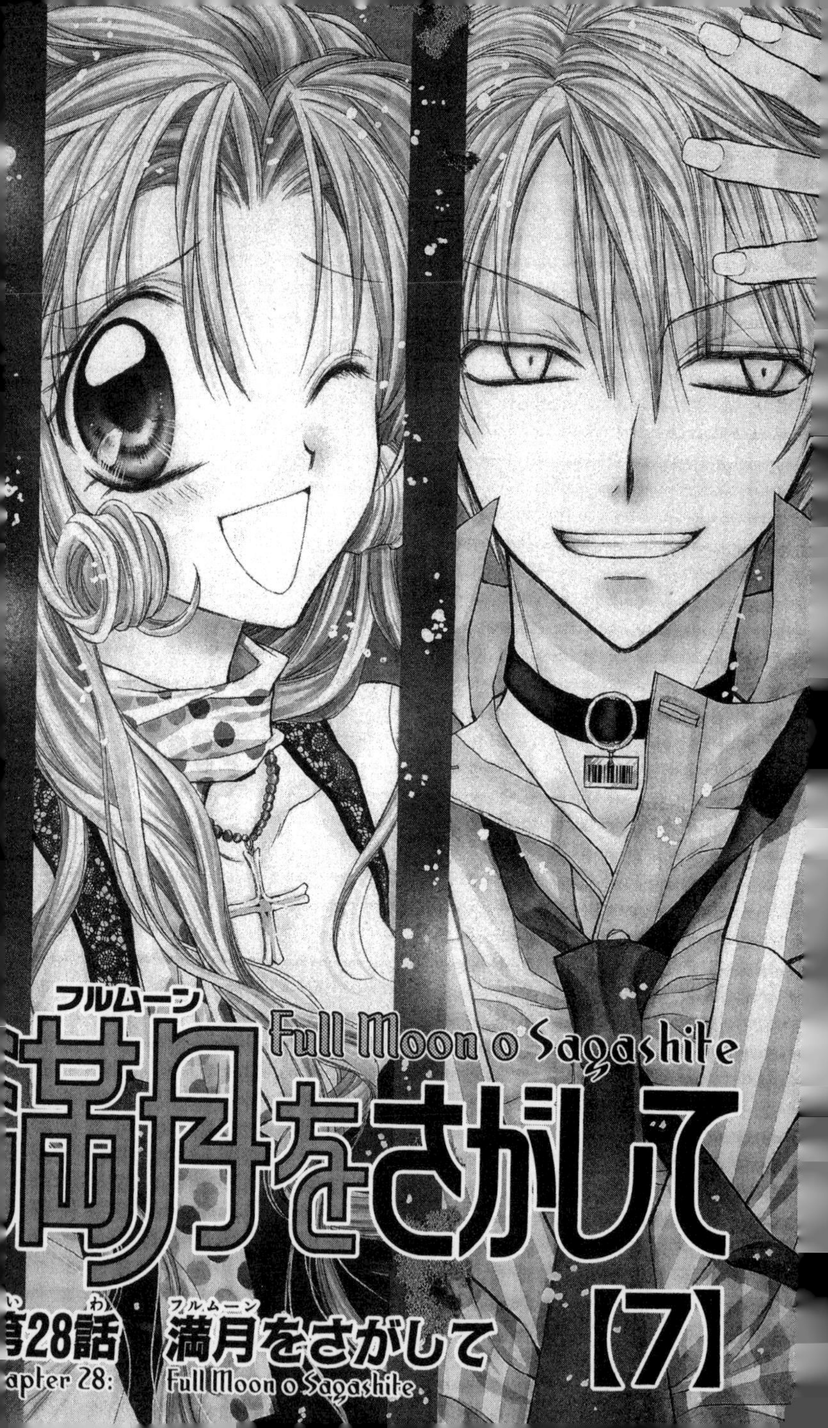
フルムーン
満月をさがして
Full Moon o Sagashite
第28話 満月をさがして【7】
apter 28: Full Moon o Sagashite

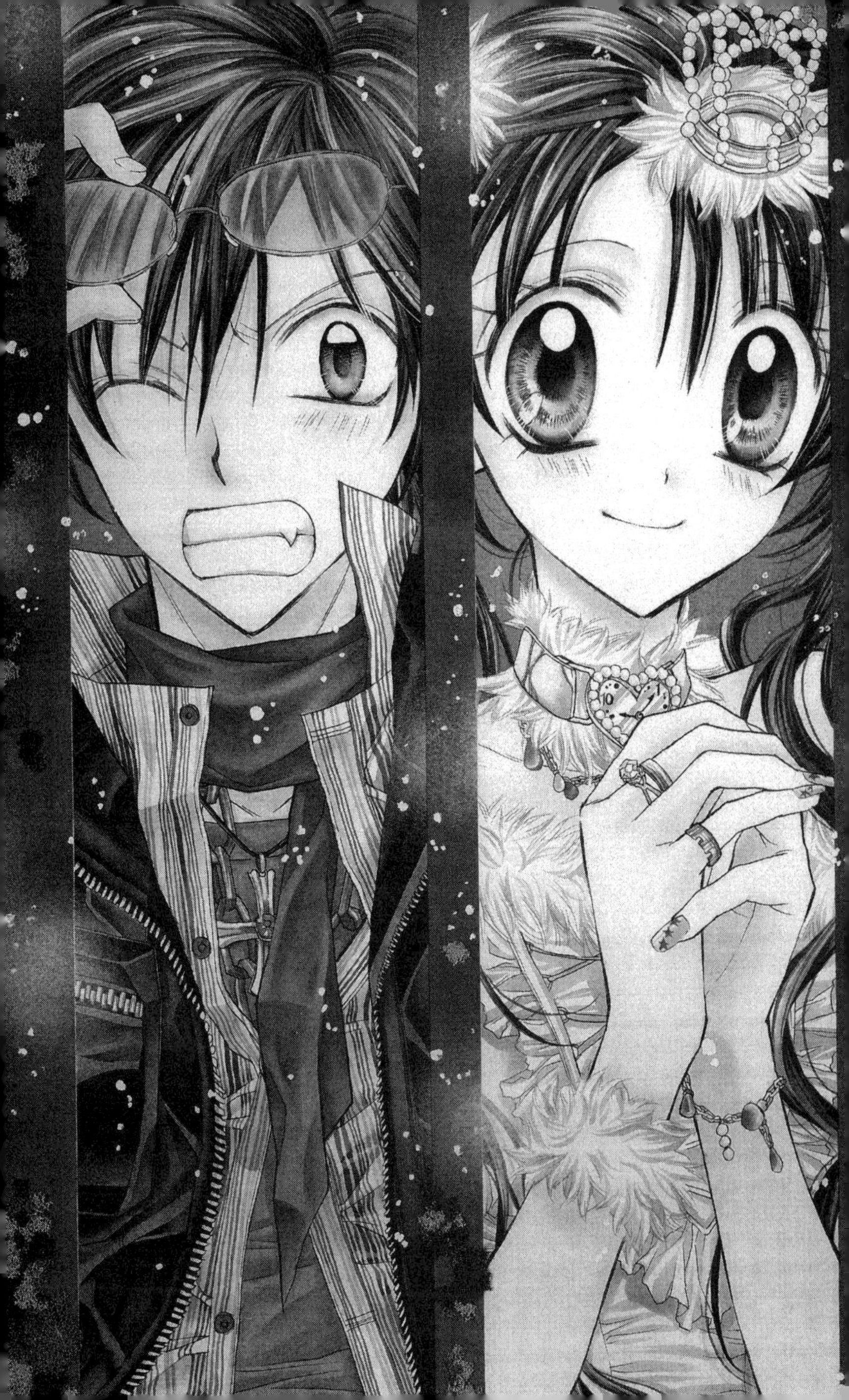

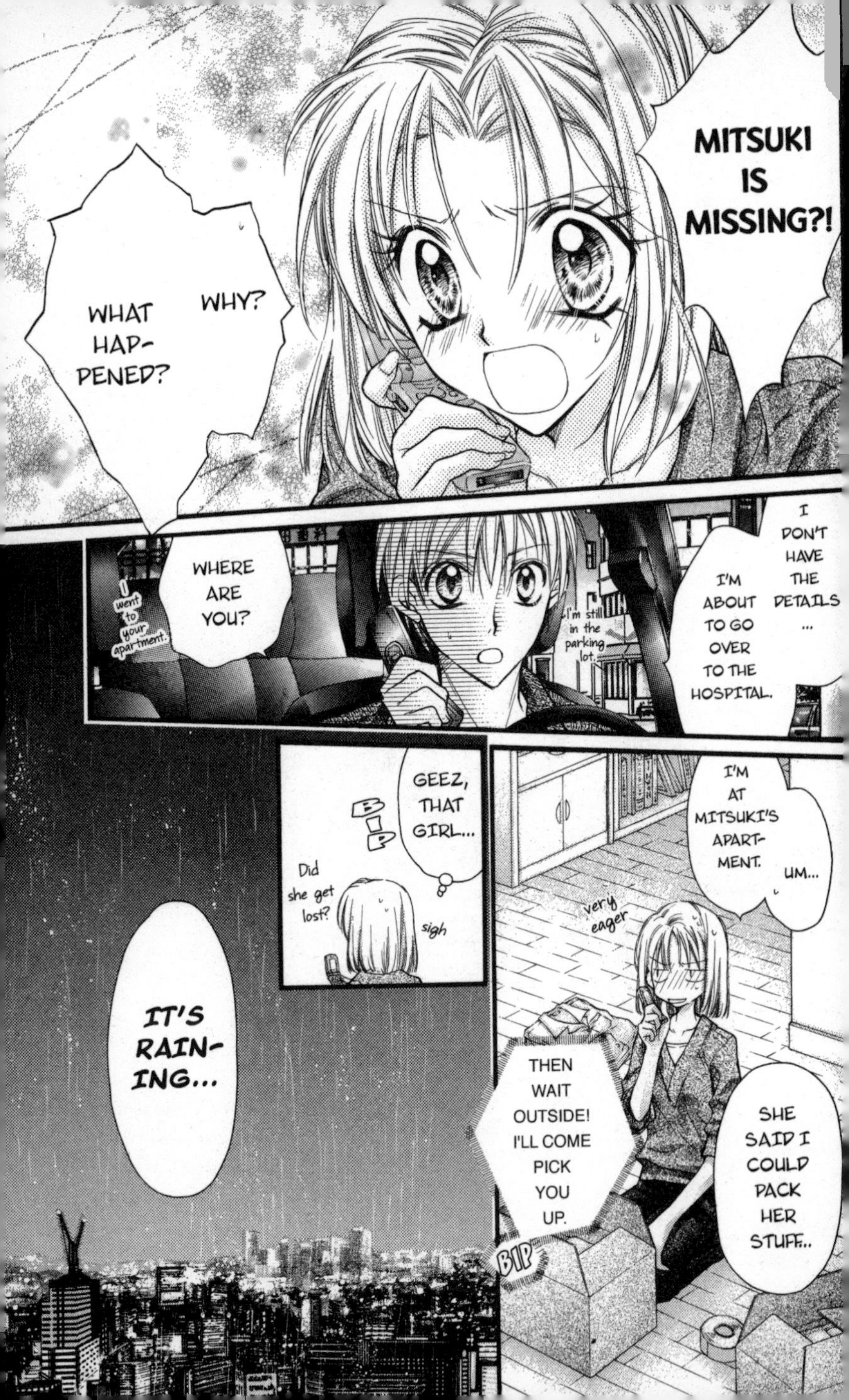
MITSUKI IS MISSING?!
WHY?
WHAT HAPPENED?
I DON'T HAVE THE DETAILS ...
I'M ABOUT TO GO OVER TO THE HOSPITAL.
I'm still in the parking lot.
WHERE ARE YOU?
I went to your apartment.
I'M AT MITSUKI'S APARTMENT.
UM...
very eager
SHE SAID I COULD PACK HER STUFF..
THEN WAIT OUTSIDE! I'LL COME PICK YOU UP.
BIP
GEEZ, THAT GIRL...
BIP
Did she get lost?
sigh
IT'S RAINING...

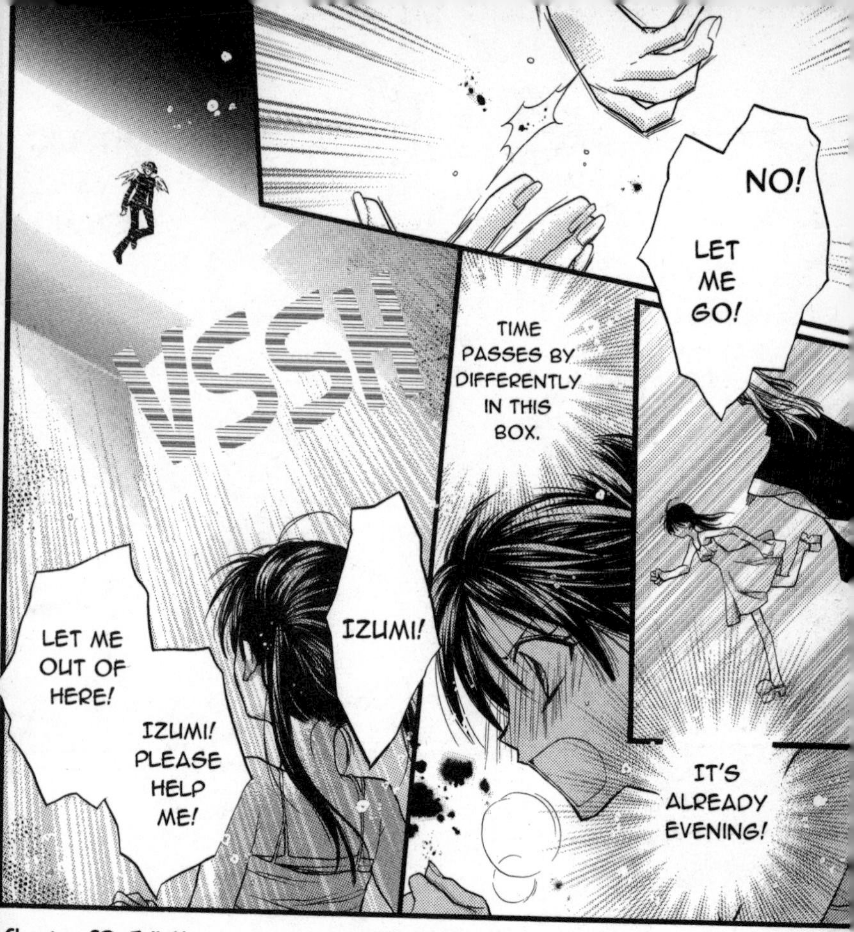
NO!
LET ME GO!
VSSH
IT'S ALREADY EVENING!
TIME PASSES BY DIFFERENTLY IN THIS BOX.
IZUMI!
LET ME OUT OF HERE!
IZUMI! PLEASE HELP ME!

Chapter 28: Full Moon o Sagashite Cover Copy I love every one of you!!

I drew this chapter in the hospital, as I was hospitalized...thank you so much, doctors and nurses. //// It was fun, although I inconvenienced a lot of people.

This chapter mainly features Shinigamiiz...well, Izumi-kun. Because I had Sakamoto Maaya-san's "Hikari Are," this chapter turned out really well!! The song really matched the chapter, so I was really able to envision everything! (I apologize to Maaya-san fans. It's just my image of the song.

Mitsuki-chan's feelings of wanting to die to become the same as Eichi-kun, and of wanting to live if there are people who need her...finally, finally came to the surface.

To chase a dead lover or to live for the moment may seem beautiful, but Mitsuki-chan wanted to find the strength of the soul that overcomes everything.

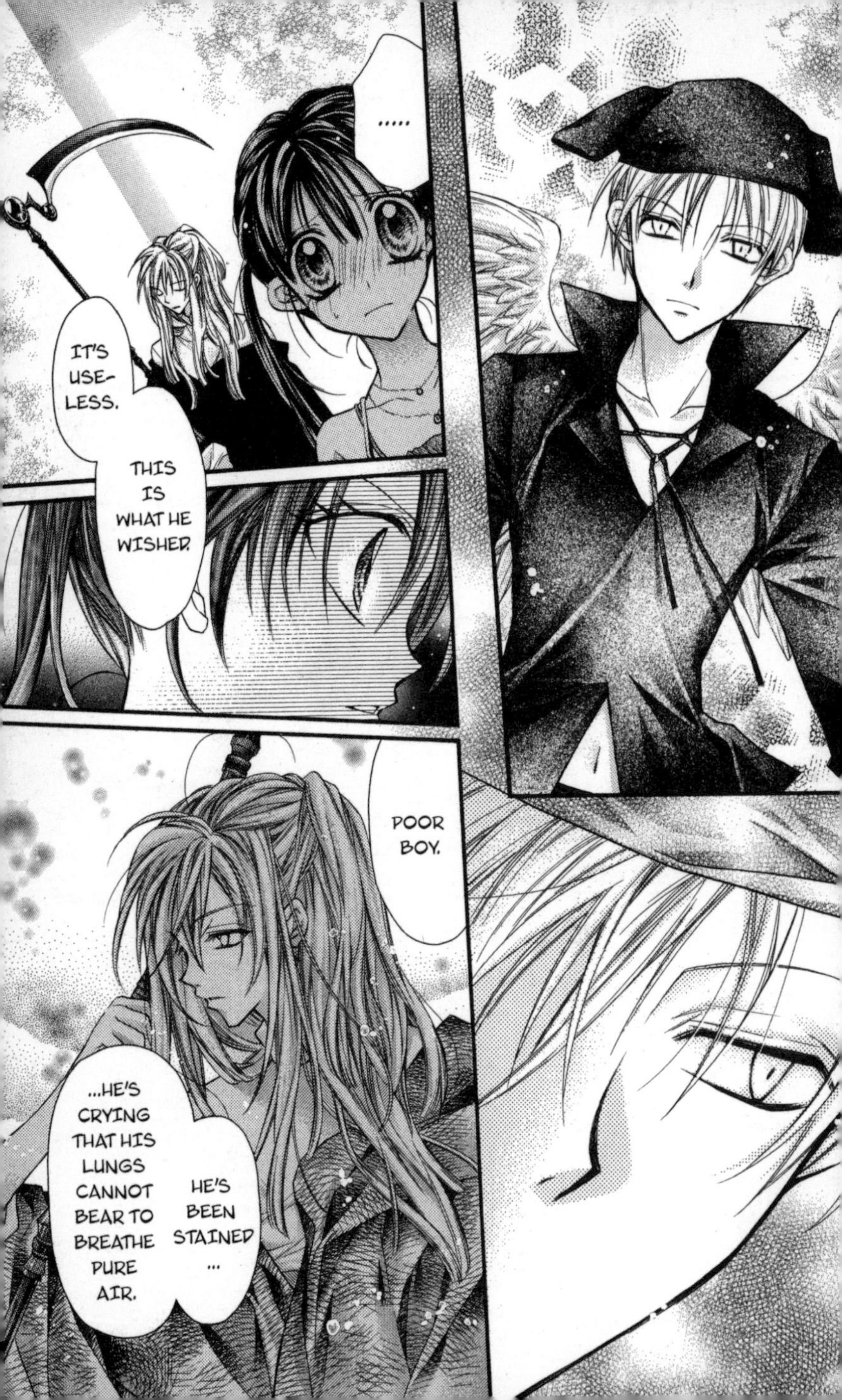
.....
IT'S USE-LESS.
THIS IS WHAT HE WISHED.
POOR BOY.
HE'S BEEN STAINED...
...HE'S CRYING THAT HIS LUNGS CANNOT BEAR TO BREATHE PURE AIR.

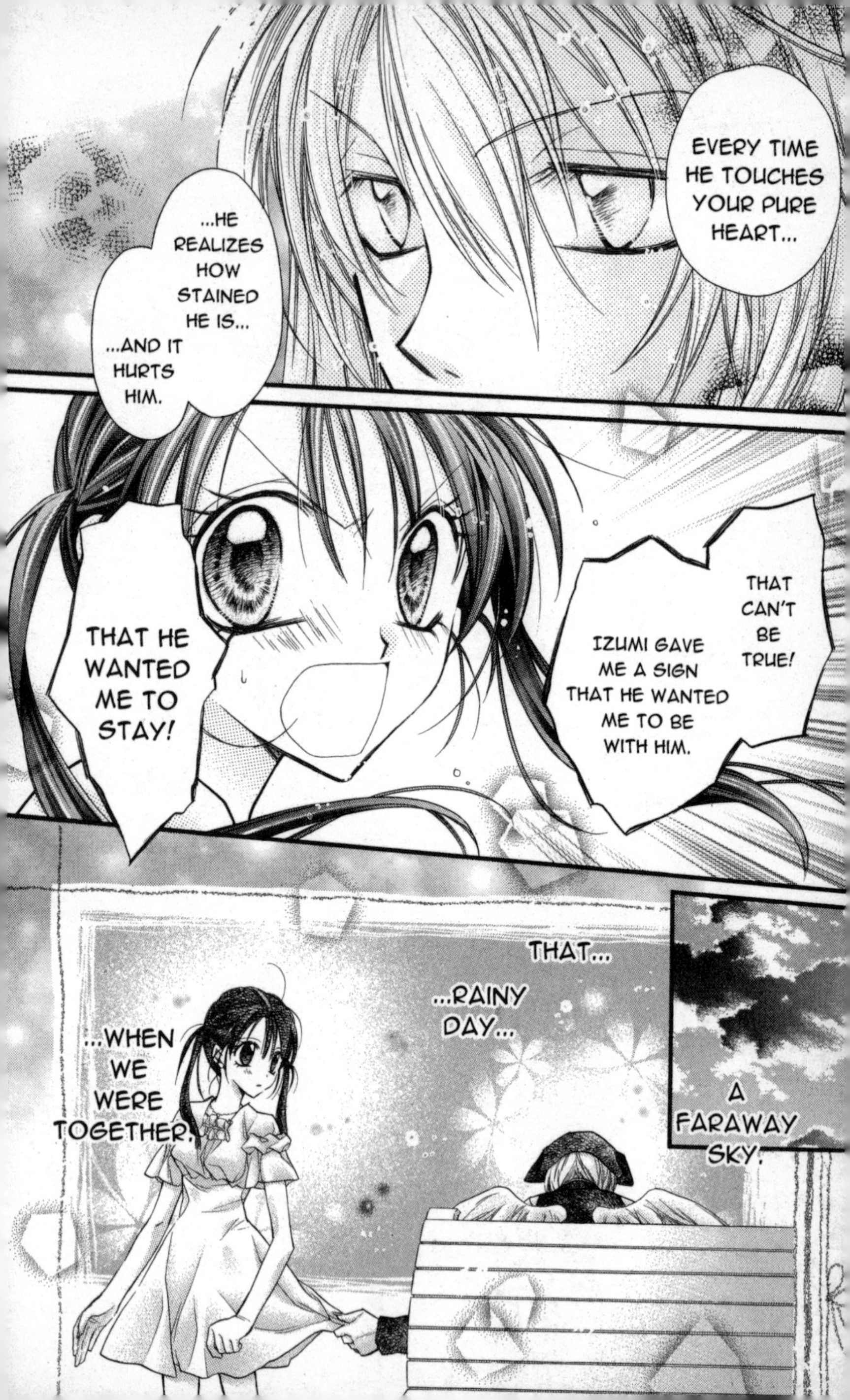
EVERY TIME HE TOUCHES YOUR PURE HEART...
...HE REALIZES HOW STAINED HE IS...
...AND IT HURTS HIM.
THAT CAN'T BE TRUE!
IZUMI GAVE ME A SIGN THAT HE WANTED ME TO BE WITH HIM.
THAT HE WANTED ME TO STAY!
A FARAWAY SKY.
THAT...
...RAINY DAY...
...WHEN WE WERE TOGETHER.

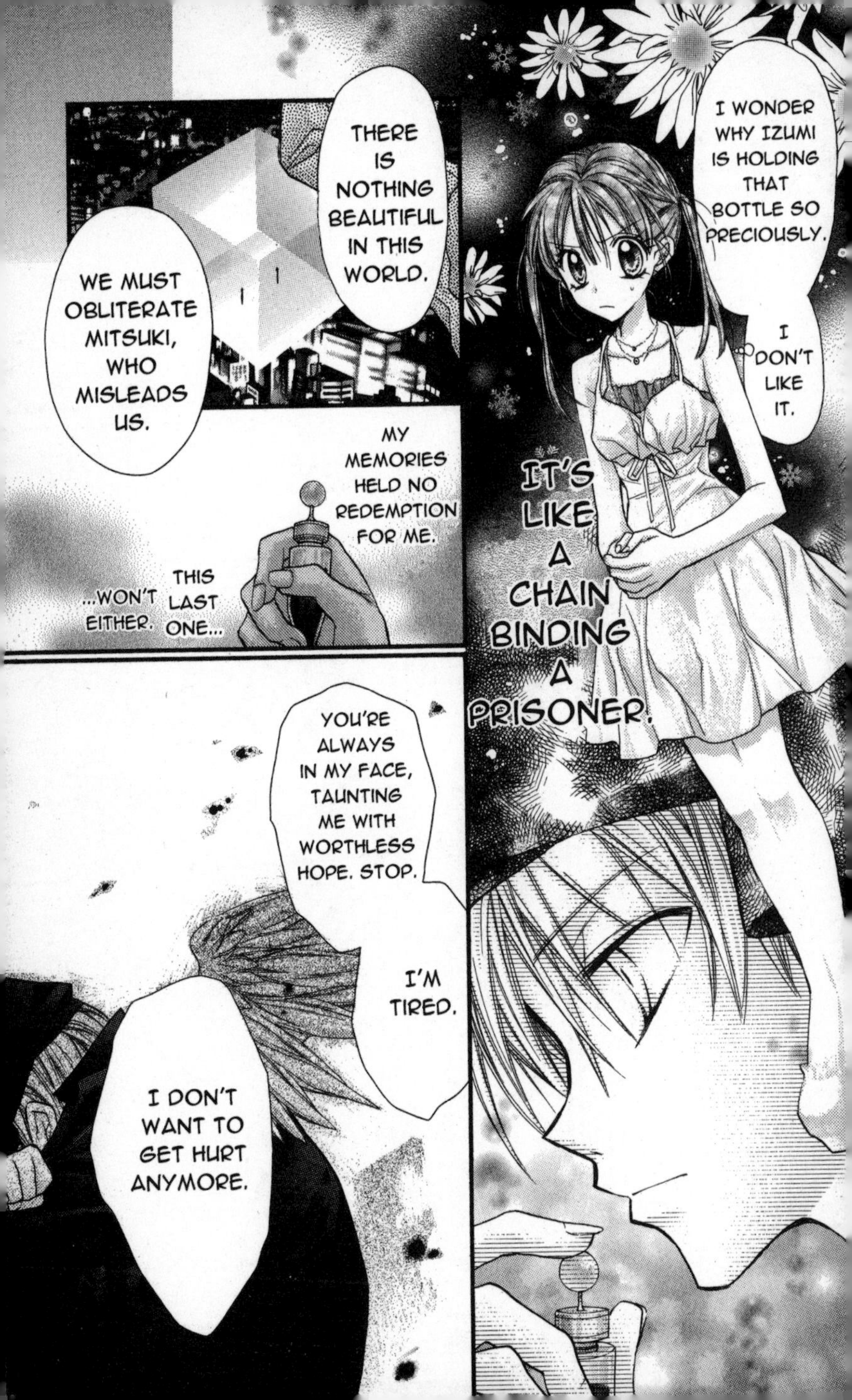
I WONDER WHY IZUMI IS HOLDING THAT BOTTLE SO PRECIOUSLY.
I DON'T LIKE IT.
IT'S LIKE A CHAIN BINDING A PRISONER.
THERE IS NOTHING BEAUTIFUL IN THIS WORLD.
WE MUST OBLITERATE MITSUKI, WHO MISLEADS US.
MY MEMORIES HELD NO REDEMPTION FOR ME.
THIS LAST ONE...
...WON'T EITHER.
YOU'RE ALWAYS IN MY FACE, TAUNTING ME WITH WORTHLESS HOPE. STOP.
I'M TIRED.
I DON'T WANT TO GET HURT ANYMORE.

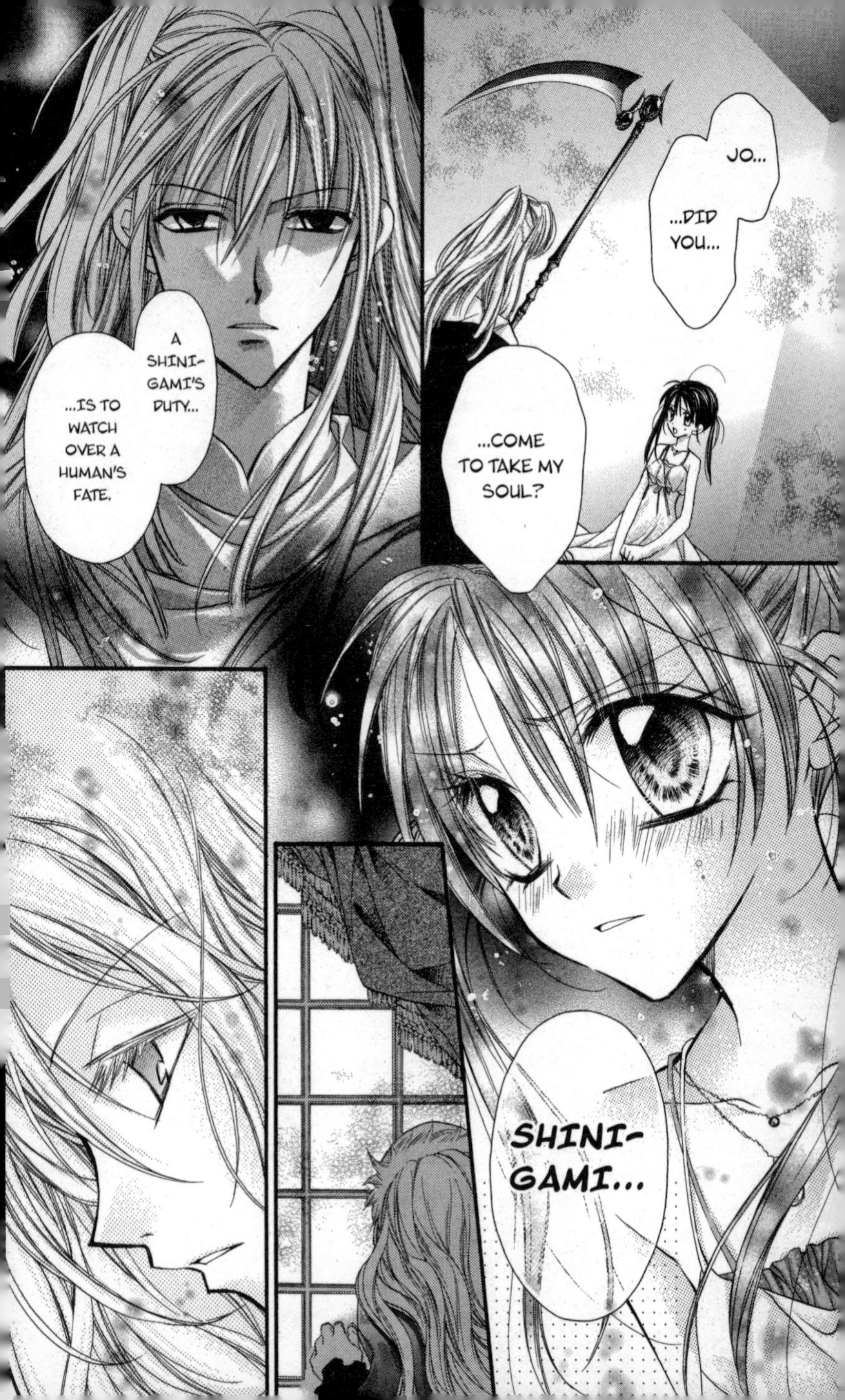
JO...
...DID YOU...
...COME TO TAKE MY SOUL?
A SHINIGAMI'S DUTY...
...IS TO WATCH OVER A HUMAN'S FATE.
SHINI-GAMI...

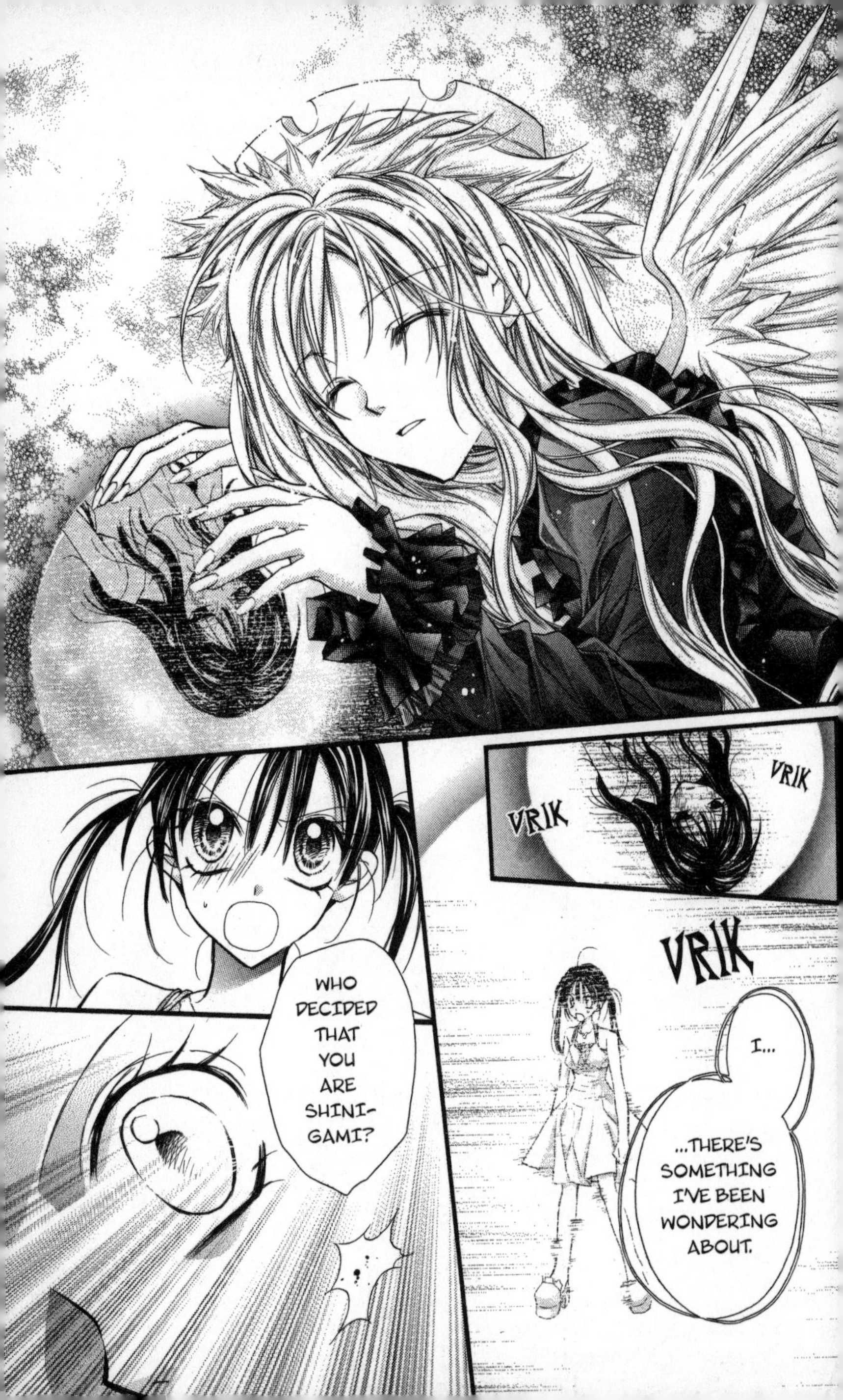
VRIK
VRIK
VRIK
I...
...THERE'S SOMETHING I'VE BEEN WONDERING ABOUT.
WHO DECIDED THAT YOU ARE SHINIGAMI?

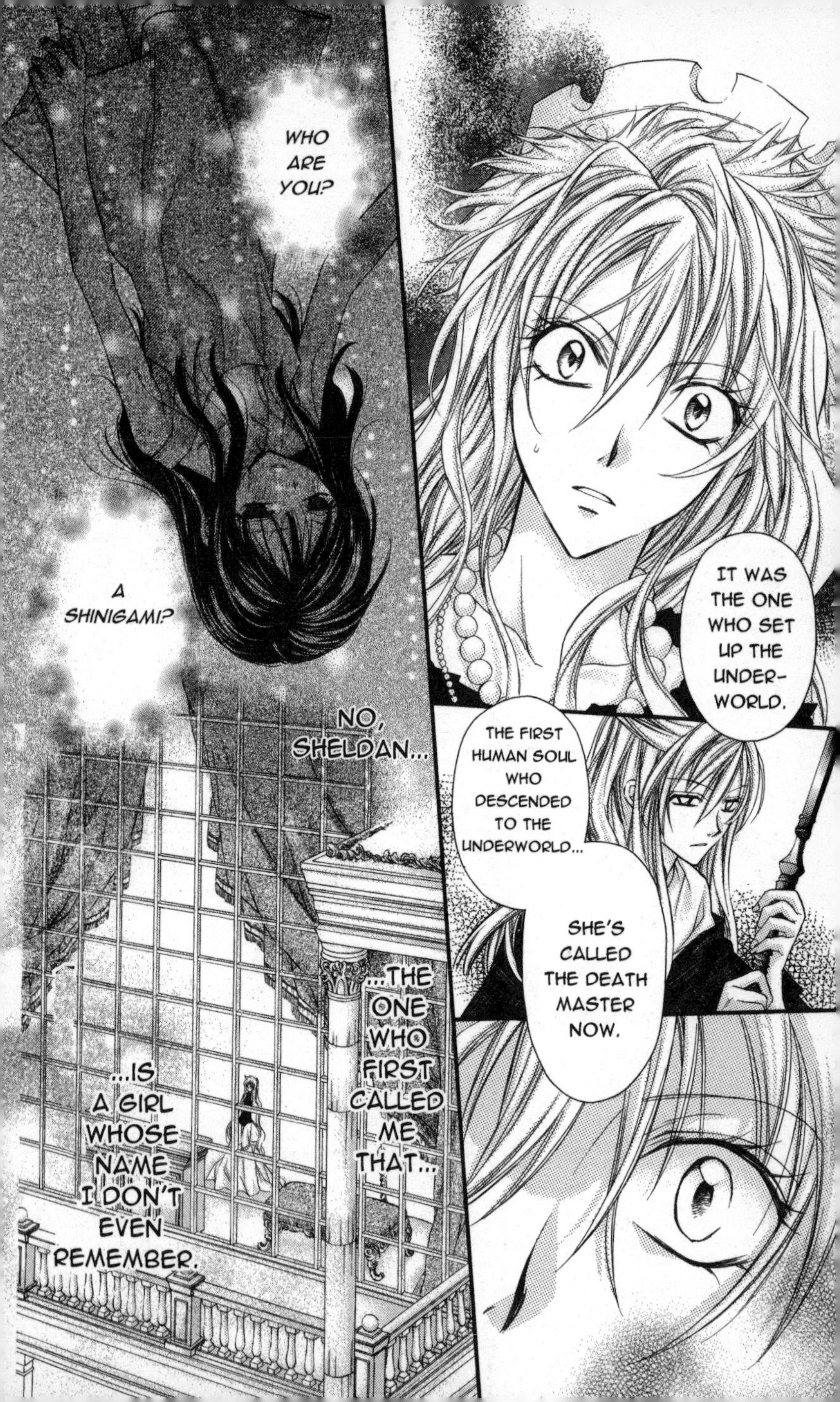
IT WAS THE ONE WHO SET UP THE UNDER-WORLD.
THE FIRST HUMAN SOUL WHO DESCENDED TO THE UNDERWORLD...
SHE'S CALLED THE DEATH MASTER NOW.
WHO ARE YOU?
A SHINIGAMI?
NO, SHELDAN...
...THE ONE WHO FIRST CALLED ME THAT...
...IS A GIRL WHOSE NAME I DON'T EVEN REMEMBER.

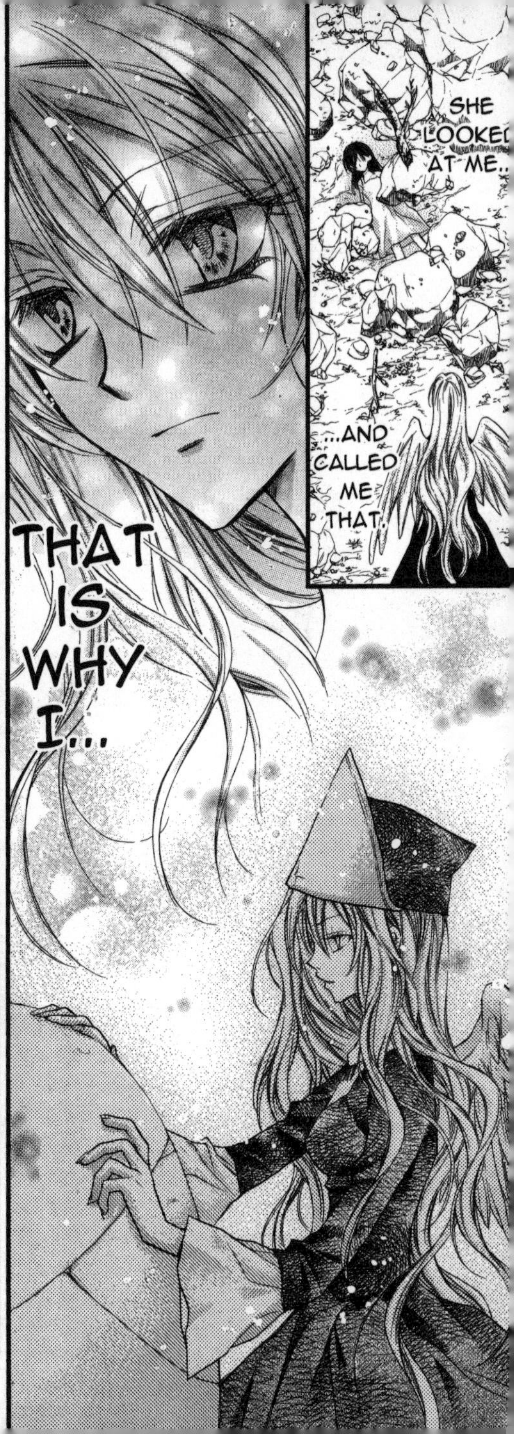
SHE LOOKED AT ME...
...AND CALLED ME THAT.
THAT IS WHY I...

Penshaki Special!!

Being Hospitalized 1

Doom!! Doom!

This is the record of what happened to me when drawing Chapter 28 of *Full Moon o Sagashite*.

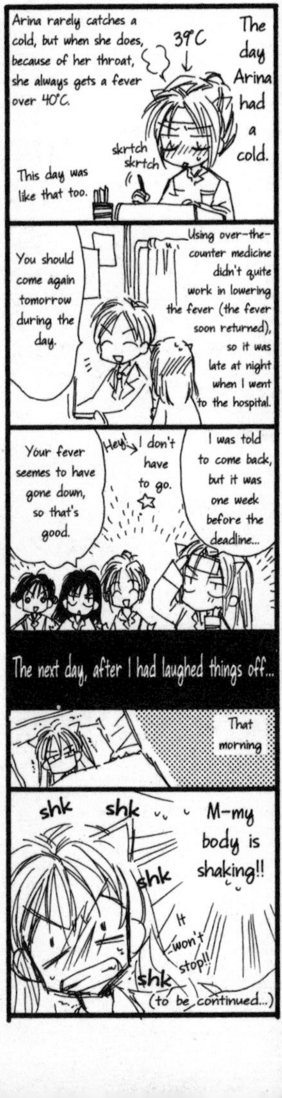
The day Arina had a cold.
Arina rarely catches a cold, but when she does, because of her throat, she always gets a fever over 40°C.
39°C
skrtch skrtch
This day was like that too.
Using over-the-counter medicine didn't quite work in lowering the fever (the fever soon returned), so it was late at night when I went to the hospital.
You should come again tomorrow during the day.
I was told to come back, but it was one week before the deadline...
Hey!
I don't have to go.
Your fever seemes to have gone down, so that's good.
The next day, after I had laughed things off...
That morning
M-my body is shaking!!
shk shk
shk
It won't stop!!
shk
(to be continued...)

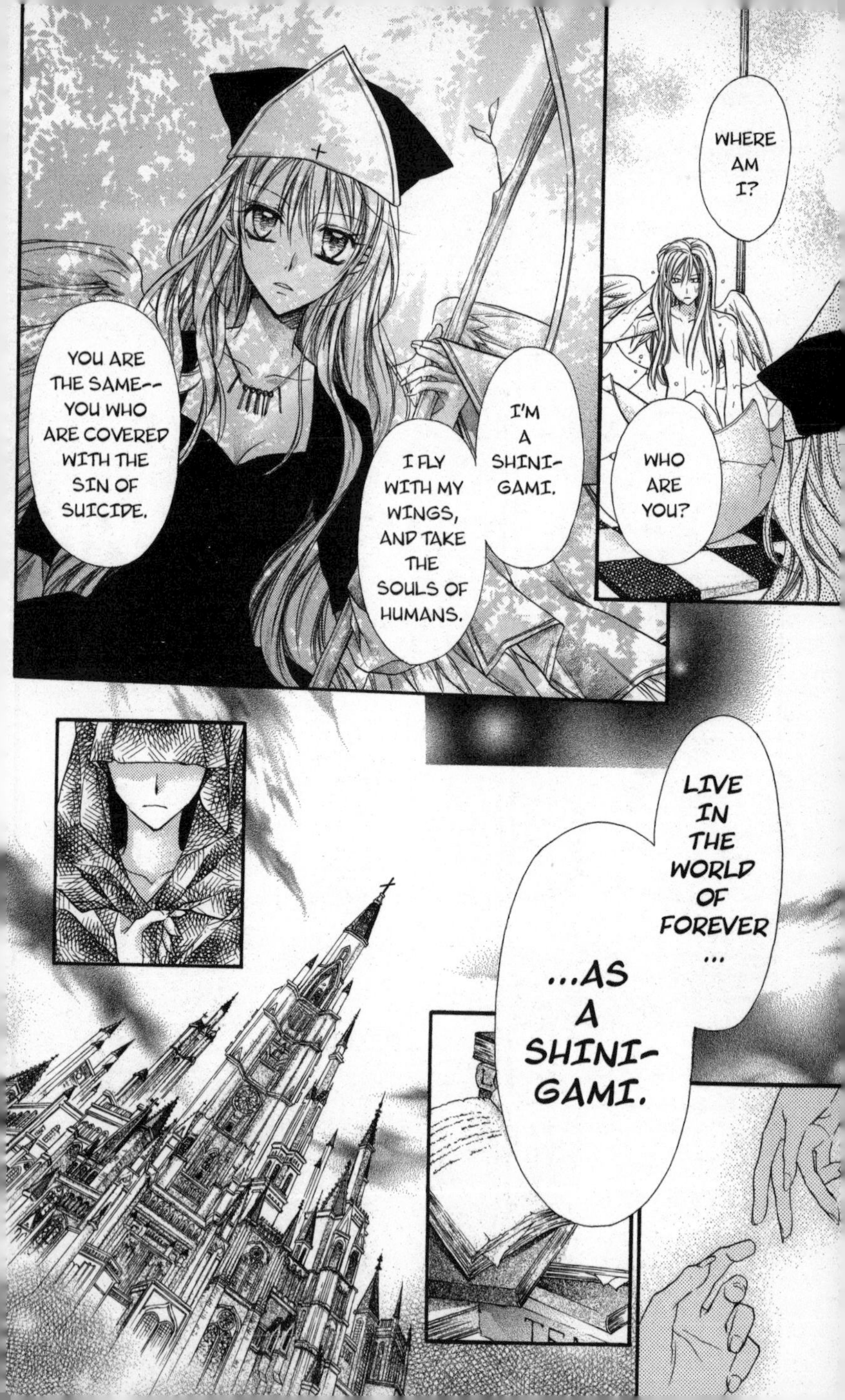
WHERE AM I?
WHO ARE YOU?
I'M A SHINI-GAMI.
I FLY WITH MY WINGS, AND TAKE THE SOULS OF HUMANS.
YOU ARE THE SAME-- YOU WHO ARE COVERED WITH THE SIN OF SUICIDE.
LIVE IN THE WORLD OF FOREVER ...
...AS A SHINI-GAMI.

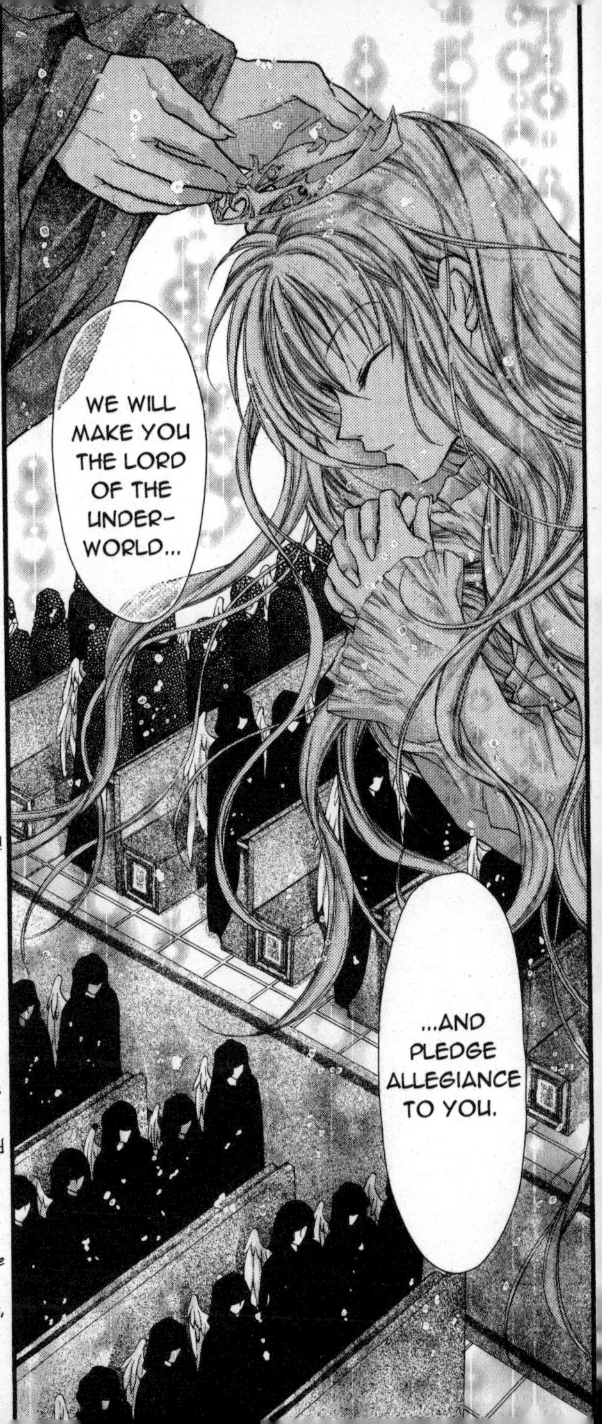
WE WILL MAKE YOU THE LORD OF THE UNDER-WORLD...
...AND PLEDGE ALLEGIANCE TO YOU.

Hello.

I'm Arina Tanemura!! I bring you the final volume of *Full Moon o Sagashite*!

In this volume, I've reversed the 1/4 space and 1/3 space, and will do my talking in the 1/4 space and the *Penshakis* in the 1/3 space. (Because it's the *Penshaki* special.)

There were so many things about *Full Moon*... nod nod

I have strong feelings for each of the characters.

I'd like to write more, but nothing comes out. It's probably because I'm satisfied that I "drew" everything. So I can't write much...

I can write about things other than the story. So here's the things that made me happy.

Arina's **BEST 5!**

1. Calendar (2004) on sale!! Yay! (Sorry—I was really happy about that...)
2. Second illustration book published!! (I'm sorry I'm only mentioning things about myself.) Woo hoo!
3. The anime being made!!! Yay! Yay! No matter how many times it happens, it's a fresh happiness.
4. Manga completed!! You tend to forget it when you are a veteran (I am?), but I'm happy every time a tankobon comes out.
5. Supplementary *Ribon* issue for *Full Moon* published! I was really happy about it...like, is this allowed?!

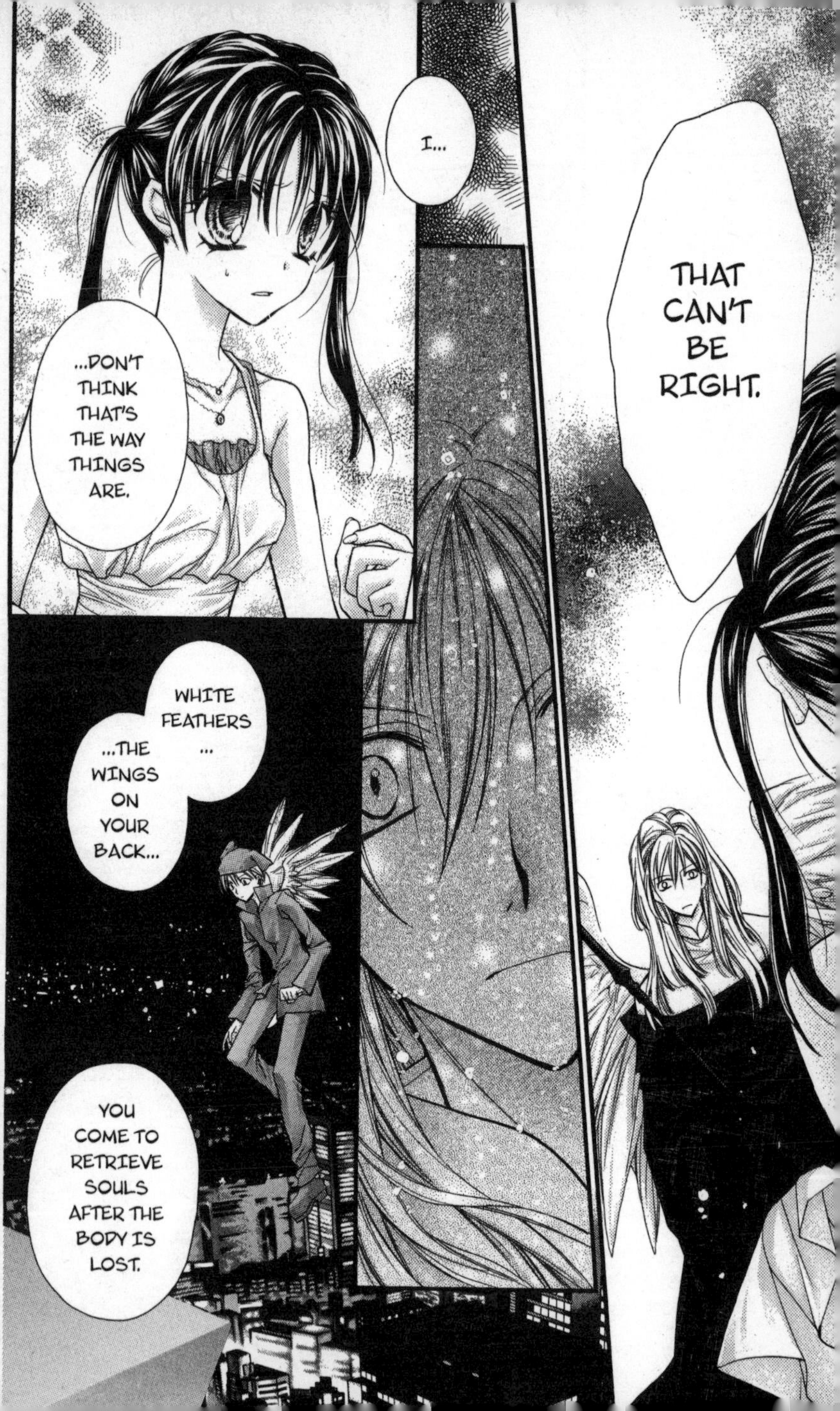
THAT CAN'T BE RIGHT.
I...
...DON'T THINK THAT'S THE WAY THINGS ARE.
WHITE FEATHERS...
...THE WINGS ON YOUR BACK...
YOU COME TO RETRIEVE SOULS AFTER THE BODY IS LOST.

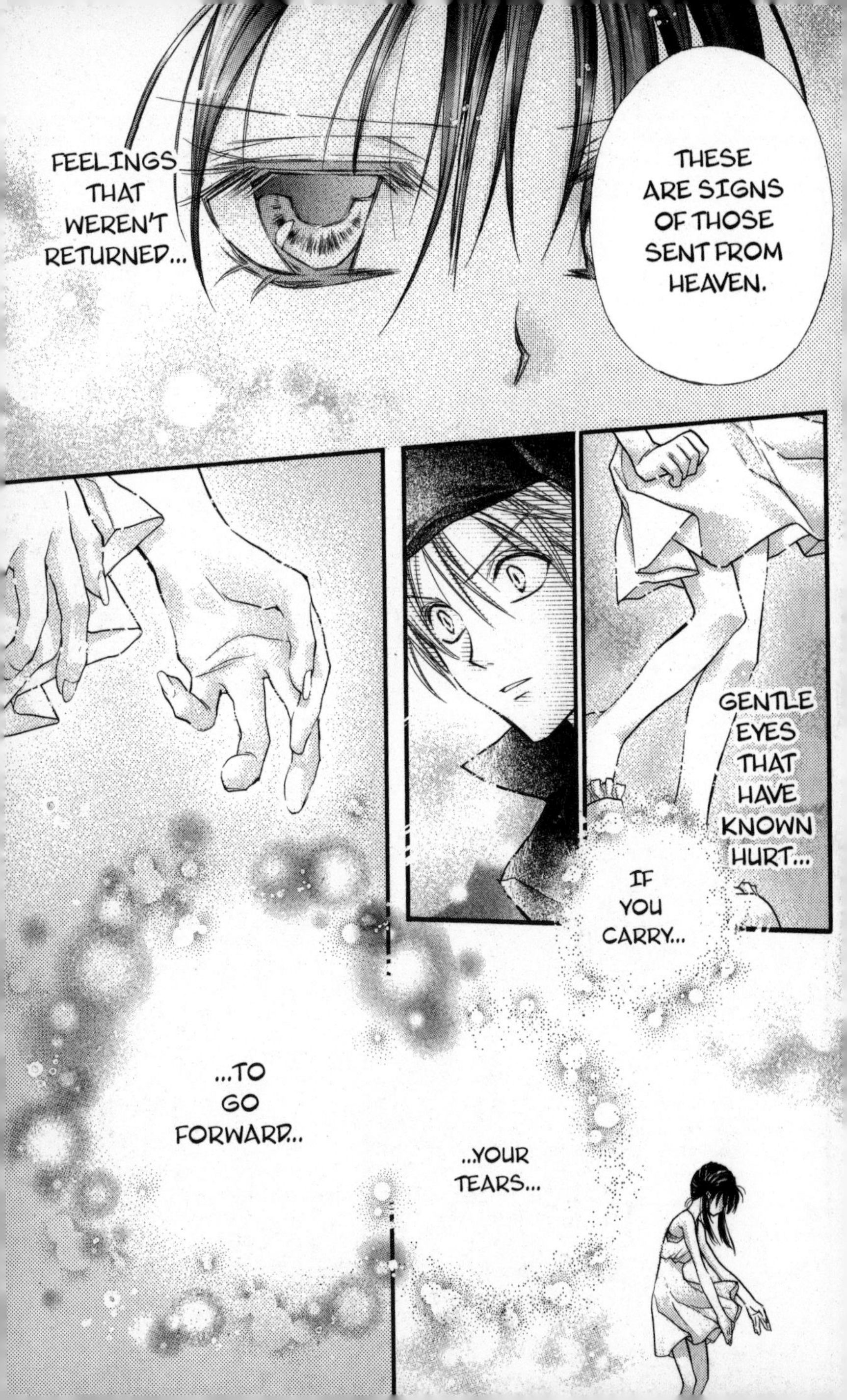
THESE ARE SIGNS OF THOSE SENT FROM HEAVEN.
FEELINGS THAT WEREN'T RETURNED...
GENTLE EYES THAT HAVE KNOWN HURT...
IF YOU CARRY...
...YOUR TEARS...
...TO GO FORWARD...

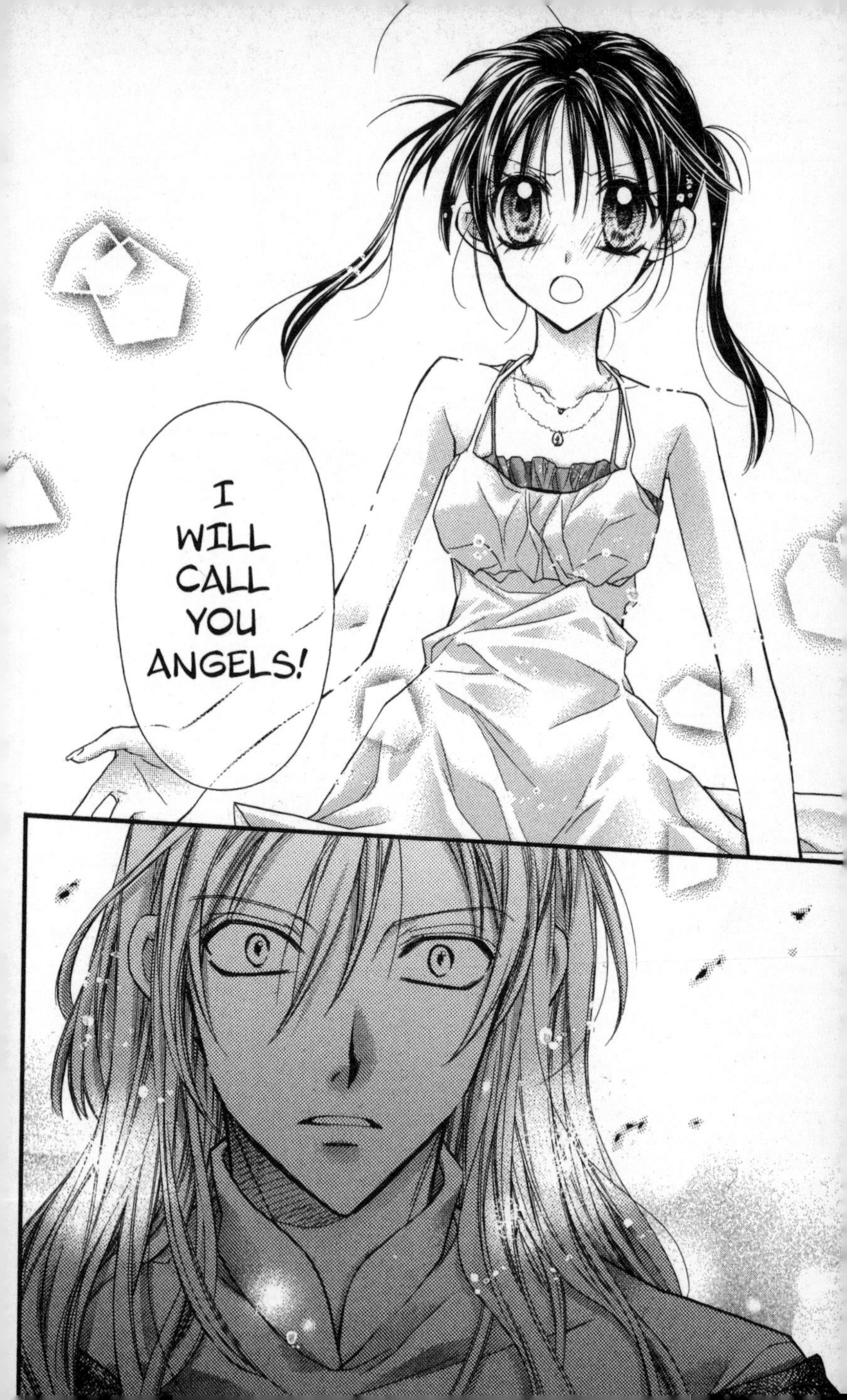
I WILL CALL YOU ANGELS!

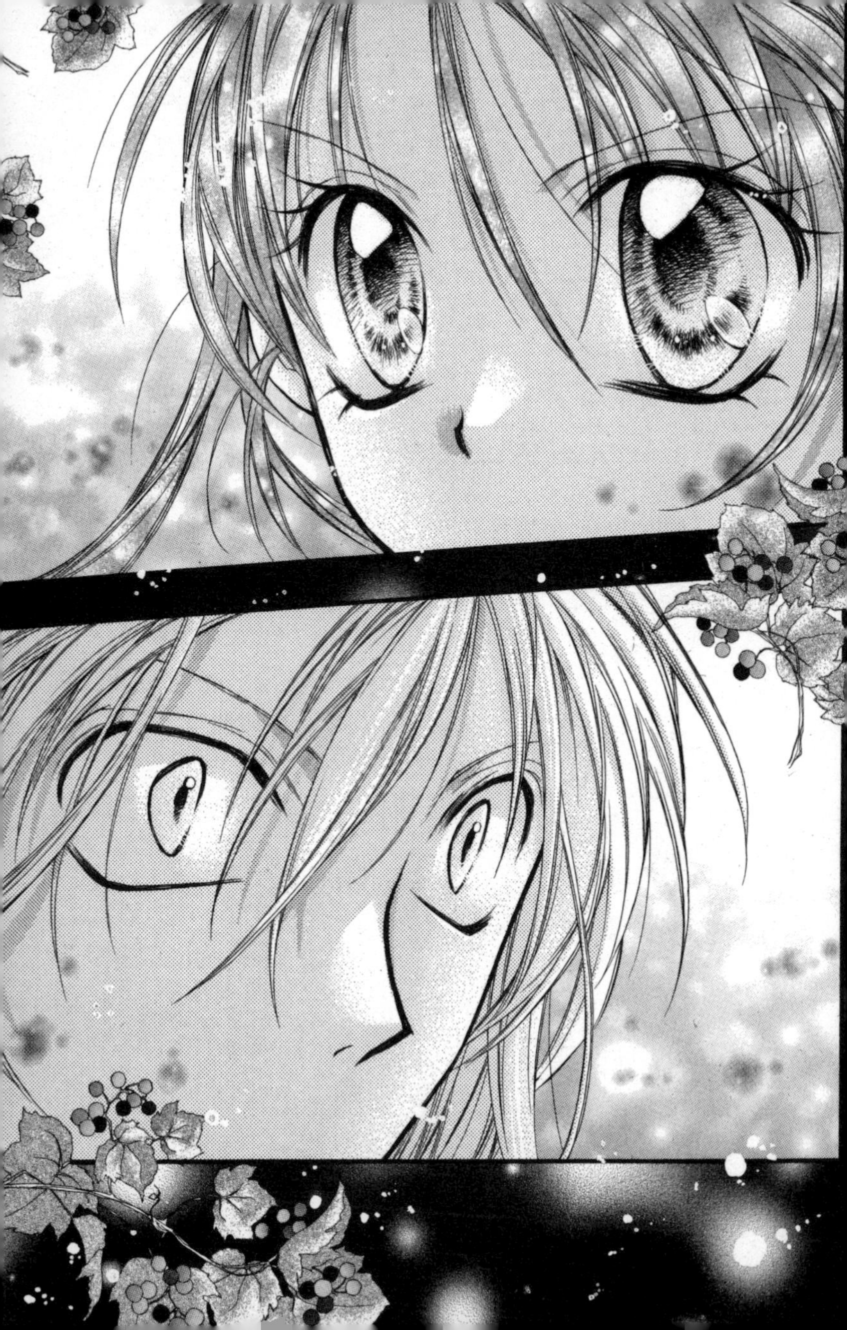

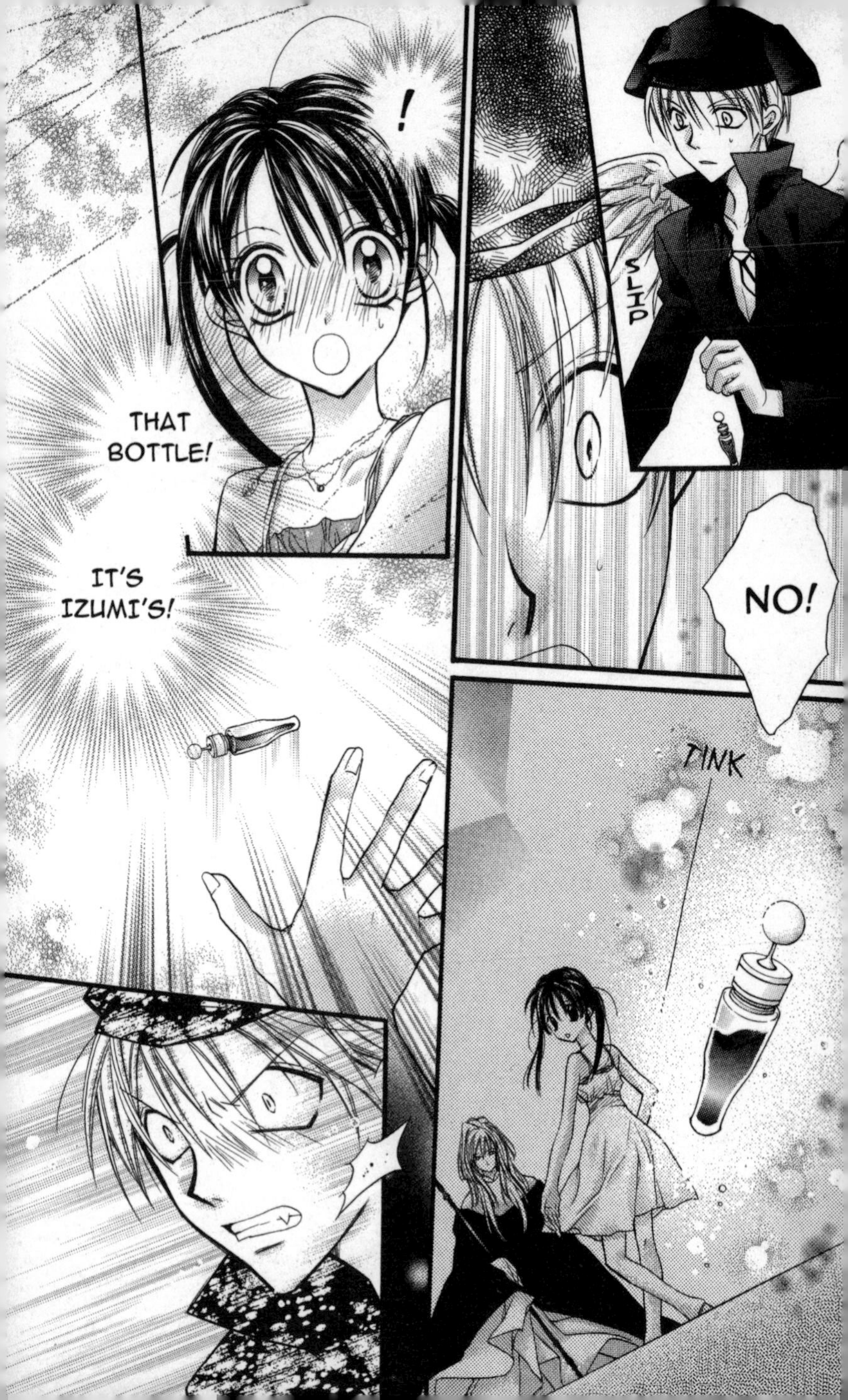
SLIP
NO!
!
THAT BOTTLE!
IT'S IZUMI'S!
TINK

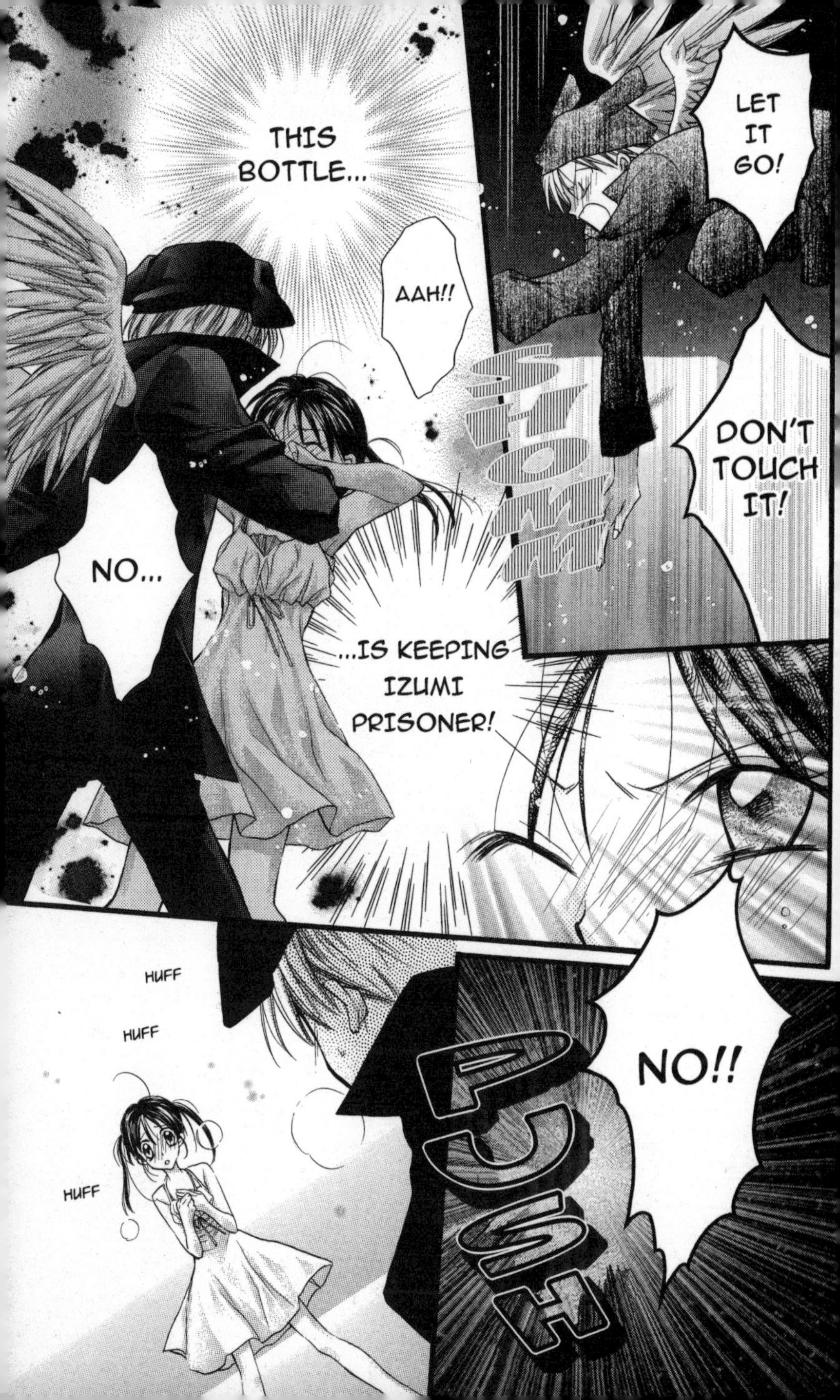
LET IT GO!
DON'T TOUCH IT!
THIS BOTTLE...
AAH!!
NO...
...IS KEEPING IZUMI PRISONER!
NO!!
PUSH
HUFF
HUFF
HUFF

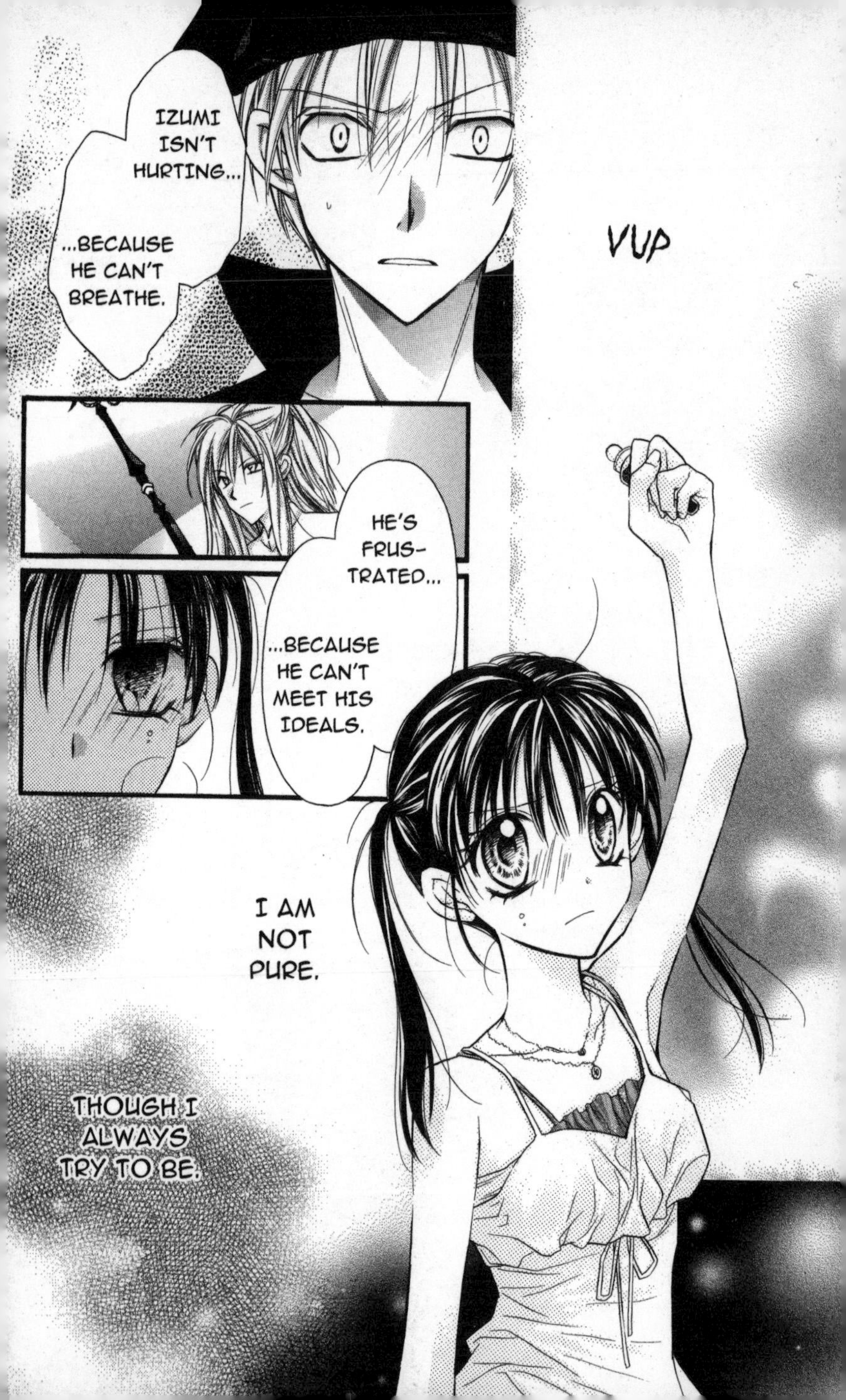
VUP
IZUMI ISN'T HURTING...
...BECAUSE HE CAN'T BREATHE.
HE'S FRUS-TRATED...
...BECAUSE HE CAN'T MEET HIS IDEALS.
I AM NOT PURE.
THOUGH I ALWAYS TRY TO BE.

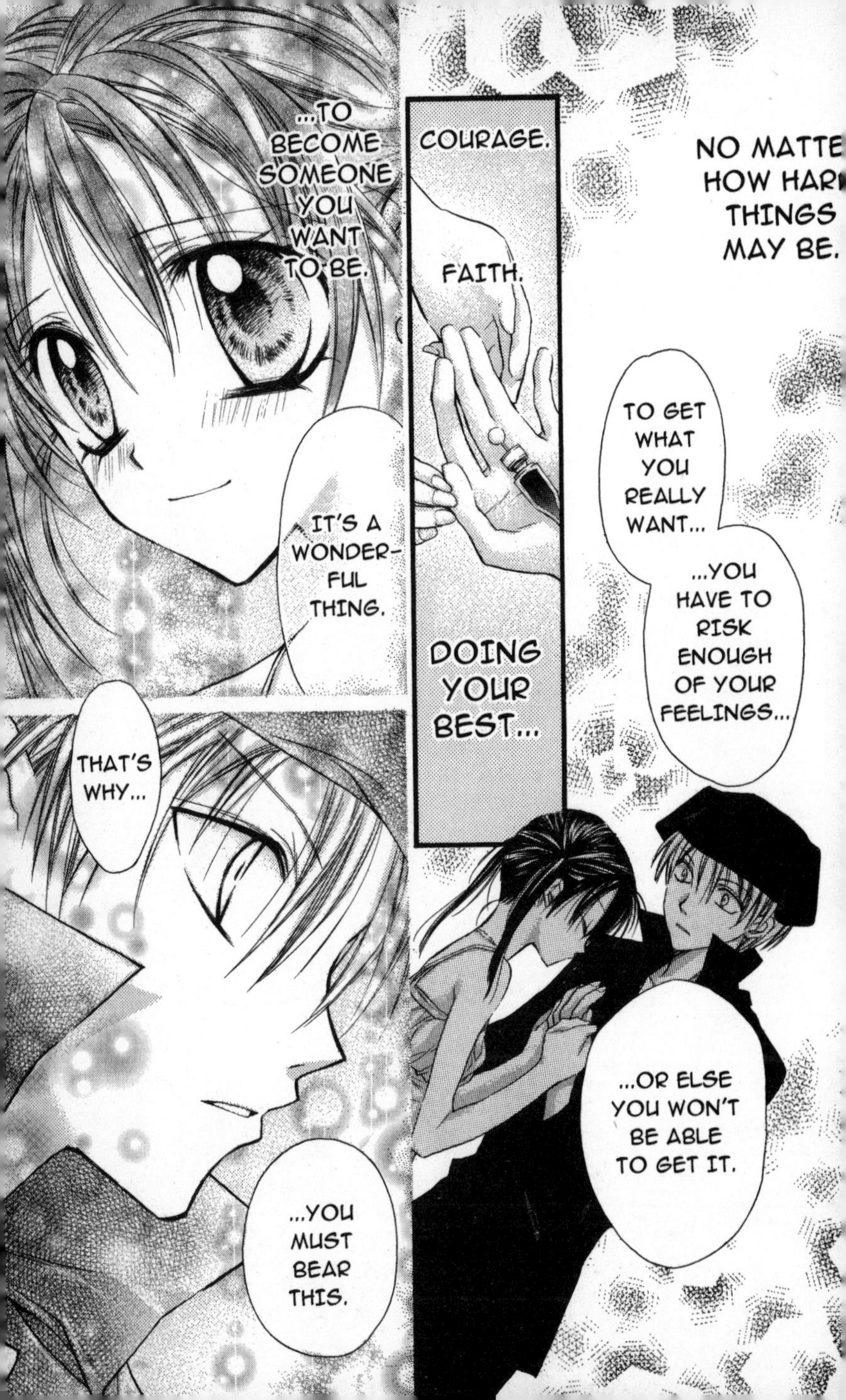
NO MATTE HOW HAR THINGS MAY BE.
TO GET WHAT YOU REALLY WANT...
...YOU HAVE TO RISK ENOUGH OF YOUR FEELINGS...
...OR ELSE YOU WON'T BE ABLE TO GET IT.
COURAGE.
FAITH.
DOING YOUR BEST...
...TO BECOME SOMEONE YOU WANT TO BE.
IT'S A WONDERFUL THING.
THAT'S WHY...
...YOU MUST BEAR THIS.

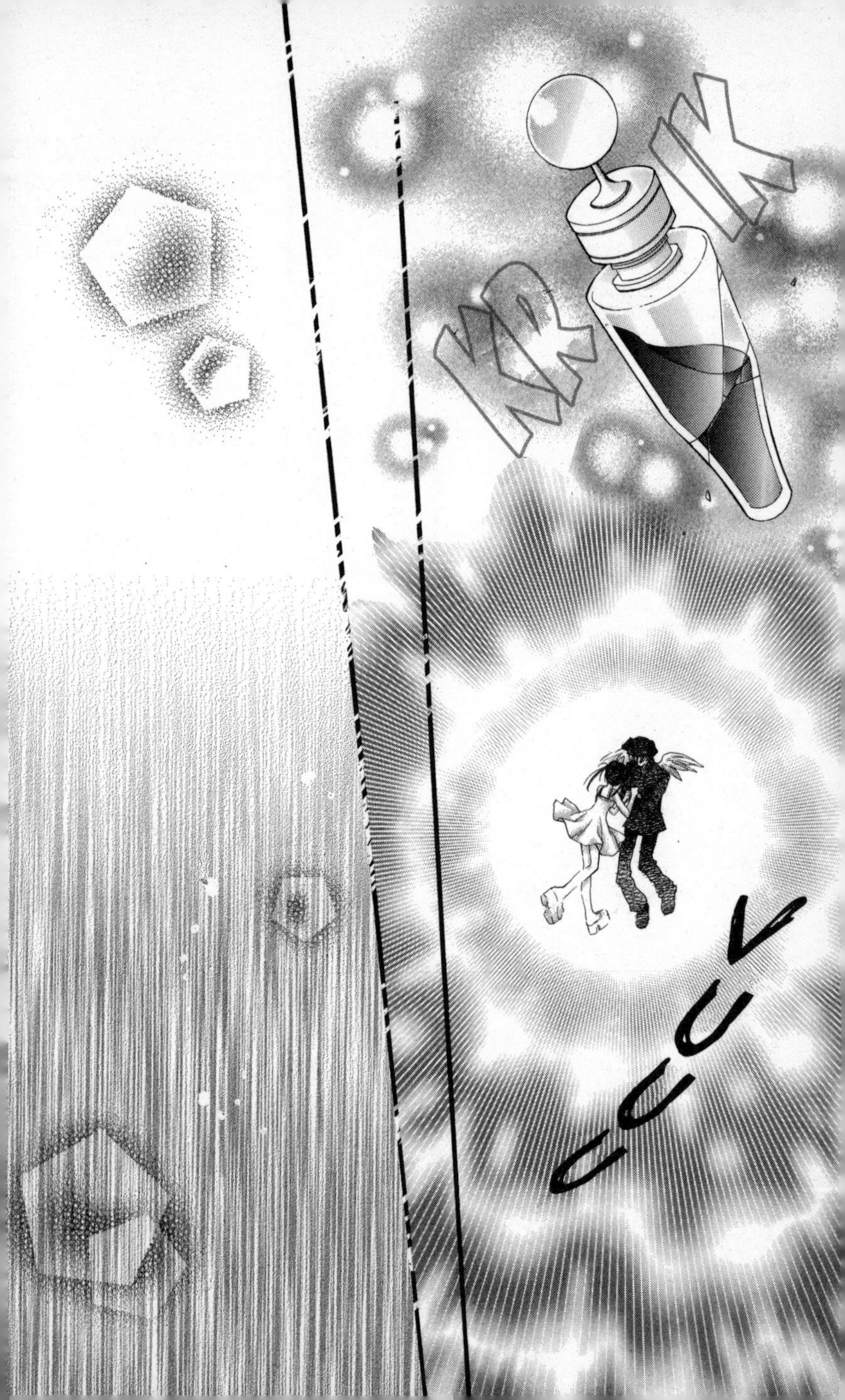
KRIK
VUUU

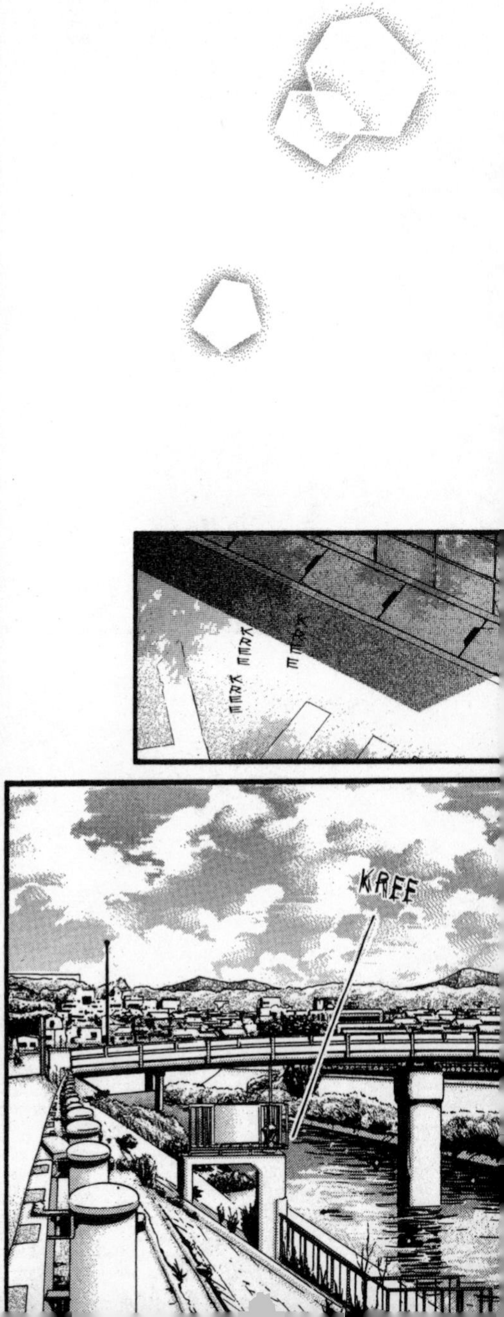

KREE KREE
KREE
KREE

Being Hospitalized ②

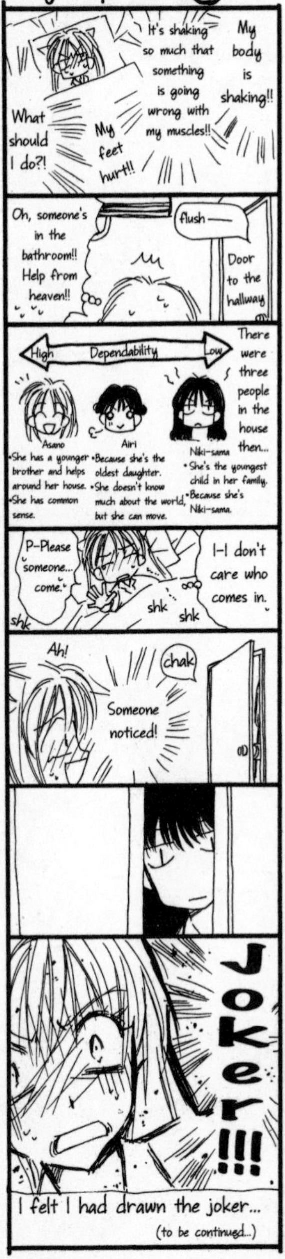

My body is shaking!!
It's shaking so much that something is going wrong with my muscles!!
My feet hurt!!
What should I do?!
flush—
Door to the hallway
Oh, someone's in the bathroom!! Help from heaven!!
There were three people in the house then...
High
Dependability
Low
Asano
•She has a younger brother and helps around her house.
•She has common sense.
Airi
•Because she's the oldest daughter.
•She doesn't know much about the world, but she can move.
Niki-sama
•She's the youngest child in her family.
•Because she's Niki-sama.
I-I don't care who comes in.
shk
shk
P-Please someone... come.
shk
chak
Someone noticed!
Ah!
Joker!!!
I felt I had drawn the joker...
(to be continued...)

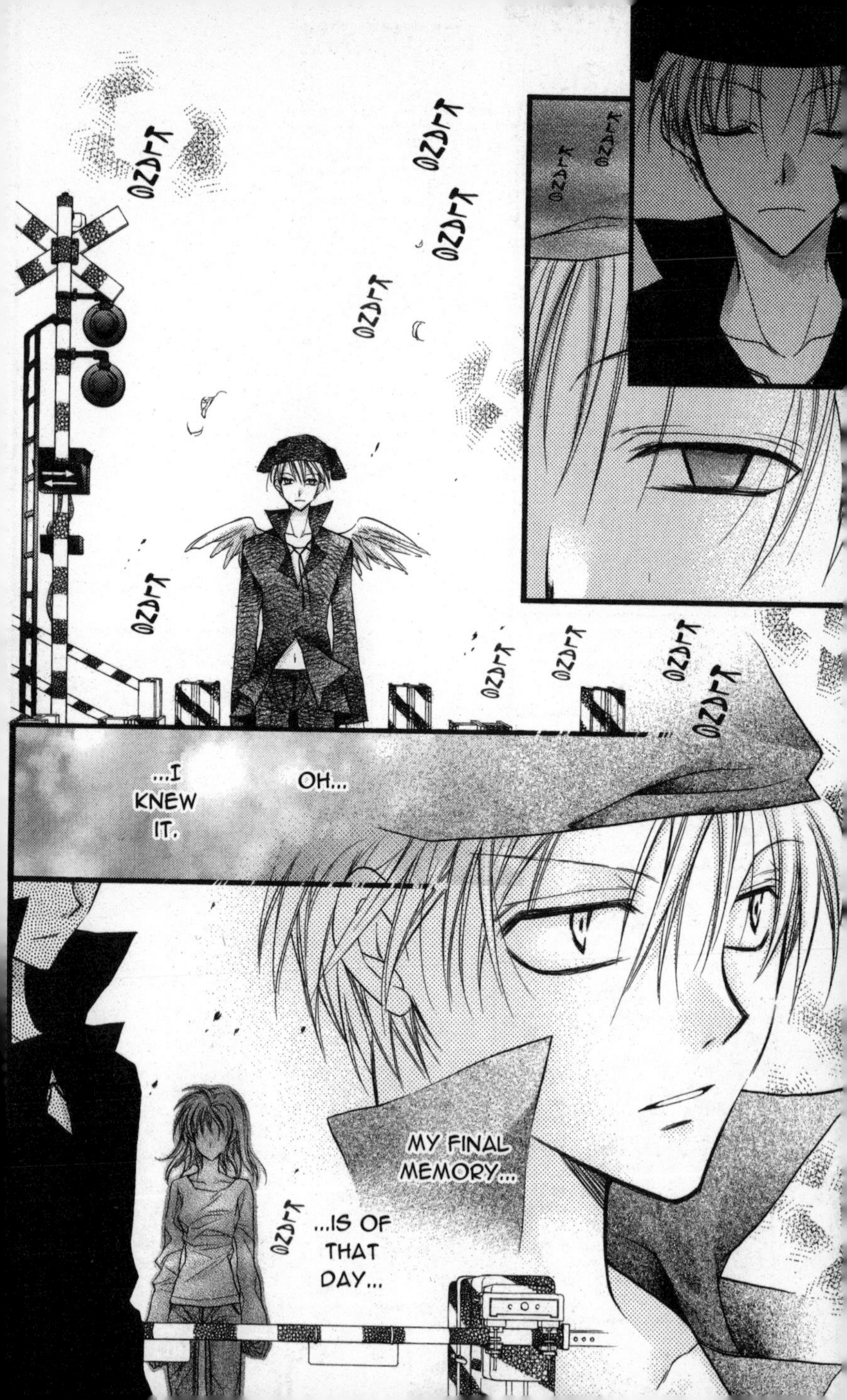
KLANG
KLANG
KLANG
KLANG
KLANG
KLANG
KLANG
KLANG
KLANG
KLANG
KLANG
OH...
...I KNEW IT.
MY FINAL MEMORY...
...IS OF THAT DAY...
KLANG

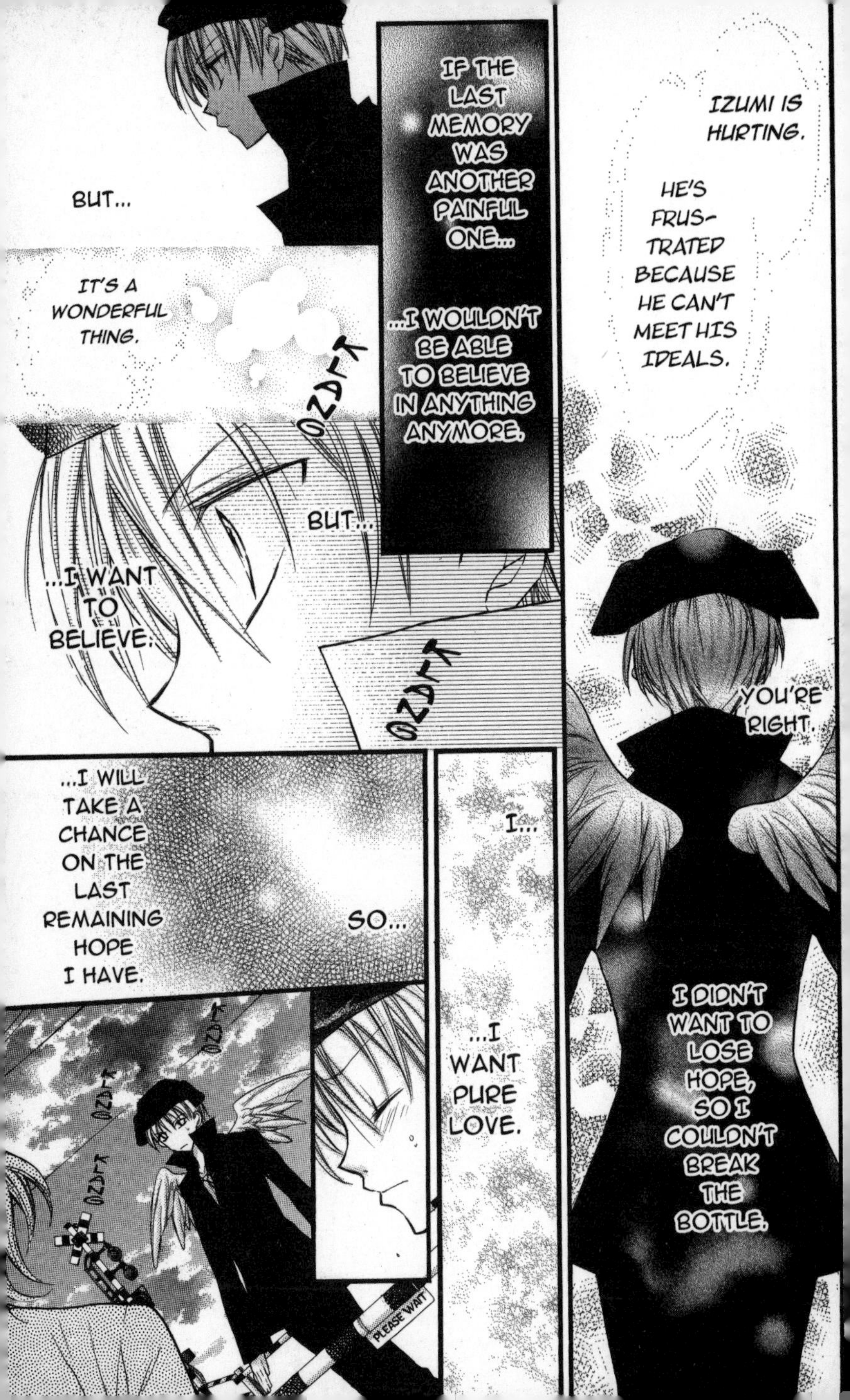
IZUMI IS HURTING.
HE'S FRUS-TRATED BECAUSE HE CAN'T MEET HIS IDEALS.
YOU'RE RIGHT.
I DIDN'T WANT TO LOSE HOPE, SO I COULDN'T BREAK THE BOTTLE.
IF THE LAST MEMORY WAS ANOTHER PAINFUL ONE...
...I WOULDN'T BE ABLE TO BELIEVE IN ANYTHING ANYMORE.
BUT...
IT'S A WONDERFUL THING.
KLANG
BUT...
...I WANT TO BELIEVE.
KLANG
I...
...I WANT PURE LOVE.
...I WILL TAKE A CHANCE ON THE LAST REMAINING HOPE I HAVE.
SO...
KLANG
KLANG
KLANG
PLEASE WAIT

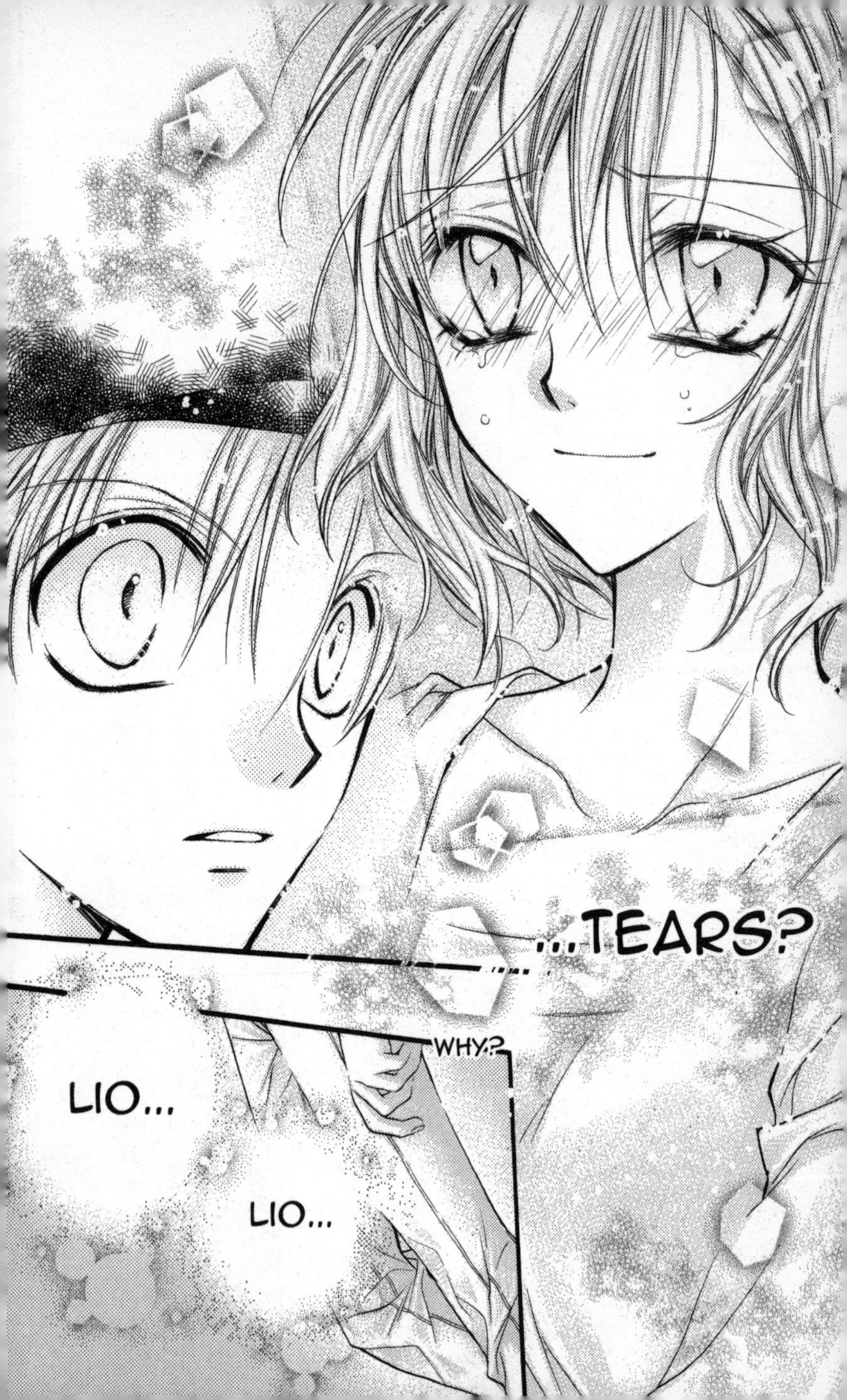
...TEARS?
WHY?
LIO...
LIO...

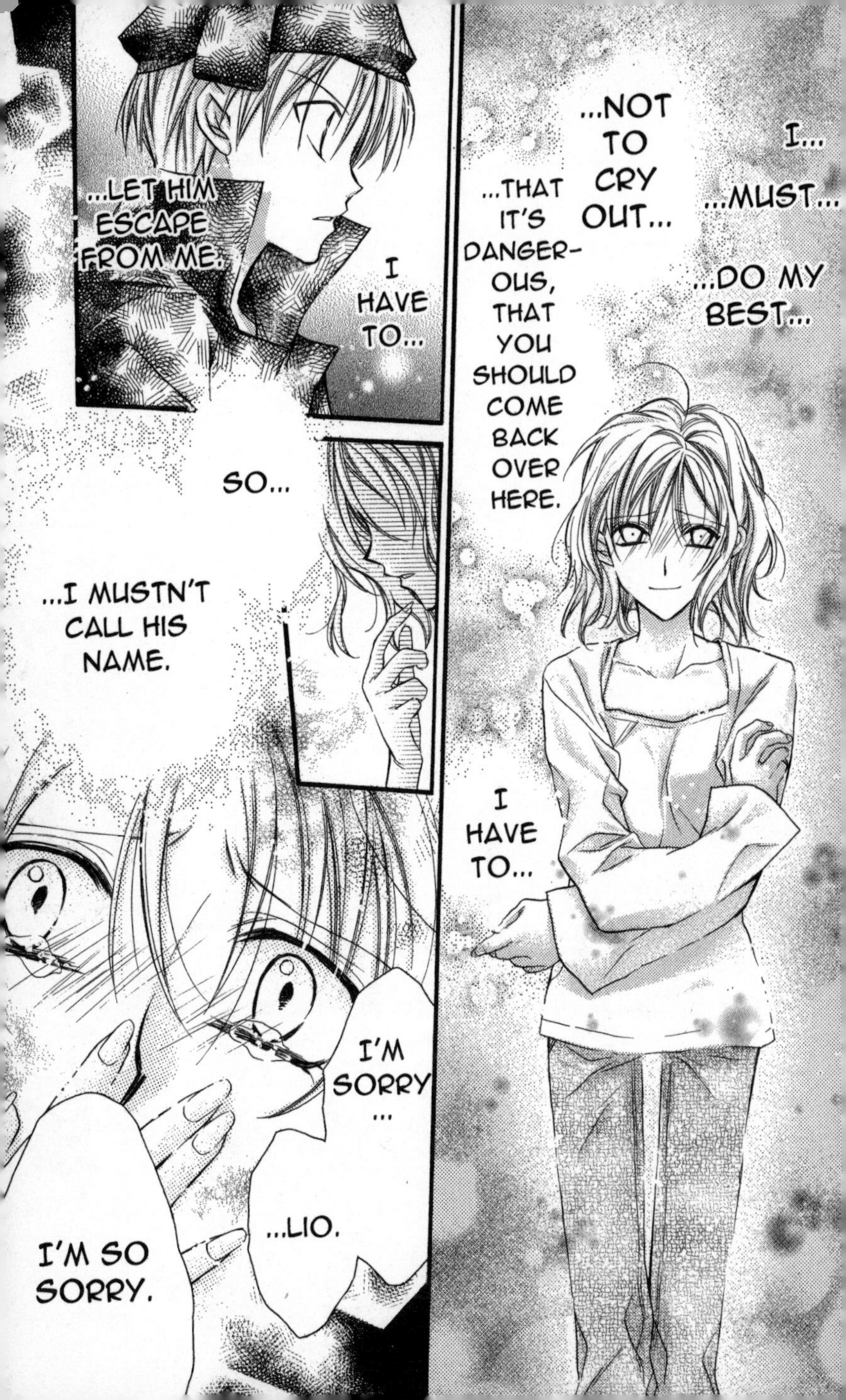
I...
...MUST...
...DO MY BEST...
...NOT TO CRY OUT...
...THAT IT'S DANGER-OUS, THAT YOU SHOULD COME BACK OVER HERE.
I HAVE TO...
I HAVE TO...
...LET HIM ESCAPE FROM ME.
SO...
...I MUSTN'T CALL HIS NAME.
I'M SORRY...
...LIO.
I'M SO SORRY.

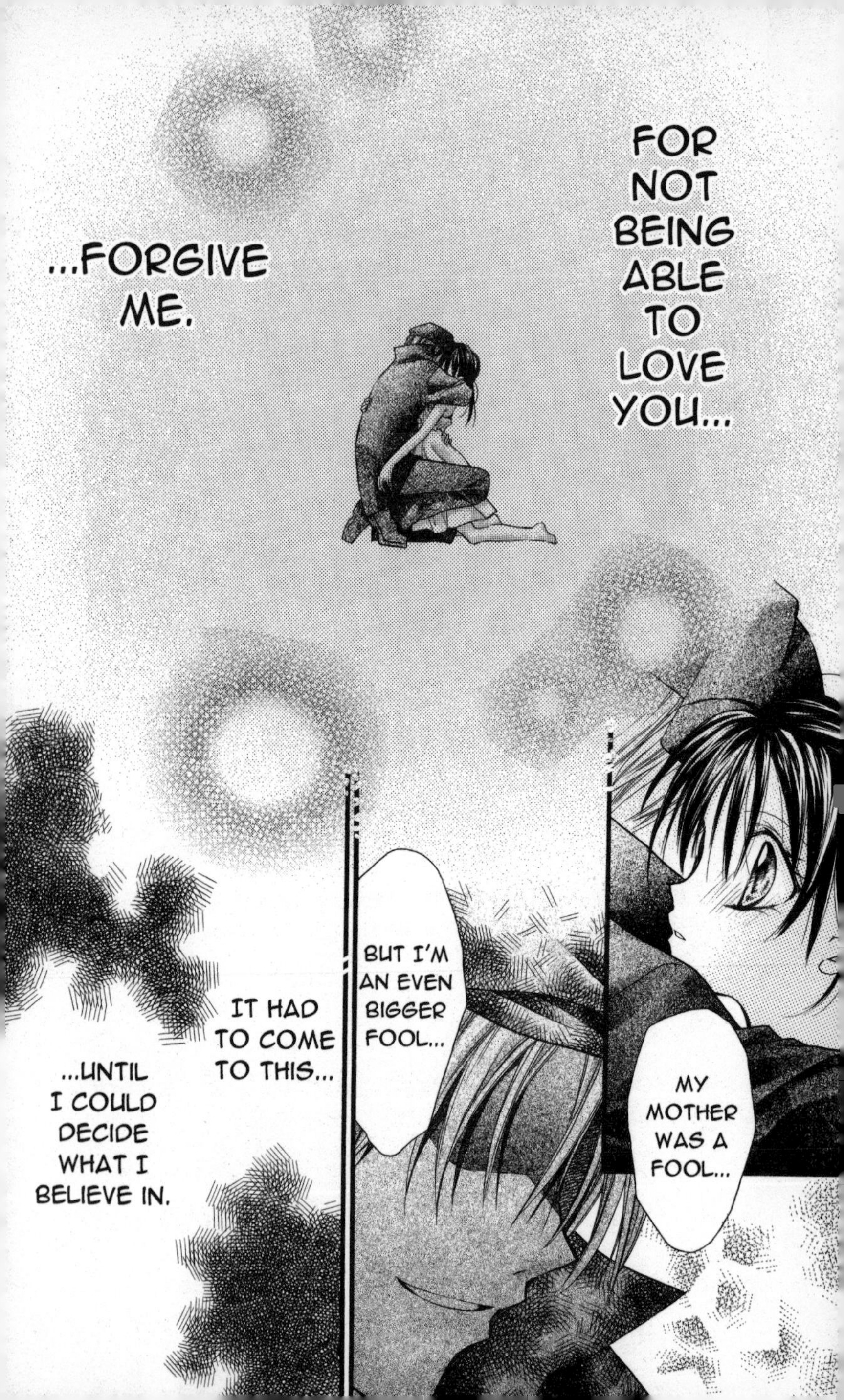
FOR NOT BEING ABLE TO LOVE YOU...
...FORGIVE ME.
MY MOTHER WAS A FOOL...
BUT I'M AN EVEN BIGGER FOOL...
IT HAD TO COME TO THIS...
...UNTIL I COULD DECIDE WHAT I BELIEVE IN.

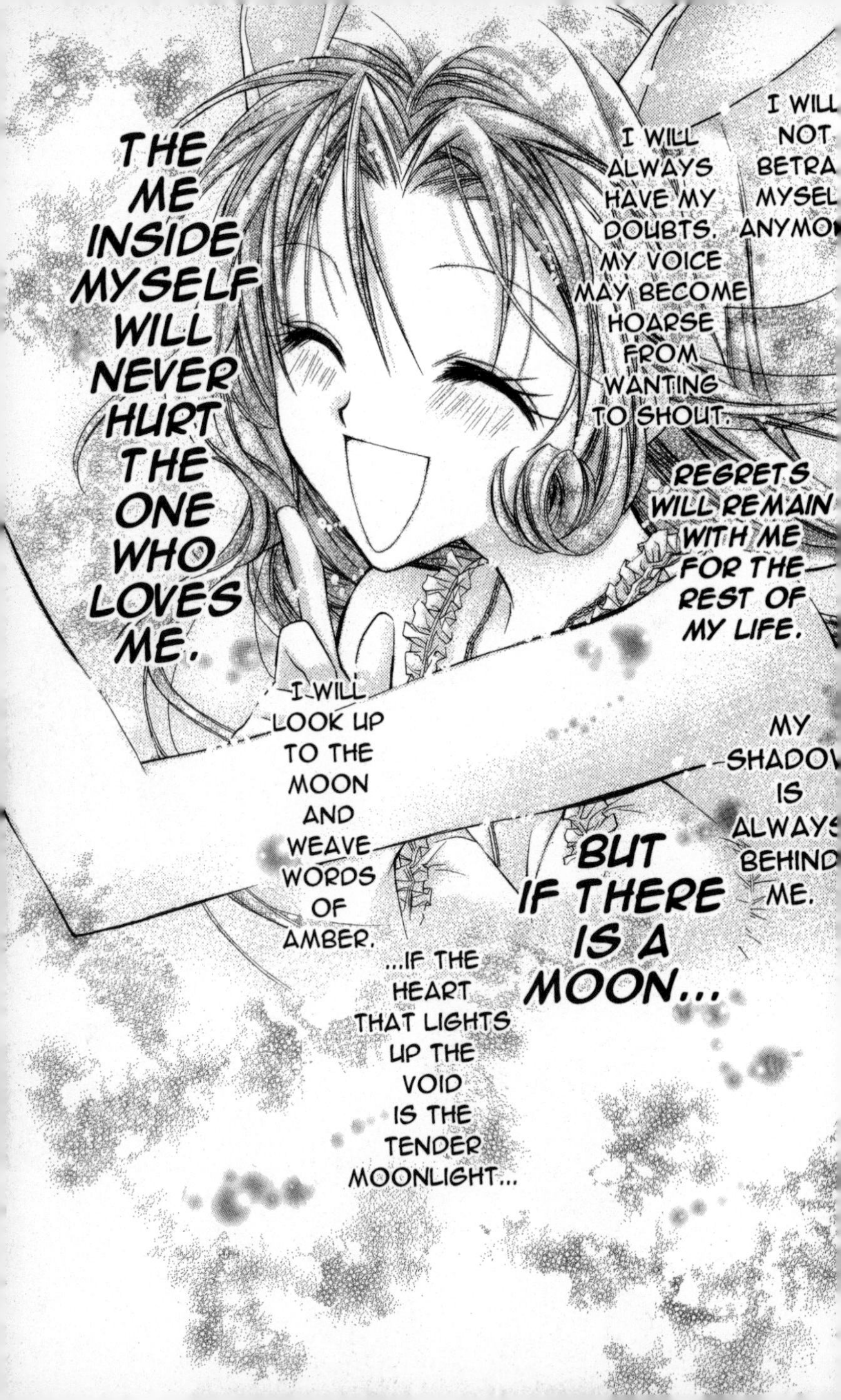
I WILL NOT BETRA MYSEL ANYMO
I WILL ALWAYS HAVE MY DOUBTS. MY VOICE MAY BECOME HOARSE FROM WANTING TO SHOUT.
THE ME INSIDE MYSELF WILL NEVER HURT THE ONE WHO LOVES ME.
REGRETS WILL REMAIN WITH ME FOR THE REST OF MY LIFE.
MY SHADO IS ALWAY BEHIND ME.
BUT IF THERE IS A MOON...
I WILL LOOK UP TO THE MOON AND WEAVE WORDS OF AMBER.
...IF THE HEART THAT LIGHTS UP THE VOID IS THE TENDER MOONLIGHT...

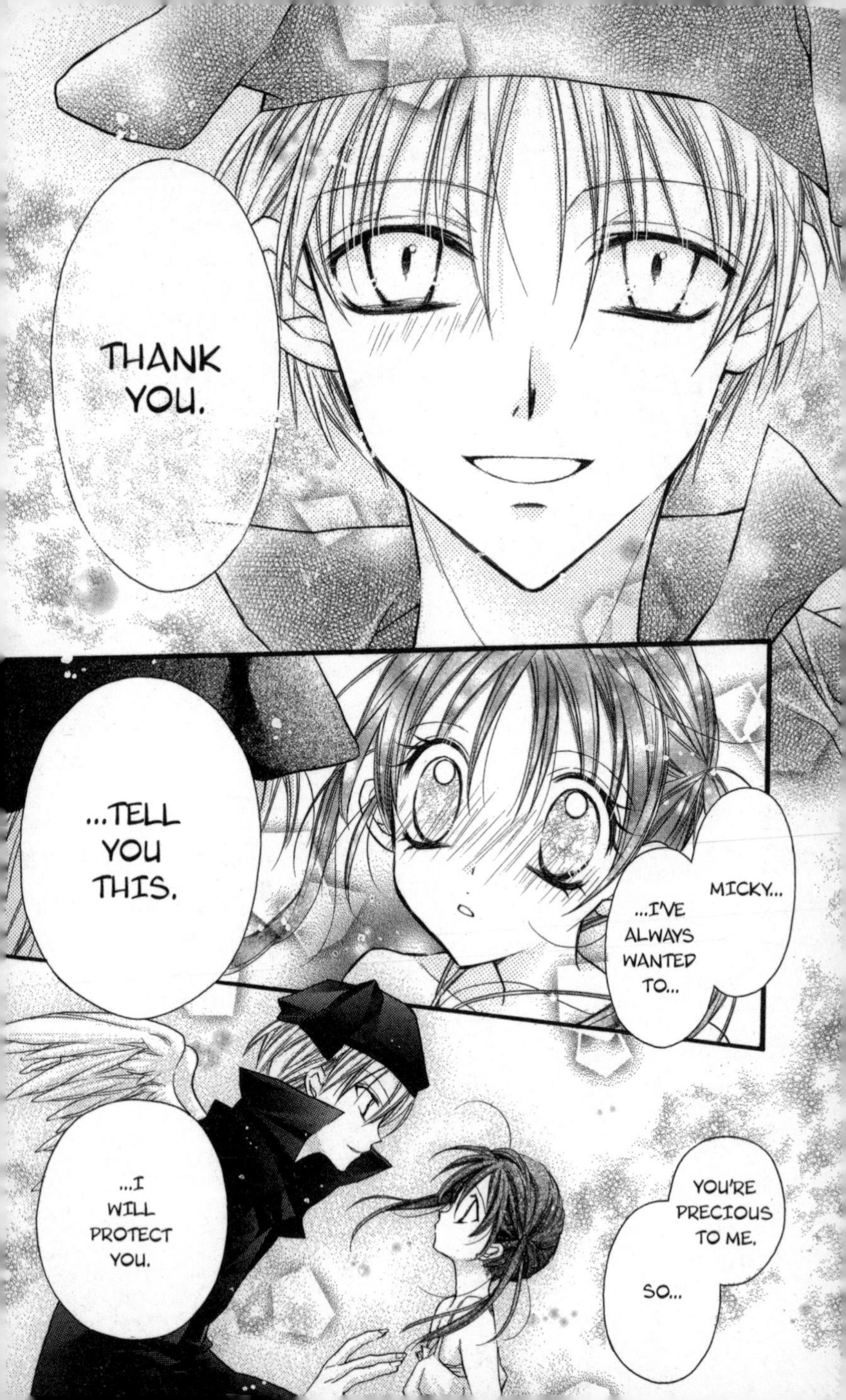
THANK YOU.
MICKY...
...I'VE ALWAYS WANTED TO...
...TELL YOU THIS.
YOU'RE PRECIOUS TO ME.
SO...
...I WILL PROTECT YOU.

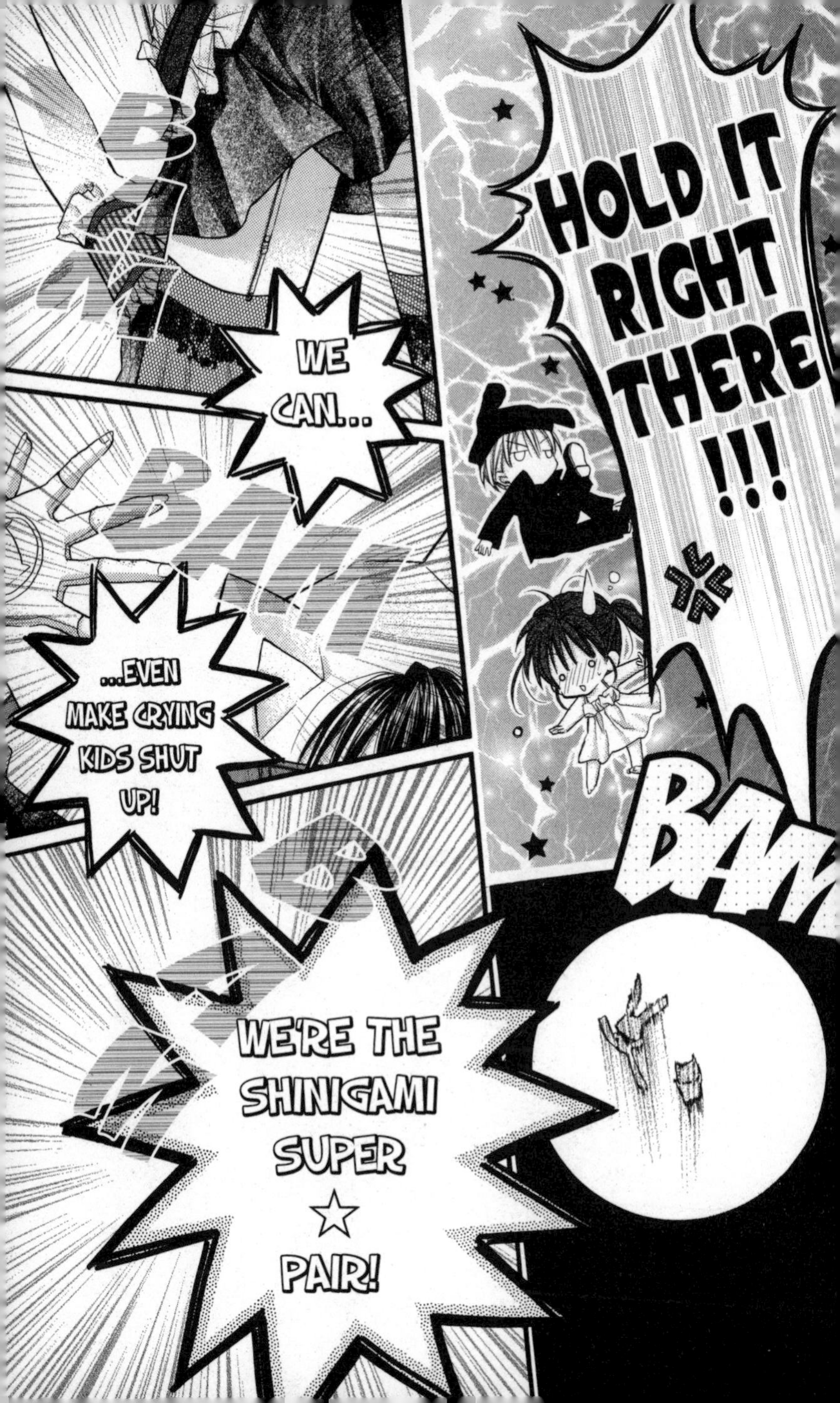
HOLD IT RIGHT THERE!!!
BAM
BAM
WE CAN...
BAM
...EVEN MAKE CRYING KIDS SHUT UP!
BAM
WE'RE THE SHINIGAMI SUPER ☆ PAIR!

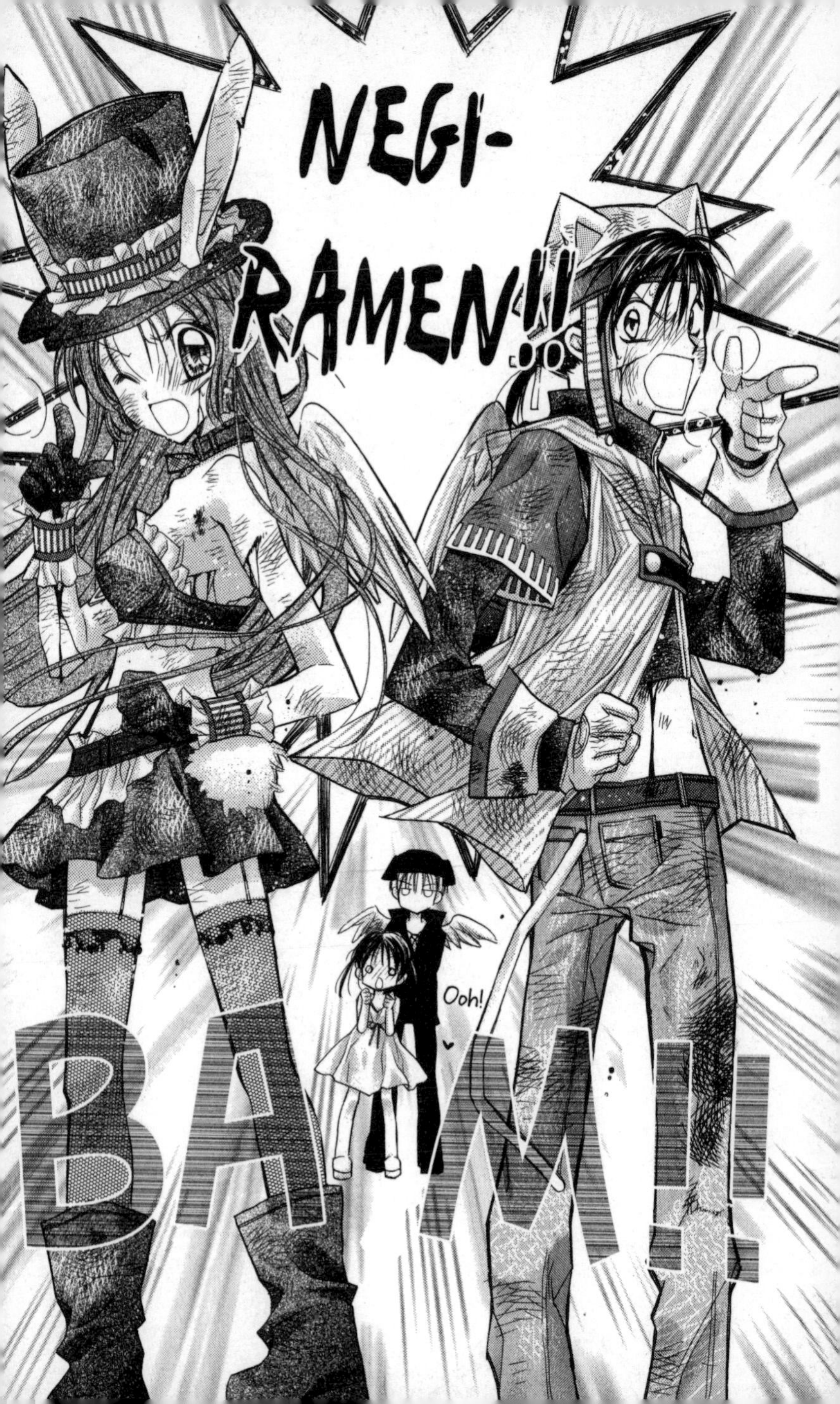
NEGI-RAMEN!!
Ooh!
BAM!!

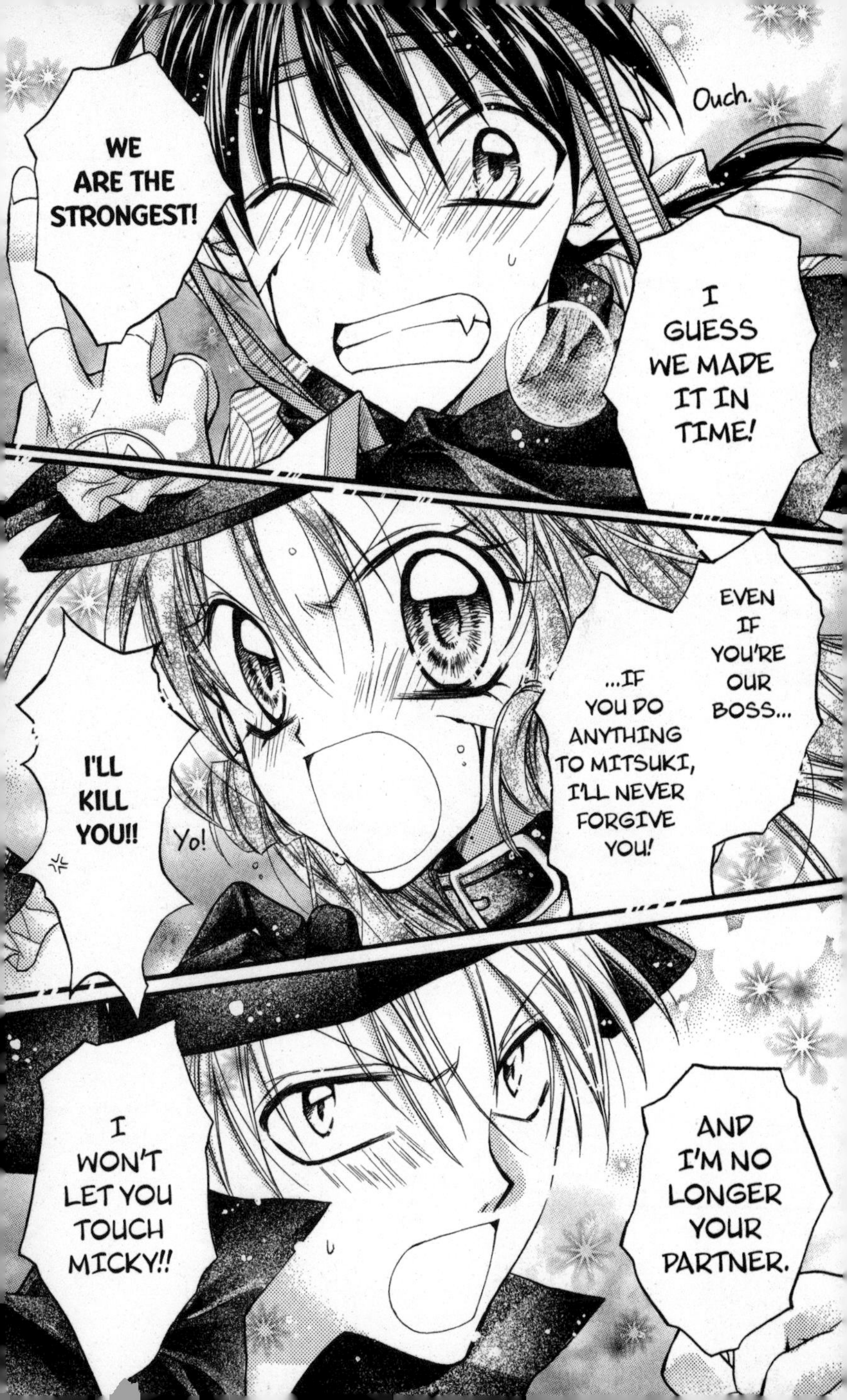
Ouch.
I GUESS WE MADE IT IN TIME!
WE ARE THE STRONGEST!
EVEN IF YOU'RE OUR BOSS...
...IF YOU DO ANYTHING TO MITSUKI, I'LL NEVER FORGIVE YOU!
Yo!
I'LL KILL YOU!!
AND I'M NO LONGER YOUR PARTNER.
I WON'T LET YOU TOUCH MICKY!!

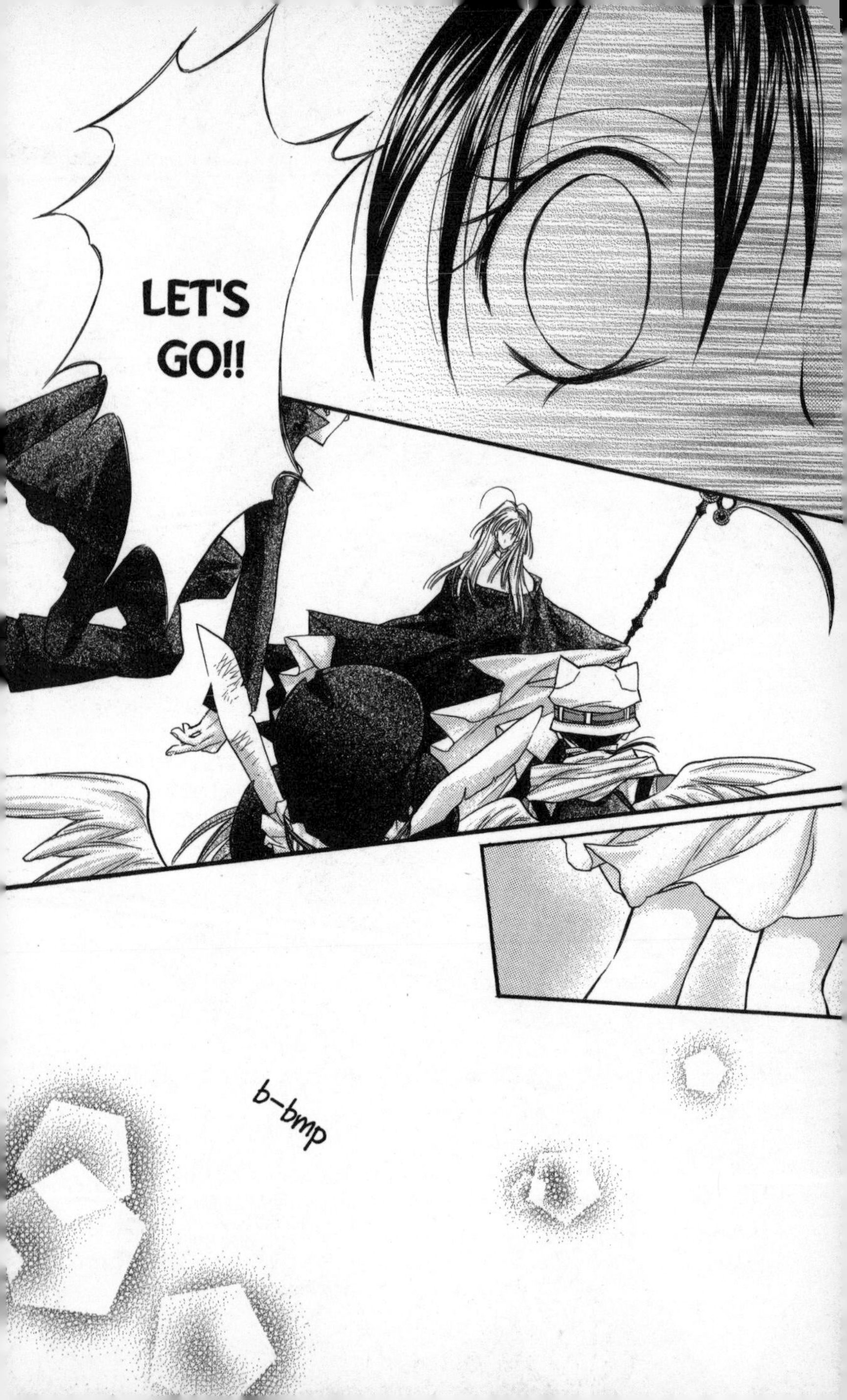
LET'S GO!!
b-bmp

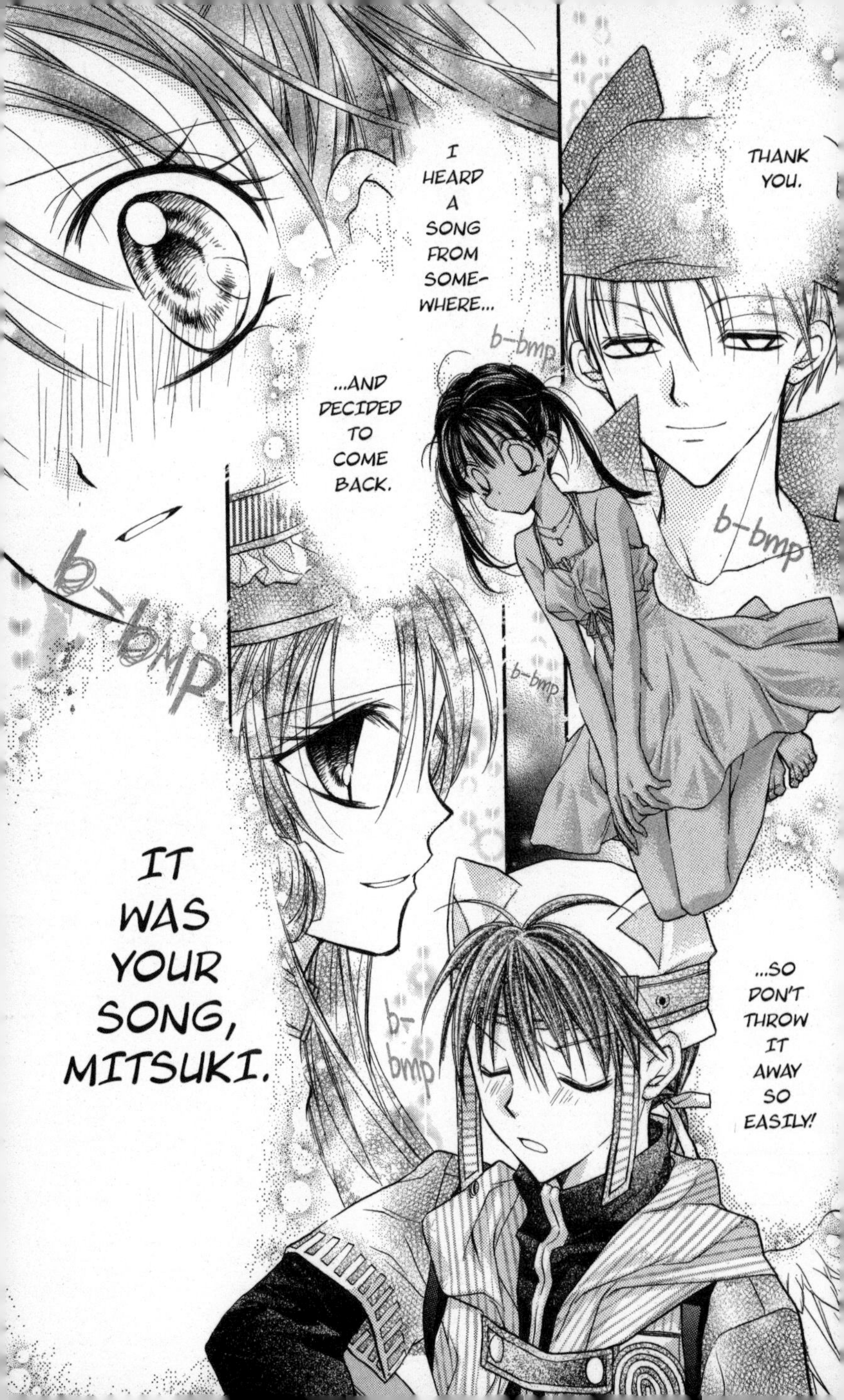
THANK YOU.
b-bmp
I HEARD A SONG FROM SOMEWHERE...
b-bmp
...AND DECIDED TO COME BACK.
b-bmp
b-bmp
IT WAS YOUR SONG, MITSUKI.
b-bmp
...SO DON'T THROW IT AWAY SO EASILY!

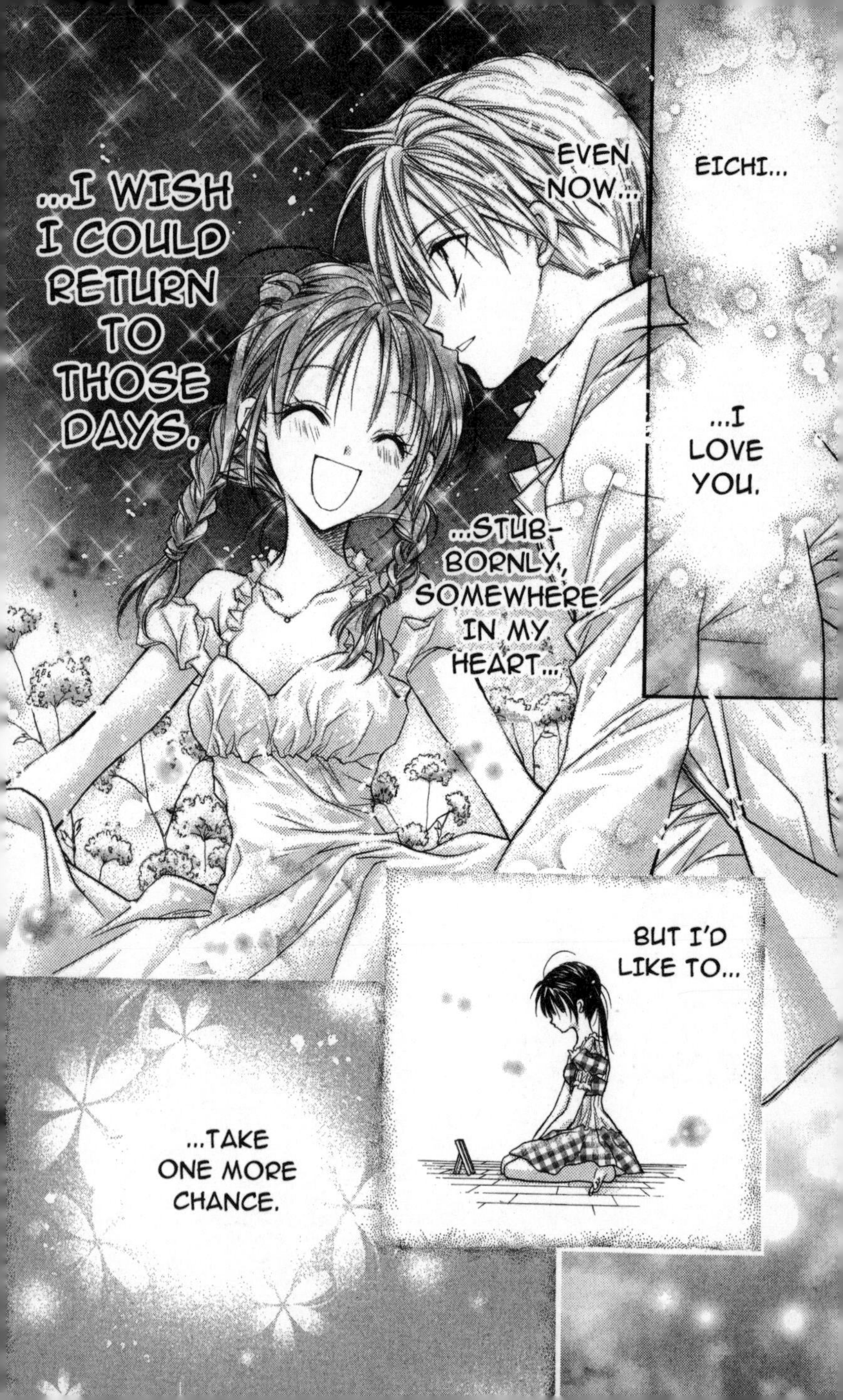
EICHI...
...I LOVE YOU.
EVEN NOW...
...STUB-BORNLY, SOMEWHERE IN MY HEART...
...I WISH I COULD RETURN TO THOSE DAYS.
BUT I'D LIKE TO...
...TAKE ONE MORE CHANCE.

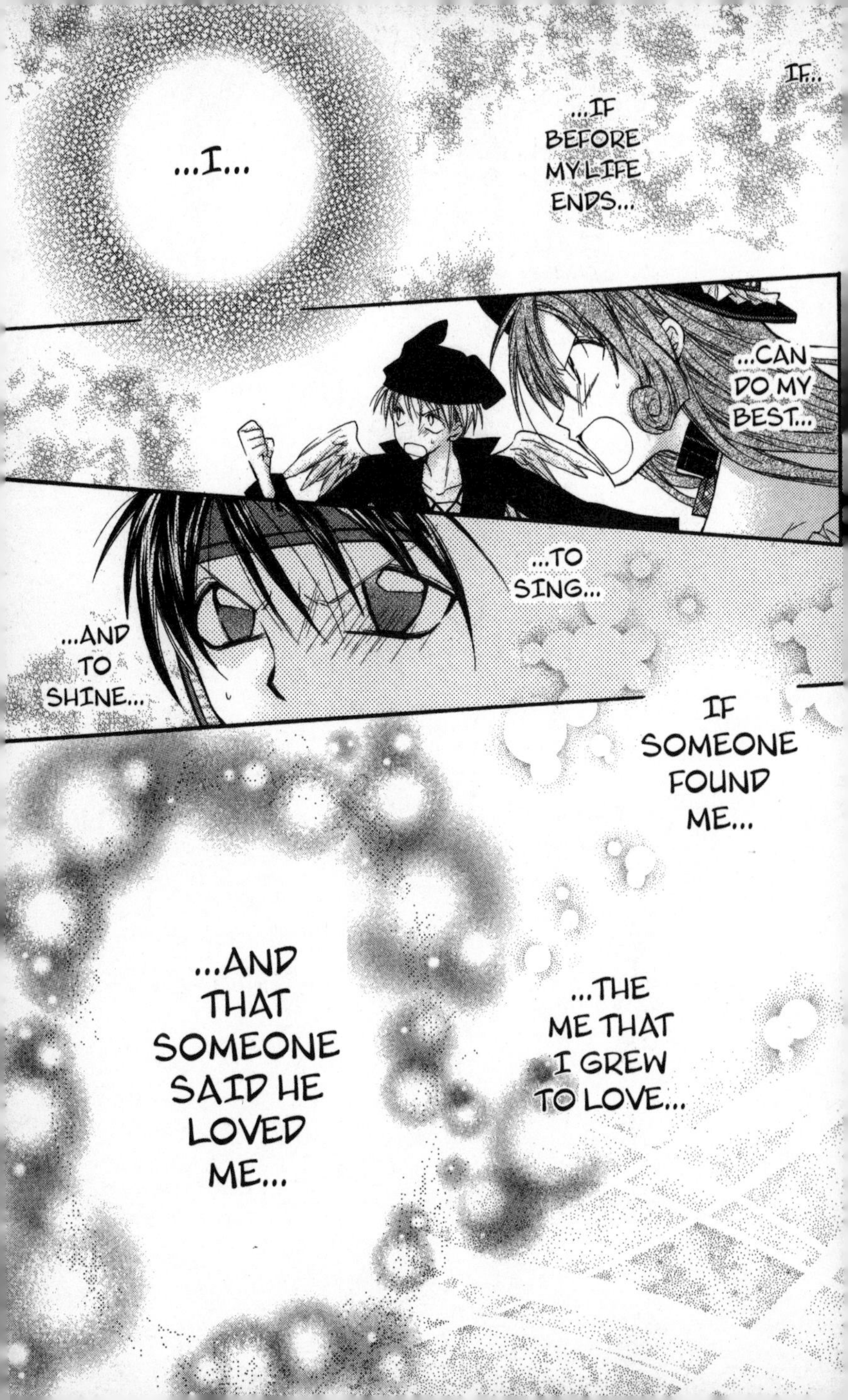
IF...
...IF BEFORE MY LIFE ENDS...
...I...
...CAN DO MY BEST...
...TO SING...
...AND TO SHINE...
IF SOMEONE FOUND ME...
...THE ME THAT I GREW TO LOVE...
...AND THAT SOMEONE SAID HE LOVED ME...

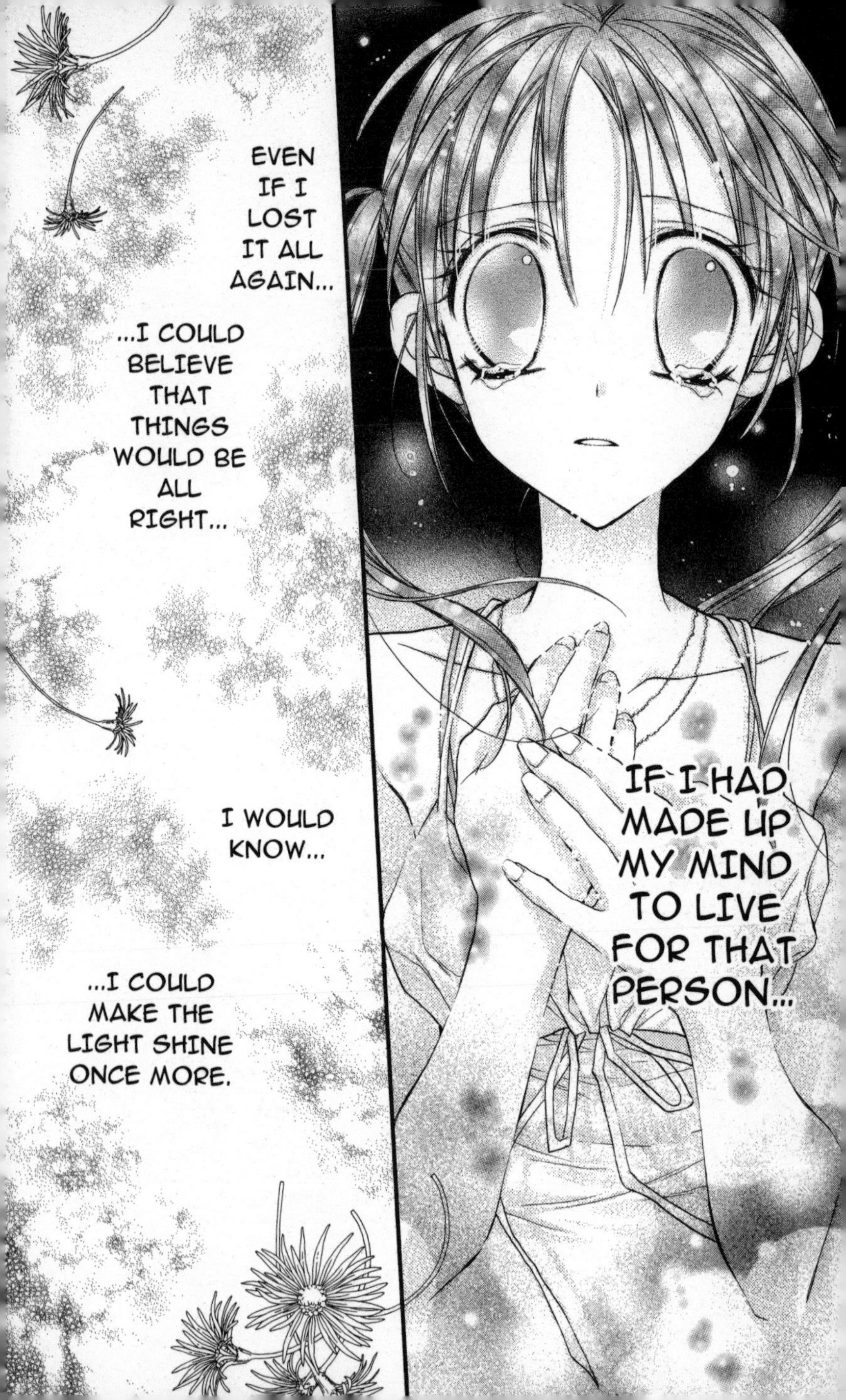
IF I HAD MADE UP MY MIND TO LIVE FOR THAT PERSON...
EVEN IF I LOST IT ALL AGAIN...
...I COULD BELIEVE THAT THINGS WOULD BE ALL RIGHT...
I WOULD KNOW...
...I COULD MAKE THE LIGHT SHINE ONCE MORE.

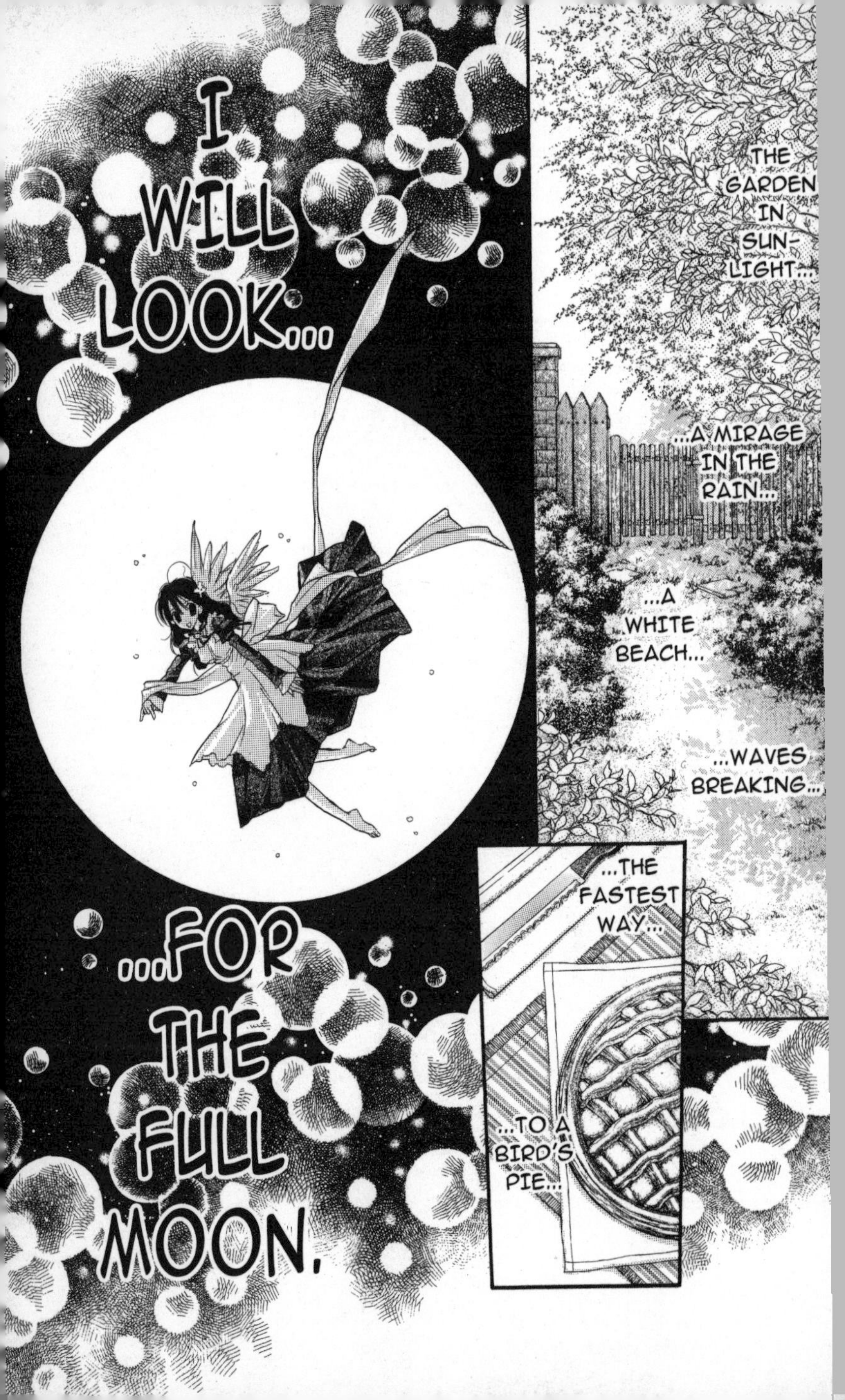
THE GARDEN IN SUN-LIGHT...
...A MIRAGE IN THE RAIN...
...A WHITE BEACH...
...WAVES BREAKING...
...THE FASTEST WAY...
...TO A BIRD'S PIE...
I WILL LOOK...
...FOR THE FULL MOON.

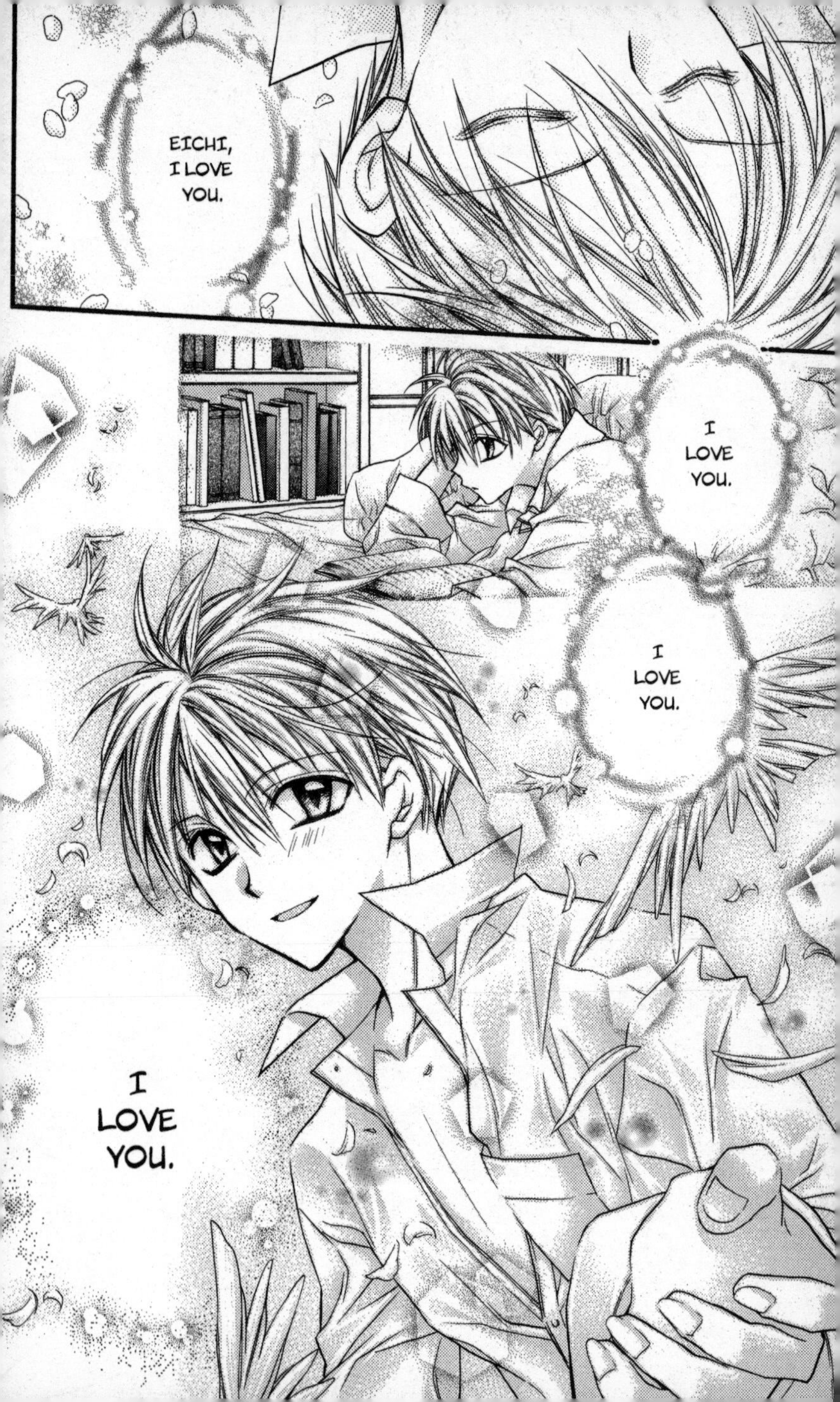
EICHI, I LOVE YOU.
I LOVE YOU.
I LOVE YOU.
I LOVE YOU.

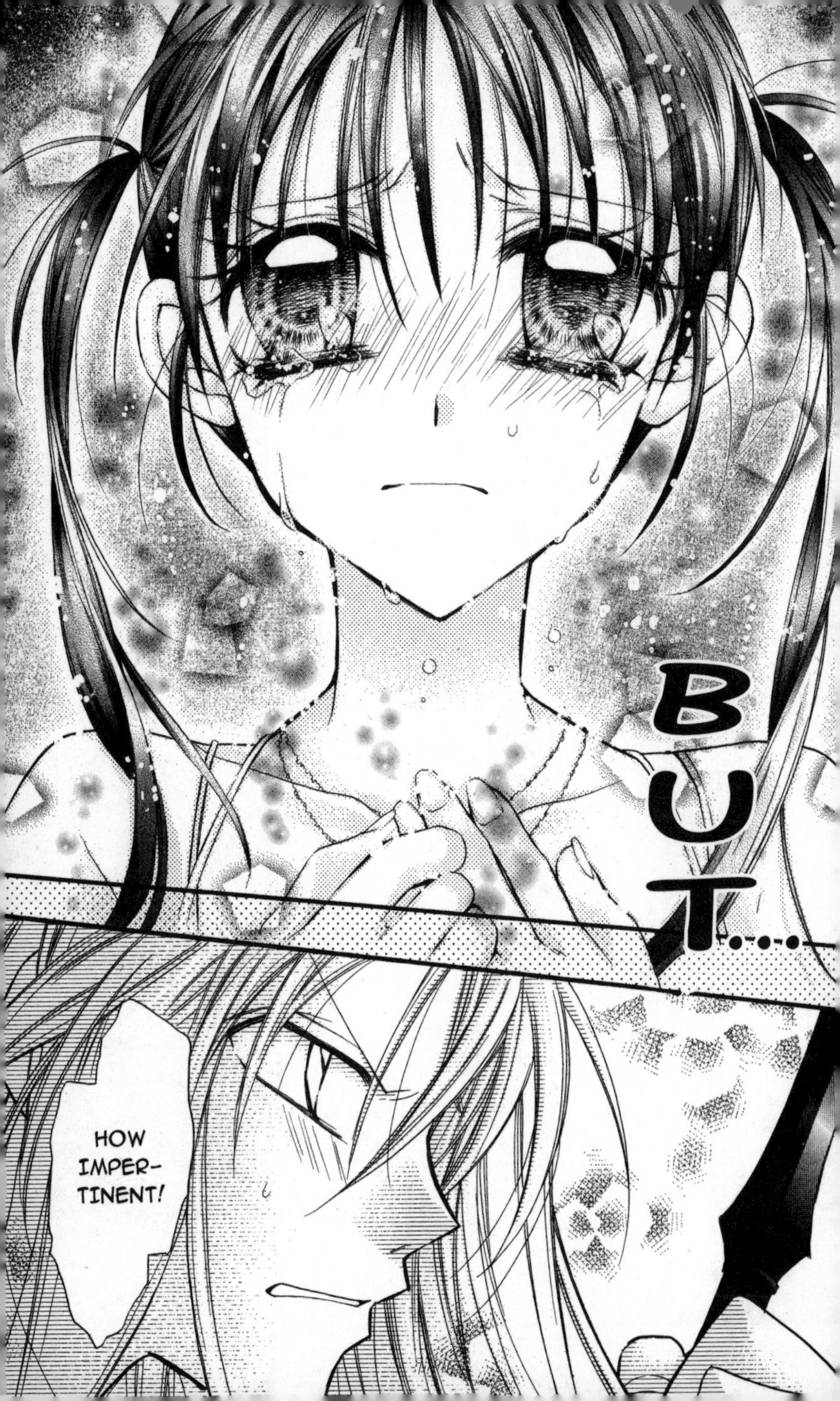
BUT...
HOW IMPER-TINENT!

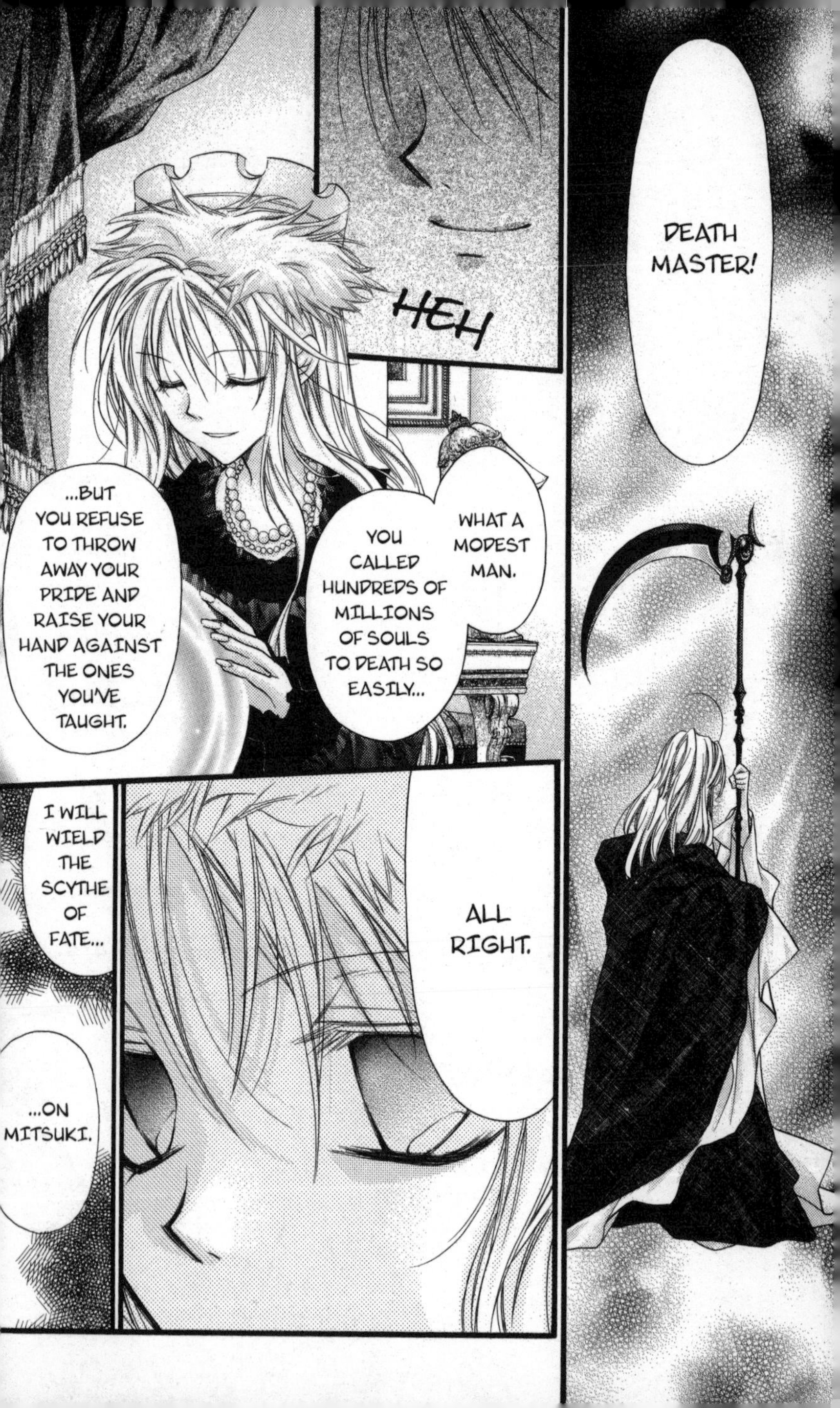
DEATH MASTER!
HEH
WHAT A MODEST MAN.
YOU CALLED HUNDREDS OF MILLIONS OF SOULS TO DEATH SO EASILY...
...BUT YOU REFUSE TO THROW AWAY YOUR PRIDE AND RAISE YOUR HAND AGAINST THE ONES YOU'VE TAUGHT.
ALL RIGHT.
I WILL WIELD THE SCYTHE OF FATE...
...ON MITSUKI.

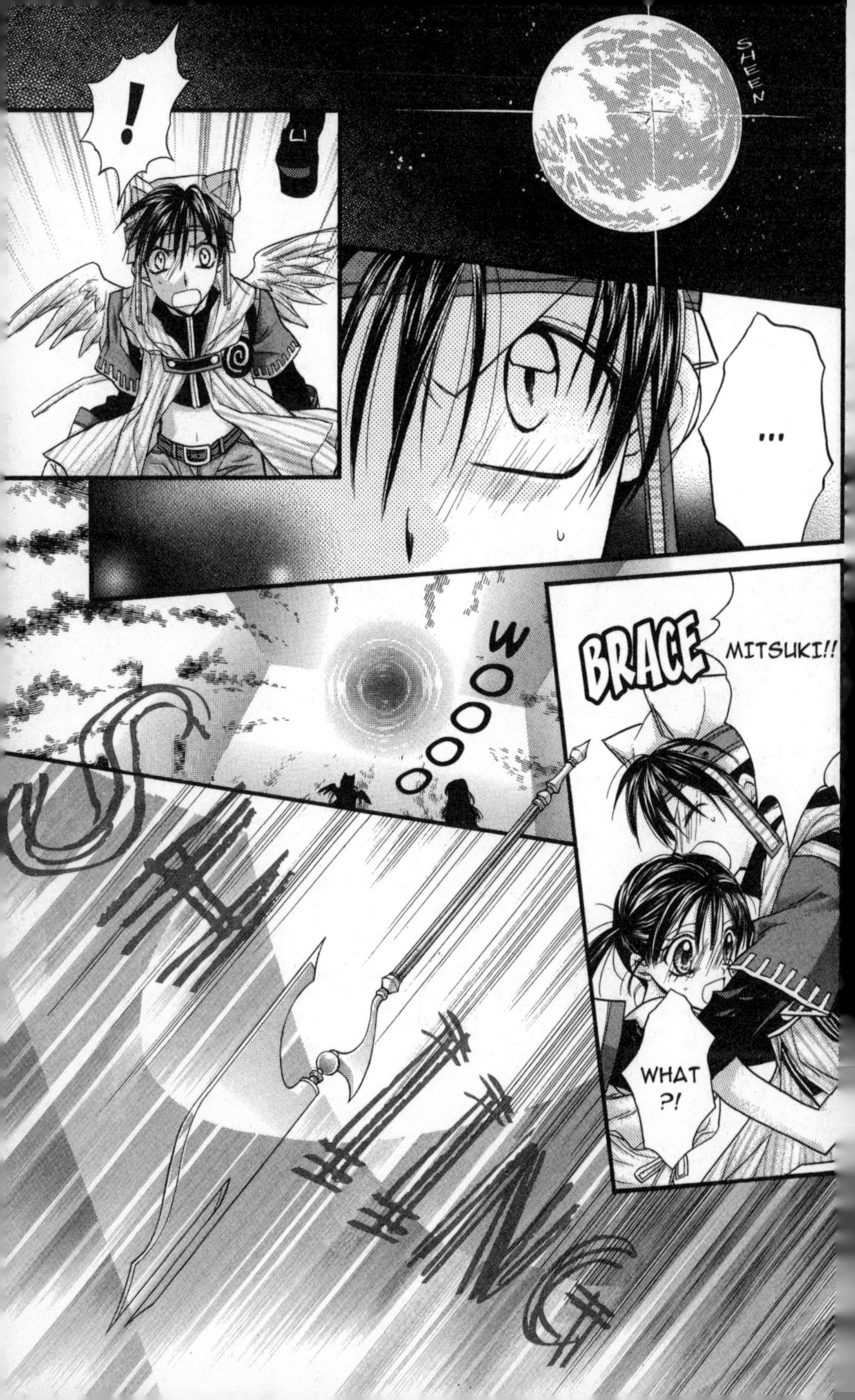
SHEEN
!
...
BRACE
MITSUKI!!
WHAT ?!
WOOOOO
SHING

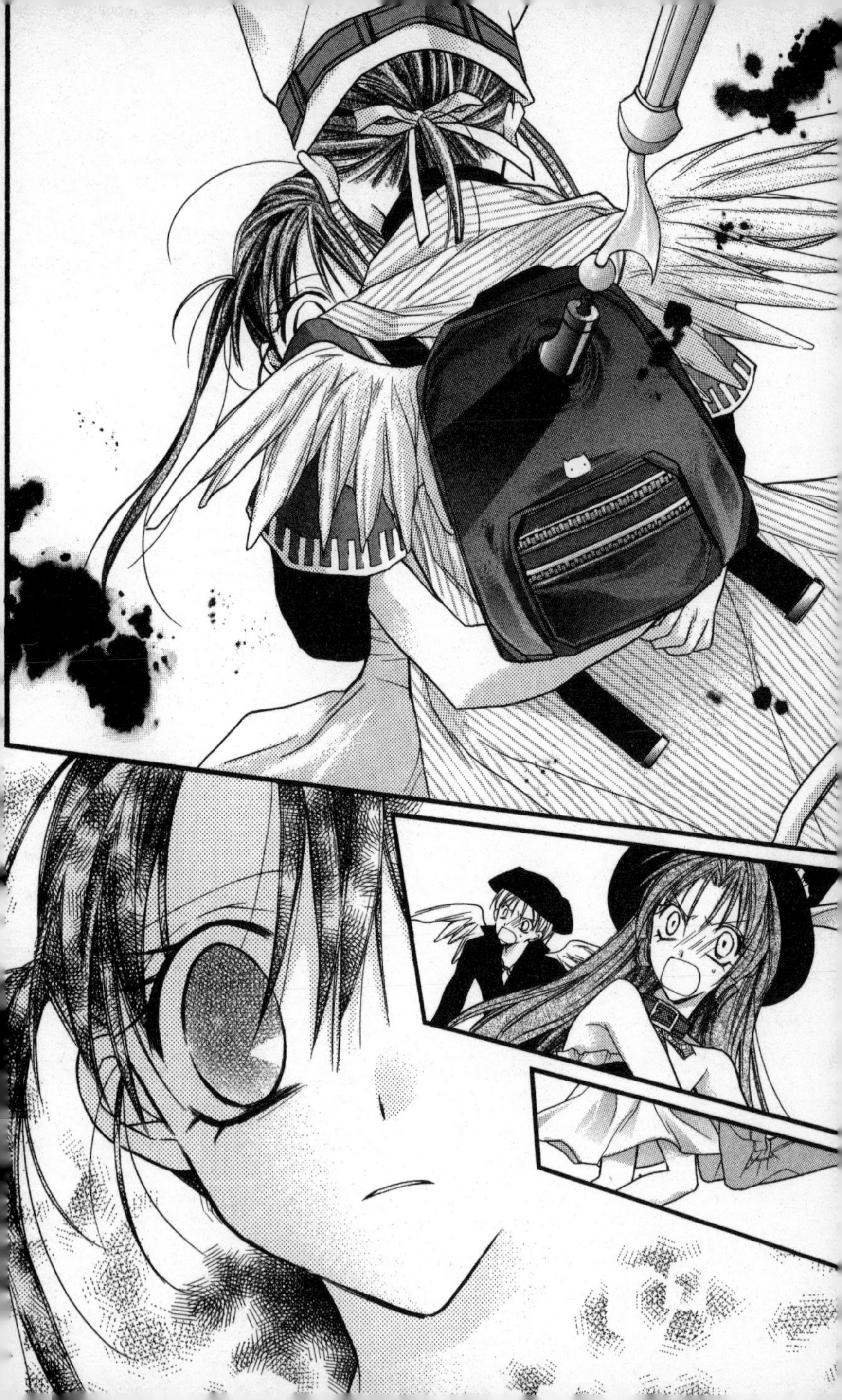

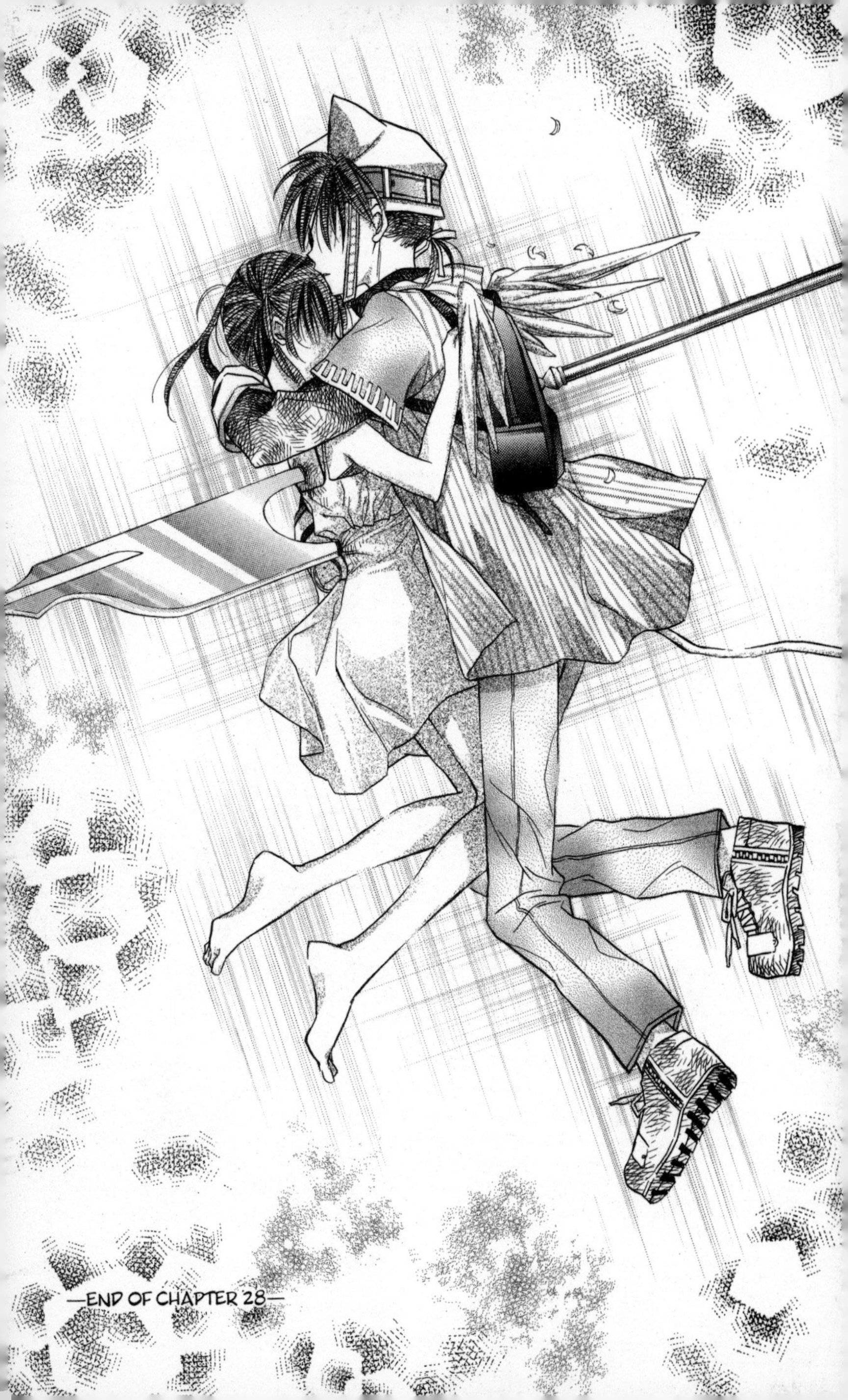
—END OF CHAPTER 28—

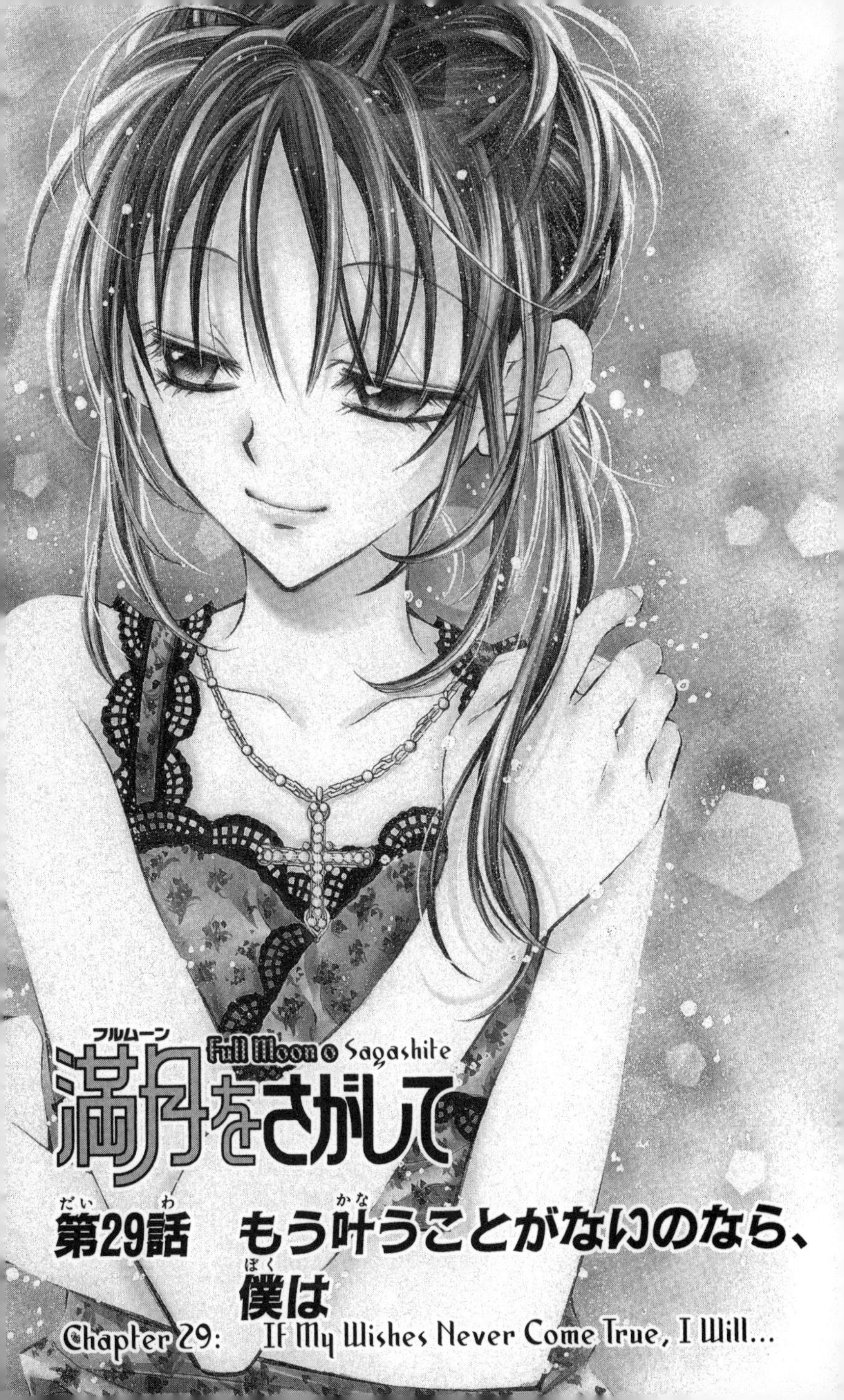
フルムーン
Full Moon o Sagashite
満月をさがして
だい わ
第29話
かな
もう叶うことがないのなら、
ぼく
僕は
Chapter 29: If My Wishes Never Come True, I Will...

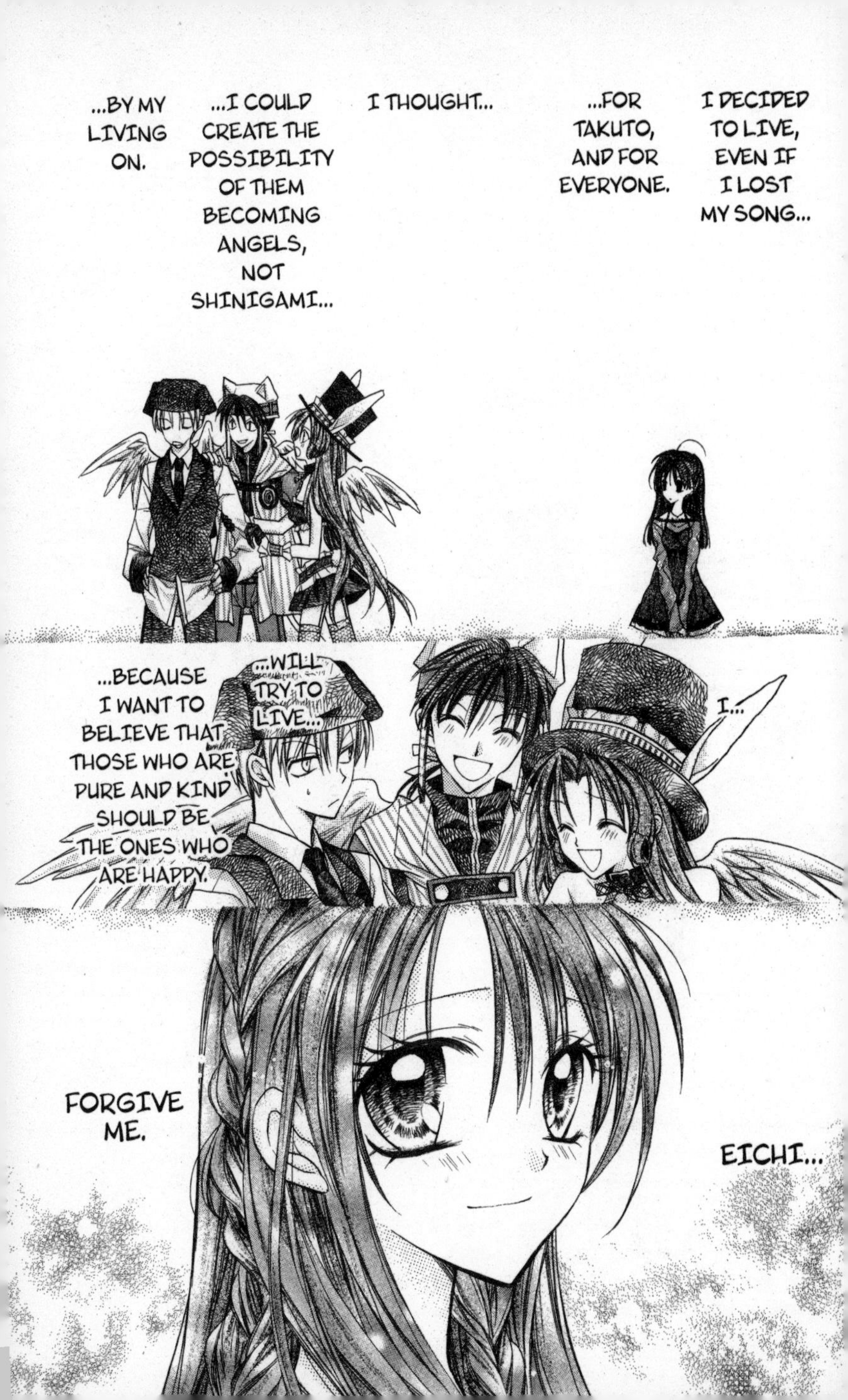
I DECIDED TO LIVE, EVEN IF I LOST MY SONG...
...FOR TAKUTO, AND FOR EVERYONE.
I THOUGHT...
...I COULD CREATE THE POSSIBILITY OF THEM BECOMING ANGELS, NOT SHINIGAMI...
...BY MY LIVING ON.
I...
...WILL TRY TO LIVE...
...BECAUSE I WANT TO BELIEVE THAT THOSE WHO ARE PURE AND KIND SHOULD BE THE ONES WHO ARE HAPPY.
EICHI...
FORGIVE ME.

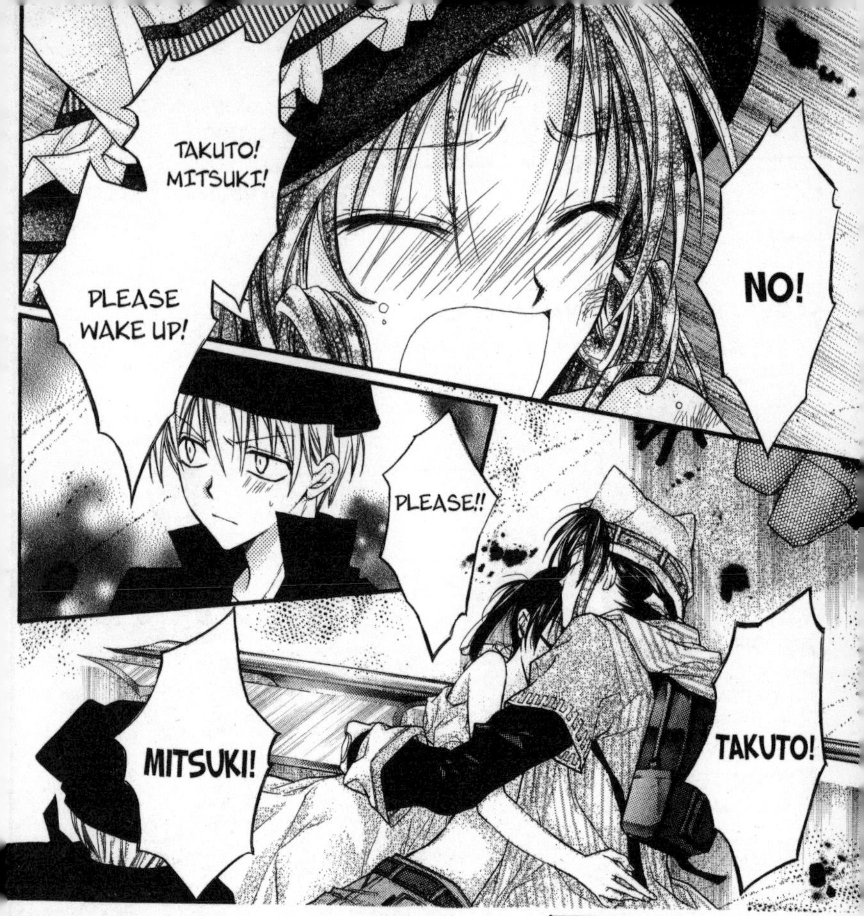
NO!
TAKUTO! MITSUKI!
PLEASE WAKE UP!
PLEASE!!
TAKUTO!
MITSUKI!

Chapter 29: If My Wishes Will Never Come True, I Will...

(spoilers follow)

Cover Copy

I wanted to be with you always...
Now I simply pray, and watch over you.
I will not look away from you anymore.

The chapter title and the cover copy are Eichi-kun's words. (Sad...)

The cherry blossoms that blew in when Dr. Wakaoji confronted Fullmoon, and the reason why the bottle Jonathan threw didn't hit her--these were Eichi-kun's doing.

Eichi-kun must have initially wanted Mitsuki-chan to come to him, somewhere in his heart... But I think he didn't want Mitsuki-chan's life to end sadly. He was watching over her so that Mitsuki-chan's heart would be healed, for her sake.

It's hard to believe "if you keep on living, things will be good," because we are still in the middle of living. But I have experienced being really, really happy several times, so I want to believe it. Dying can be done without striving for it. We all eventually die. To use your strength for such a thing is a waste!! So let's at least move toward believing. I will too.

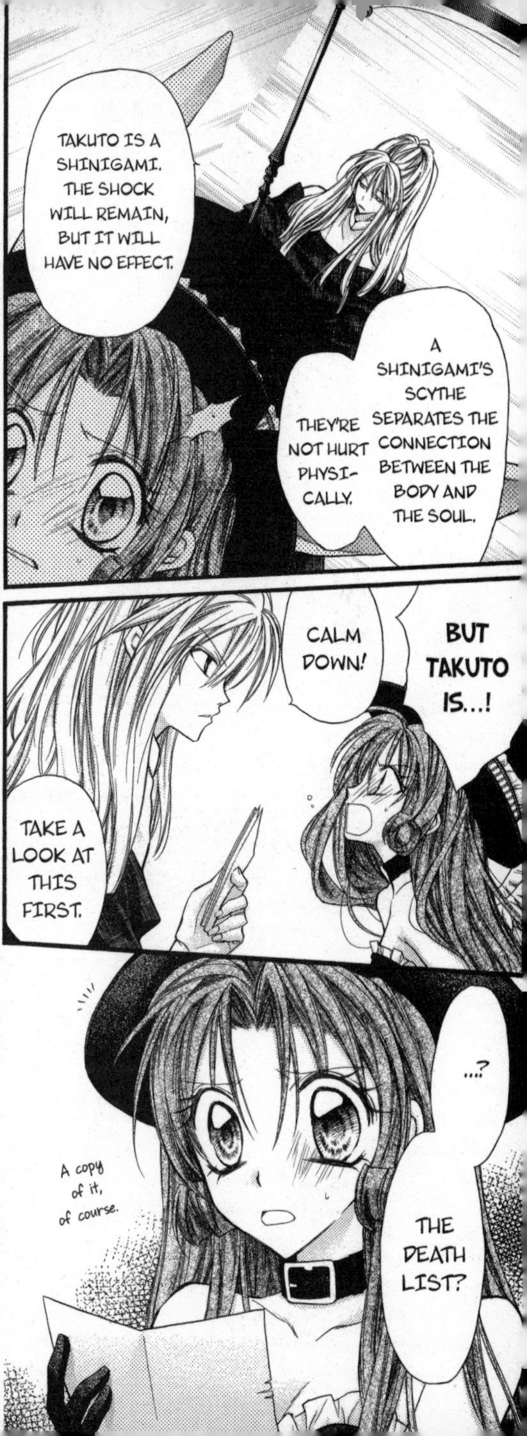
A SHINIGAMI'S SCYTHE SEPARATES THE CONNECTION BETWEEN THE BODY AND THE SOUL.
THEY'RE NOT HURT PHYSI-CALLY.
TAKUTO IS A SHINIGAMI. THE SHOCK WILL REMAIN, BUT IT WILL HAVE NO EFFECT.
BUT TAKUTO IS...!
CALM DOWN!
TAKE A LOOK AT THIS FIRST.
...?
THE DEATH LIST?
A copy of it, of course.

Being Hospitalized ③

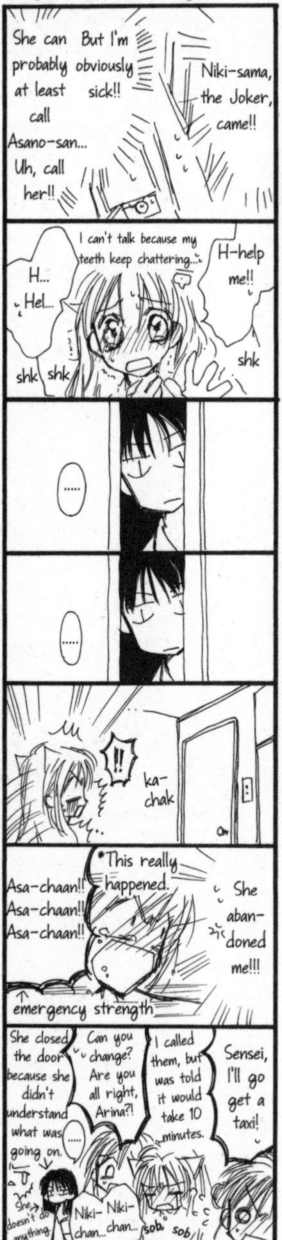
Niki-sama, the Joker, came!!
But I'm obviously sick!!
She can probably at least call Asano-san... Uh, call her!!
H-help me!!
I can't talk because my teeth keep chattering...
H... Hel...
shk shk
shk
.....
.....
!!
ka-chak
She aban-doned me!!!
*This really happened.
Asa-chaan!! Asa-chaan!! Asa-chaan!!
emergency strength
Sensei, I'll go get a taxi!
I called them, but was told it would take 10 minutes.
Can you change? Are you all right, Arina?!
She closed the door because she didn't understand what was going on.
.....
She doesn't do anything.
Niki-chan... Niki-chan...
sob sob

(to be continued...)

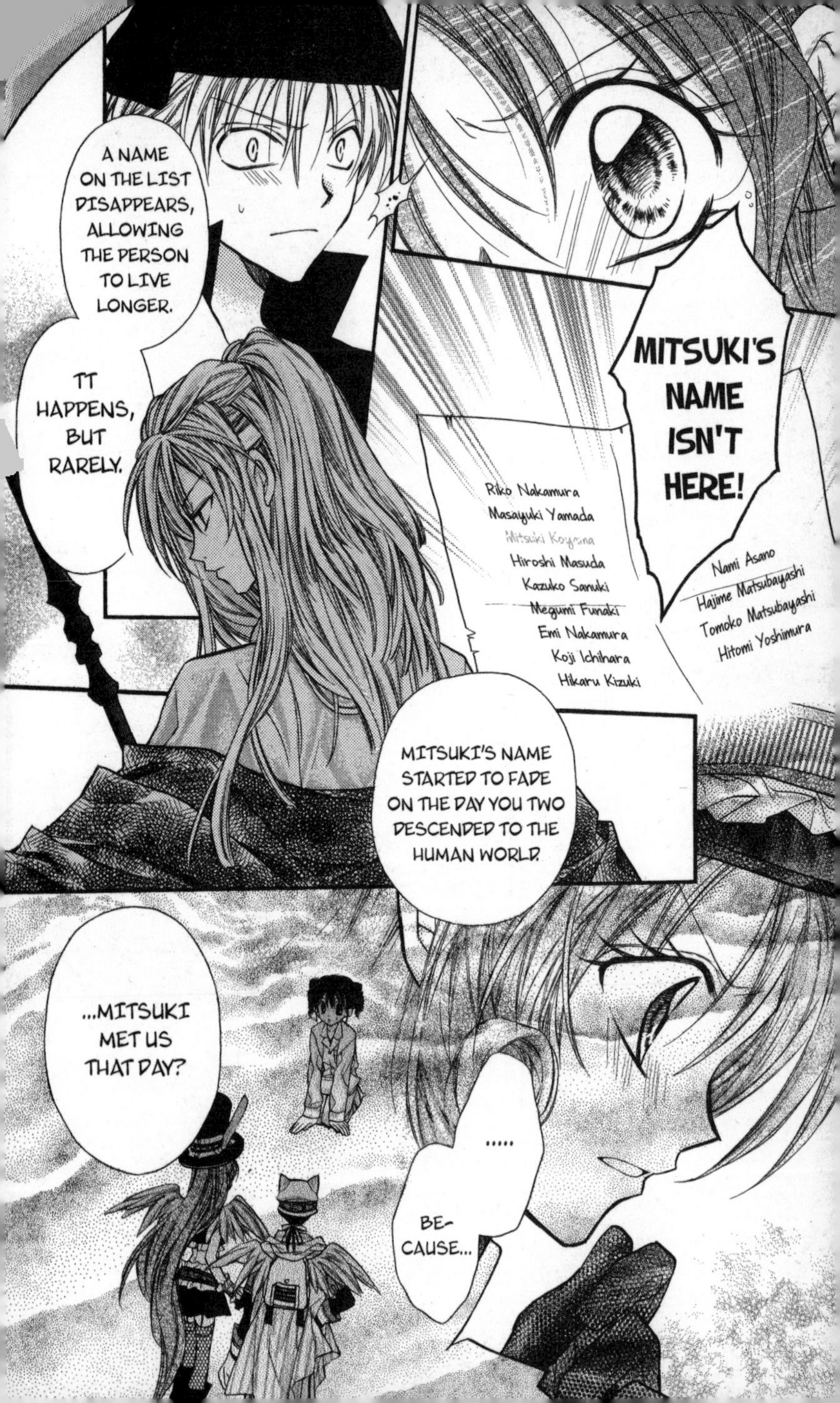

MITSUKI'S NAME ISN'T HERE!
Riko Nakamura
Masayuki Yamada
Mitsuki Koyama
Hiroshi Masuda
Kazuko Sanuki
Megumi Funaki
Emi Nakamura
Koji Ichihara
Hikaru Kizuki
Nami Asano
Hajime Matsubayashi
Tomoko Matsubayashi
Hitomi Yoshimura
A NAME ON THE LIST DISAPPEARS, ALLOWING THE PERSON TO LIVE LONGER.
IT HAPPENS, BUT RARELY.
MITSUKI'S NAME STARTED TO FADE ON THE DAY YOU TWO DESCENDED TO THE HUMAN WORLD.
...MITSUKI MET US THAT DAY?
.....
BE-CAUSE...

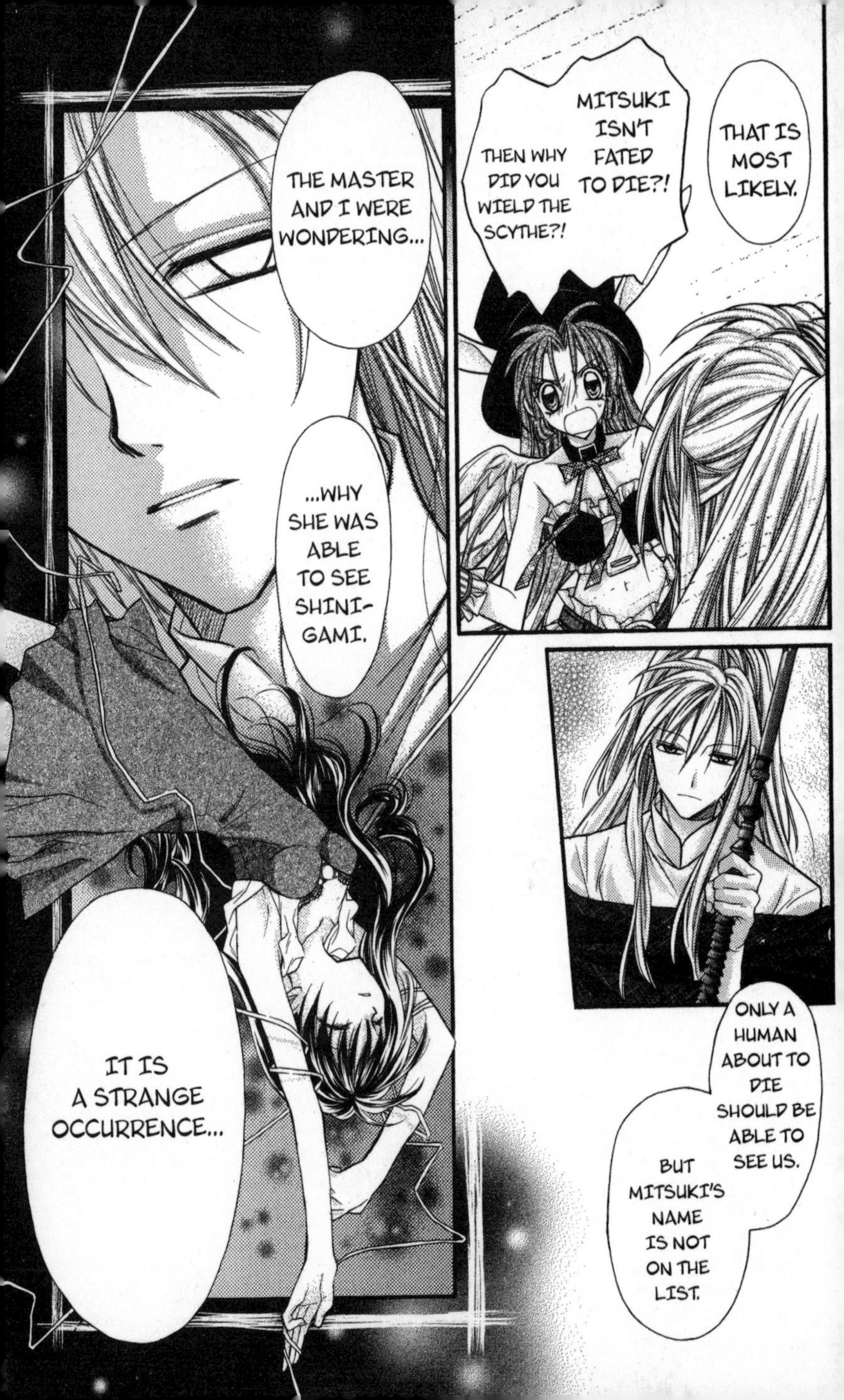
THAT IS MOST LIKELY.
MITSUKI ISN'T FATED TO DIE?!
THEN WHY DID YOU WIELD THE SCYTHE?!
ONLY A HUMAN ABOUT TO DIE SHOULD BE ABLE TO SEE US.
BUT MITSUKI'S NAME IS NOT ON THE LIST.
THE MASTER AND I WERE WONDERING...
...WHY SHE WAS ABLE TO SEE SHINIGAMI.
IT IS A STRANGE OCCURRENCE...

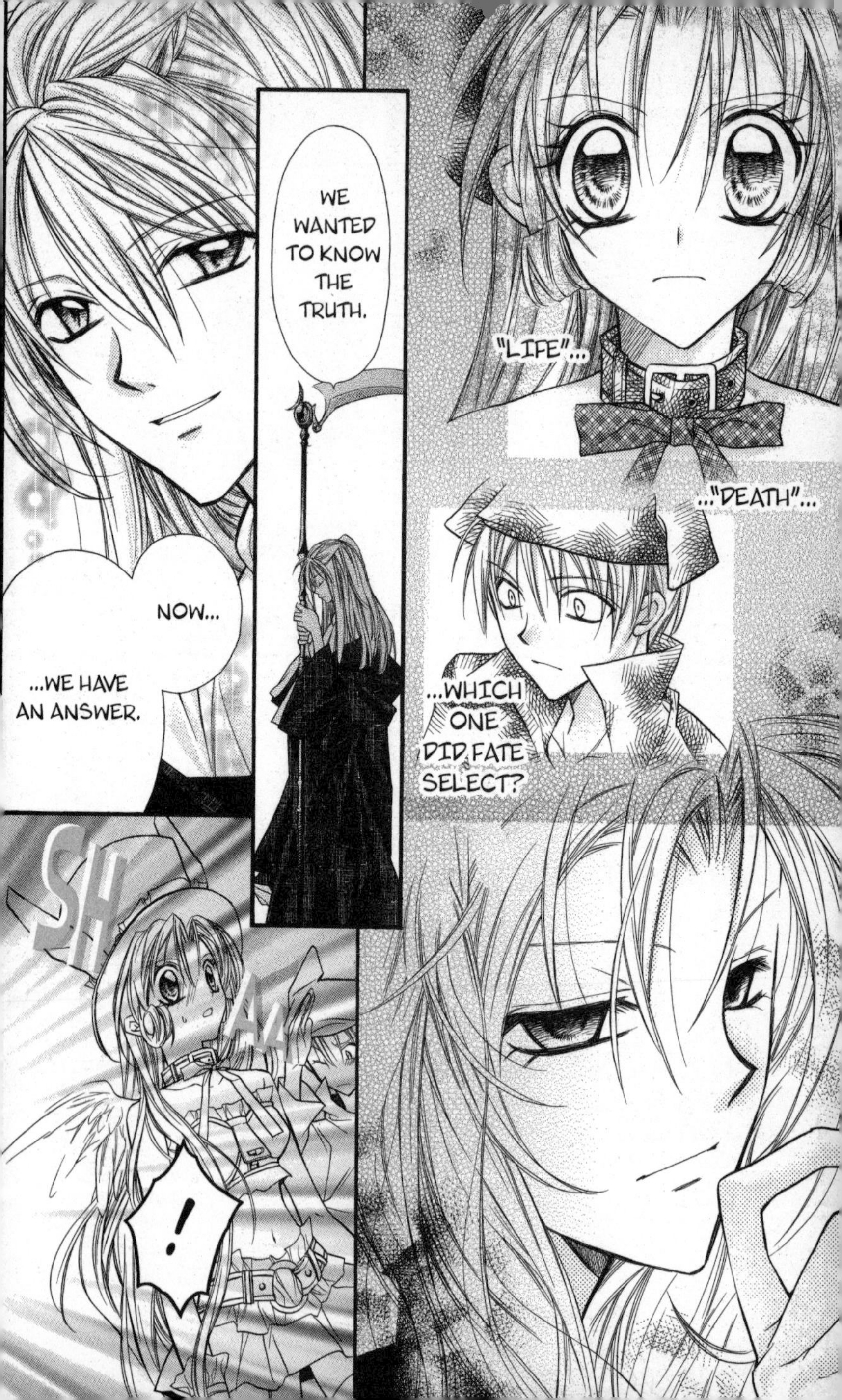
"LIFE"...
..."DEATH"...
...WHICH ONE DID FATE SELECT?
WE WANTED TO KNOW THE TRUTH.
NOW...
...WE HAVE AN ANSWER.
SHAA
!

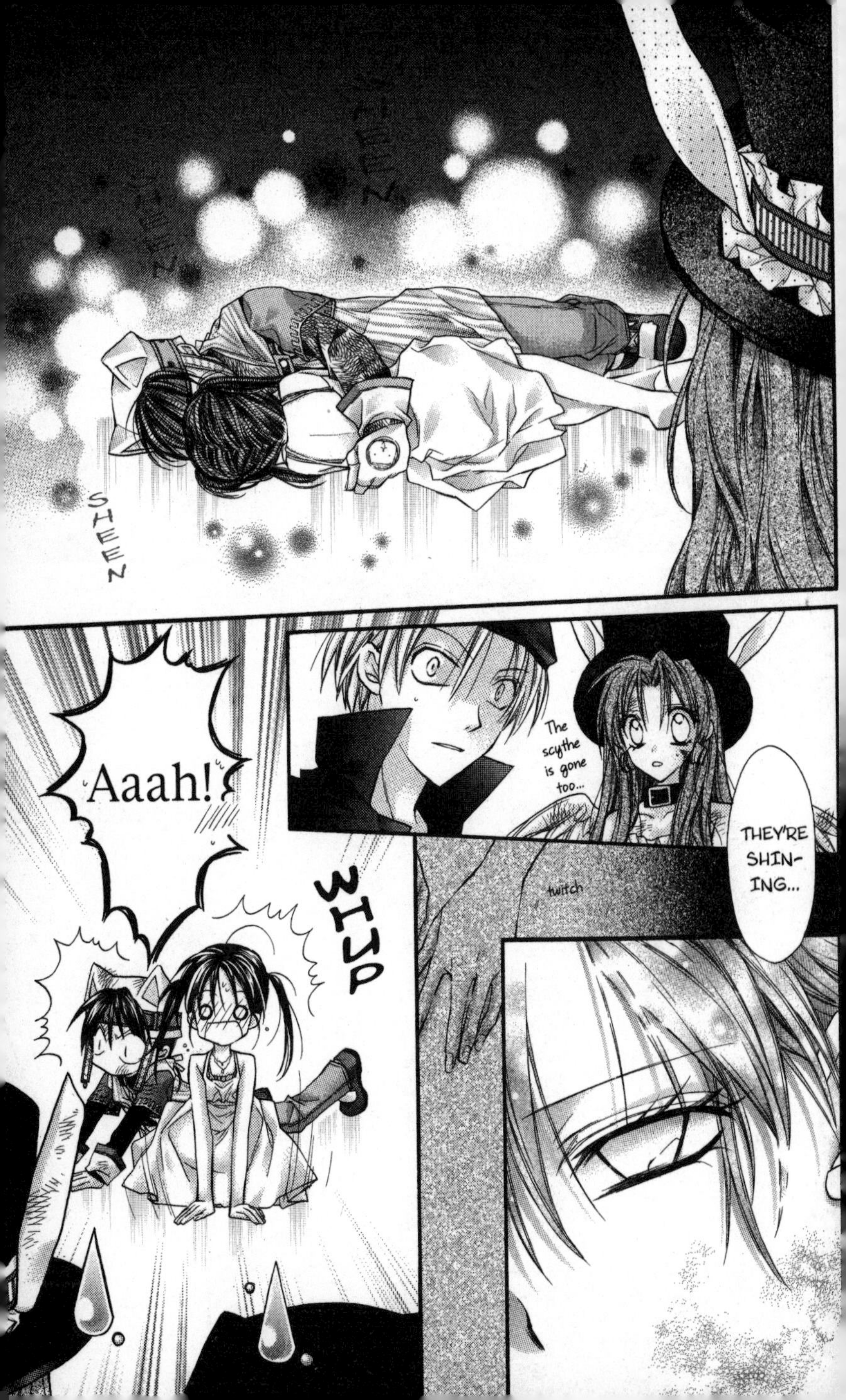
SHEEN
The scythe is gone too...
THEY'RE SHIN-ING...
twitch
Aaah!
WHUP

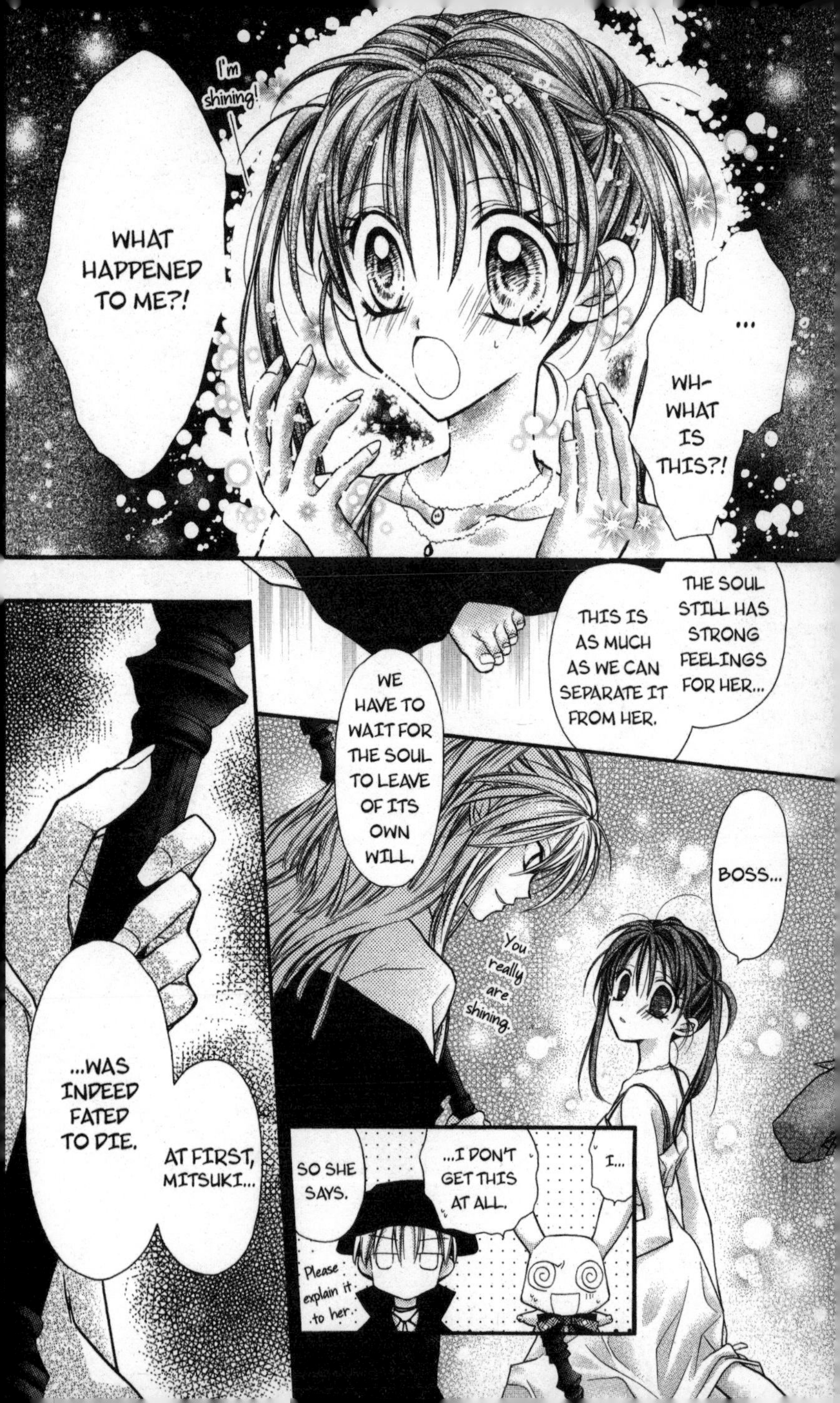
...
WH-WHAT IS THIS?!
I'm shining!
WHAT HAPPENED TO ME?!
THE SOUL STILL HAS STRONG FEELINGS FOR HER...
THIS IS AS MUCH AS WE CAN SEPARATE IT FROM HER.
WE HAVE TO WAIT FOR THE SOUL TO LEAVE OF ITS OWN WILL.
BOSS...
You really are shining.
I...
...I DON'T GET THIS AT ALL.
SO SHE SAYS.
Please explain it to her.
AT FIRST, MITSUKI...
...WAS INDEED FATED TO DIE.

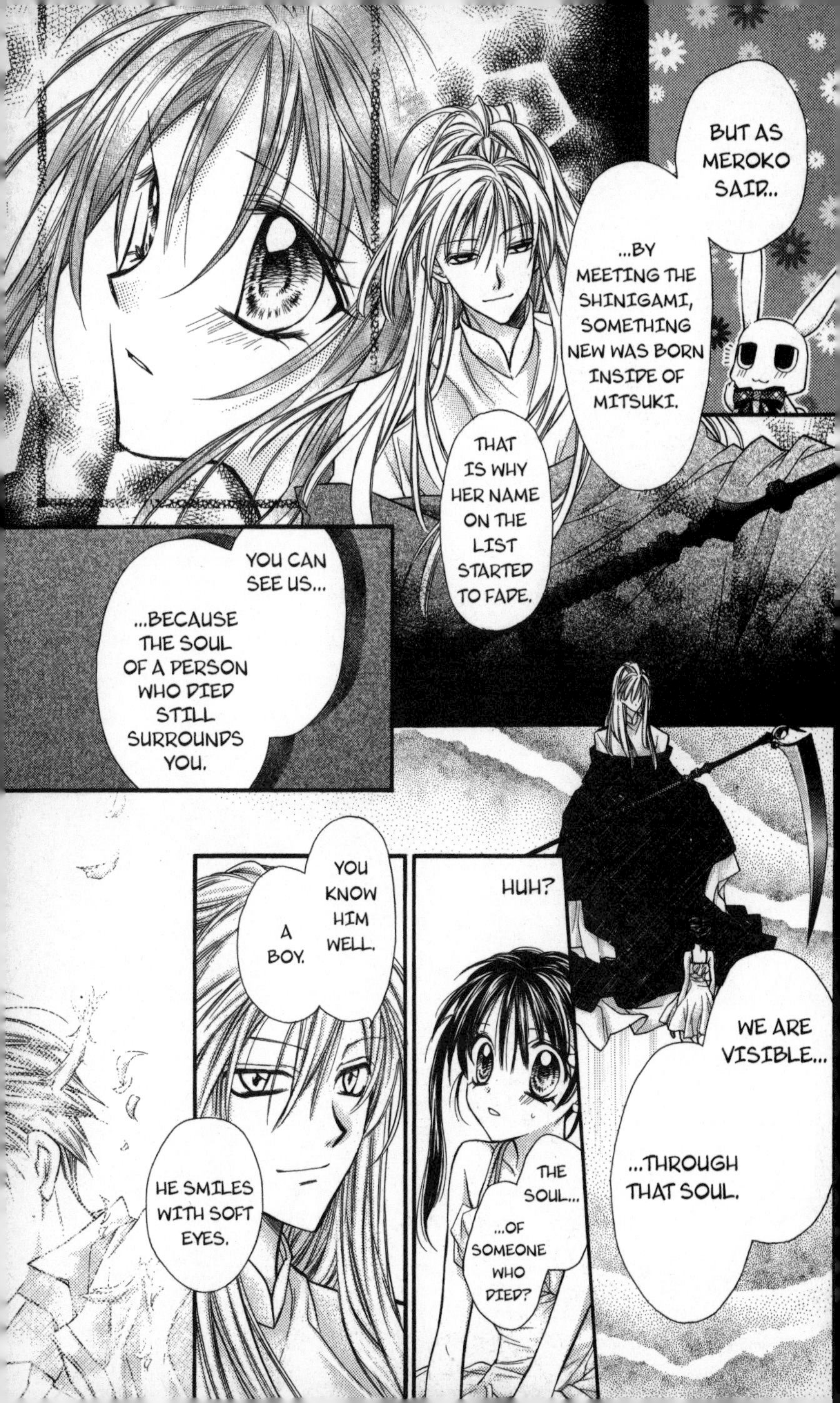
BUT AS MEROKO SAID...
...BY MEETING THE SHINIGAMI, SOMETHING NEW WAS BORN INSIDE OF MITSUKI.
THAT IS WHY HER NAME ON THE LIST STARTED TO FADE.
YOU CAN SEE US...
...BECAUSE THE SOUL OF A PERSON WHO DIED STILL SURROUNDS YOU.
WE ARE VISIBLE...
...THROUGH THAT SOUL.
HUH?
THE SOUL...
...OF SOMEONE WHO DIED?
YOU KNOW HIM WELL.
A BOY.
HE SMILES WITH SOFT EYES.

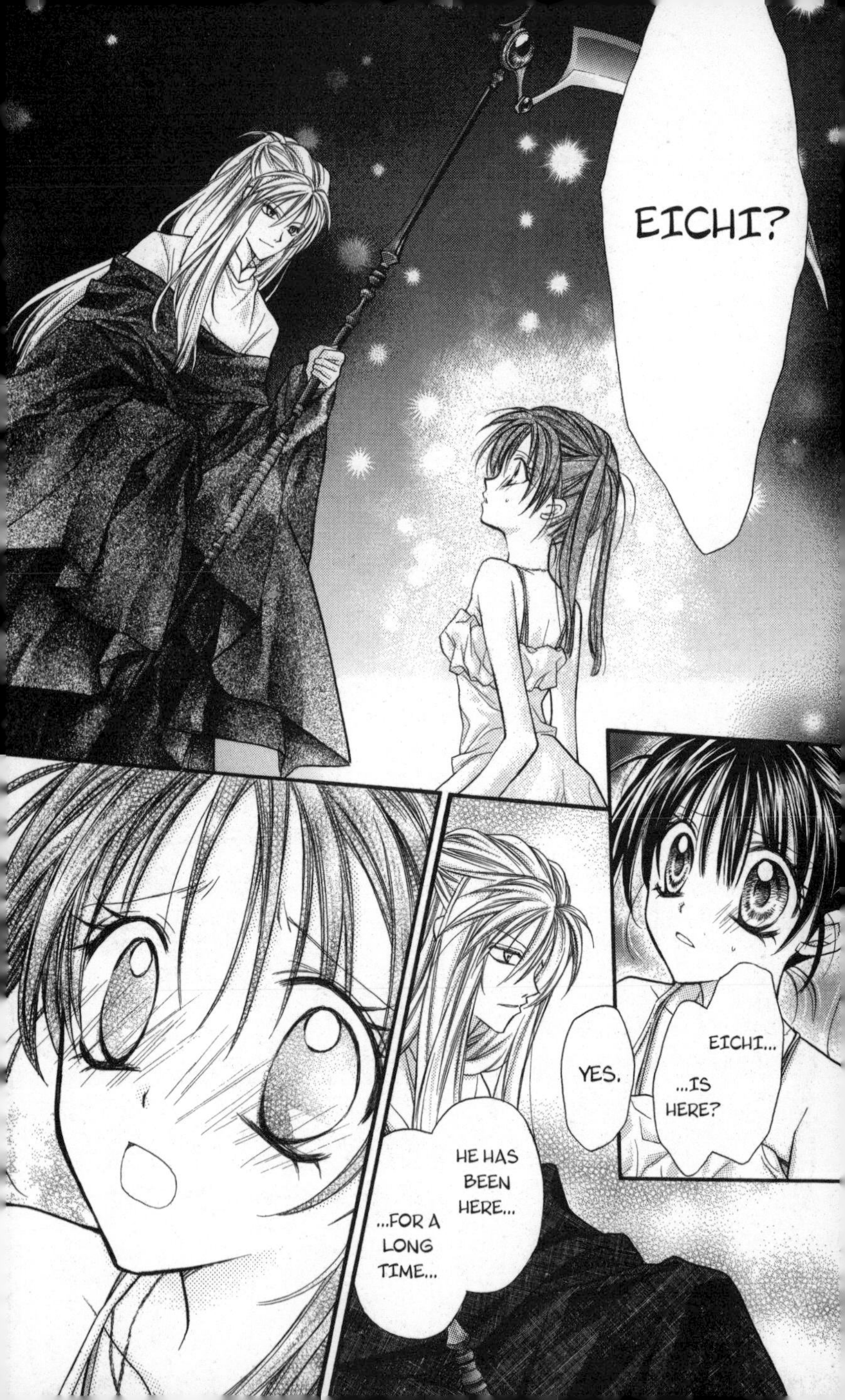
EICHI?
EICHI...
...IS HERE?
YES.
HE HAS BEEN HERE...
...FOR A LONG TIME...

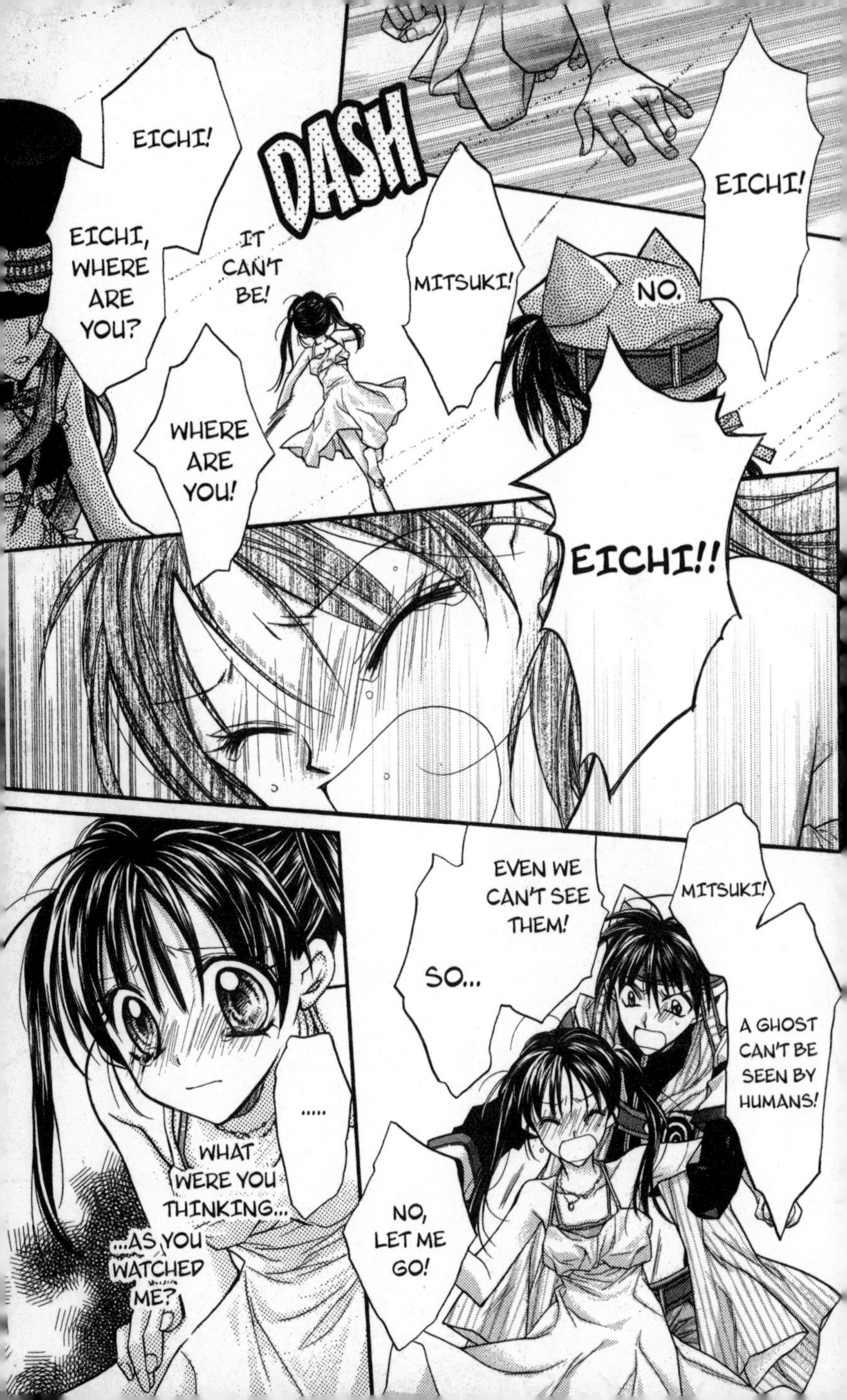
EICHI!
NO.
MITSUKI!
DASH
IT CAN'T BE!
EICHI!
EICHI, WHERE ARE YOU?
WHERE ARE YOU!
EICHI!!
MITSUKI!
EVEN WE CAN'T SEE THEM!
SO...
A GHOST CAN'T BE SEEN BY HUMANS!
NO, LET ME GO!
.....
WHAT WERE YOU THINKING...
...AS YOU WATCHED ME?

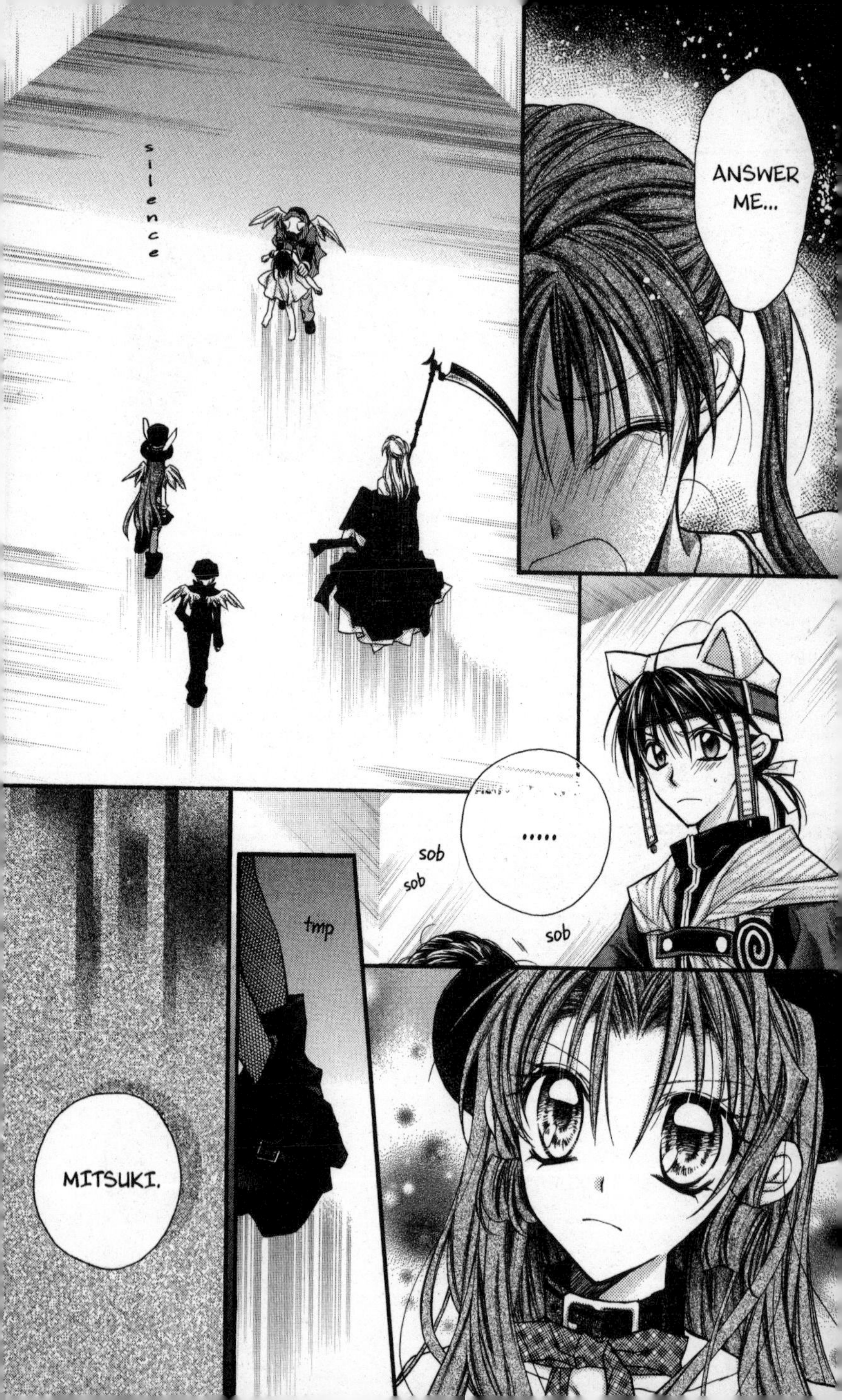
ANSWER ME...
silence
......
sob
sob
sob
tmp
MITSUKI.

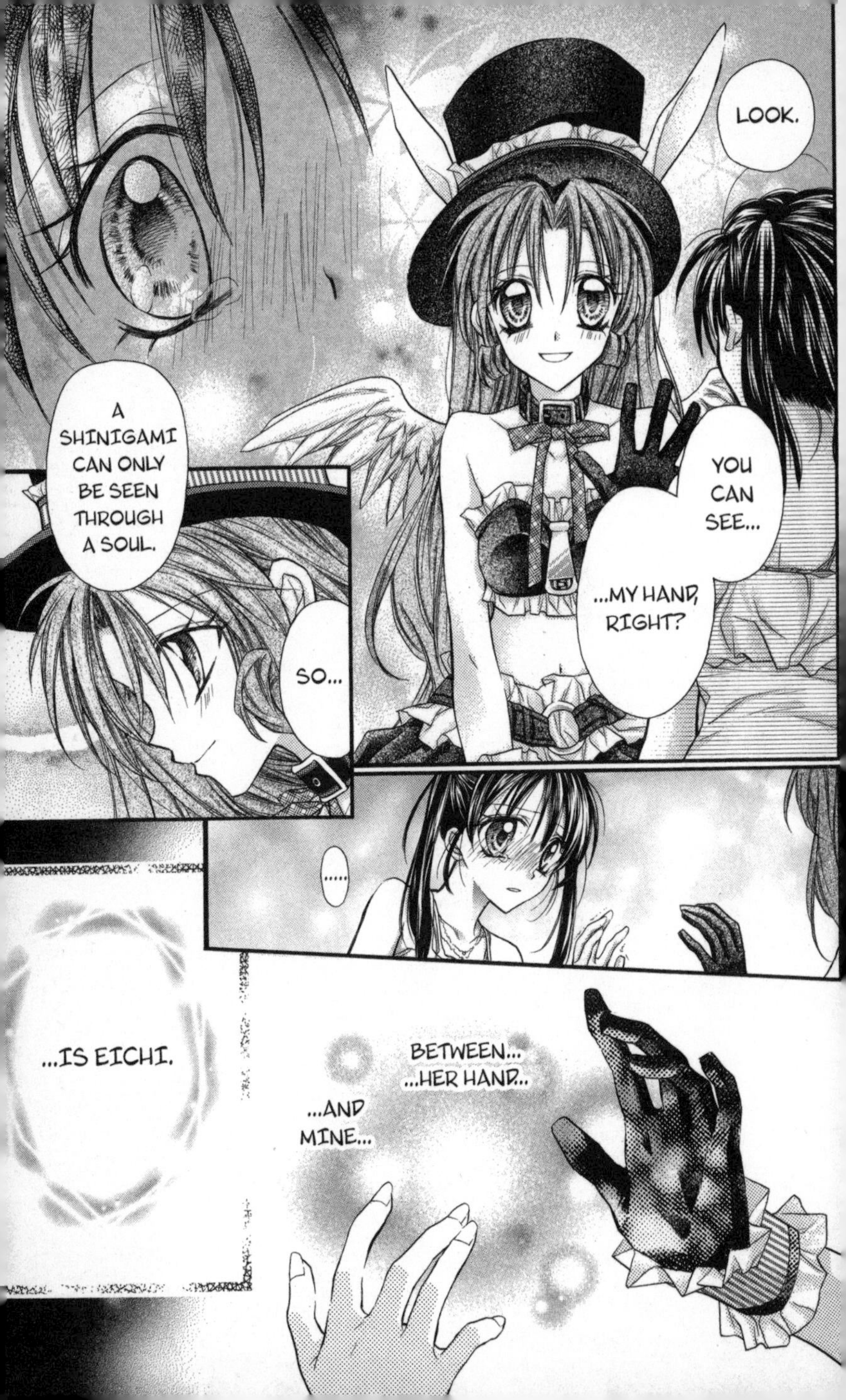
LOOK.
YOU CAN SEE...
...MY HAND, RIGHT?
A SHINIGAMI CAN ONLY BE SEEN THROUGH A SOUL.
SO...
.....
BETWEEN... ...HER HAND...
...AND MINE...
...IS EICHI.

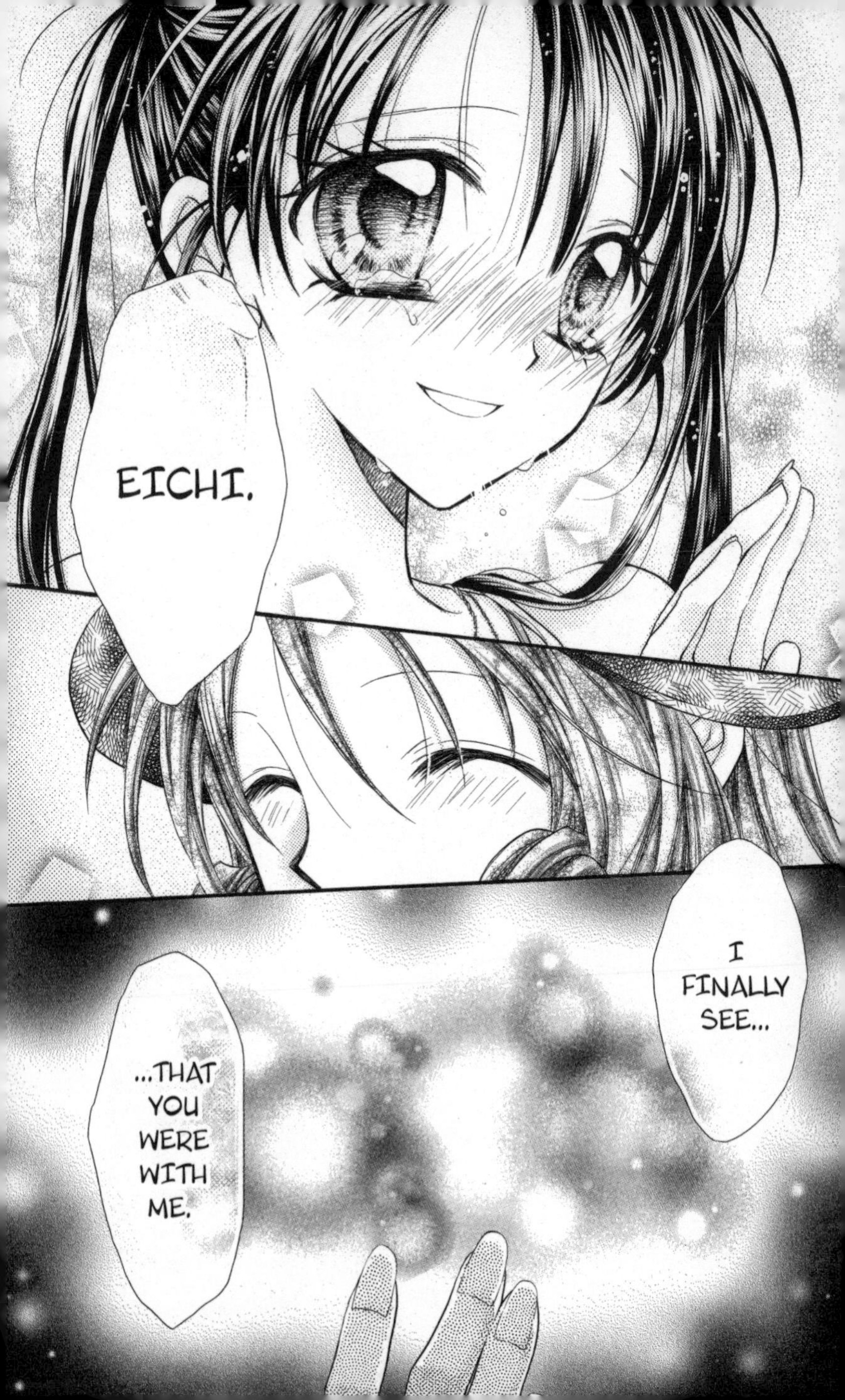
EICHI.
I FINALLY SEE...
...THAT YOU WERE WITH ME.

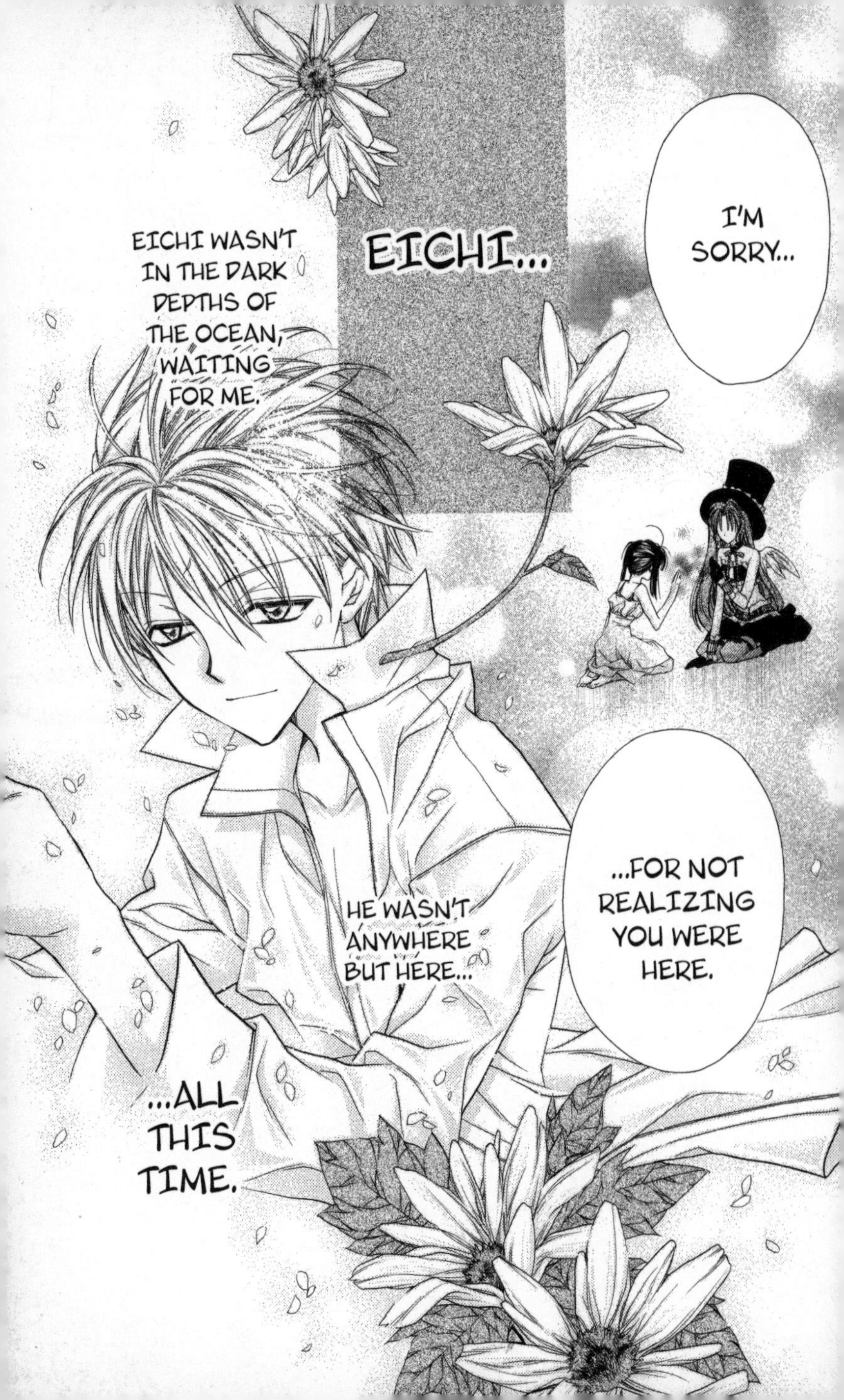

I'M SORRY...
EICHI...
EICHI WASN'T IN THE DARK DEPTHS OF THE OCEAN, WAITING FOR ME.
...FOR NOT REALIZING YOU WERE HERE.
HE WASN'T ANYWHERE BUT HERE...
...ALL THIS TIME.

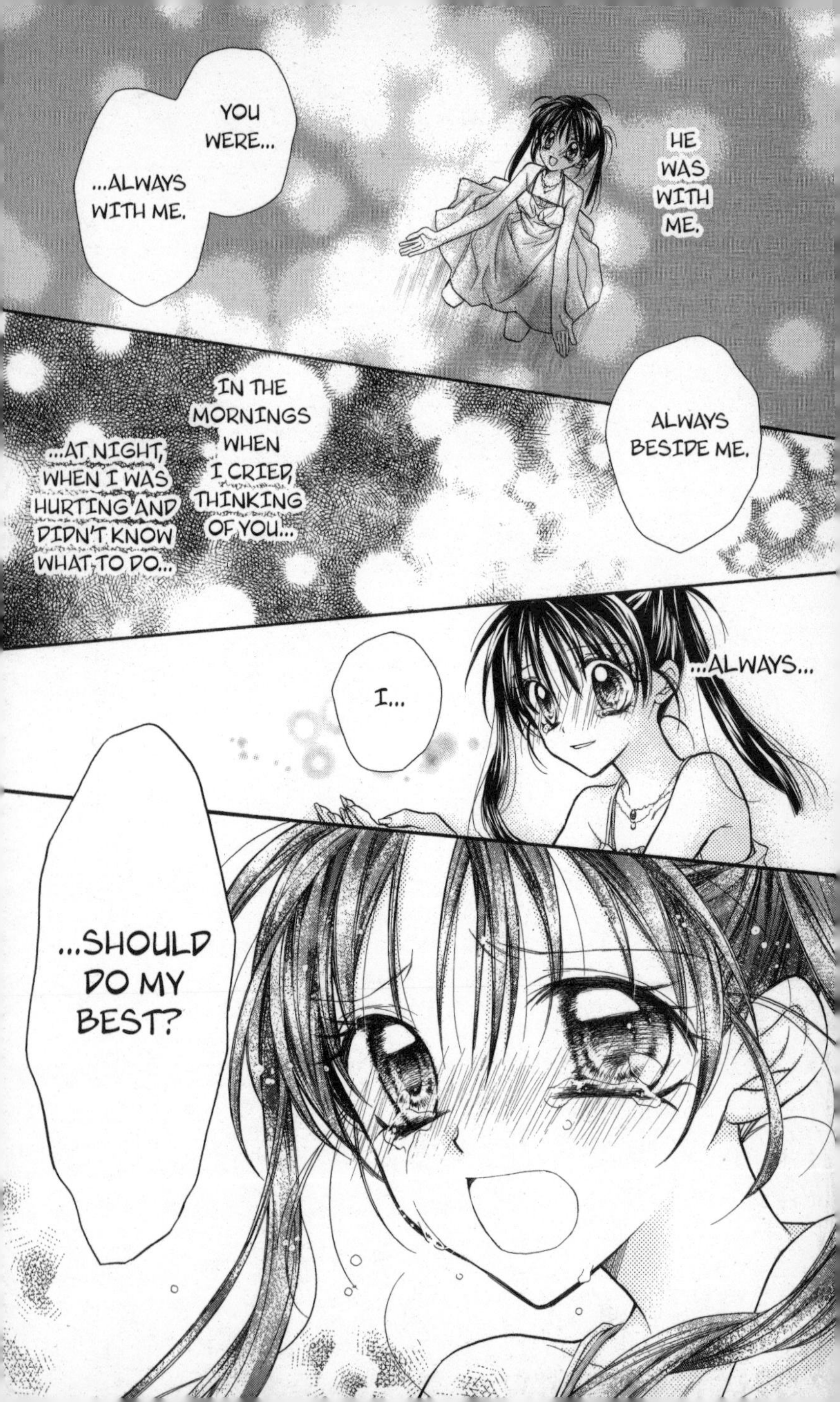
HE WAS WITH ME.
YOU WERE...
...ALWAYS WITH ME.
ALWAYS BESIDE ME.
IN THE MORNINGS WHEN I CRIED, THINKING OF YOU...
...AT NIGHT, WHEN I WAS HURTING AND DIDN'T KNOW WHAT TO DO...
...ALWAYS...
I...
...SHOULD DO MY BEST?

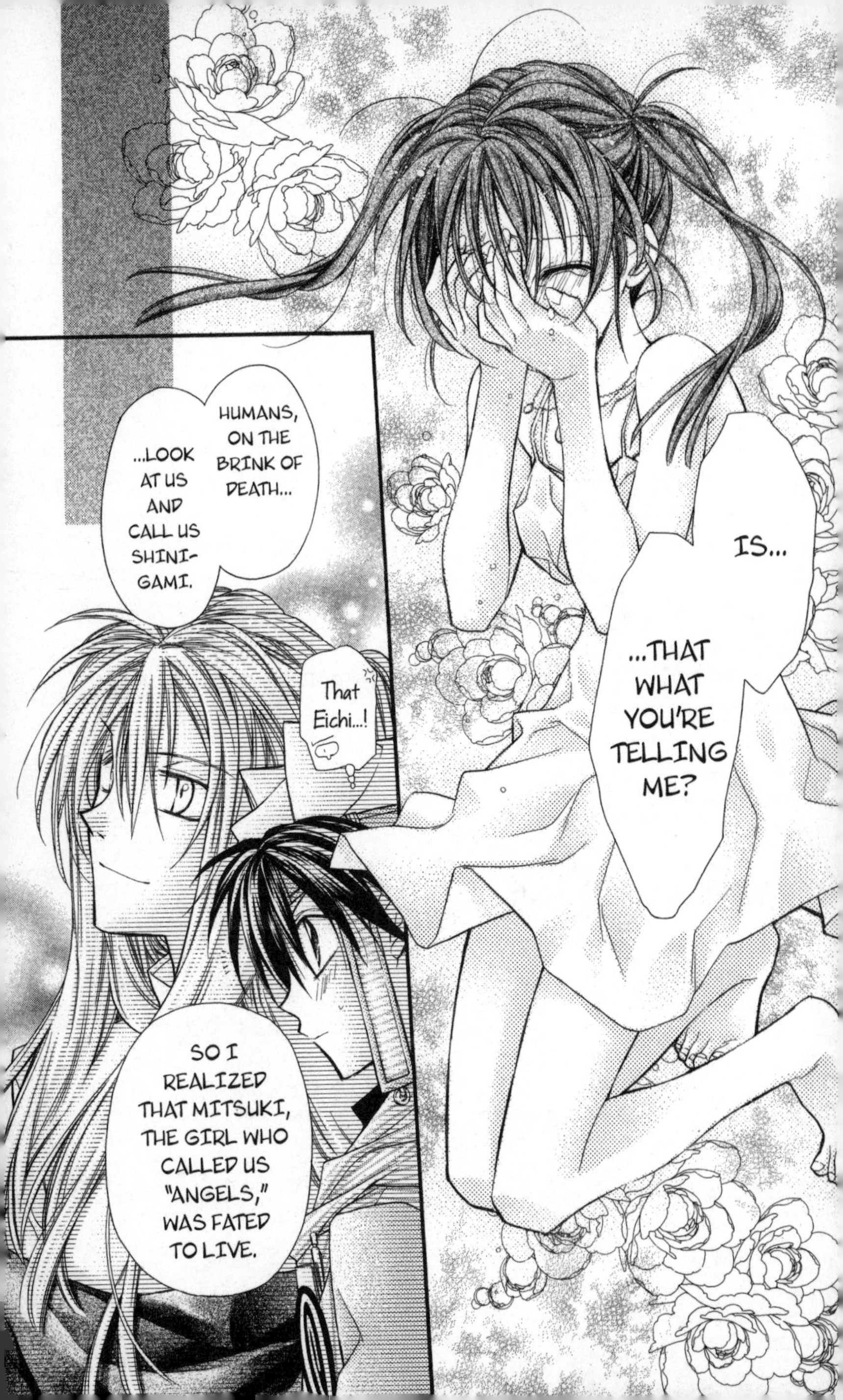
IS...
...THAT WHAT YOU'RE TELLING ME?
HUMANS, ON THE BRINK OF DEATH...
...LOOK AT US AND CALL US SHINI-GAMI.
That Eichi...!
SO I REALIZED THAT MITSUKI, THE GIRL WHO CALLED US "ANGELS," WAS FATED TO LIVE.

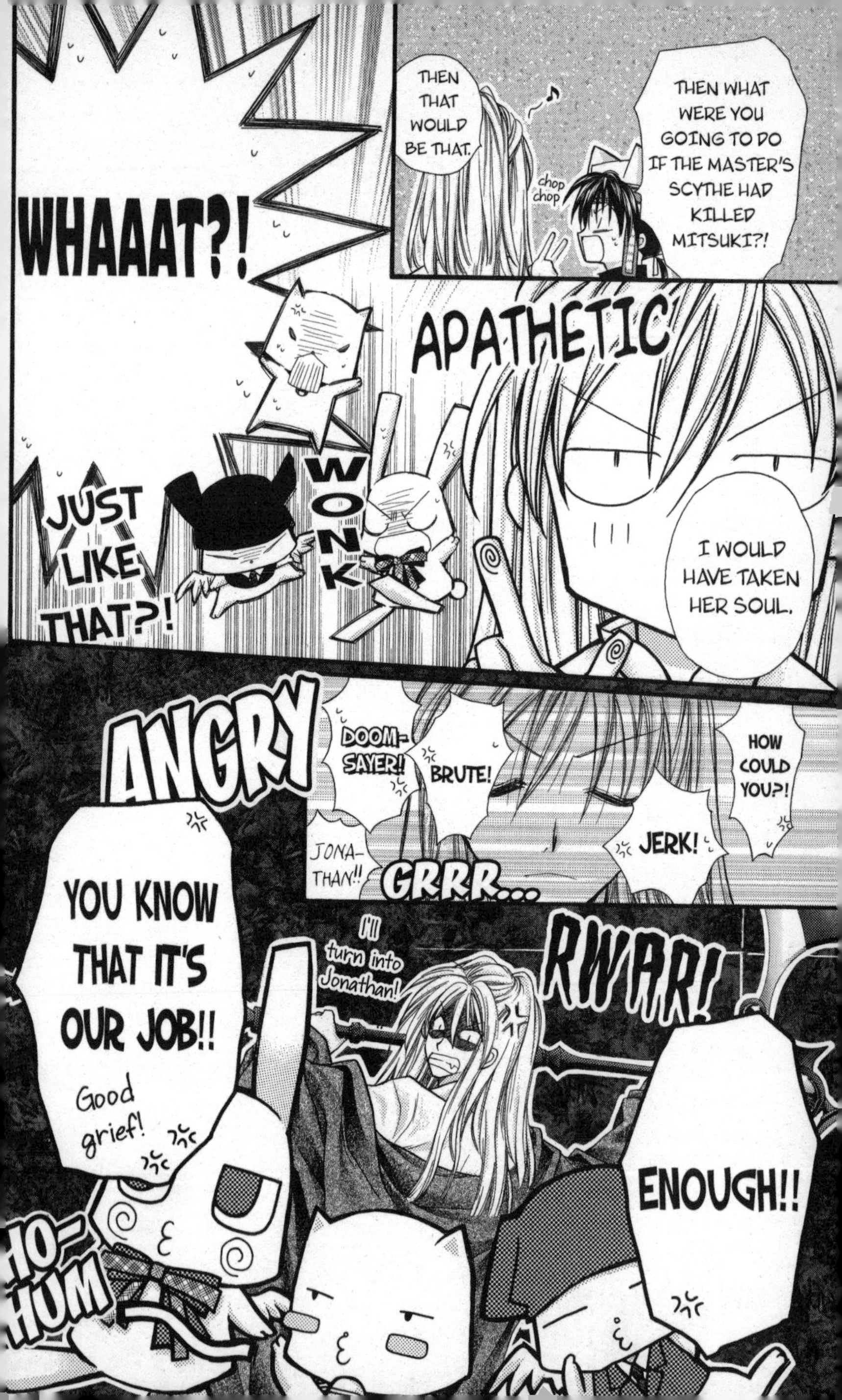
THEN WHAT WERE YOU GOING TO DO IF THE MASTER'S SCYTHE HAD KILLED MITSUKI?!
chop chop
THEN THAT WOULD BE THAT.
APATHETIC
I WOULD HAVE TAKEN HER SOUL.
WHAAAT?!
WONK
JUST LIKE THAT?!
ANGRY
HOW COULD YOU?!
JERK!
BRUTE!
DOOM-SAYER!!
JONA-THAN!!
GRRR...
RWAR!
ENOUGH!!
I'll turn into Jonathan!
YOU KNOW THAT IT'S OUR JOB!!
Good grief!
HO-HUM

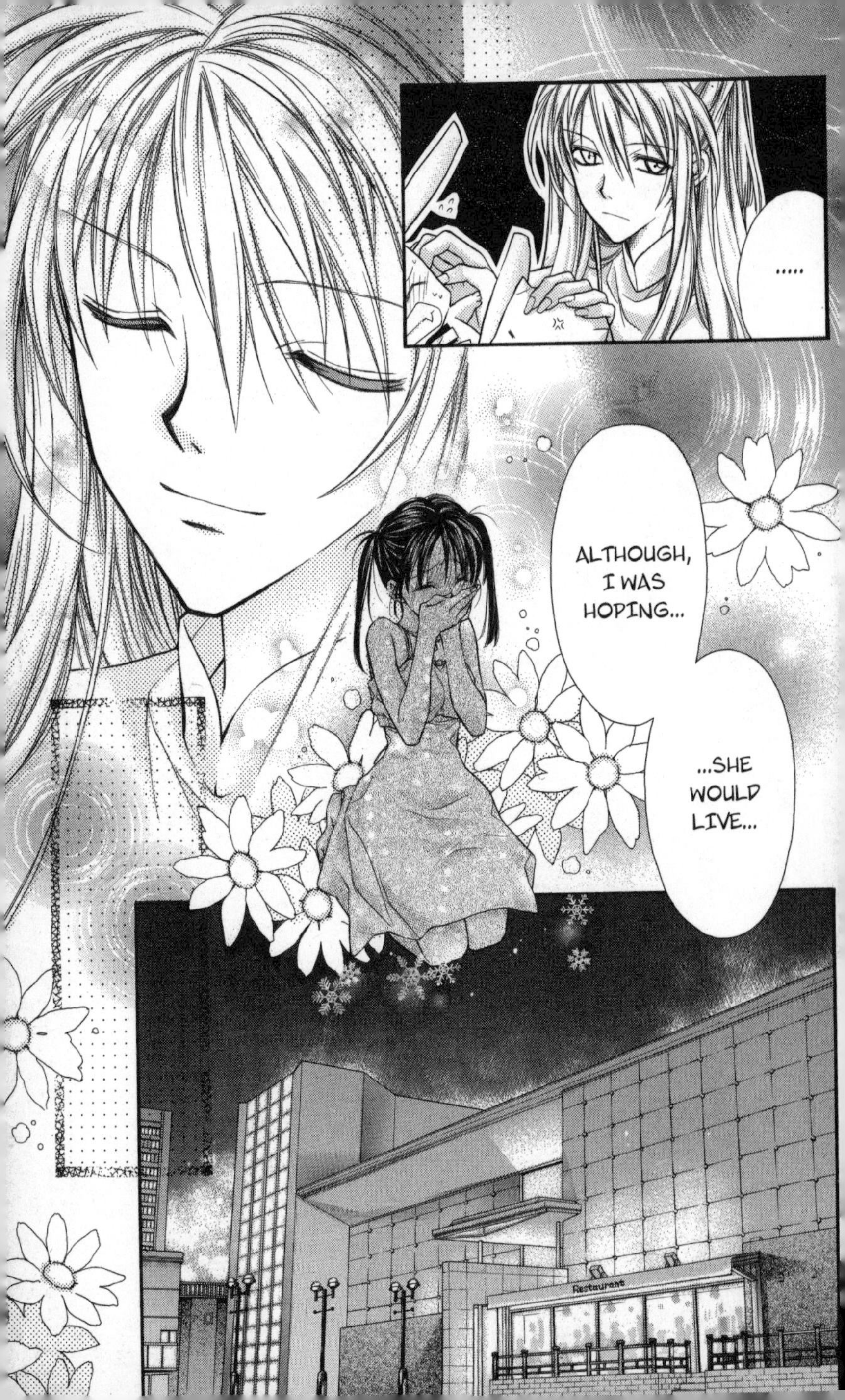
.....
ALTHOUGH, I WAS HOPING...
...SHE WOULD LIVE...
Restaurant

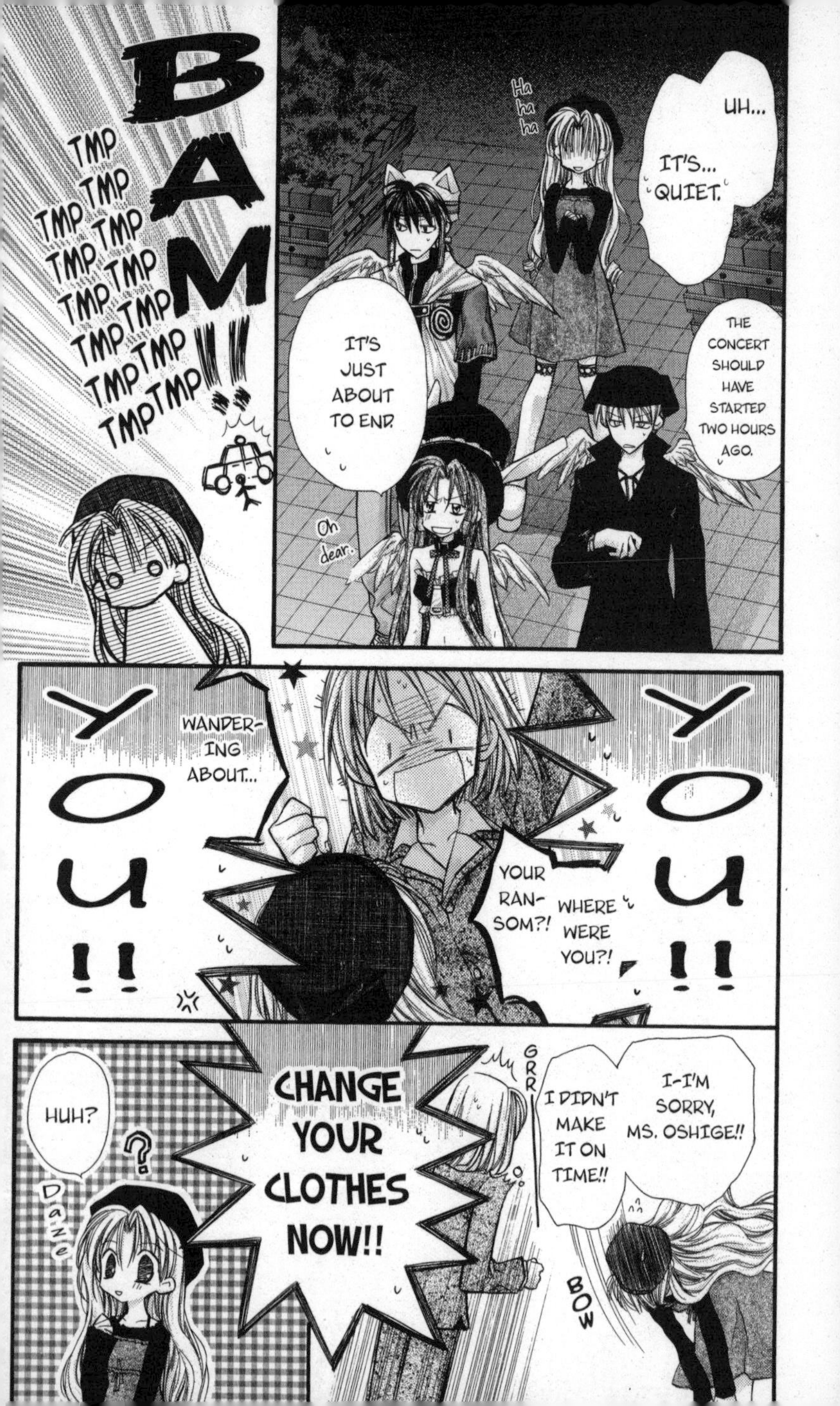
UH...
IT'S... QUIET.
Ha ha ha
THE CONCERT SHOULD HAVE STARTED TWO HOURS AGO.
IT'S JUST ABOUT TO END.
Oh dear.
BAM!!
TMP TMP TMP TMP TMP TMP TMP TMP TMP TMP TMP TMP TMP TMP TMP
YOU!!
WHERE WERE YOU?!
YOUR RAN-SOM?!
WANDER-ING ABOUT...
YOU!!
I-I'M SORRY, MS. OSHIGE!!
I DIDN'T MAKE IT ON TIME!!
GRR
BOW
CHANGE YOUR CLOTHES NOW!!
HUH?
Daze

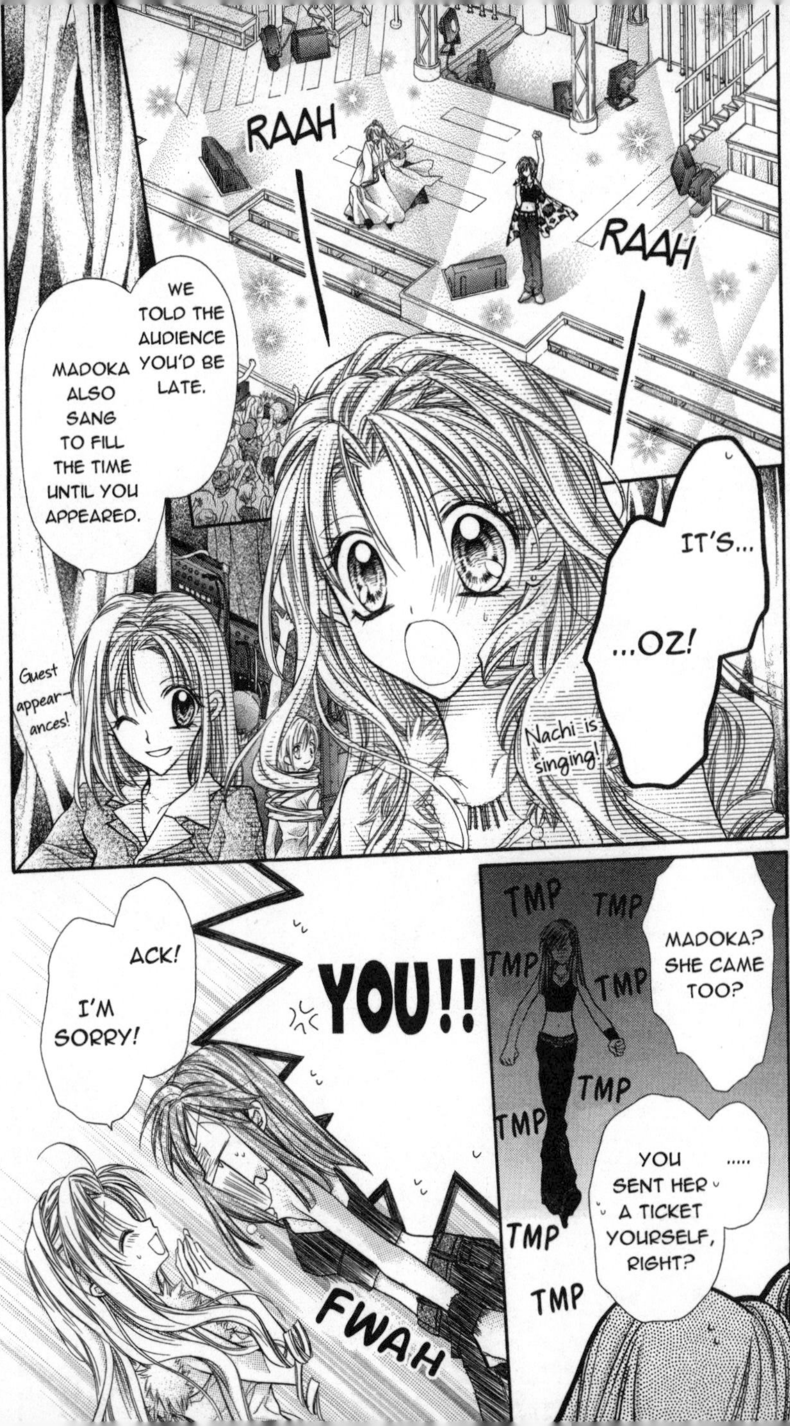
RAAH
RAAH
IT'S...
...OZ!
WE TOLD THE AUDIENCE YOU'D BE LATE. MADOKA ALSO SANG TO FILL THE TIME UNTIL YOU APPEARED.
Nachi is singing!
Guest appearances!
TMP TMP TMP TMP
MADOKA? SHE CAME TOO?
TMP TMP TMP TMP
YOU SENT HER A TICKET YOURSELF, RIGHT?
.....
YOU!!
ACK! I'M SORRY!
FWAH

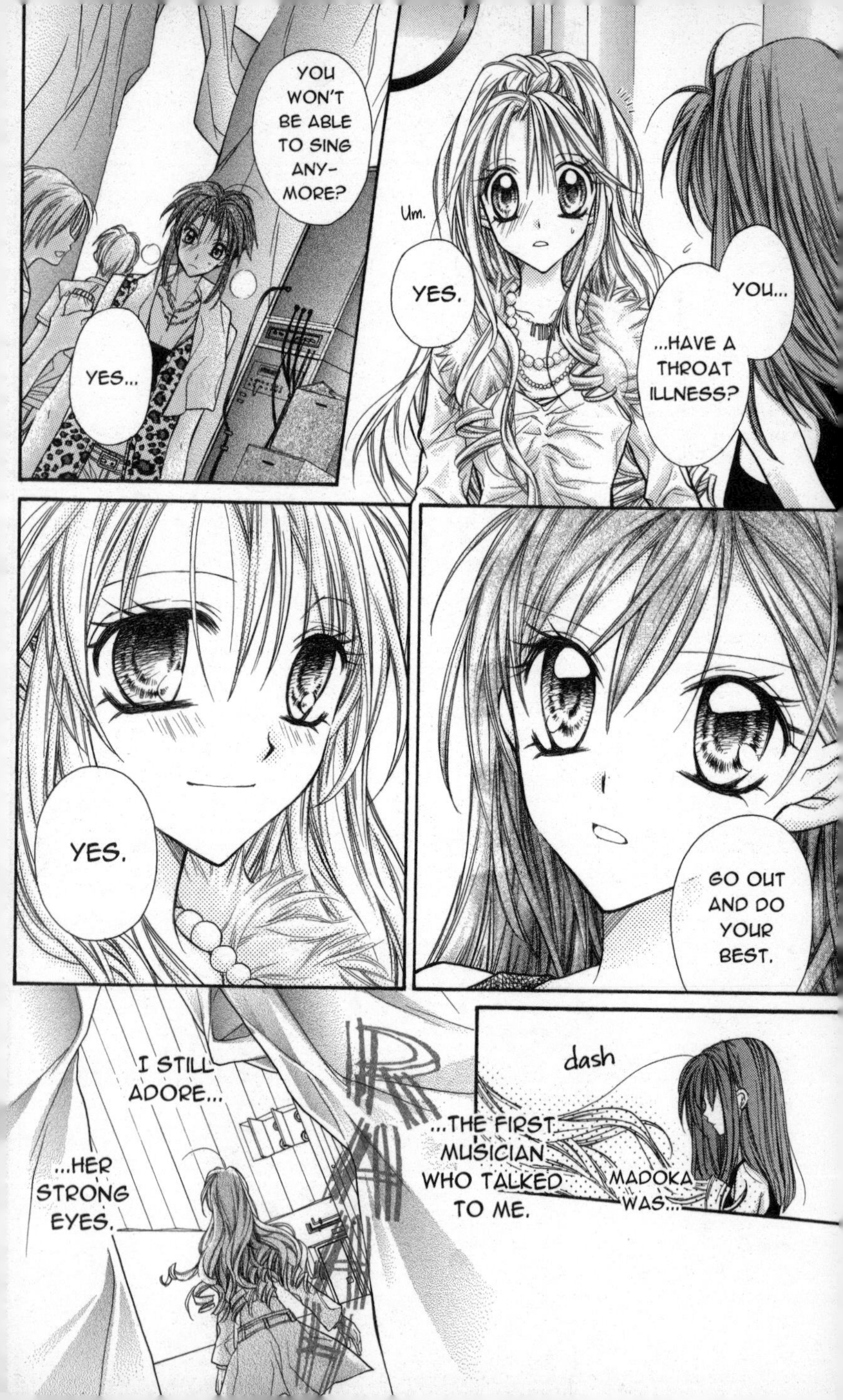
YOU... ...HAVE A THROAT ILLNESS?
Um.
YES.
YOU WON'T BE ABLE TO SING ANY-MORE?
YES...
GO OUT AND DO YOUR BEST.
YES.
dash
MADOKA WAS...
...THE FIRST MUSICIAN WHO TALKED TO ME.
I STILL ADORE...
...HER STRONG EYES.

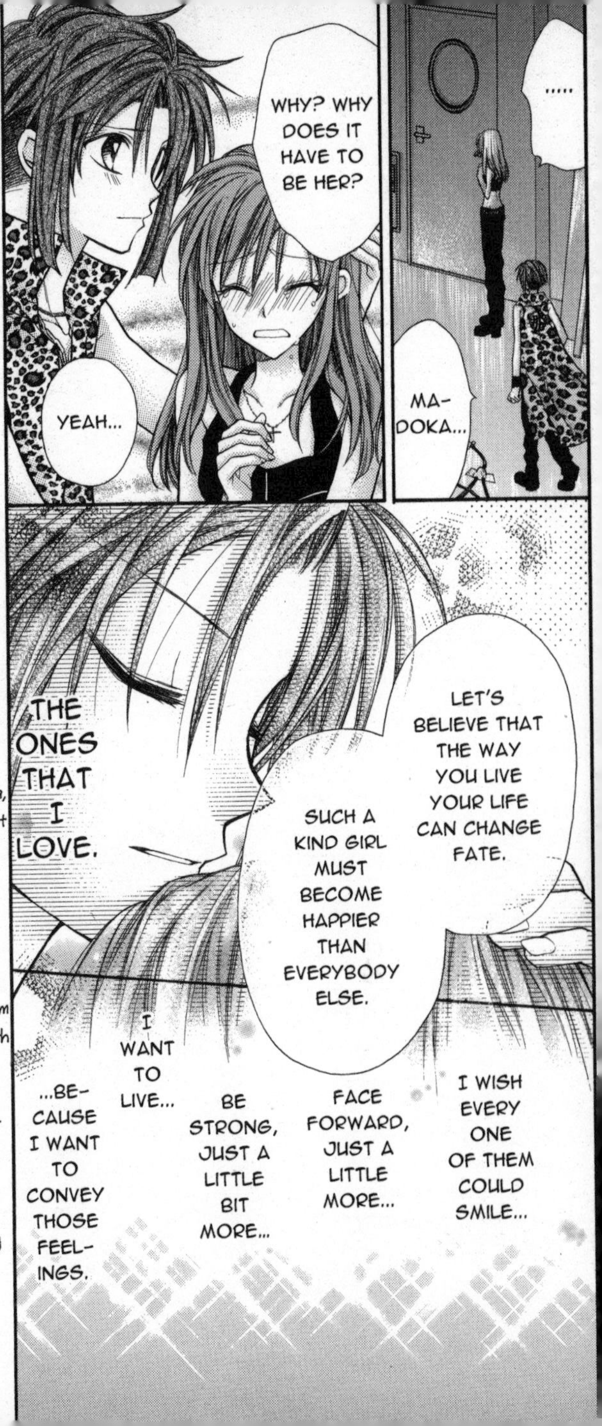
.....
MA-DOKA...
WHY? WHY DOES IT HAVE TO BE HER?
YEAH...
LET'S BELIEVE THAT THE WAY YOU LIVE YOUR LIFE CAN CHANGE FATE.
SUCH A KIND GIRL MUST BECOME HAPPIER THAN EVERYBODY ELSE.
THE ONES THAT I LOVE.
I WISH EVERY ONE OF THEM COULD SMILE...
FACE FORWARD, JUST A LITTLE MORE...
BE STRONG, JUST A LITTLE BIT MORE...
I WANT TO LIVE...
...BE-CAUSE I WANT TO CONVEY THOSE FEEL-INGS.

Me Recently

I can't talk about *Full Moon*, so please forgive me... (I wrote a little in the chapter comments.)

Recently, I've been working as usual. Wait a minute! Am I being duped?! What are holidays?! Where are my holidays?!!

Well, it's a relief to not have my monthly deadlines (since my brain is full of work)!! Now it's full of my new series.

And! I took my assistants on a trip! ✧ (Generous me!) We went to Hokkaido.✧ Even now, when I remember it, I just can't help but want to go back. (Shintsuki-chan lives in Hokkaido...) ← A female fan of mine.

Twelve of us rode *Cassiopeia*, ✧ the sleeper express. (I got a suite for myself!!) The food was really delicious. (You need to reserve it.) I had a full-course French meal. It was really delicious...

Airi stayed in the same room as me (because she came with me to get the tickets--in the early morning, one month before the trip...). At night, we turned off the lights and talked, facing each other while watching the nightscape. It was really relaxing and good!!

Sigh...

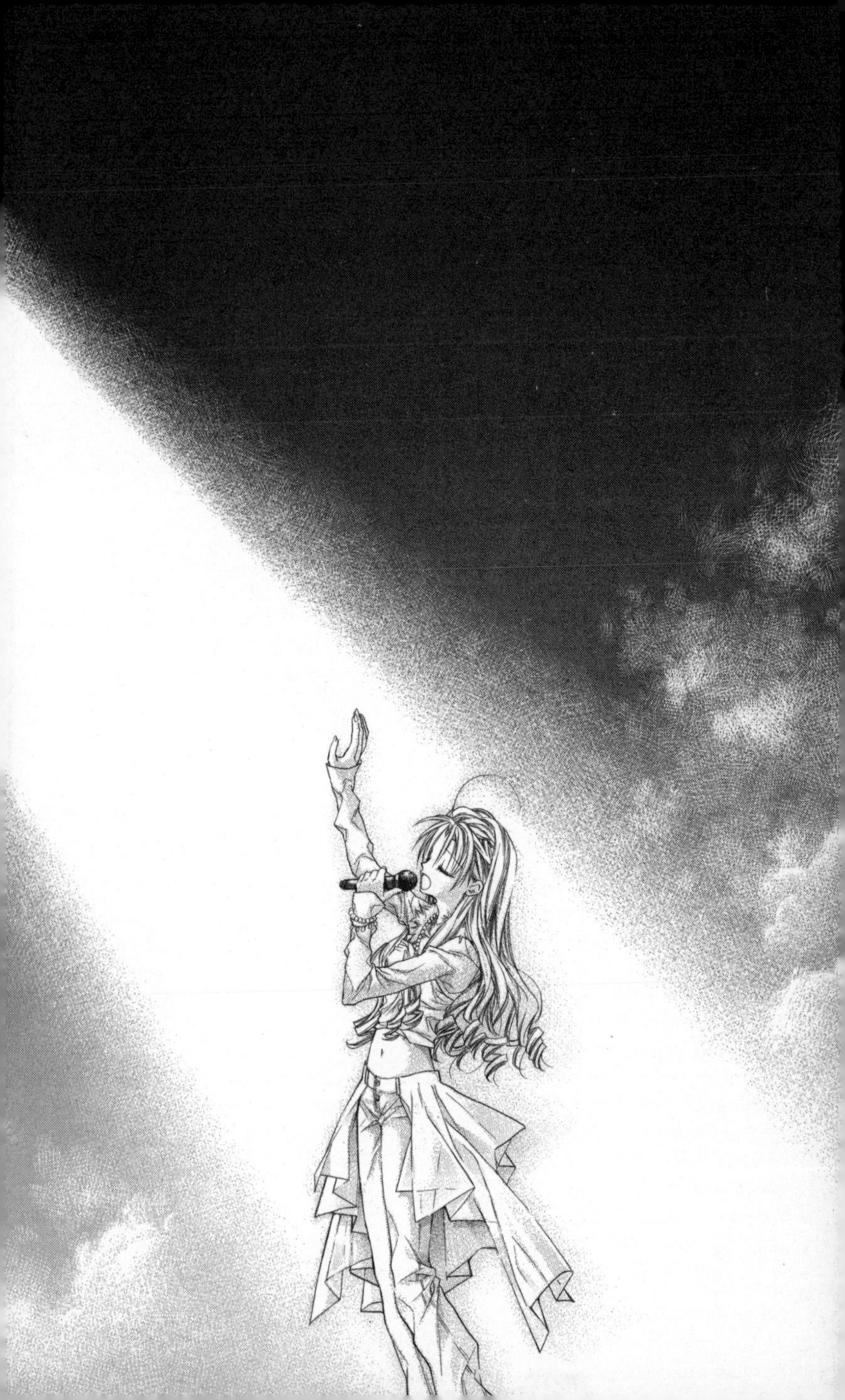

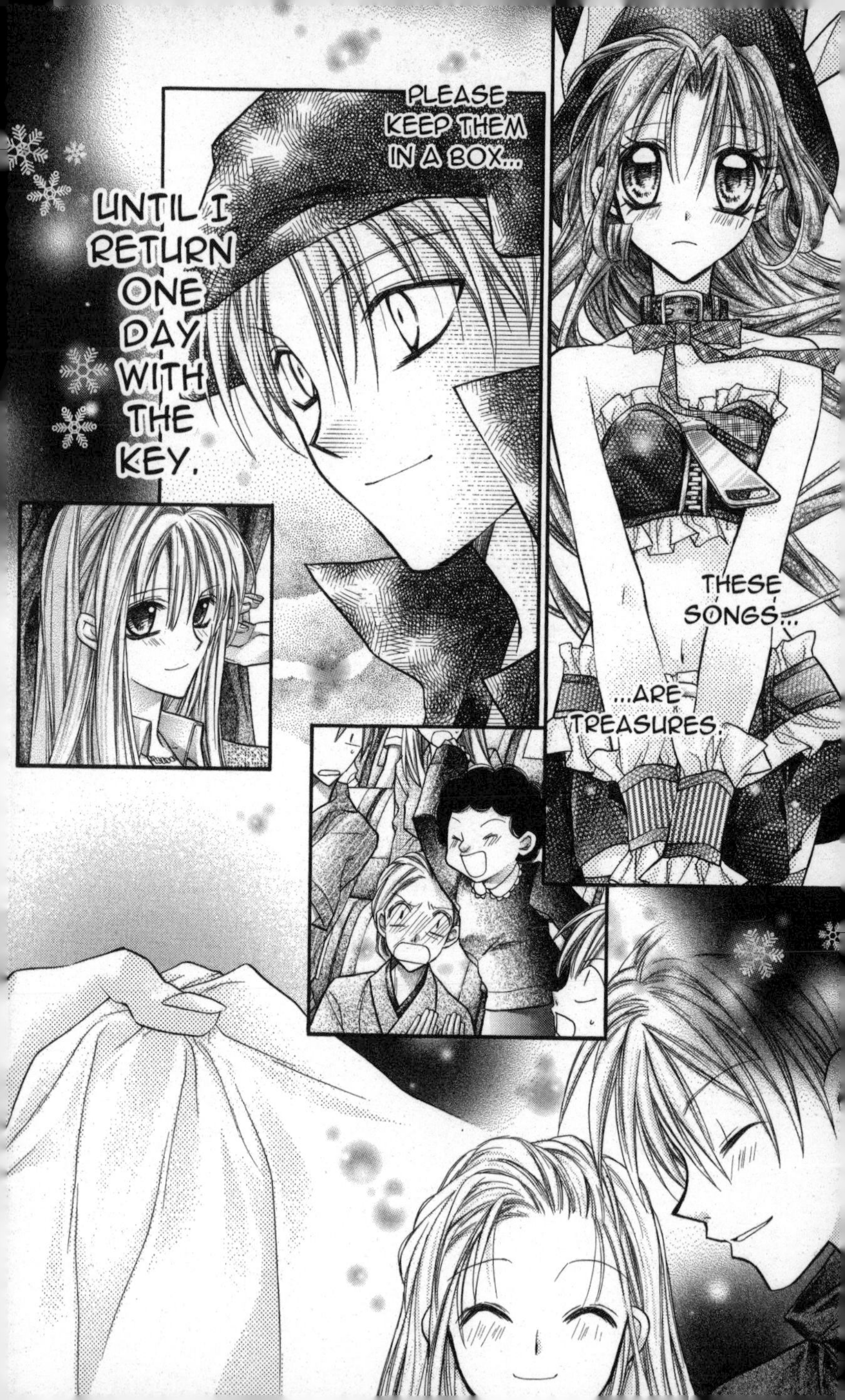
THESE SONGS...
...ARE TREASURES.
PLEASE KEEP THEM IN A BOX...
UNTIL I RETURN ONE DAY WITH THE KEY.

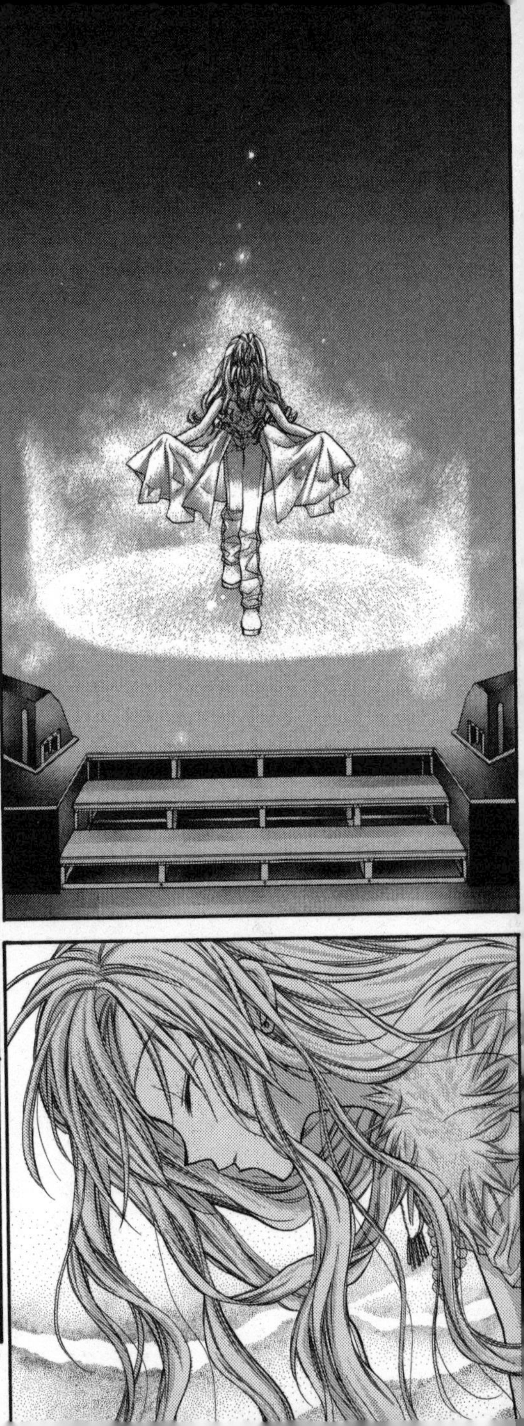

Being Hospitalized ④

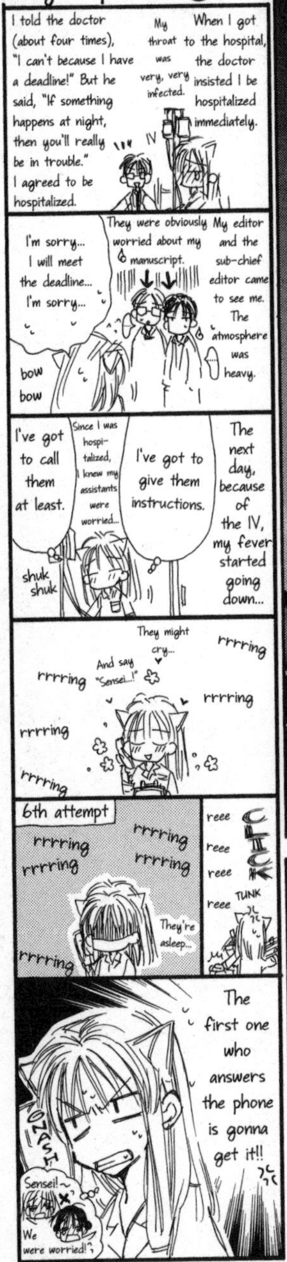

When I got to the hospital, the doctor insisted I be hospitalized immediately.
My throat was very, very infected.
IV
I told the doctor (about four times), "I can't because I have a deadline!" But he said, "If something happens at night, then you'll really be in trouble." I agreed to be hospitalized.
My editor and the sub-chief editor came to see me. The atmosphere was heavy.
They were obviously worried about my manuscript.
I'm sorry... I will meet the deadline... I'm sorry...
bow bow
The next day, because of the IV, my fever started going down...
I've got to give them instructions.
Since I was hospitalized, I knew my assistants were worried...
I've got to call them at least.
shuk shuk
rrrring
They might cry...
And say "Sensei...!"
rrrring
rrrring
rrrring
rrrring
reee
CLICK
reee
reee
reee
TUNK
6th attempt
rrrring
rrrring
rrrring
rrrring
They're asleep...
rrrring
The first one who answers the phone is gonna get it!!
GNASH
Sensei!~
We were worried!

(to be continued...)

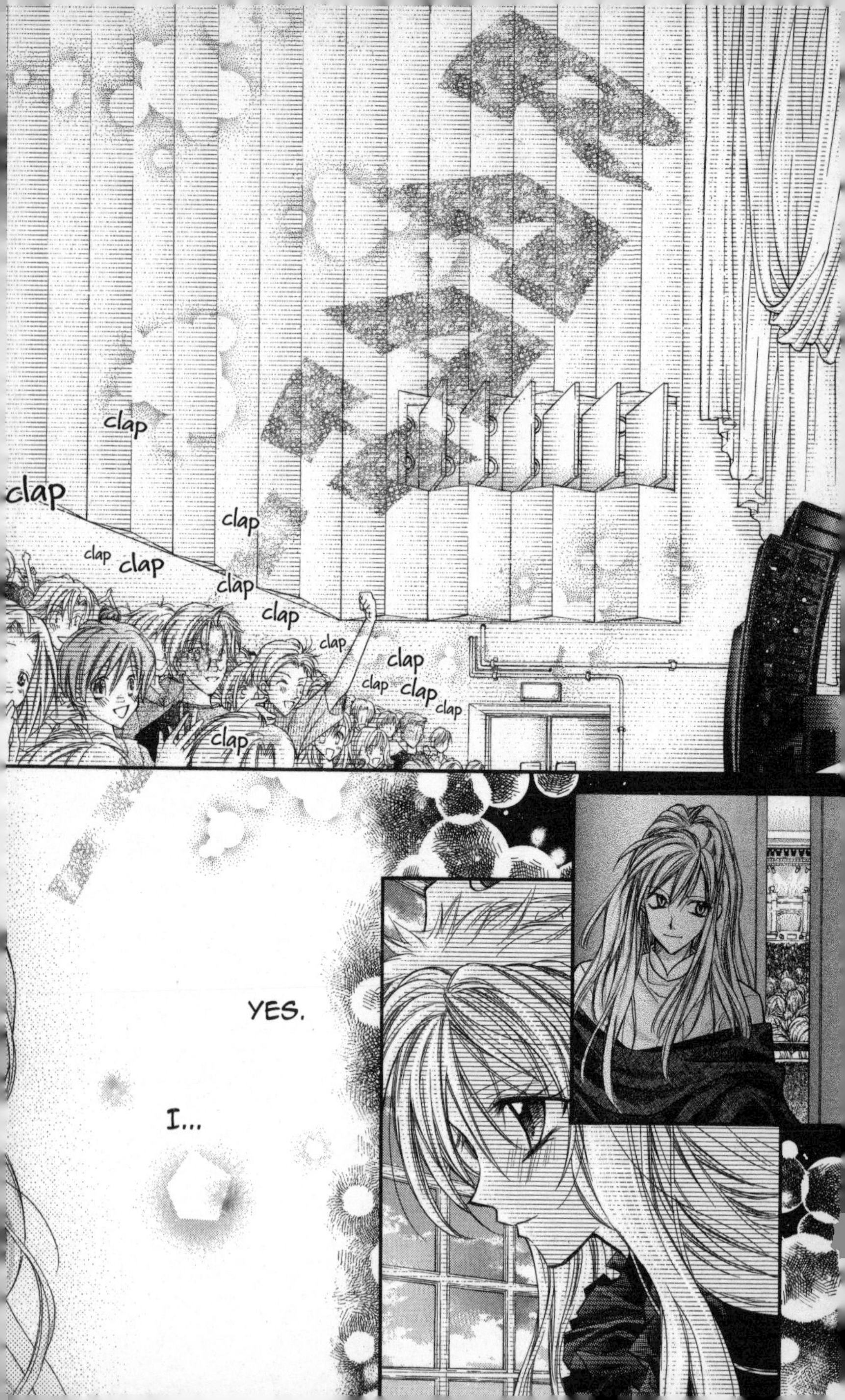
clap
clap
clap
clap clap
clap
clap
clap
clap
clap clap
clap
clap
clap
YES.
I...

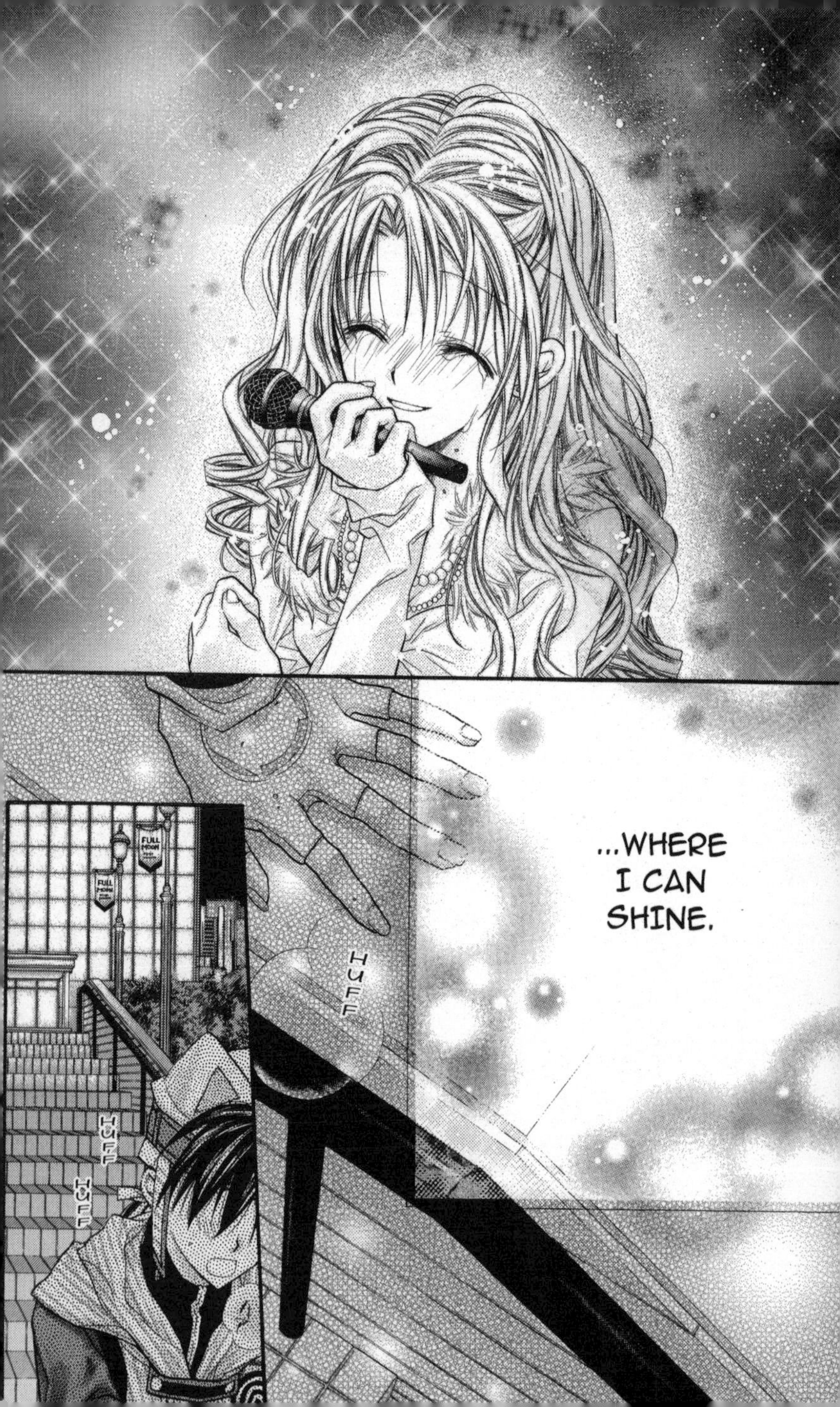
...WHERE I CAN SHINE.
HUFF
HUFF
HUFF

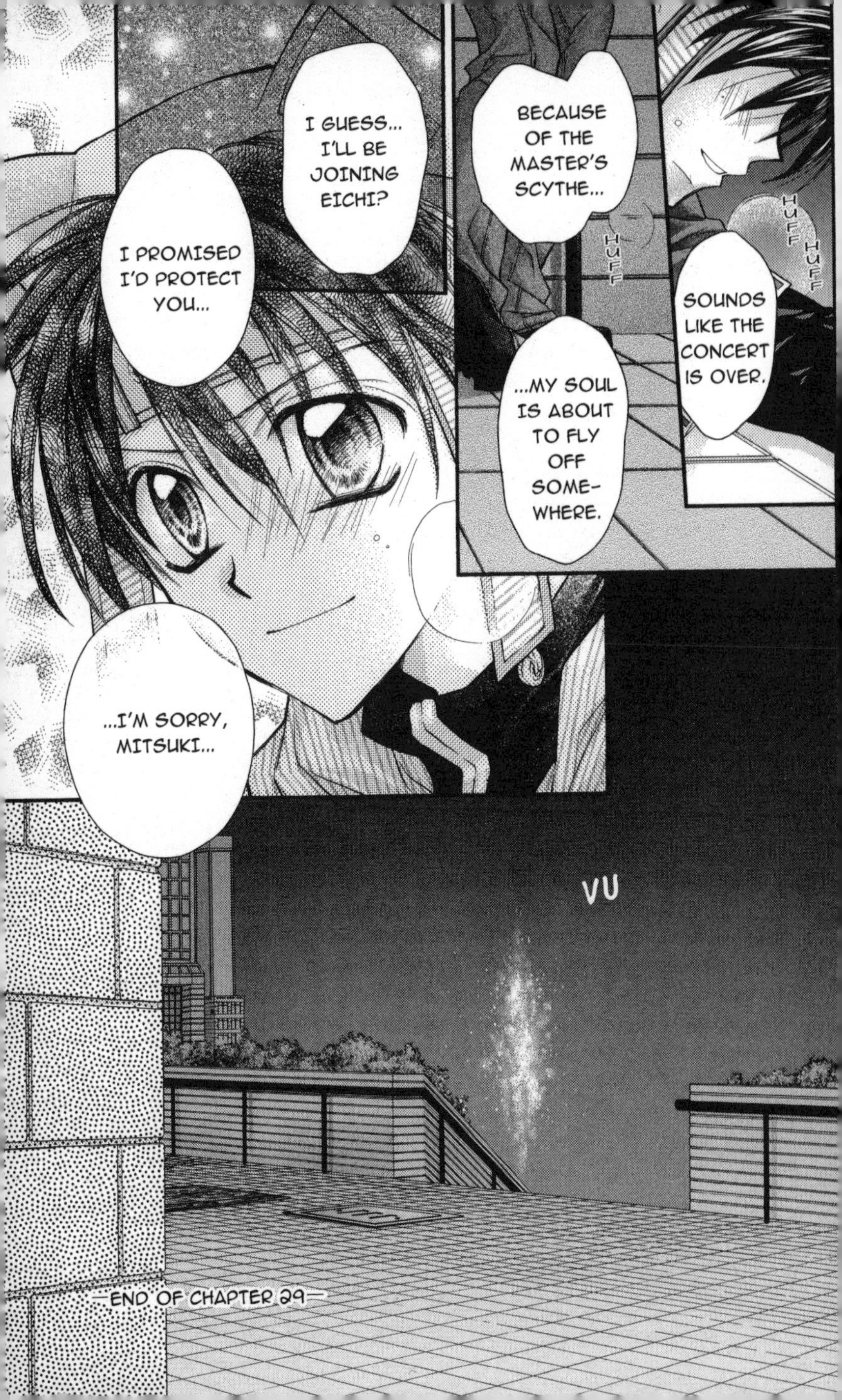
HUFF
HUFF
SOUNDS LIKE THE CONCERT IS OVER.
BECAUSE OF THE MASTER'S SCYTHE...
HUFF
...MY SOUL IS ABOUT TO FLY OFF SOME-WHERE.
I GUESS... I'LL BE JOINING EICHI?
I PROMISED I'D PROTECT YOU...
...I'M SORRY, MITSUKI...
VU
—END OF CHAPTER 29—

満月(フルムーン)をさがして

Full Moon o Sagashite

最終話(さいしゅうわ)　たった１人(り)の、英知君(えいちくん)へ。

Final Chapter:　To My One and Only Eichi

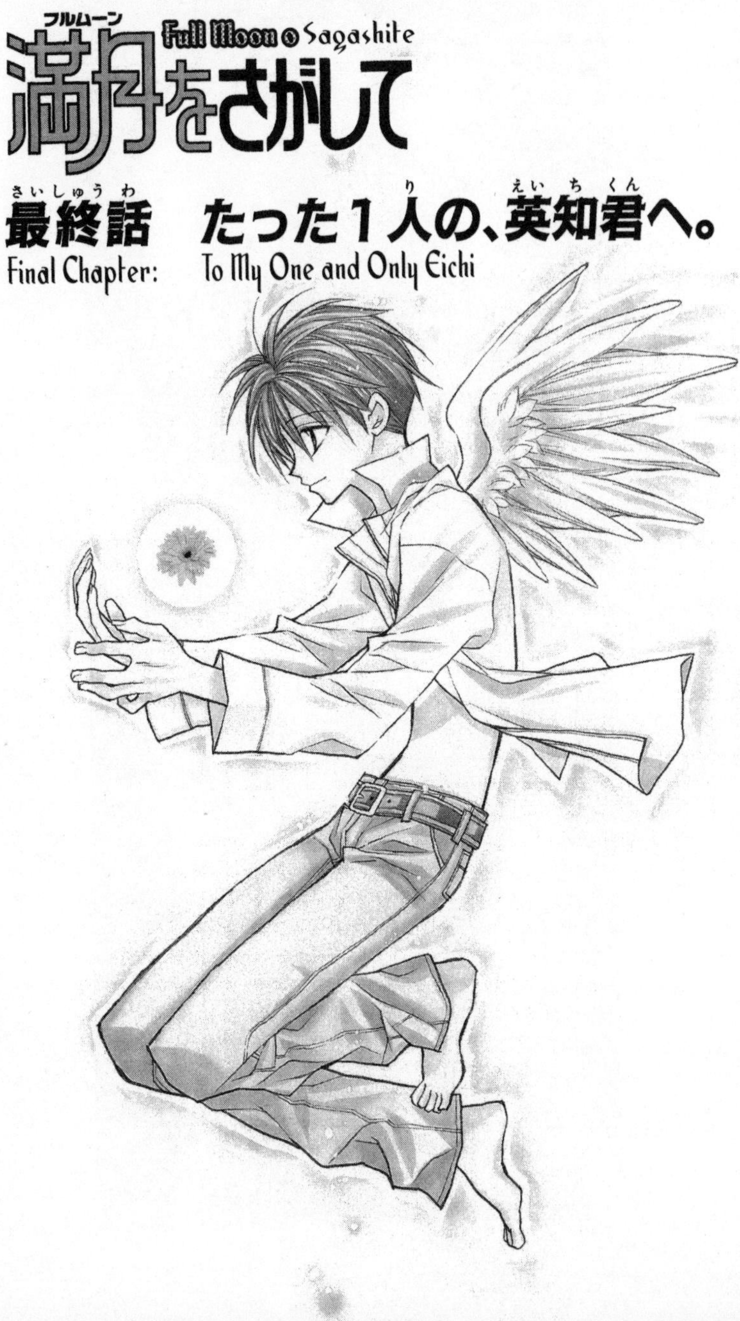

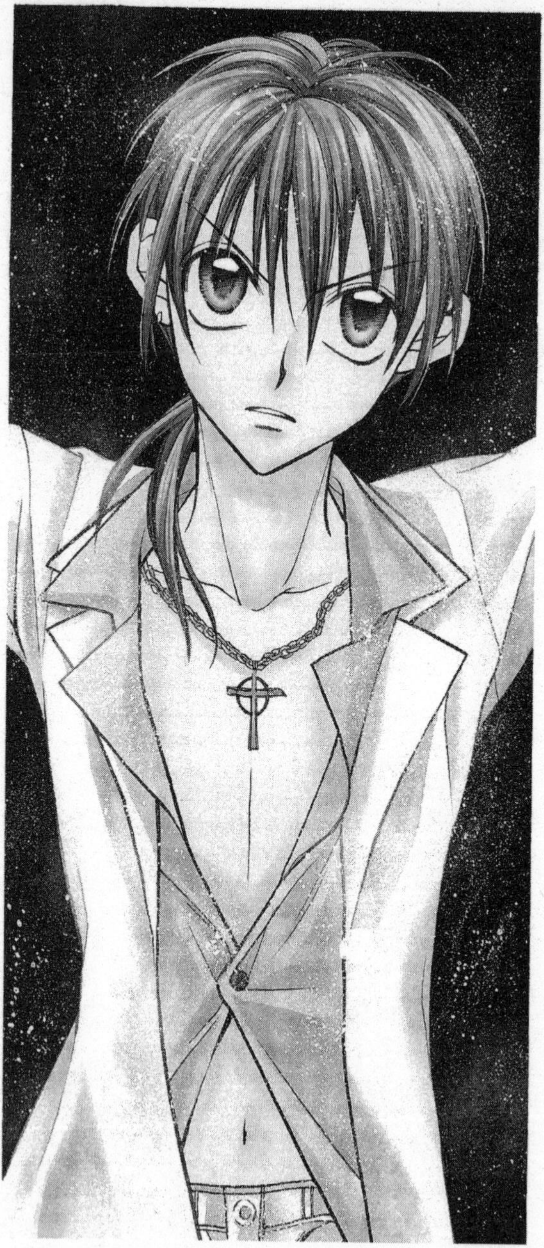

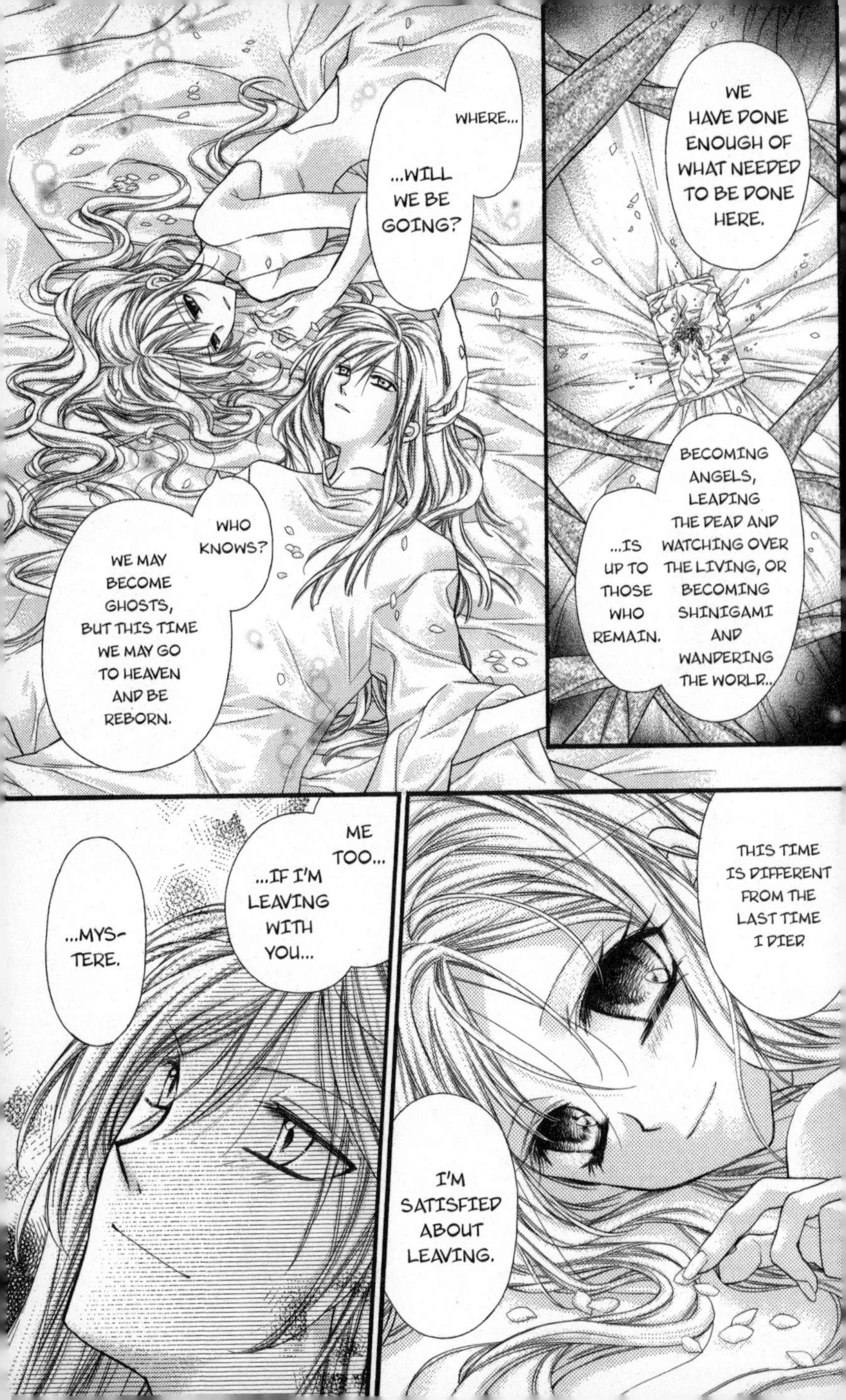
WE HAVE DONE ENOUGH OF WHAT NEEDED TO BE DONE HERE.
BECOMING ANGELS, LEADING THE DEAD AND WATCHING OVER THE LIVING, OR BECOMING SHINIGAMI AND WANDERING THE WORLD...
...IS UP TO THOSE WHO REMAIN.
WHERE...
...WILL WE BE GOING?
WHO KNOWS?
WE MAY BECOME GHOSTS, BUT THIS TIME WE MAY GO TO HEAVEN AND BE REBORN.
THIS TIME IS DIFFERENT FROM THE LAST TIME I DIED.
I'M SATISFIED ABOUT LEAVING.
ME TOO...
...IF I'M LEAVING WITH YOU...
...MYS-TERE.

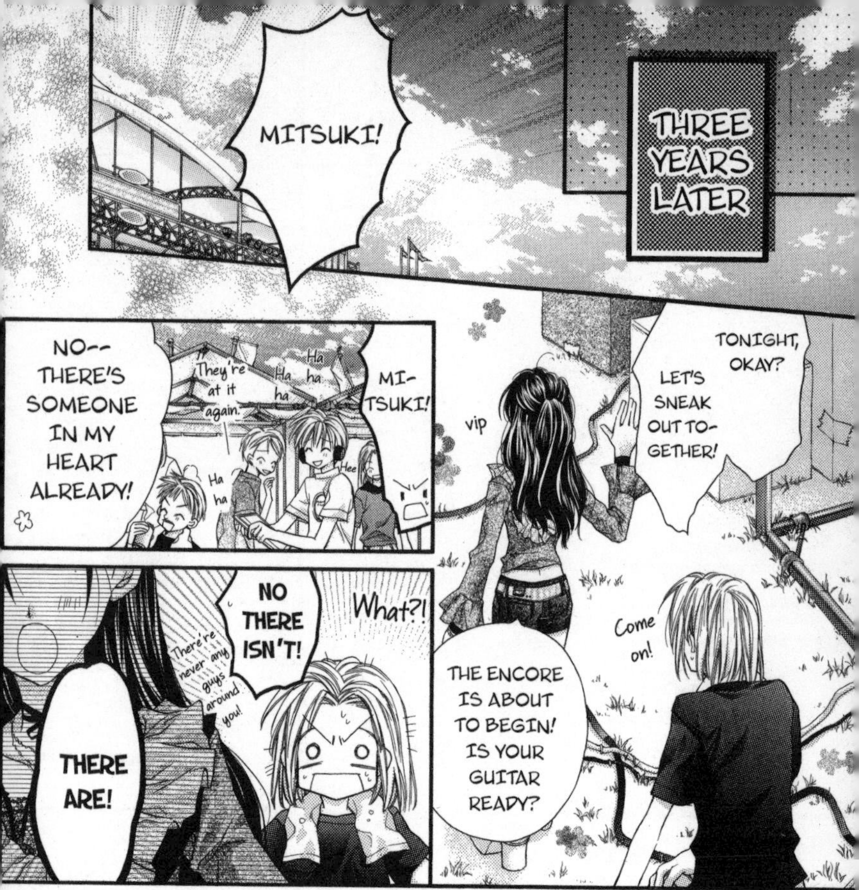
THREE YEARS LATER
MITSUKI!
TONIGHT, OKAY?
LET'S SNEAK OUT TO-GETHER!
vip
Come on!
THE ENCORE IS ABOUT TO BEGIN! IS YOUR GUITAR READY?
MI-TSUKI!
Ha ha
Ha ha
They're at it again.
Hee
Ha ha
NO-- THERE'S SOMEONE IN MY HEART ALREADY!
What?!
NO THERE ISN'T!
There're never any guys around you!
THERE ARE!

Final Chapter: To My One and Only Eichi

Cover Copy: I sing today too, thinking of you... songs of love.

※(spoilers follow)

...And, it's over. Emo.

I wanted to make it happy, and a bit lonely...did it come through? For readers of *Ribon*, it seemed to have been pretty popular. Everyone seemed to be surprised by the end credits (smile). Some people said, "It was original and fresh," while others said, "I was returned to reality feeling shocked." Yes, yes. I understand. I felt what the second set of people felt. (Hey!)
I did it because I wanted to express my appreciation for my staff. My name appears all over, but I created this work with all my staff.

And I tried to be tactful. (I didn't write Mitsuki-chan and others as "cast"...) So please forgive me! Bow, bow.
About using Changin' My Life's songs--people who are worriers said, "If you haven't watched the anime, you won't get it..." However, in the manga, the song isn't played.
It could've been a poem I wrote, but it's better to use songs that people are happy about!
I also thought that this would hopefully get people to listen to songs by Changin' My Life.

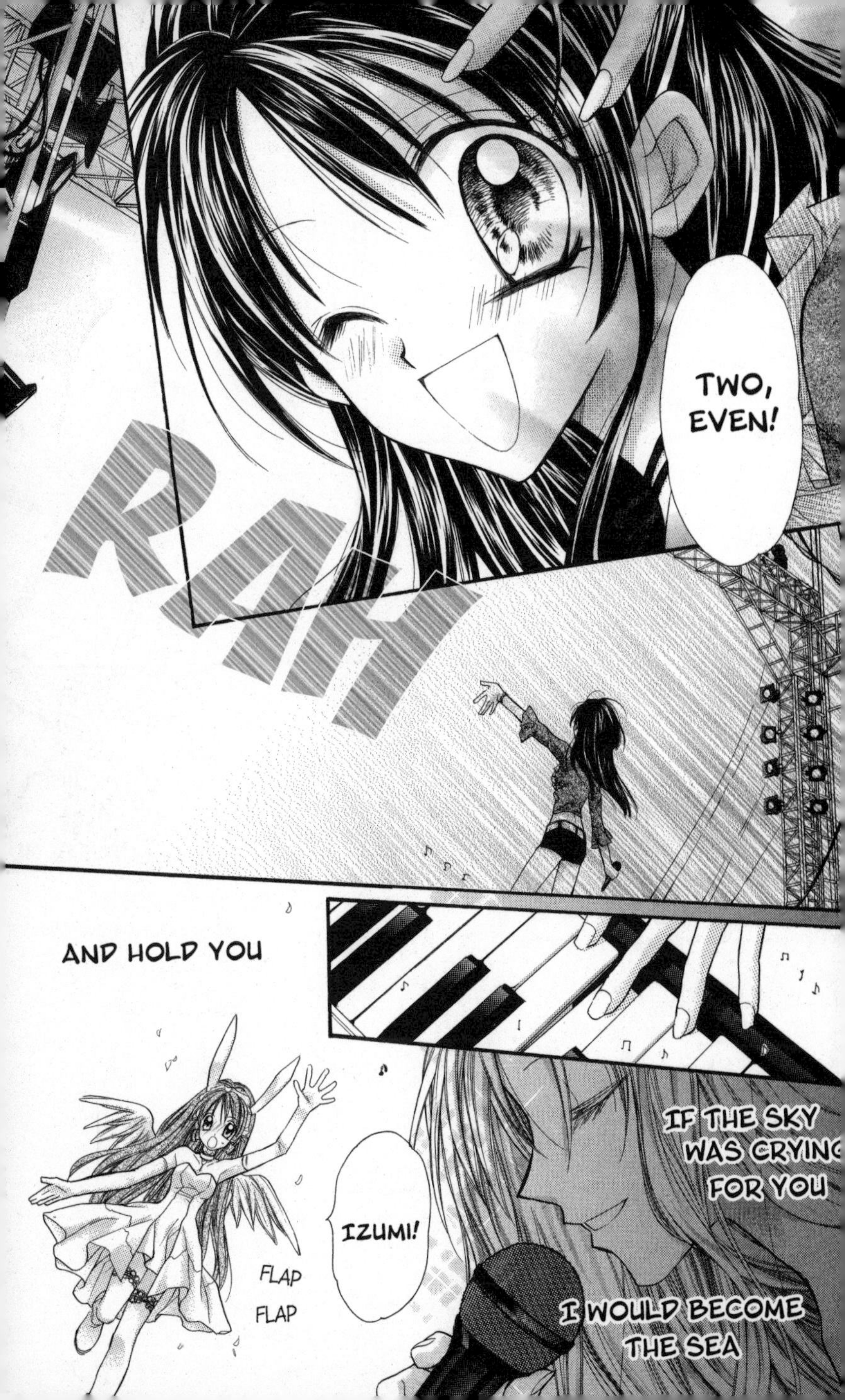
TWO, EVEN!
RAH
AND HOLD YOU
IF THE SKY
WAS CRYIN
FOR YOU
I WOULD BECOME
THE SEA
IZUMI!
FLAP
FLAP

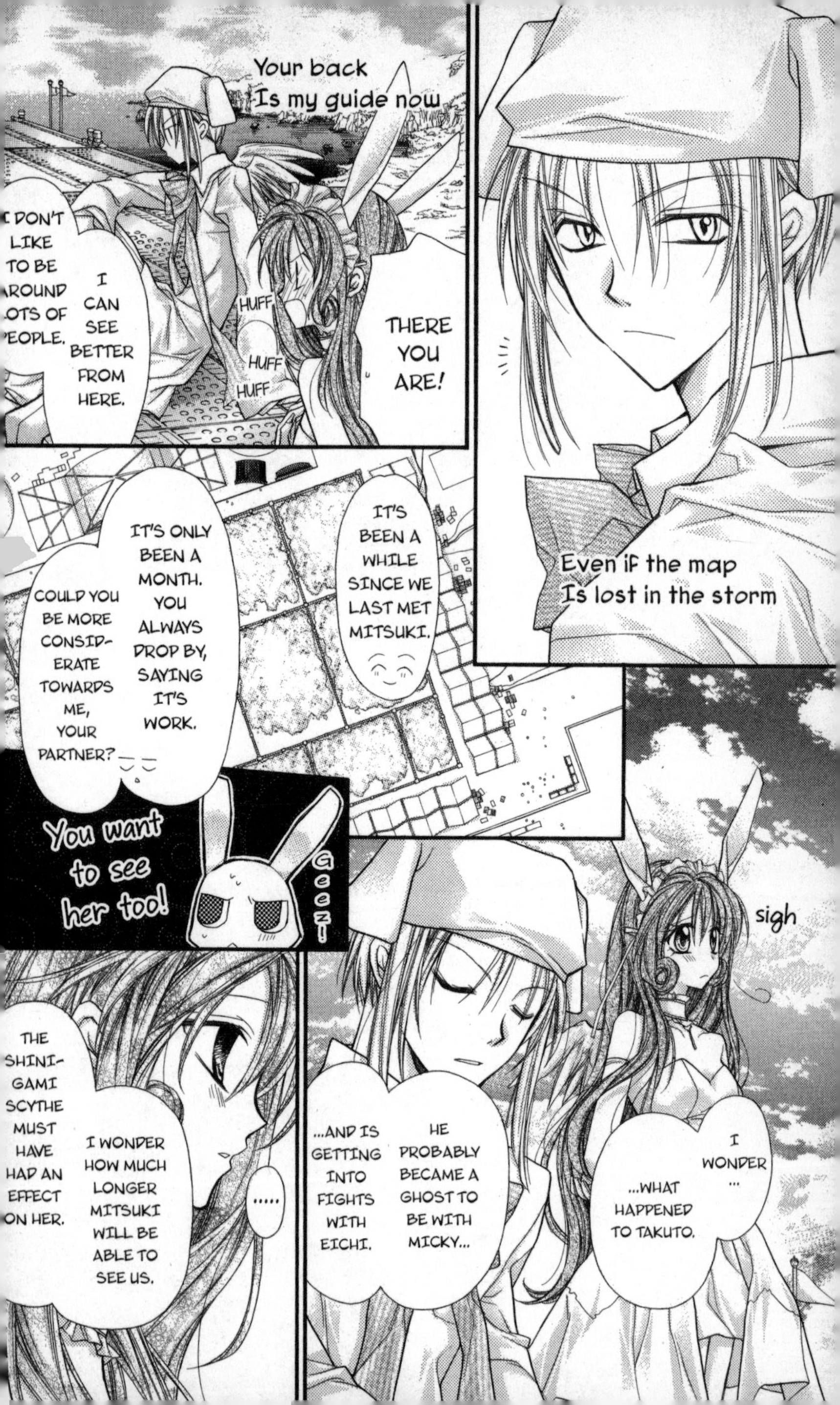
Even if the map
Is lost in the storm
Your back
Is my guide now
THERE YOU ARE!
HUFF
HUFF
HUFF
I CAN SEE BETTER FROM HERE.
I DON'T LIKE TO BE AROUND LOTS OF PEOPLE.
IT'S BEEN A WHILE SINCE WE LAST MET MITSUKI.
IT'S ONLY BEEN A MONTH. YOU ALWAYS DROP BY, SAYING IT'S WORK.
COULD YOU BE MORE CONSID-ERATE TOWARDS ME, YOUR PARTNER?
You want to see her too!
Geez!
sigh
I WONDER ...
...WHAT HAPPENED TO TAKUTO.
HE PROBABLY BECAME A GHOST TO BE WITH MICKY...
...AND IS GETTING INTO FIGHTS WITH EICHI.
.....
I WONDER HOW MUCH LONGER MITSUKI WILL BE ABLE TO SEE US.
THE SHINI-GAMI SCYTHE MUST HAVE HAD AN EFFECT ON HER.

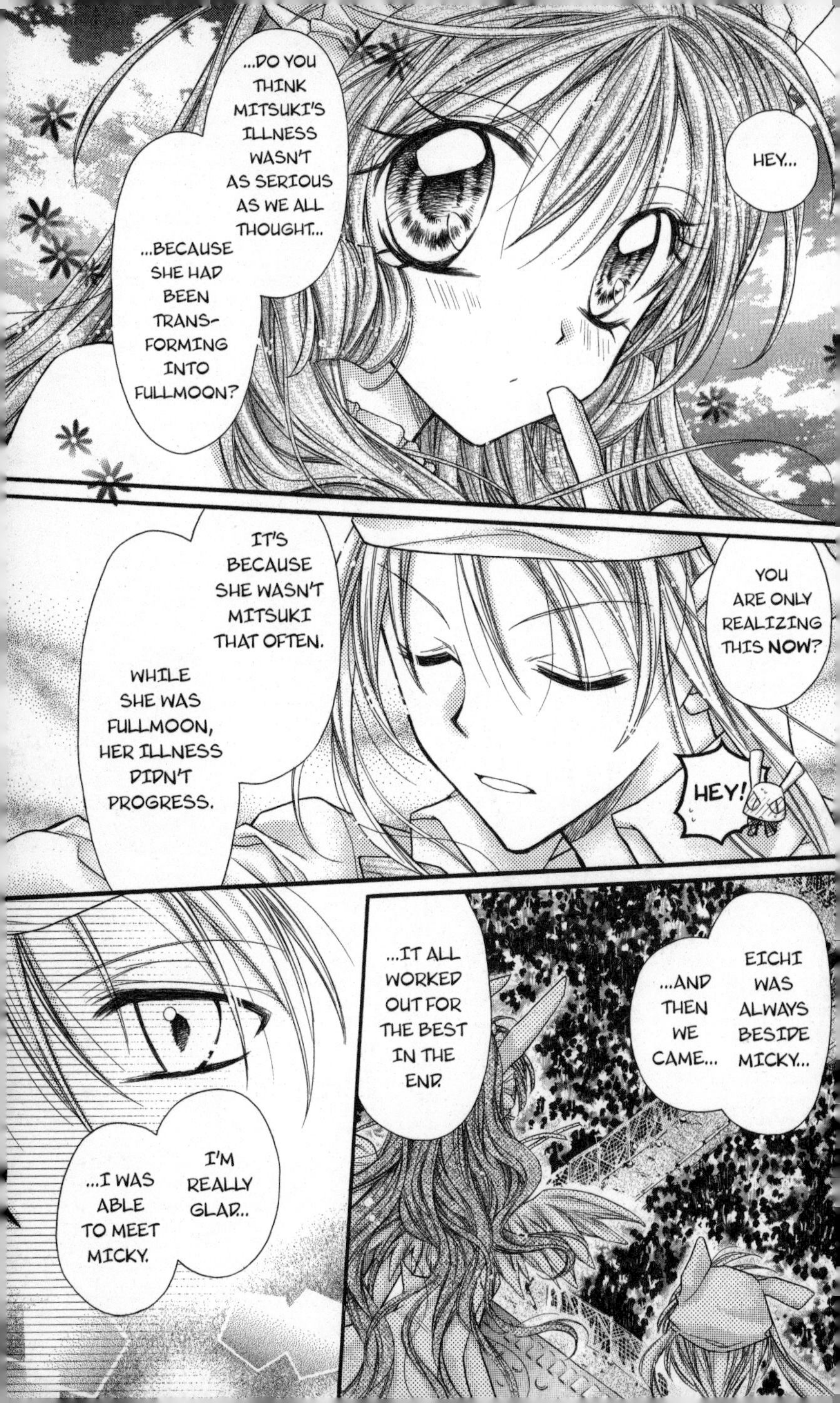
HEY...
...DO YOU THINK MITSUKI'S ILLNESS WASN'T AS SERIOUS AS WE ALL THOUGHT...
...BECAUSE SHE HAD BEEN TRANS-FORMING INTO FULLMOON?
YOU ARE ONLY REALIZING THIS **NOW**?
HEY!
IT'S BECAUSE SHE WASN'T MITSUKI THAT OFTEN.
WHILE SHE WAS FULLMOON, HER ILLNESS DIDN'T PROGRESS.
EICHI WAS ALWAYS BESIDE MICKY...
...AND THEN WE CAME...
...IT ALL WORKED OUT FOR THE BEST IN THE END.
I'M REALLY GLAD...
...I WAS ABLE TO MEET MICKY.

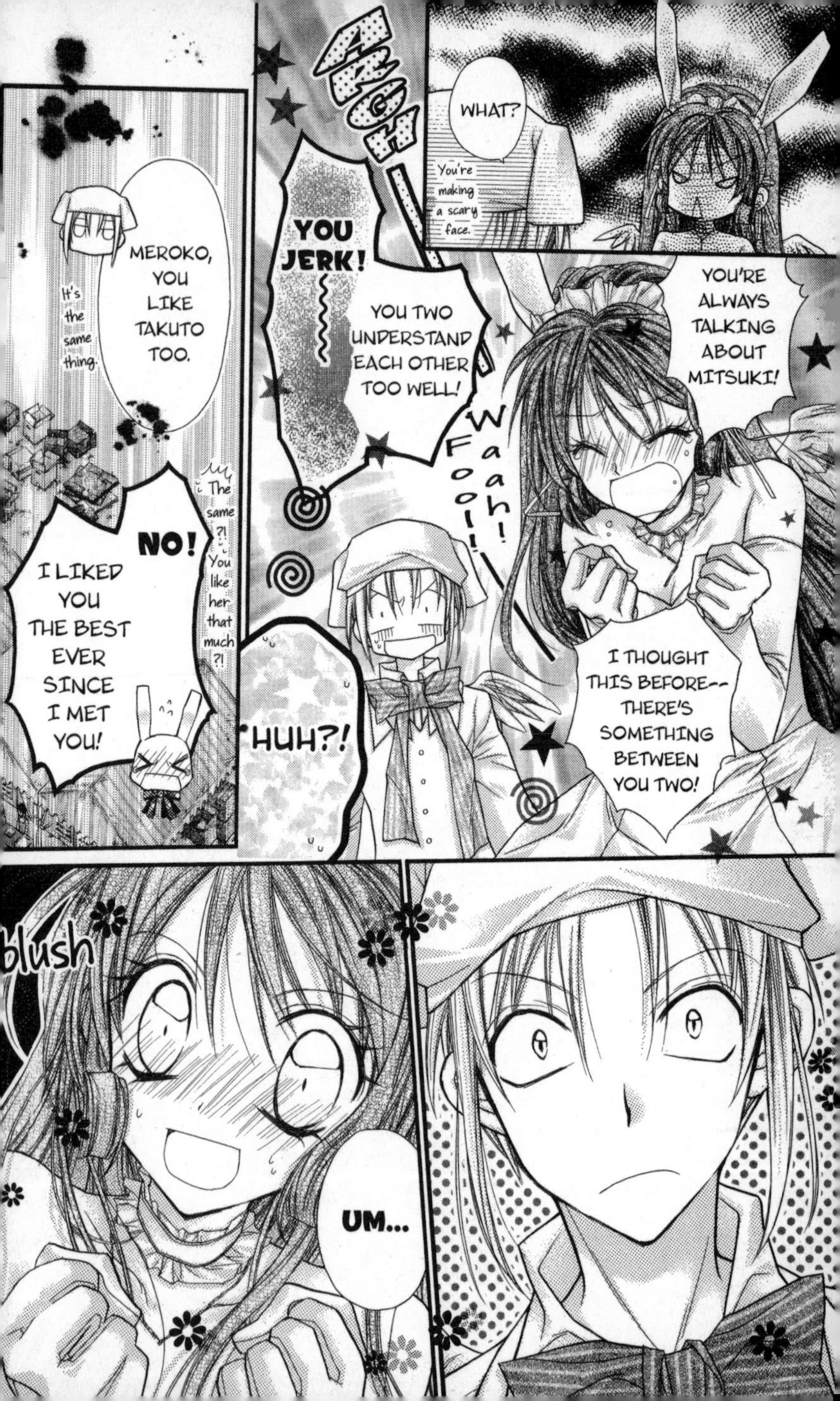
WHAT?
You're making a scary face.
AAUGH
YOU JERK!
YOU TWO UNDERSTAND EACH OTHER TOO WELL!
YOU'RE ALWAYS TALKING ABOUT MITSUKI!
Waah!
Fool!
I THOUGHT THIS BEFORE-- THERE'S SOMETHING BETWEEN YOU TWO!
HUH?!
MEROKO, YOU LIKE TAKUTO TOO.
It's the same thing.
NO! I LIKED YOU THE BEST EVER SINCE I MET YOU!
The same?! You like her that much?!
UM...
blush

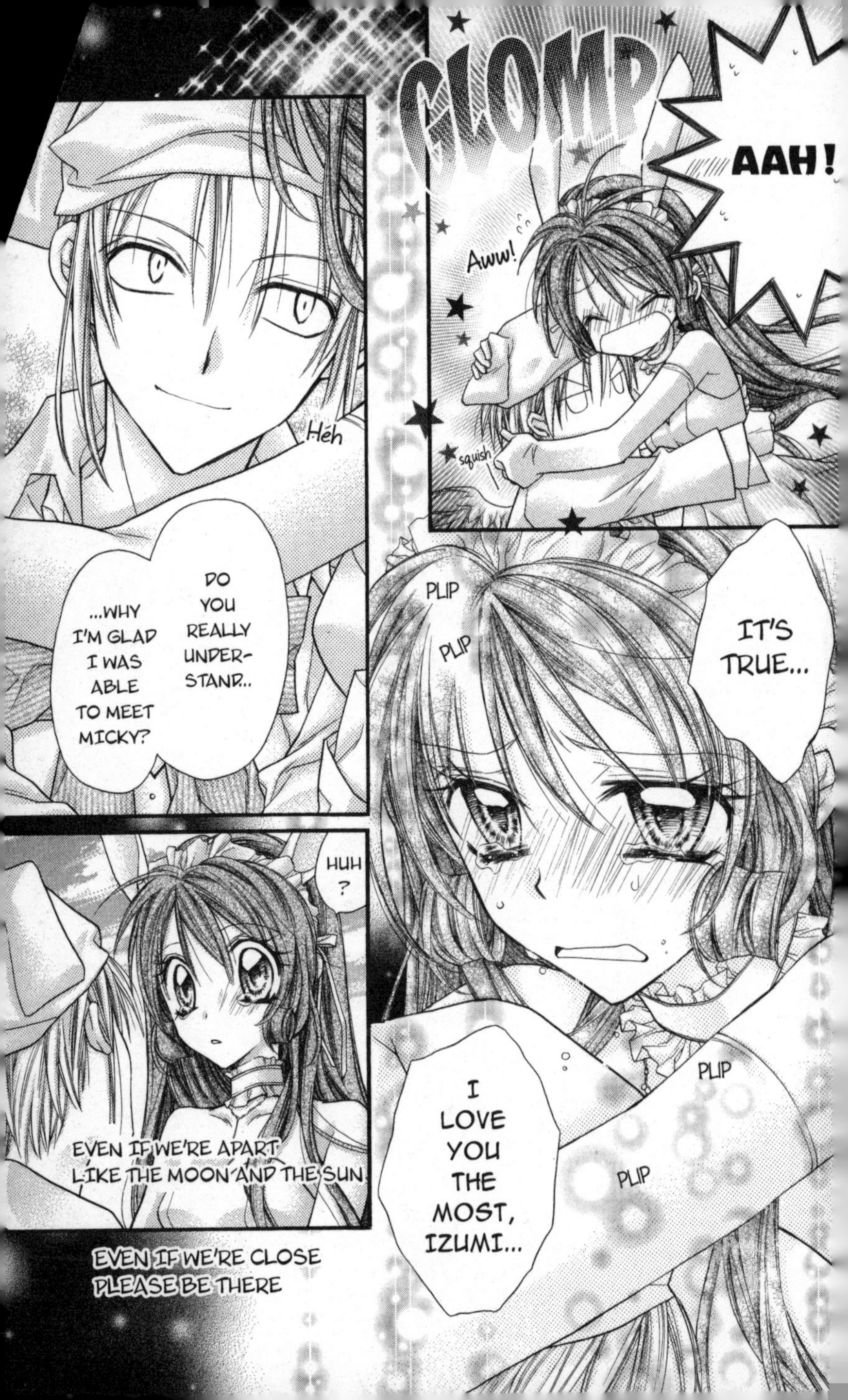
Heh
DO YOU REALLY UNDERSTAND...
...WHY I'M GLAD I WAS ABLE TO MEET MICKY?
HUH ?
EVEN IF WE'RE APART LIKE THE MOON AND THE SUN
EVEN IF WE'RE CLOSE PLEASE BE THERE
GLOMP
AAH!
Aww!
squish
PLIP
PLIP
IT'S TRUE...
PLIP
PLIP
I LOVE YOU THE MOST, IZUMI...

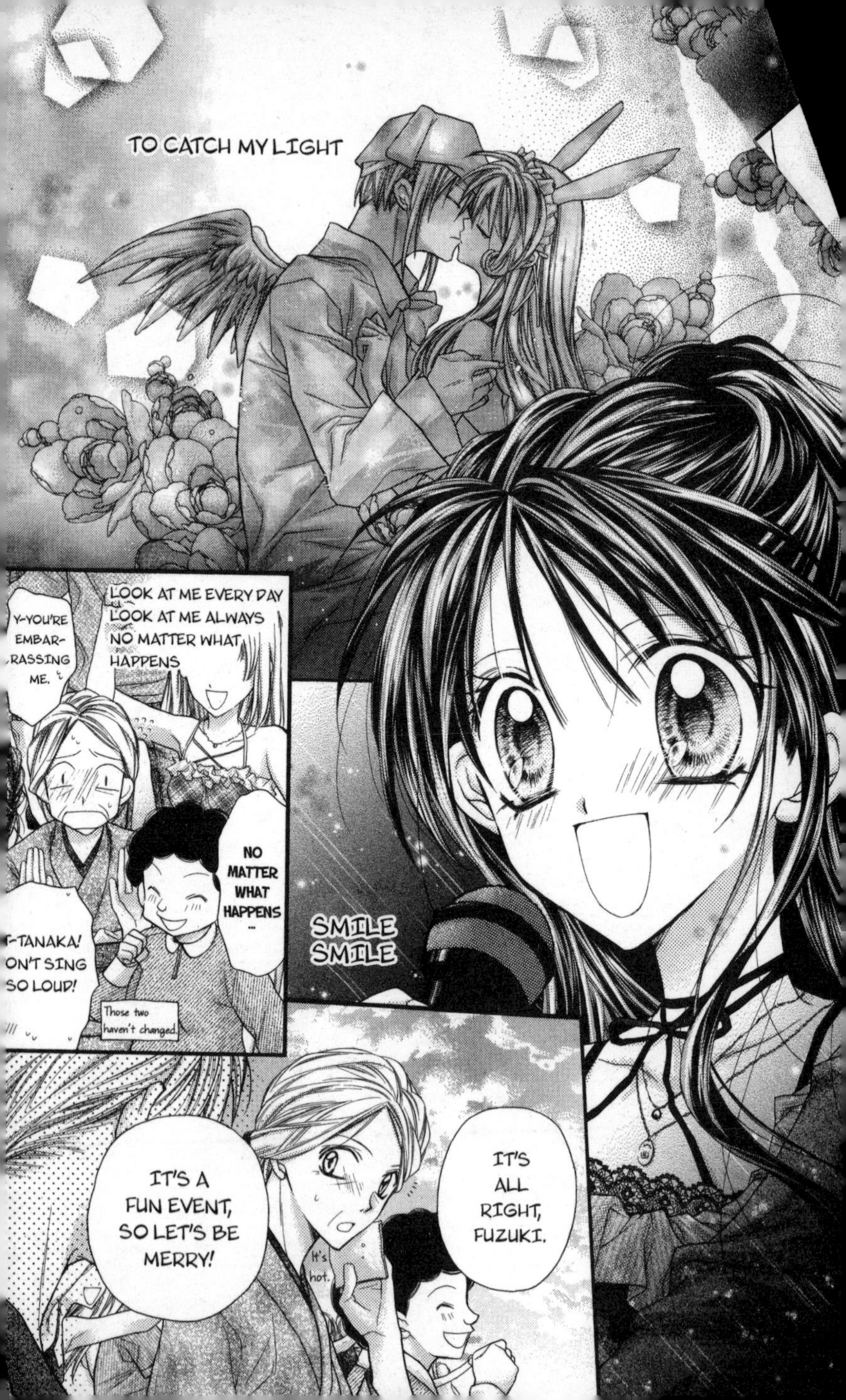
TO CATCH MY LIGHT
SMILE SMILE
LOOK AT ME EVERY DAY LOOK AT ME ALWAYS NO MATTER WHAT HAPPENS
Y-YOU'RE EMBAR-RASSING ME.
NO MATTER WHAT HAPPENS ...
-TANAKA! ON'T SING SO LOUD!
Those two haven't changed.
IT'S ALL RIGHT, FUZUKI.
It's hot.
IT'S A FUN EVENT, SO LET'S BE MERRY!

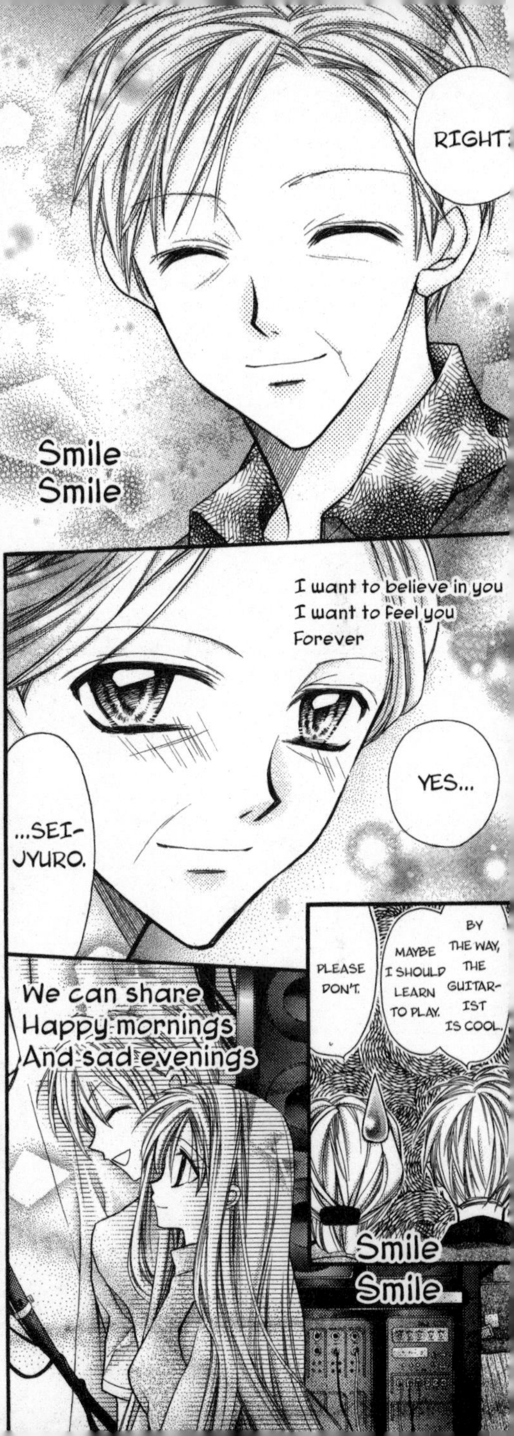
RIGHT?
Smile Smile
I want to believe in you
I want to feel you
Forever
YES...
...SEI-JYURO.
BY THE WAY, THE GUITARIST IS COOL.
MAYBE I SHOULD LEARN TO PLAY.
PLEASE DON'T.
Smile Smile
We can share
Happy mornings
And sad evenings

Being Hospitalized ⑤

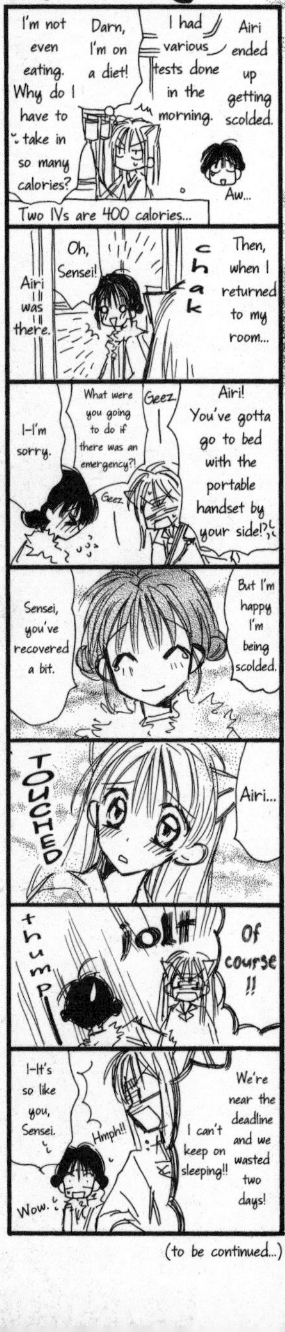
Airi ended up getting scolded.
I had various tests done in the morning.
Darn, I'm on a diet!
I'm not even eating. Why do I have to take in so many calories?
Aw...
Two IVs are 400 calories...
Then, when I returned to my room...
chak
Oh, Sensei!
Airi was there.
Airi! You've gotta go to bed with the portable handset by your side!?
Geez
What were you going to do if there was an emergency?!
Geez
I-I'm sorry.
But I'm happy I'm being scolded.
Sensei, you've recovered a bit.
Airi...
TOUCHED
Of course!!
jolt
thump
We're near the deadline and we wasted two days!
I can't keep on sleeping!!
Hmph!!
I-It's so like you, Sensei.
Wow.

(to be continued...)

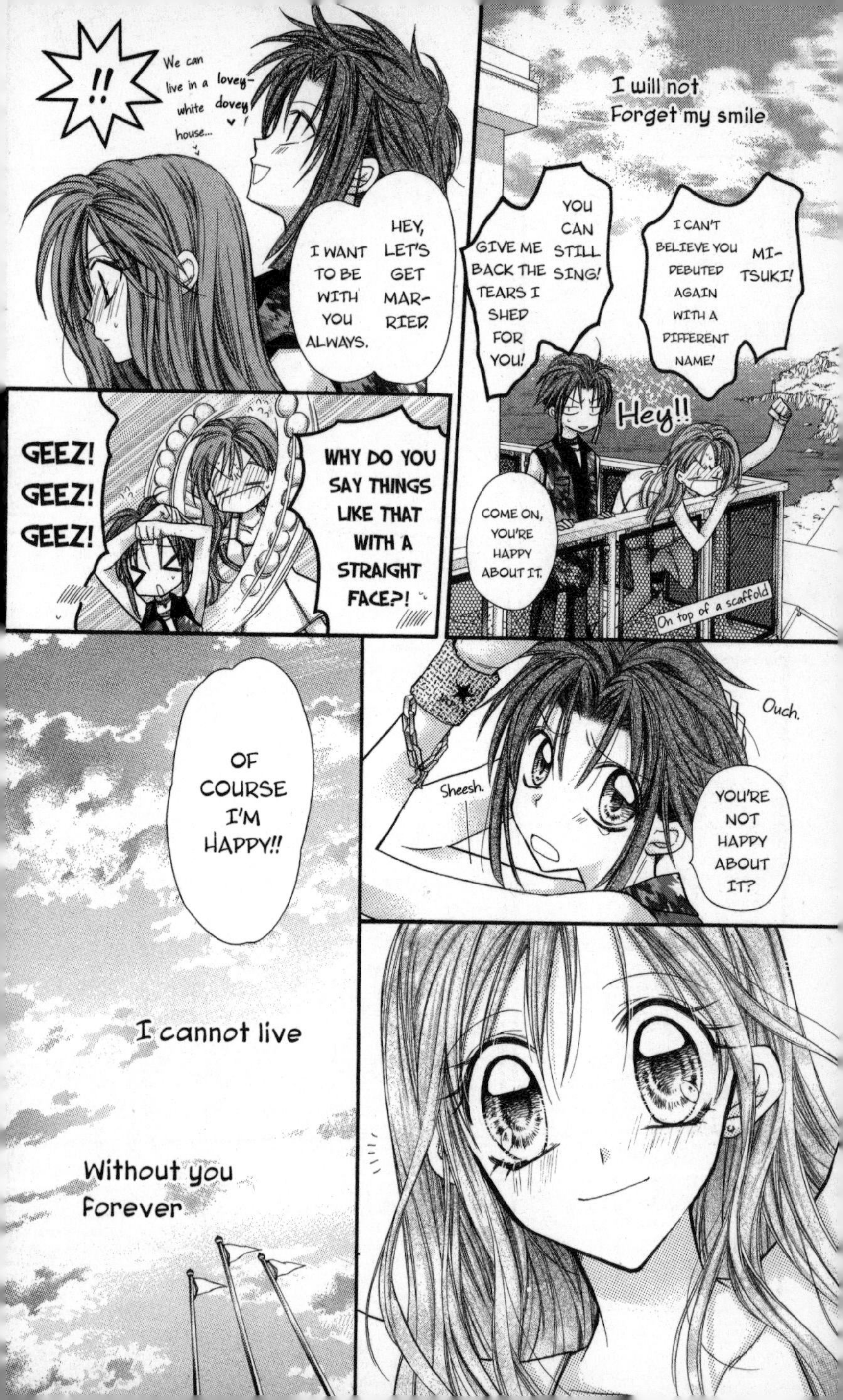
I will not Forget my smile
MI-TSUKI!
I CAN'T BELIEVE YOU DEBUTED AGAIN WITH A DIFFERENT NAME!
YOU CAN STILL SING!
GIVE ME BACK THE TEARS I SHED FOR YOU!
Hey!!
COME ON, YOU'RE HAPPY ABOUT IT.
On top of a scaffold
We can live in a lovey-dovey white house...
!!
HEY, LET'S GET MAR-RIED.
I WANT TO BE WITH YOU ALWAYS.
WHY DO YOU SAY THINGS LIKE THAT WITH A STRAIGHT FACE?!
GEEZ! GEEZ! GEEZ!
Ouch.
YOU'RE NOT HAPPY ABOUT IT?
Sheesh.
OF COURSE I'M HAPPY!!
I cannot live
Without you forever

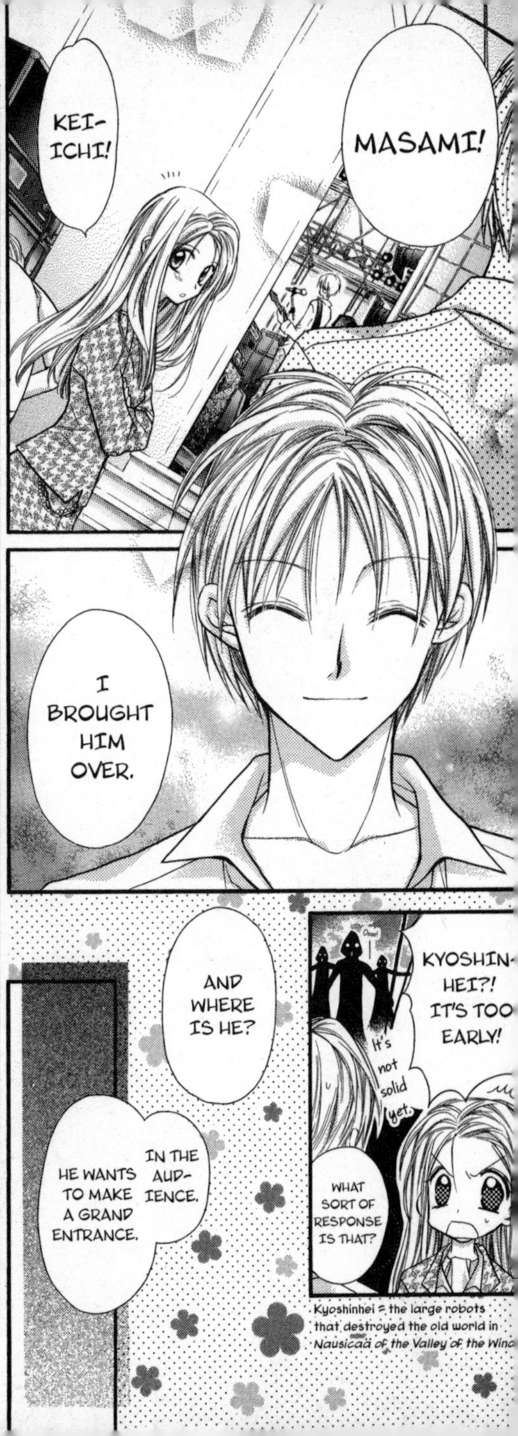
MASAMI!
KEI-ICHI!
I BROUGHT HIM OVER.
Oooo!
KYOSHIN-HEI?! IT'S TOO EARLY!
It's not solid yet.
WHAT SORT OF RESPONSE IS THAT?
AND WHERE IS HE?
IN THE AUDIENCE.
HE WANTS TO MAKE A GRAND ENTRANCE.
Kyoshinhei = the large robots that destroyed the old world in *Nausicaä of the Valley of the Wind*

Being Hospitalized ⑥

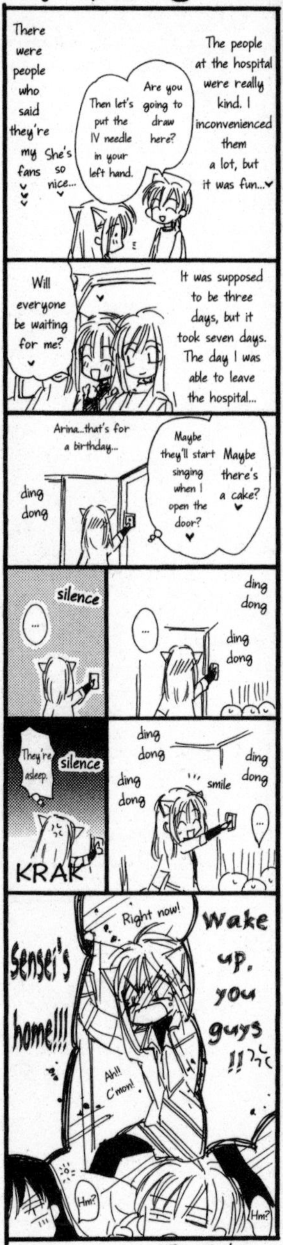
The people at the hospital were really kind. I inconvenienced them a lot, but it was fun...♥
Are you going to draw here?
Then let's put the IV needle in your left hand.
There were people who said they're my fans ♥♥♥
She's so nice...
It was supposed to be three days, but it took seven days. The day I was able to leave the hospital...
Will everyone be waiting for me? ♥
Maybe there's a cake? ♥
Maybe they'll start singing when I open the door? ♥
Arina...that's for a birthday...
ding dong
ding dong
ding dong
...
silence
...
ding dong
ding dong
smile
ding dong
ding dong
...
silence
They're asleep.
KRAK
Wake up, you guys!!
Right now!
Sensei's home!!!
Ah!! C'mon!
Hm?
Hm?

♡The End♡

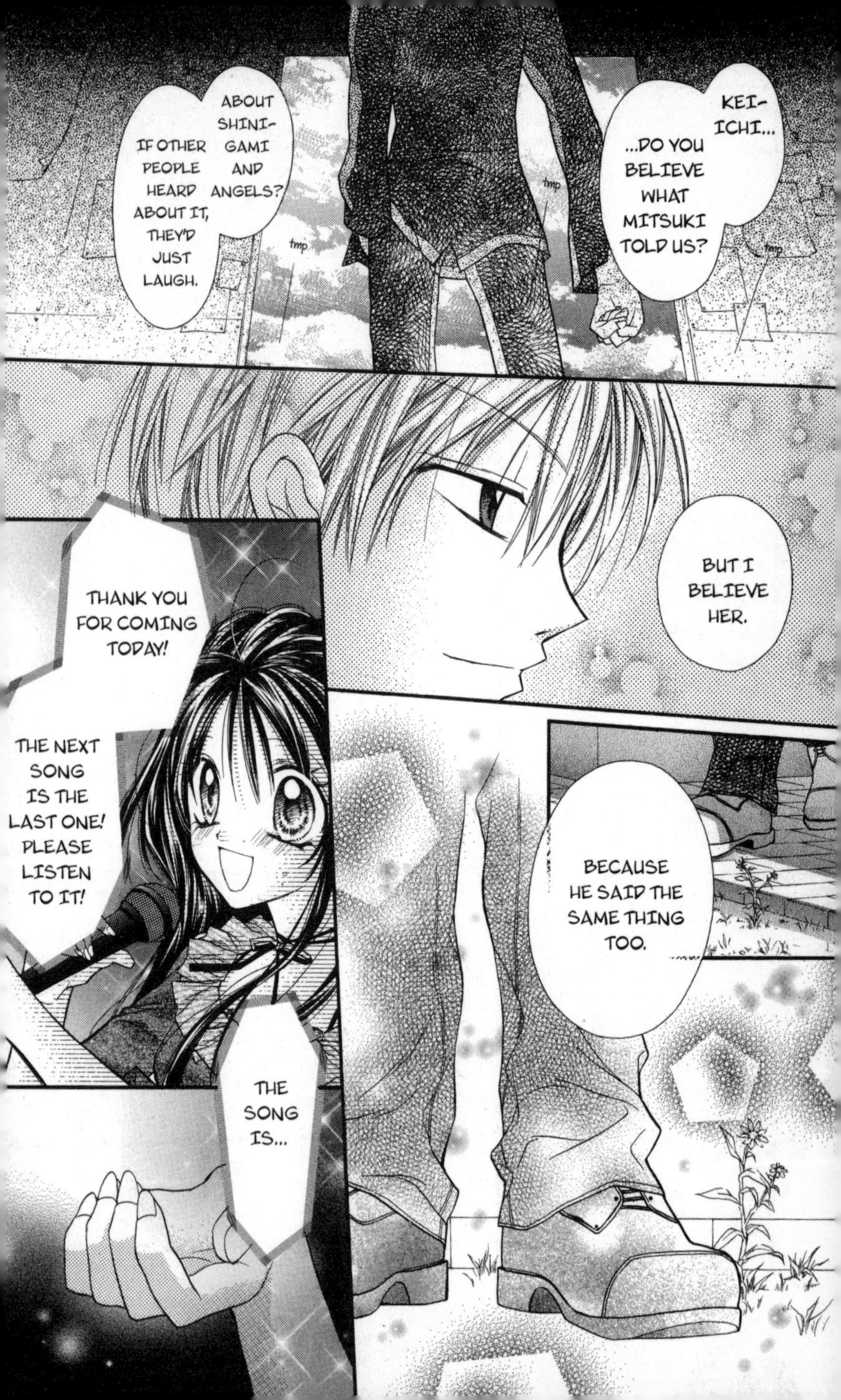
KEI-ICHI...
...DO YOU BELIEVE WHAT MITSUKI TOLD US?
tmp
tmp
tmp
ABOUT SHINI-GAMI AND ANGELS?
IF OTHER PEOPLE HEARD ABOUT IT, THEY'D JUST LAUGH.
BUT I BELIEVE HER.
THANK YOU FOR COMING TODAY!
THE NEXT SONG IS THE LAST ONE! PLEASE LISTEN TO IT!
BECAUSE HE SAID THE SAME THING TOO.
THE SONG IS...

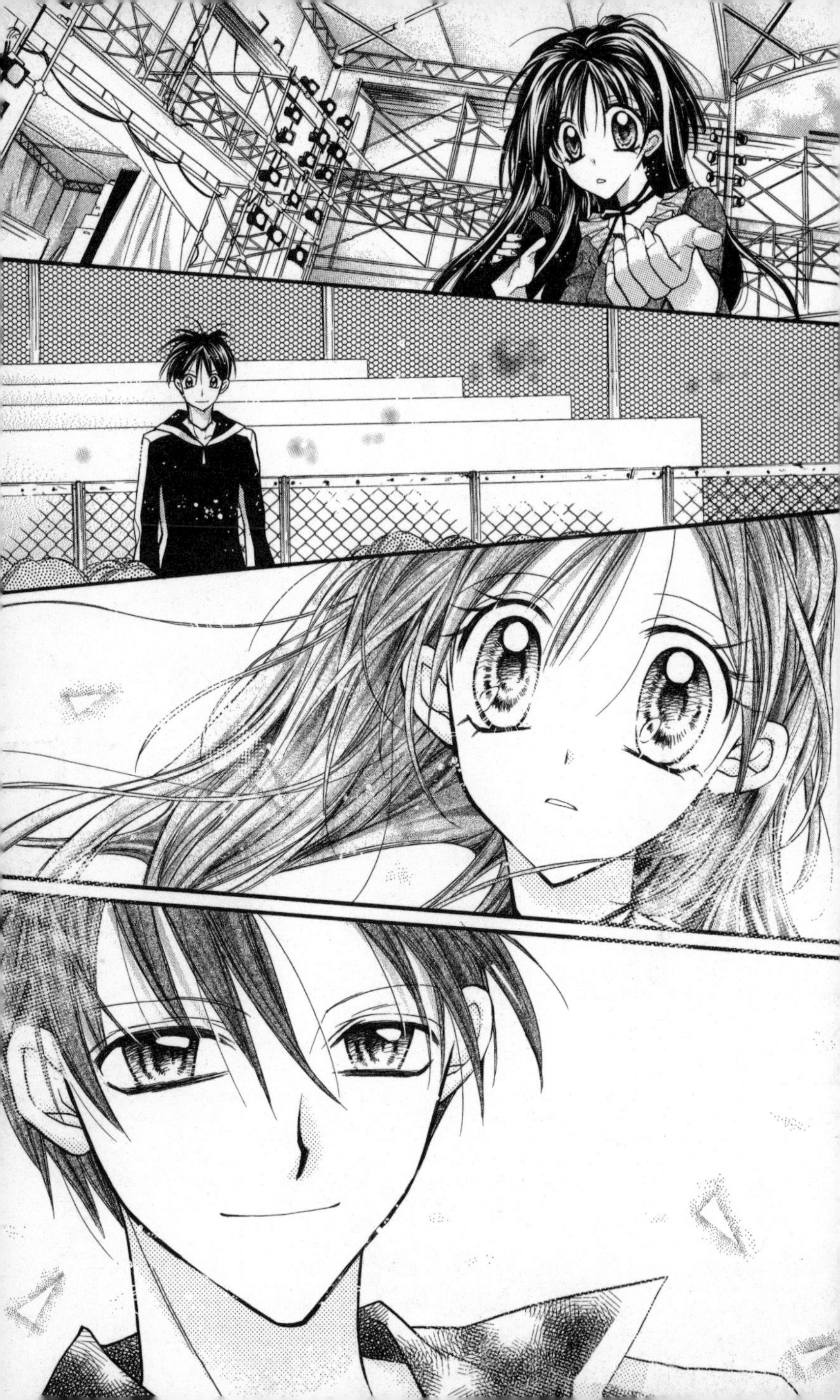

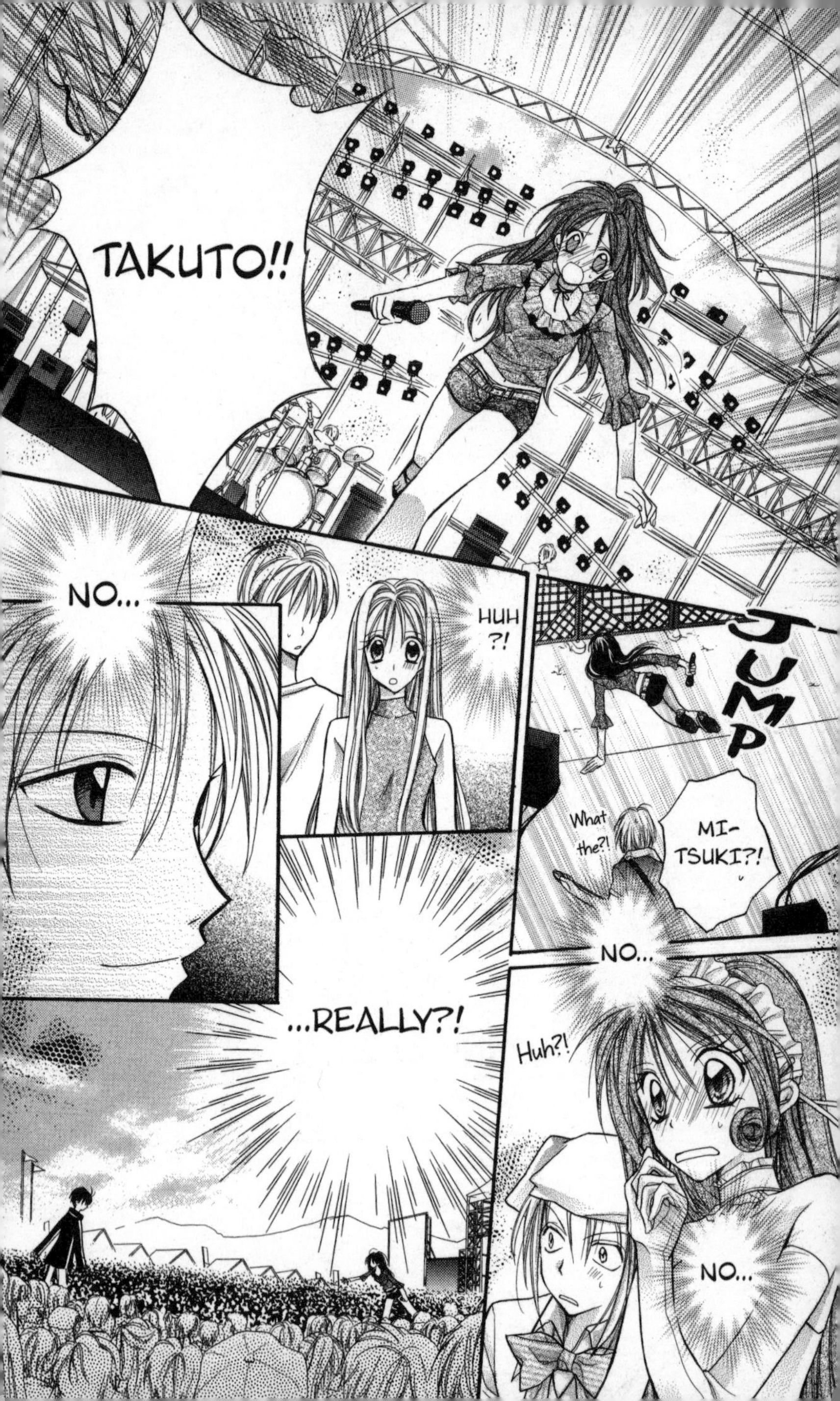
TAKUTO!!
JUMP
MI-TSUKI?!
What the?!
HUH?!
NO...
...REALLY?!
NO...
Huh?!
NO...

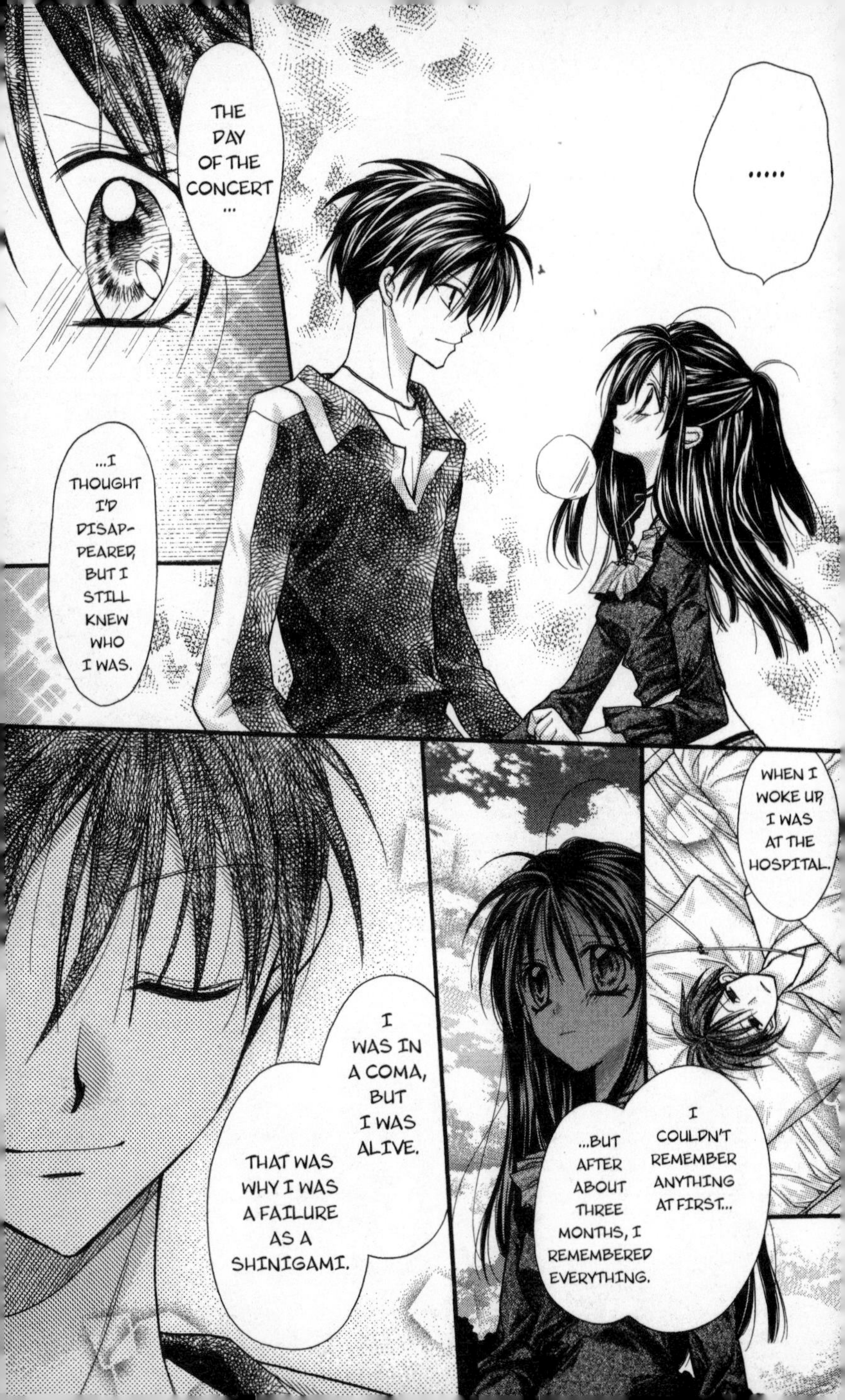
.....
THE DAY OF THE CONCERT...
...I THOUGHT I'D DISAPPEARED, BUT I STILL KNEW WHO I WAS.
WHEN I WOKE UP, I WAS AT THE HOSPITAL.
I COULDN'T REMEMBER ANYTHING AT FIRST...
...BUT AFTER ABOUT THREE MONTHS, I REMEMBERED EVERYTHING.
I WAS IN A COMA, BUT I WAS ALIVE.
THAT WAS WHY I WAS A FAILURE AS A SHINIGAMI.

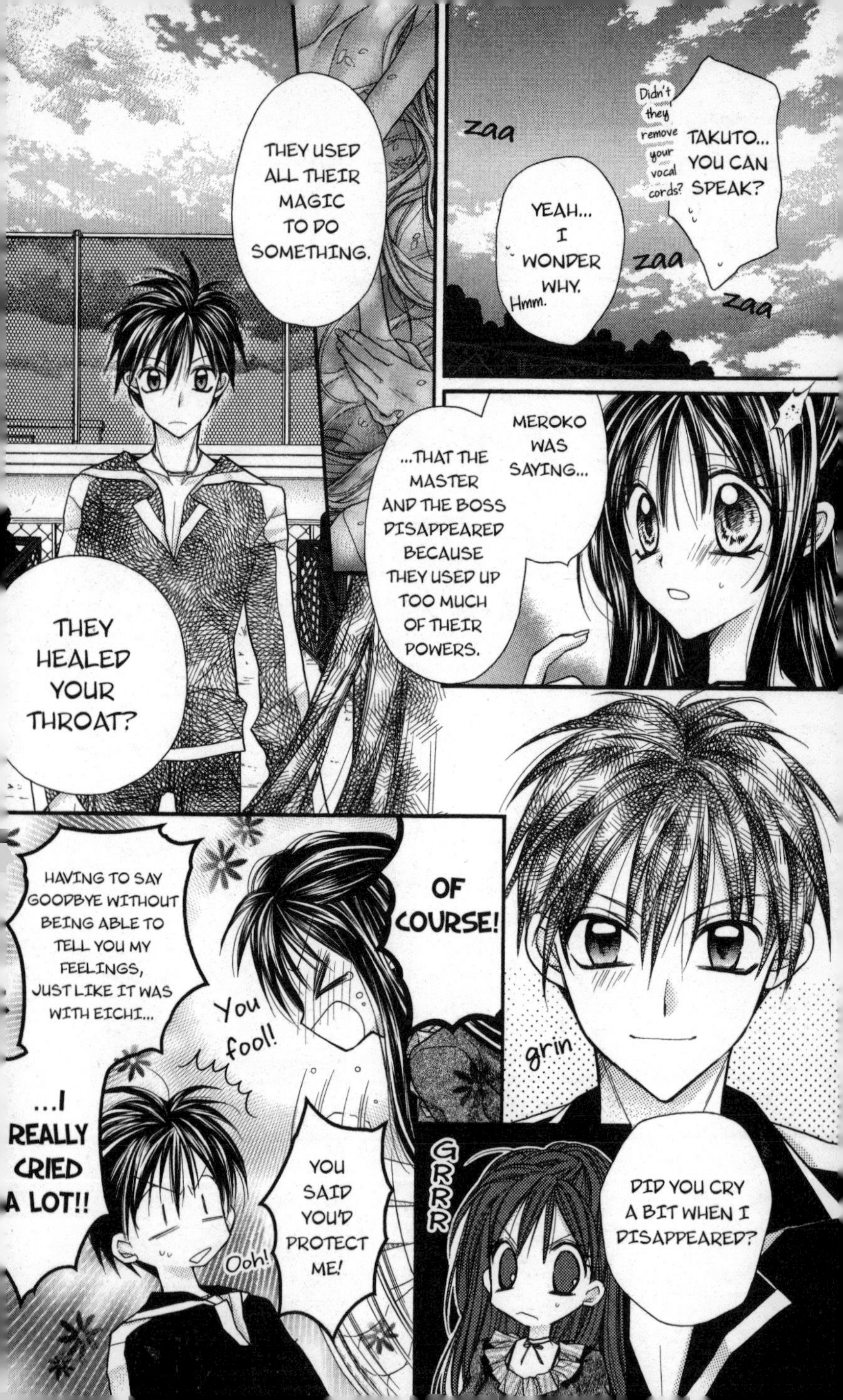
Didn't they remove your vocal cords?
TAKUTO... YOU CAN SPEAK?
zaa
YEAH... I WONDER WHY.
Hmm.
zaa
zaa
MEROKO WAS SAYING...
...THAT THE MASTER AND THE BOSS DISAPPEARED BECAUSE THEY USED UP TOO MUCH OF THEIR POWERS.
THEY USED ALL THEIR MAGIC TO DO SOMETHING.
THEY HEALED YOUR THROAT?
grin
DID YOU CRY A BIT WHEN I DISAPPEARED?
GRRR
OF COURSE!
You fool!
HAVING TO SAY GOODBYE WITHOUT BEING ABLE TO TELL YOU MY FEELINGS, JUST LIKE IT WAS WITH EICHI...
...I REALLY CRIED A LOT!!
YOU SAID YOU'D PROTECT ME!
Ooh!

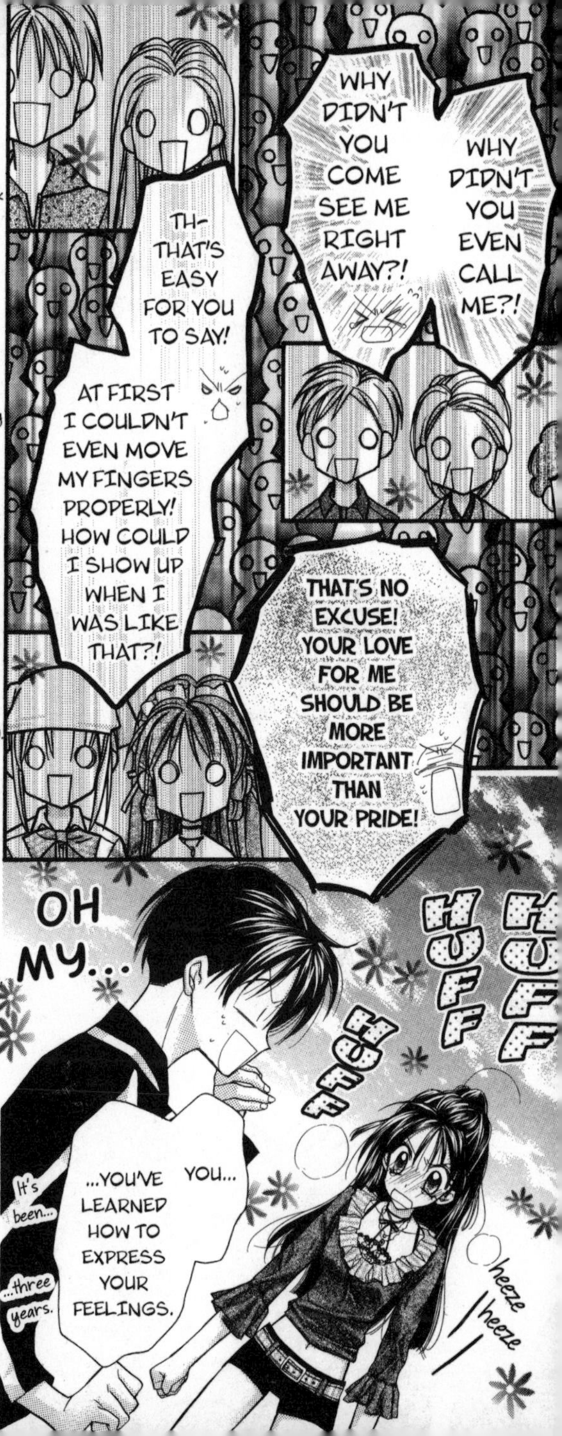
WHY DIDN'T YOU COME SEE ME RIGHT AWAY?!
WHY DIDN'T YOU EVEN CALL ME?!
TH-THAT'S EASY FOR YOU TO SAY!
AT FIRST I COULDN'T EVEN MOVE MY FINGERS PROPERLY! HOW COULD I SHOW UP WHEN I WAS LIKE THAT?!
THAT'S NO EXCUSE! YOUR LOVE FOR ME SHOULD BE MORE IMPORTANT THAN YOUR PRIDE!
HUFF HUFF
HUFF
OH MY...
YOU...
...YOU'VE LEARNED HOW TO EXPRESS YOUR FEELINGS.
It's been...
...three years.
heeze heeze

Continuation of Me Recently

We arrived in Sapporo around nine in the morning, and we took a two-and-a-half hour bus ride to Rusutsu resort.

We'd planned to go here and there, so I thought the bus ride might be boring, but the landscape was so beautiful that you couldn't pull your eyes away even for a second. ✧ The bus ride was great too!!

There were lots of dandelions in bloom--like it was overflowing--in the city and in the suburbs. They were big and really alive and wild. It was a culture shock!

At Rusutsu, my assistants held a surprise party for me (they hadn't told me, and they had a cake and other things prepared). And! They got a message for me from a doujin mangaka acquaintance, and they had even made a book (not for sale! ~ ;///). I was really moved! Thank you so much, everybody! ~~/// ;;

On the last day we went cycling for about four hours in Biei-cho. Twelve women (indoor types) going down hills!! Of course Arina is in front!

At a potato cuisine place named PUU, we had gratin. (It was really delicious ~~!!)

It was a really fulfilling trip!!

Oh... I want to go again...

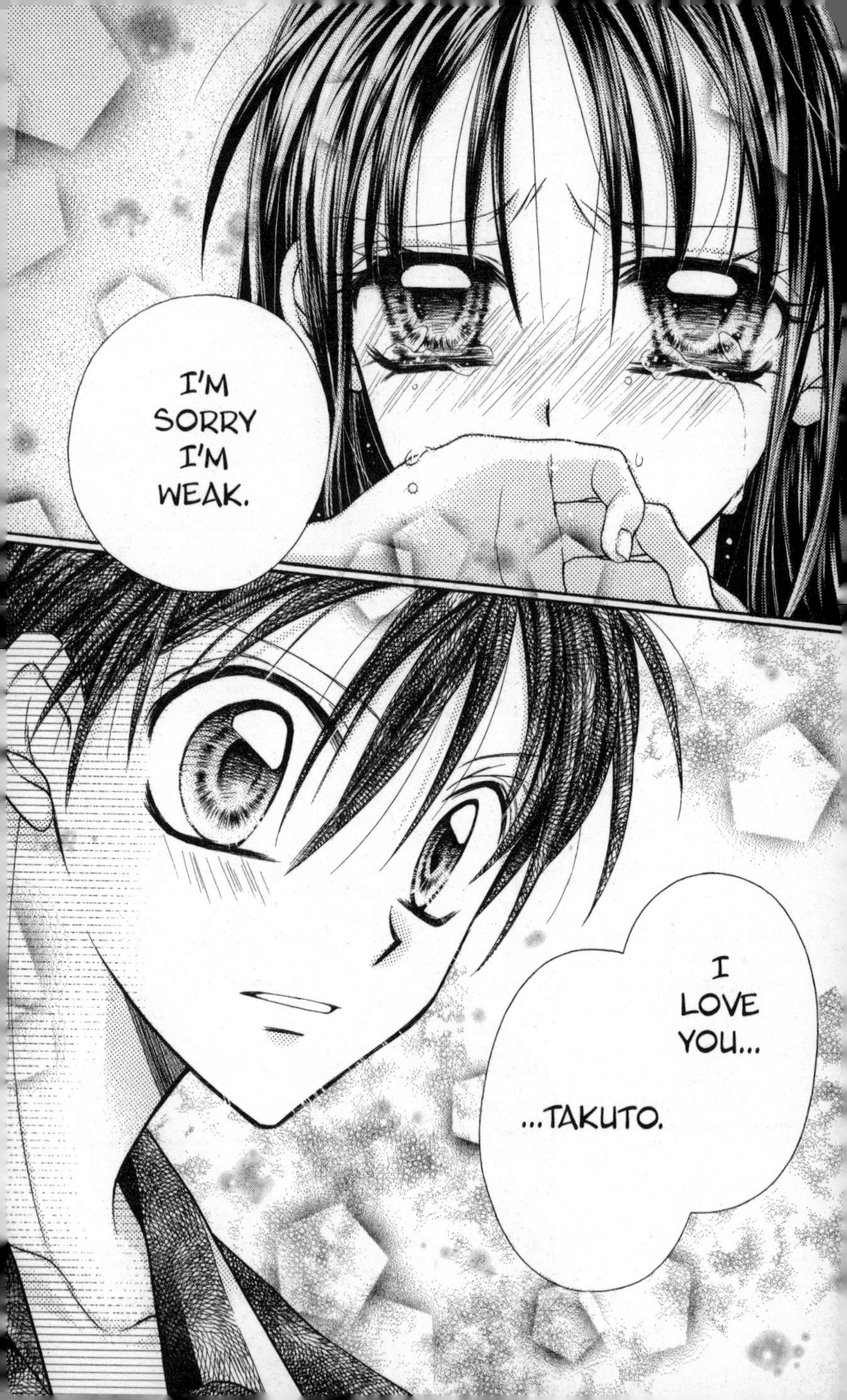
I'M SORRY I'M WEAK.
I LOVE YOU...
...TAKUTO.

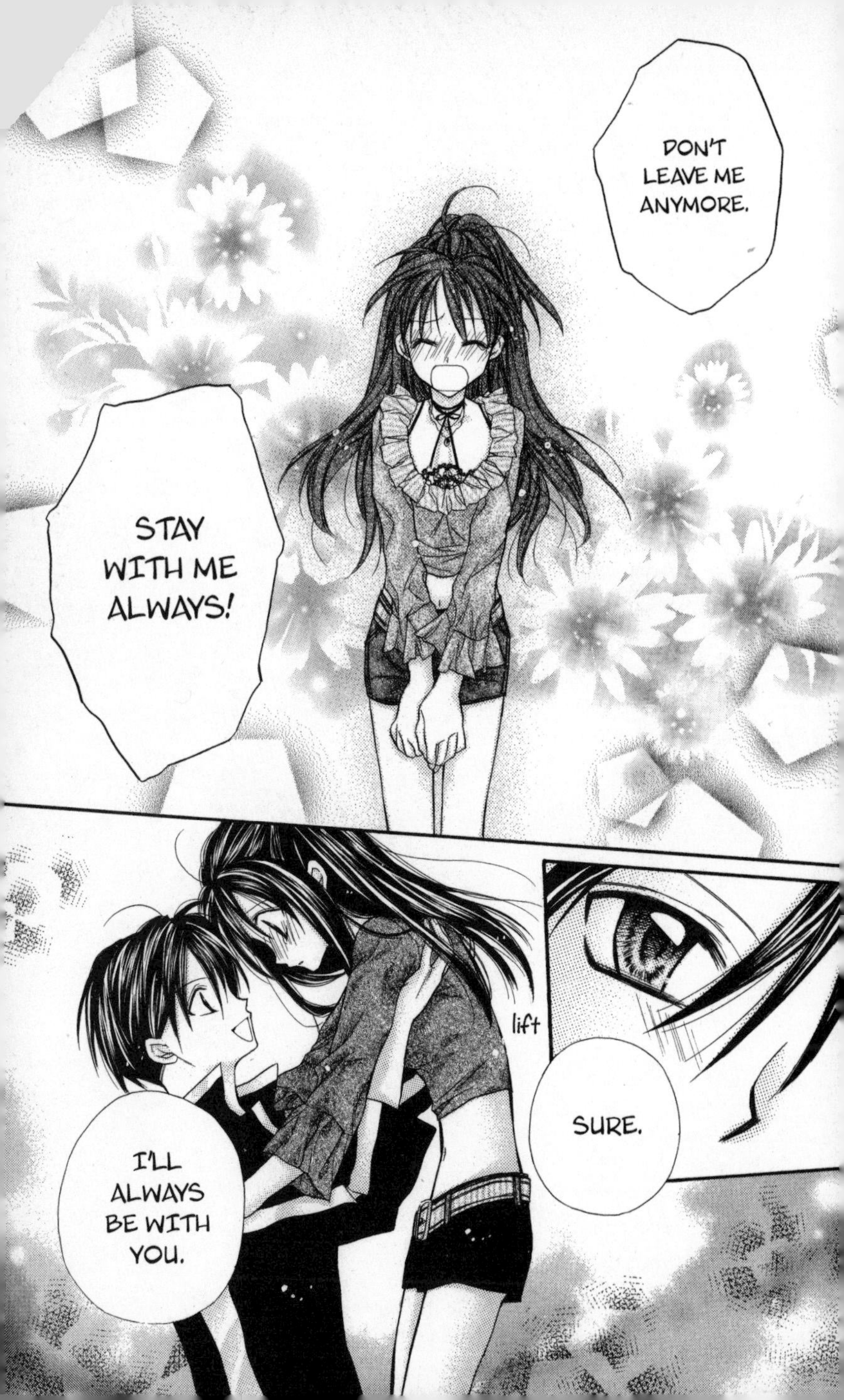
DON'T LEAVE ME ANYMORE.
STAY WITH ME ALWAYS!
SURE.
lift
I'LL ALWAYS BE WITH YOU.

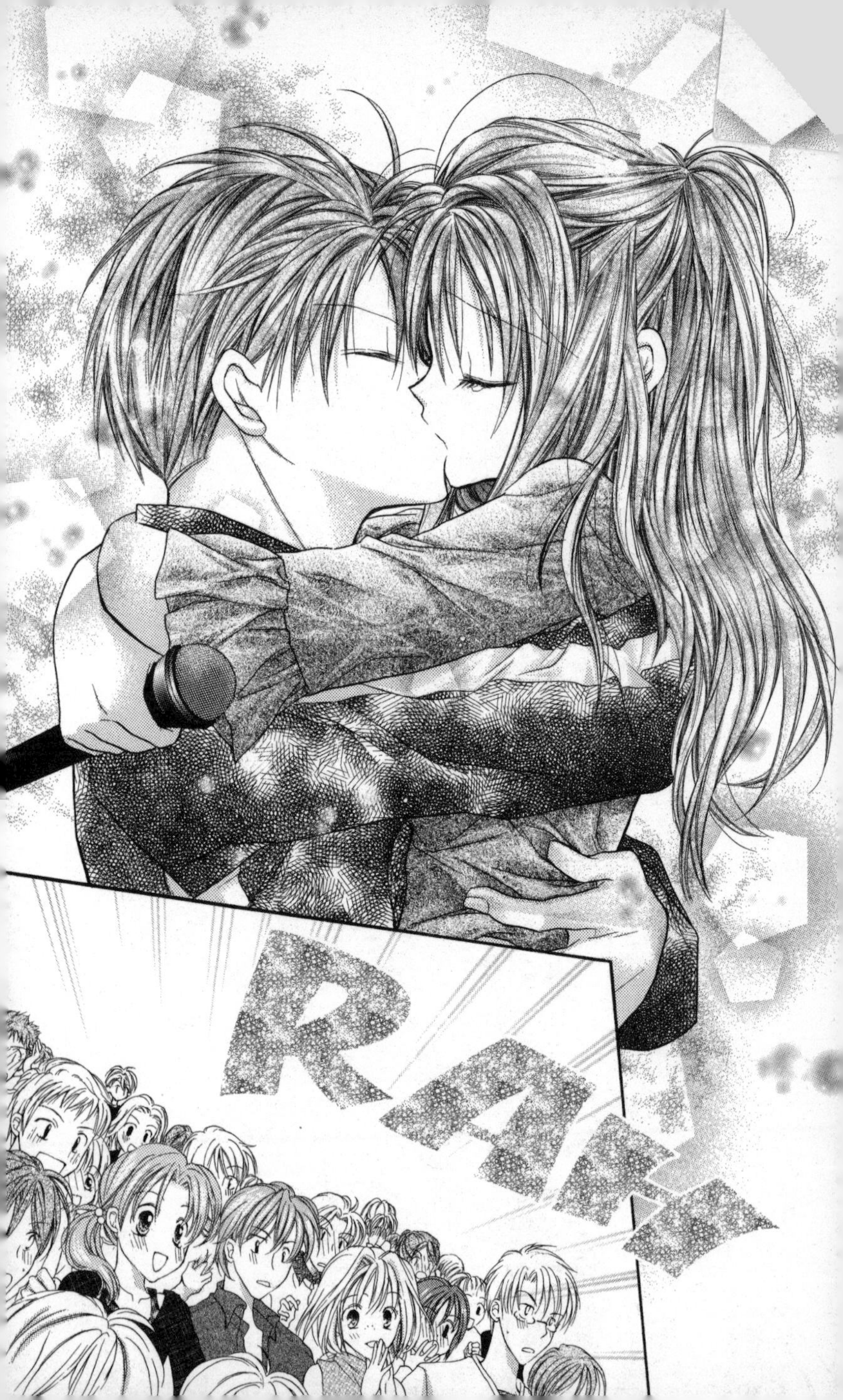
RAAAA

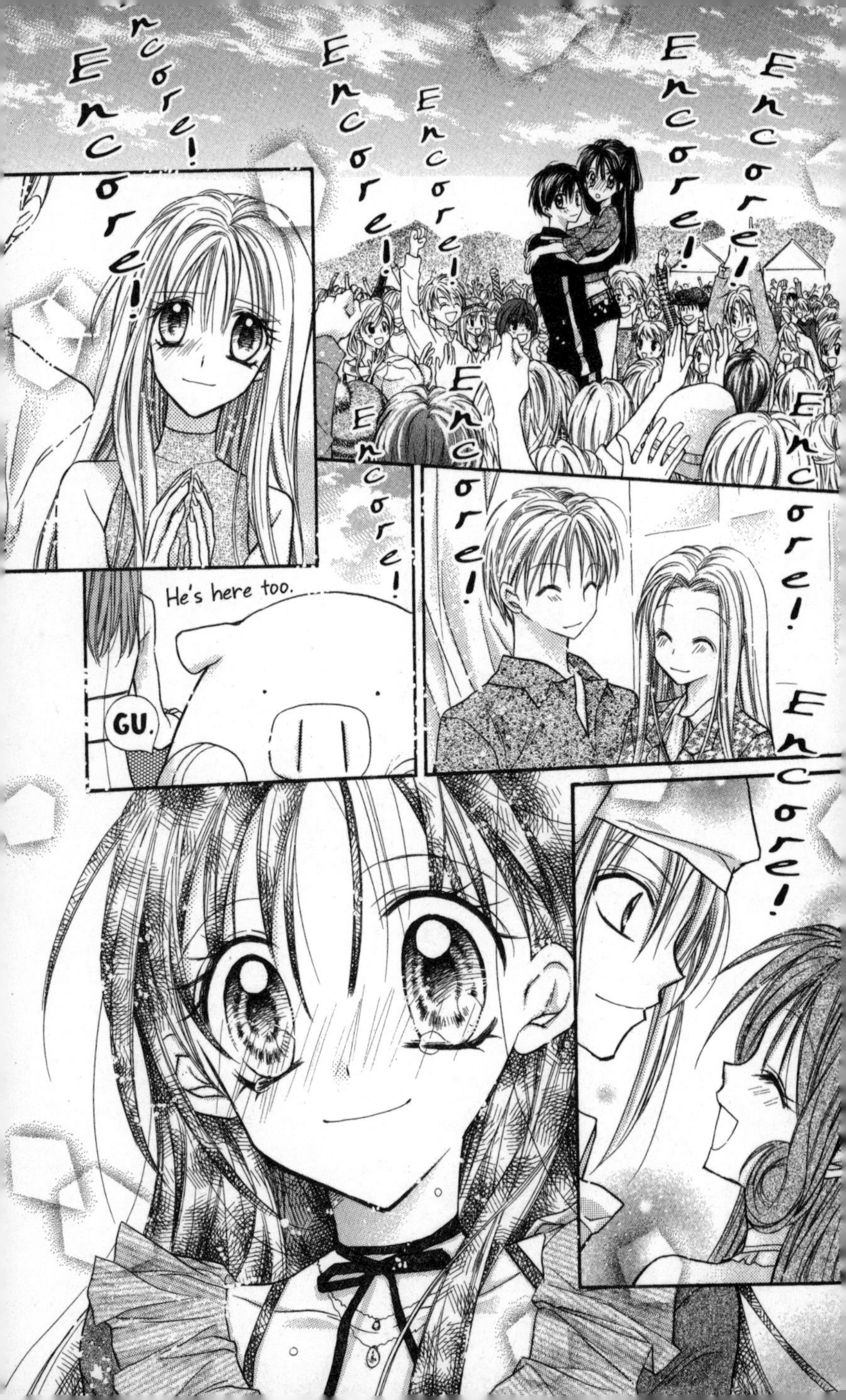

Encore!
Encore!
Encore!
Encore!
Encore!
Encore!
Encore!
Encore!
Encore!
Encore!
He's here too.
GU.

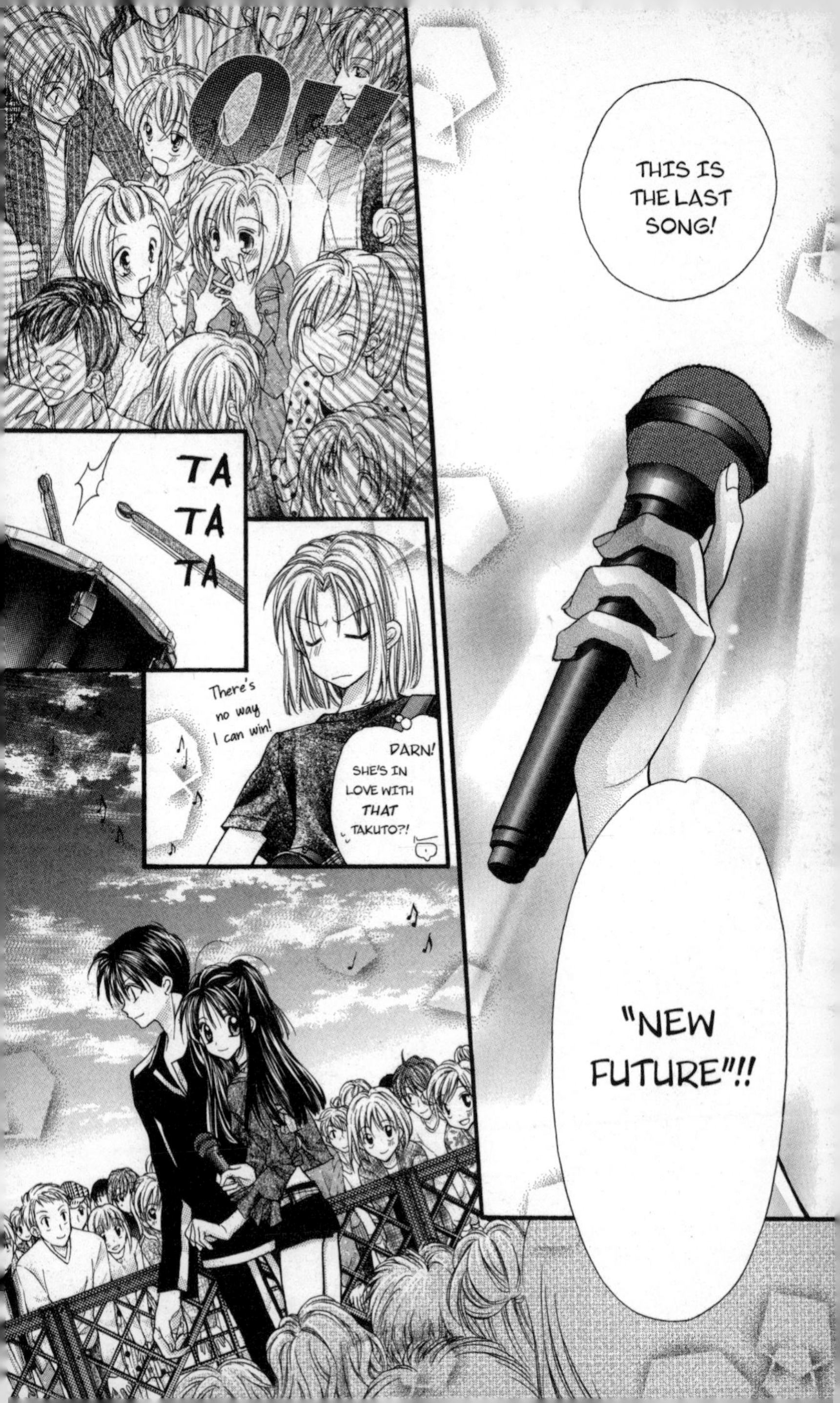
THIS IS THE LAST SONG!
"NEW FUTURE"!!
OH
TA TA TA
DARN! SHE'S IN LOVE WITH THAT TAKUTO?!
There's no way I can win!

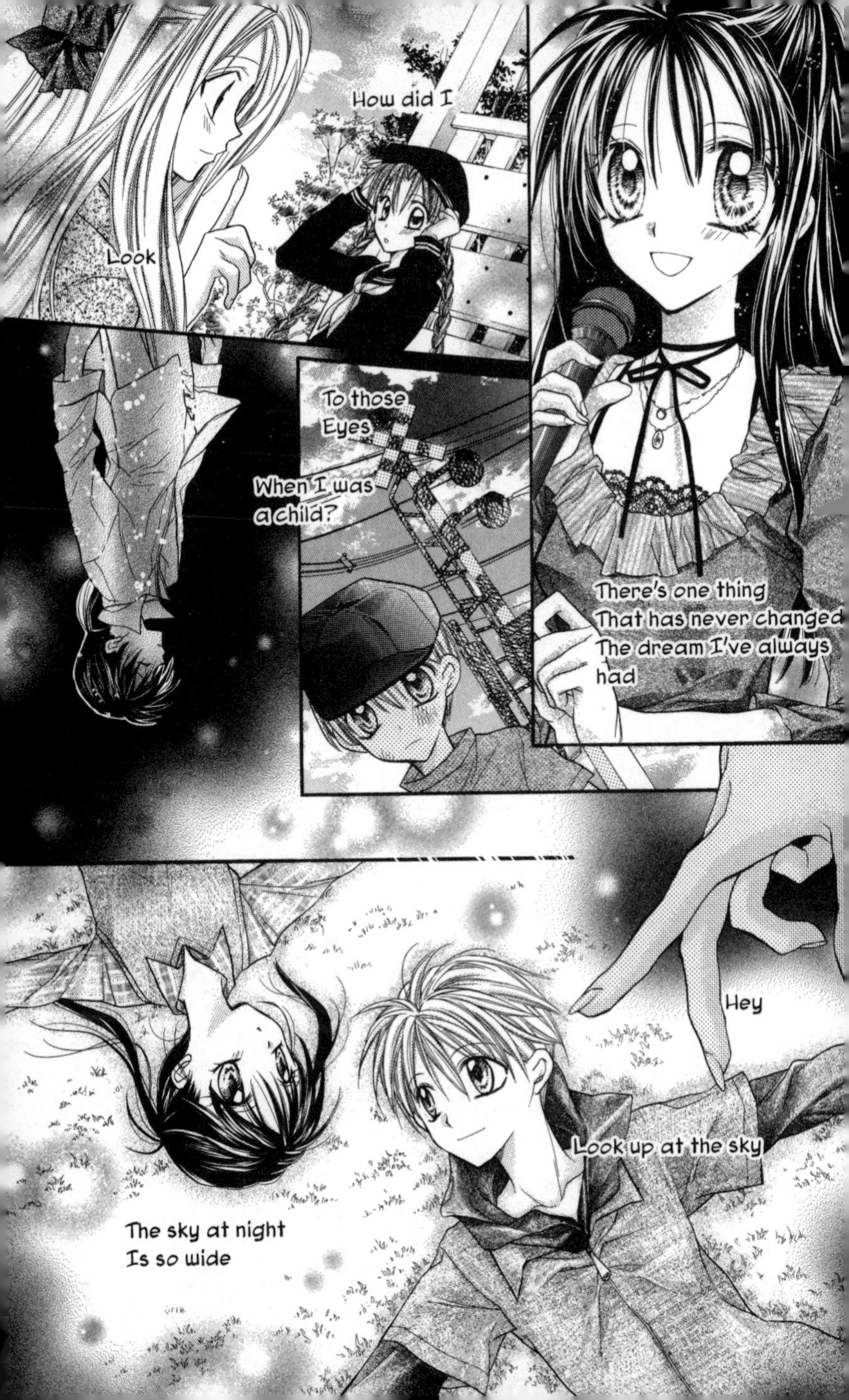
How did I
Look
To those
Eyes
When I was
a child?
There's one thing
That has never changed
The dream I've always
had
Hey
Look up at the sky
The sky at night
Is so wide

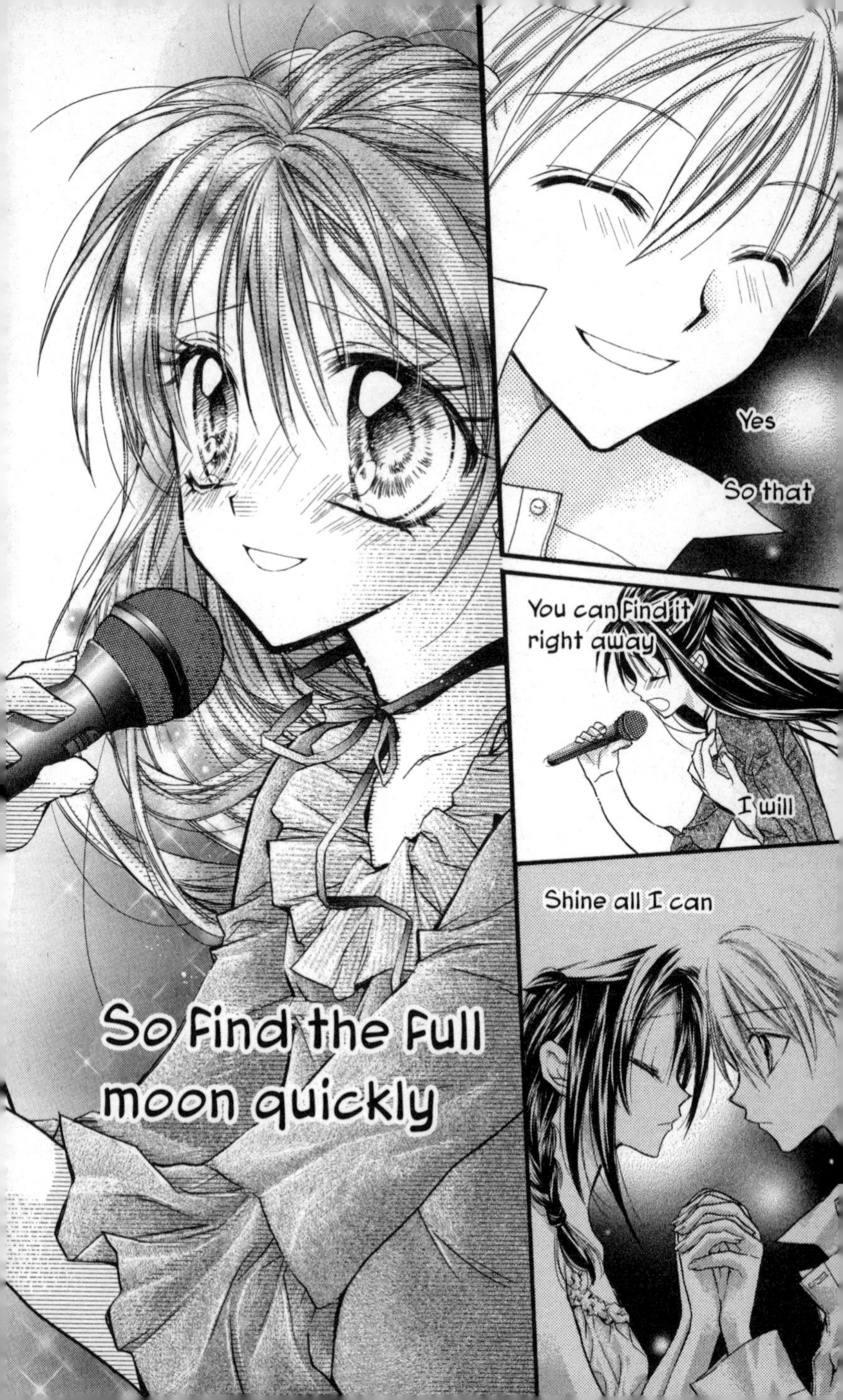
Yes
So that
You can find it right away
I will
Shine all I can
So find the full moon quickly

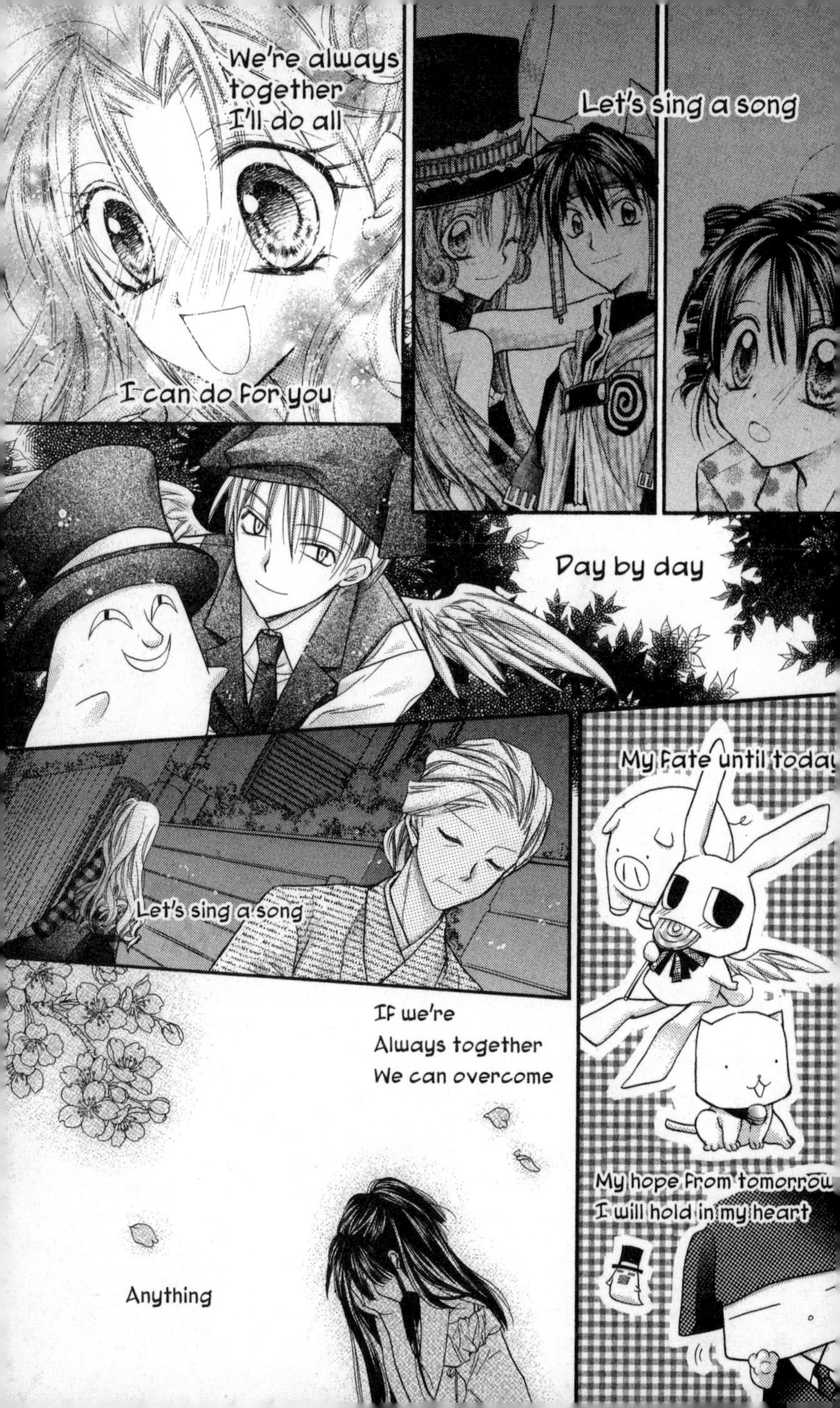

Let's sing a song
We're always together I'll do all
I can do for you
Day by day
My fate until today
My hope from tomorrow
I will hold in my heart
Let's sing a song
If we're
Always together
We can overcome
Anything

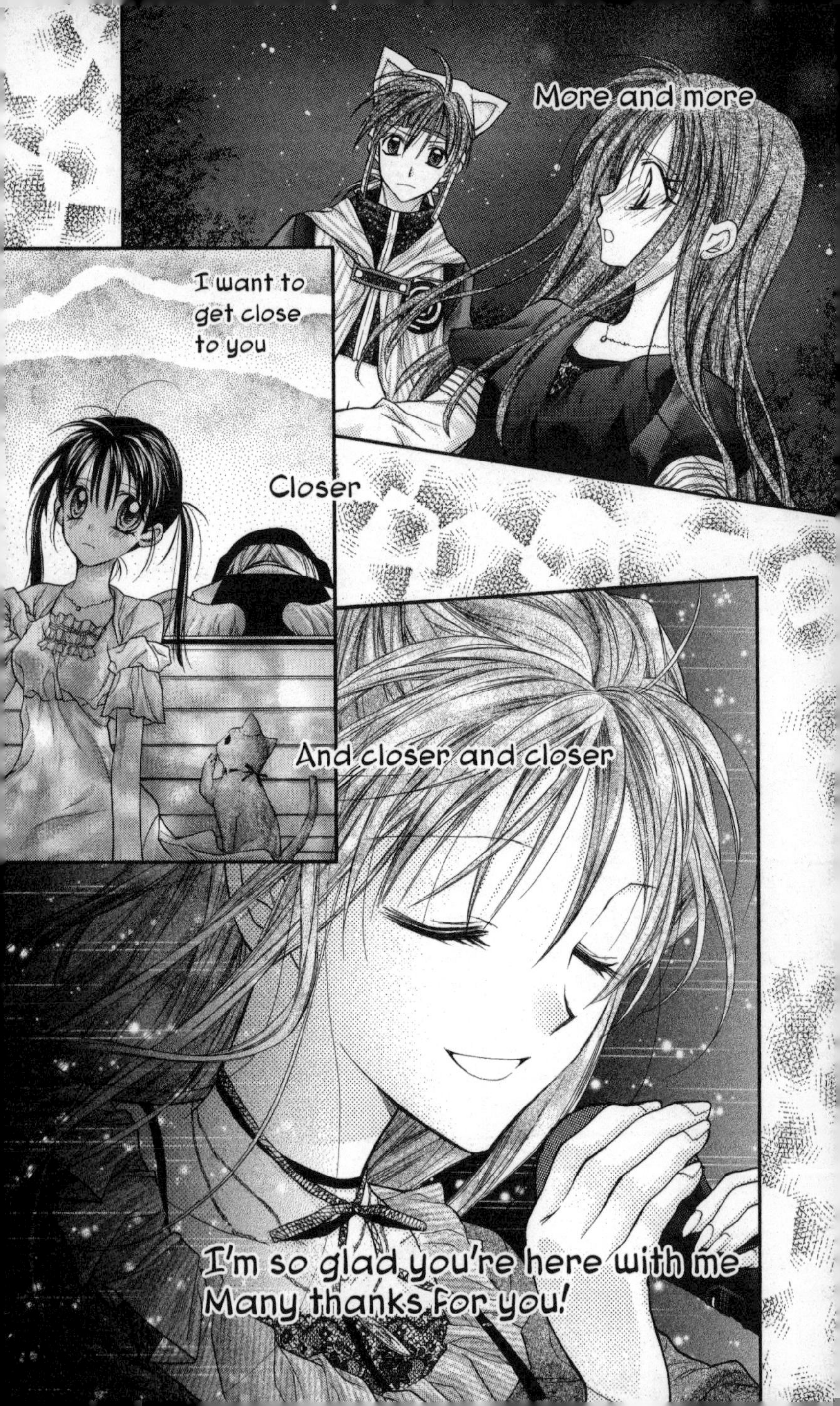
More and more
I want to get close to you
Closer
And closer and closer
I'm so glad you're here with me
Many thanks for you!

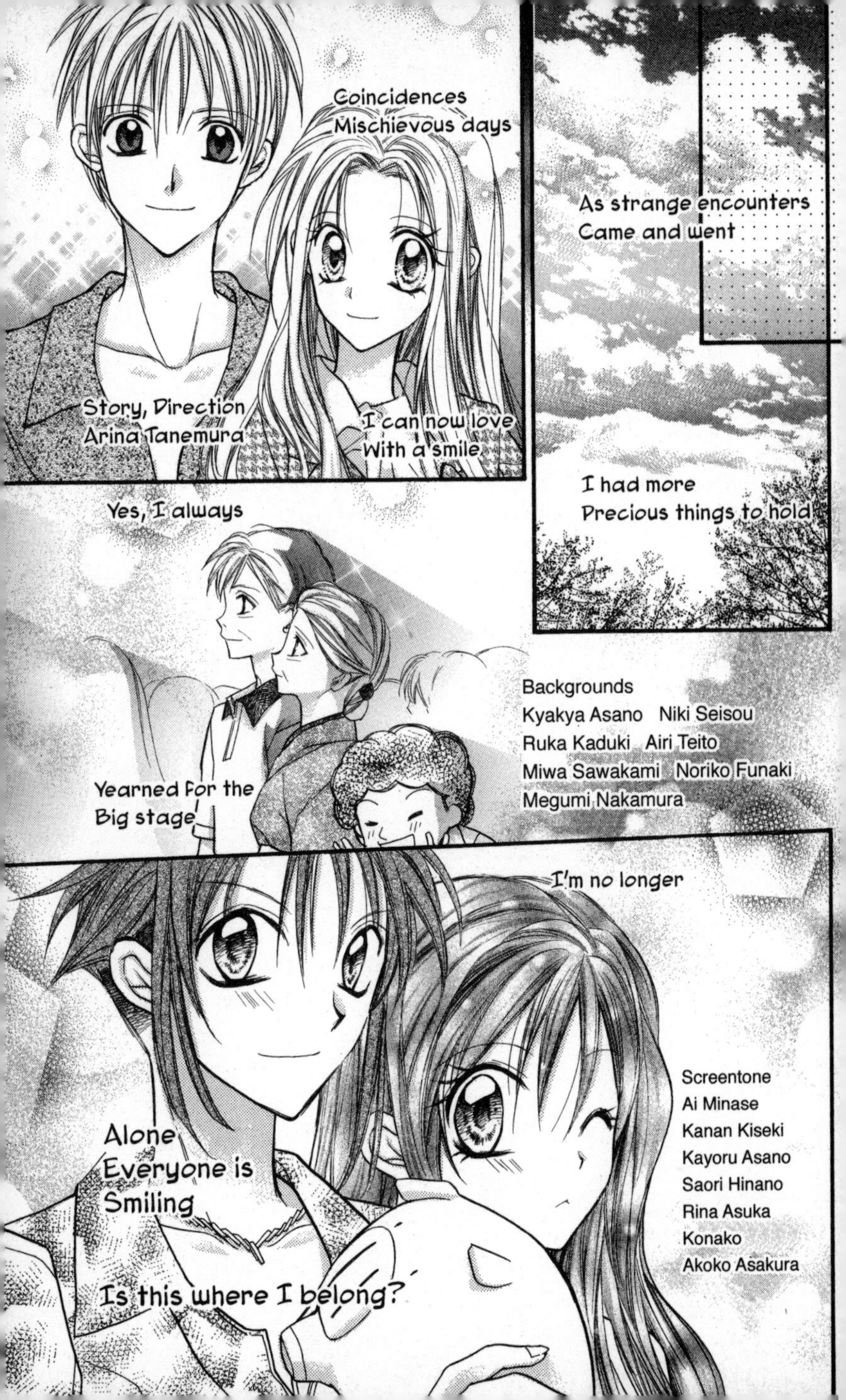
As strange encounters
Came and went
I had more
Precious things to hold
Coincidences
Mischievous days
I can now love
With a smile
Story, Direction
Arina Tanemura
Yes, I always
Yearned for the
Big stage
Backgrounds
Kyakya Asano Niki Seisou
Ruka Kaduki Airi Teito
Miwa Sawakami Noriko Funaki
Megumi Nakamura
I'm no longer
Alone
Everyone is
Smiling
Is this where I belong?
Screentone
Ai Minase
Kanan Kiseki
Kayoru Asano
Saori Hinano
Rina Asuka
Konako
Akoko Asakura

Tonight makes me shine

Production Assistance
Shueisha Ribon Department
Ammonite Limited

More than the spotlight

Let's sing a song

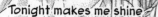

Day by day

Passionate looks and cheers
My dripping sweat shines

Let's sing a song

Special Thanks
Mitsuki Koyama
Kira Takuto
Yui Meroko
Lio Izumi
Jonathan
(Sheldan, the boss)
Keiichi Wakaoji
Masami Oshige
(Yuina Hanakazari)
Aoi Koga
Hazuki Koga
Fuzuki Koyama
Yone Tanaka
Seijyuro Koga
Madoka Wakamatsu
(Chisato Kurebayashi)
Nachi
(Soichiro Shido)
Gutchan
Mystere
(the Death Master)

Tonight will never change
I want to believe that
passionate love exists

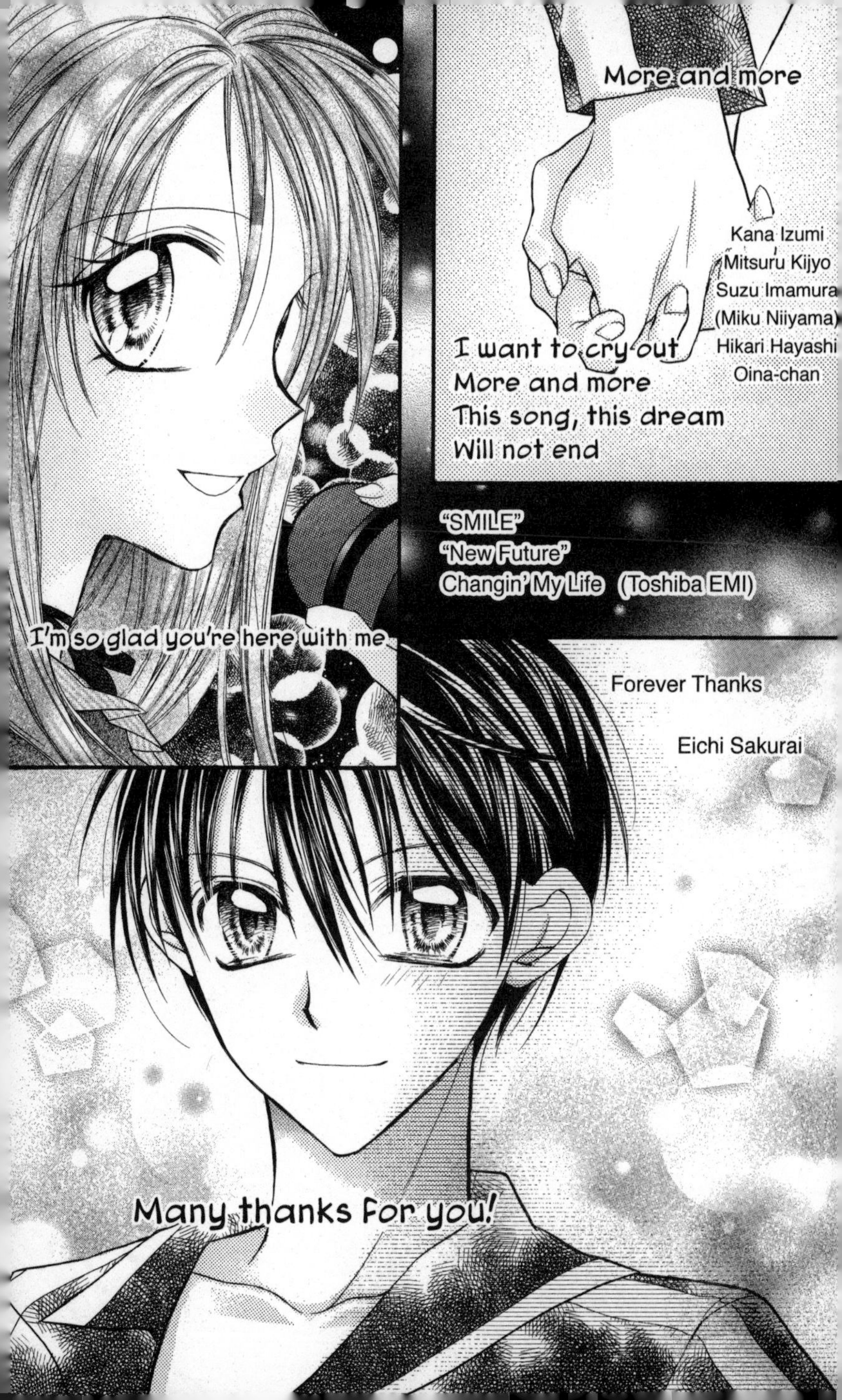
More and more
Kana Izumi
Mitsuru Kijyo
Suzu Imamura
(Miku Niiyama)
Hikari Hayashi
Oina-chan
I want to cry out
More and more
This song, this dream
Will not end
"SMILE"
"New Future"
Changin' My Life (Toshiba EMI)
I'm so glad you're here with me
Forever Thanks
Eichi Sakurai
Many thanks for you!

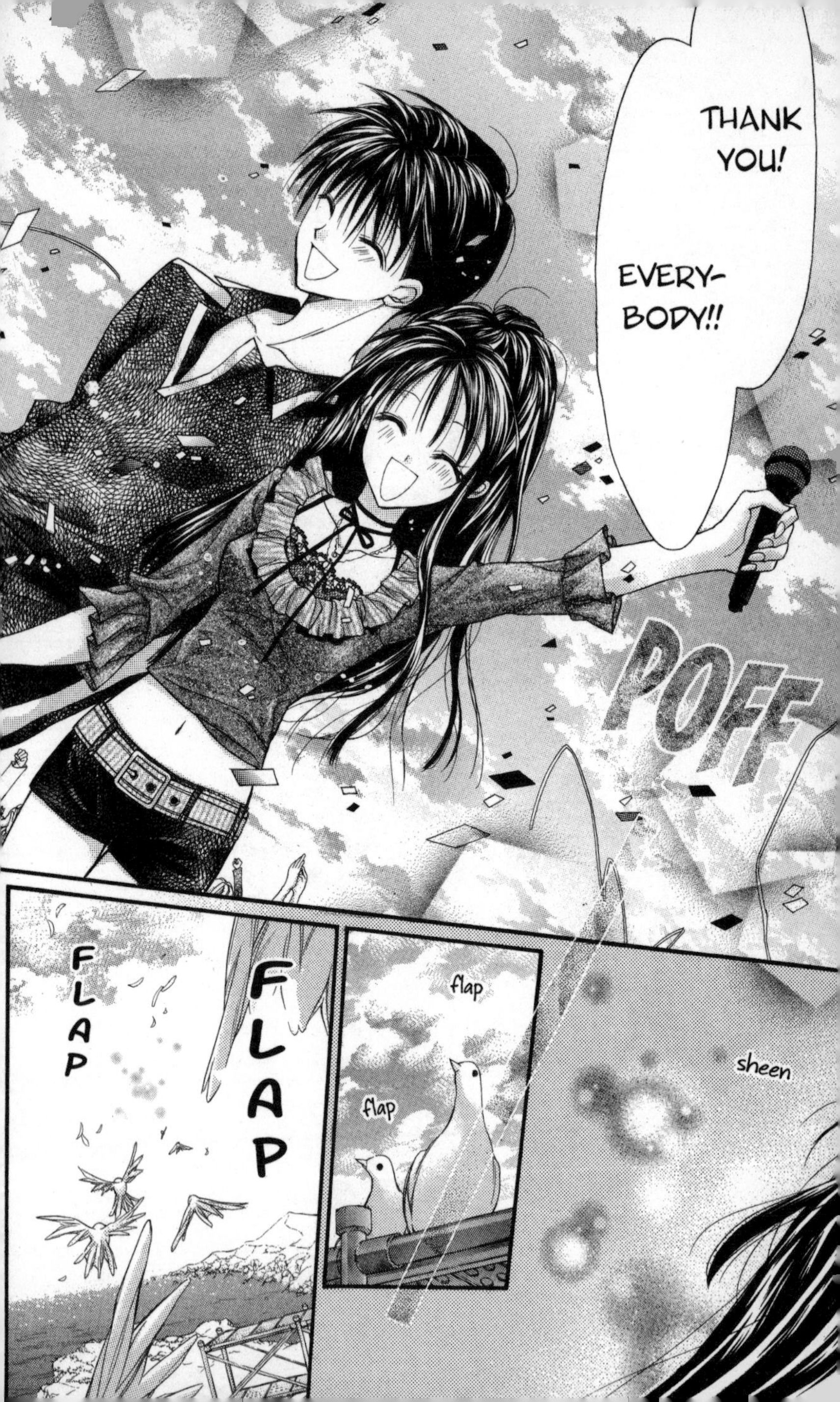
THANK YOU!
EVERY-BODY!!
POFF
sheen
flap
flap
FLAP
FLAP

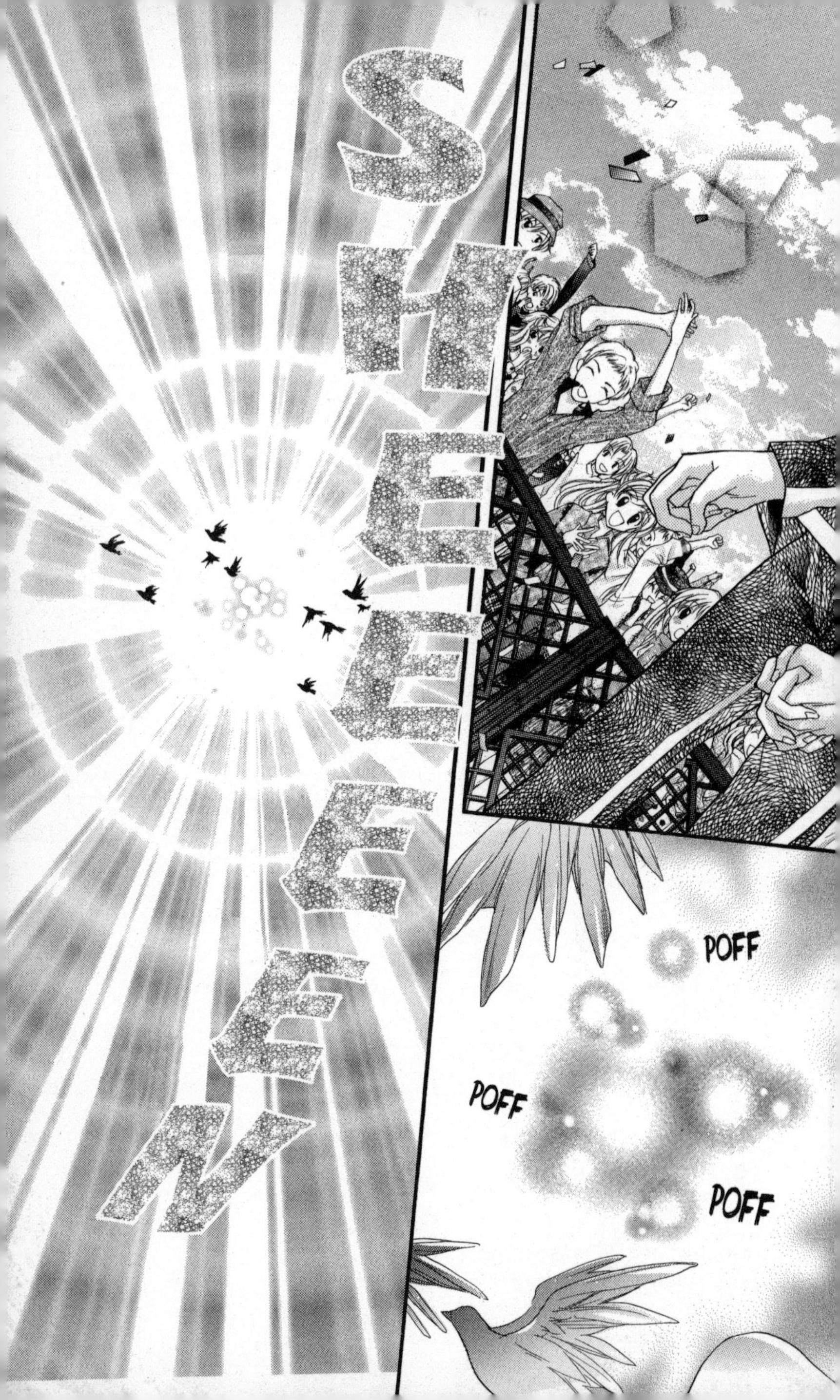
SHEEEEEW
POFF
POFF
POFF

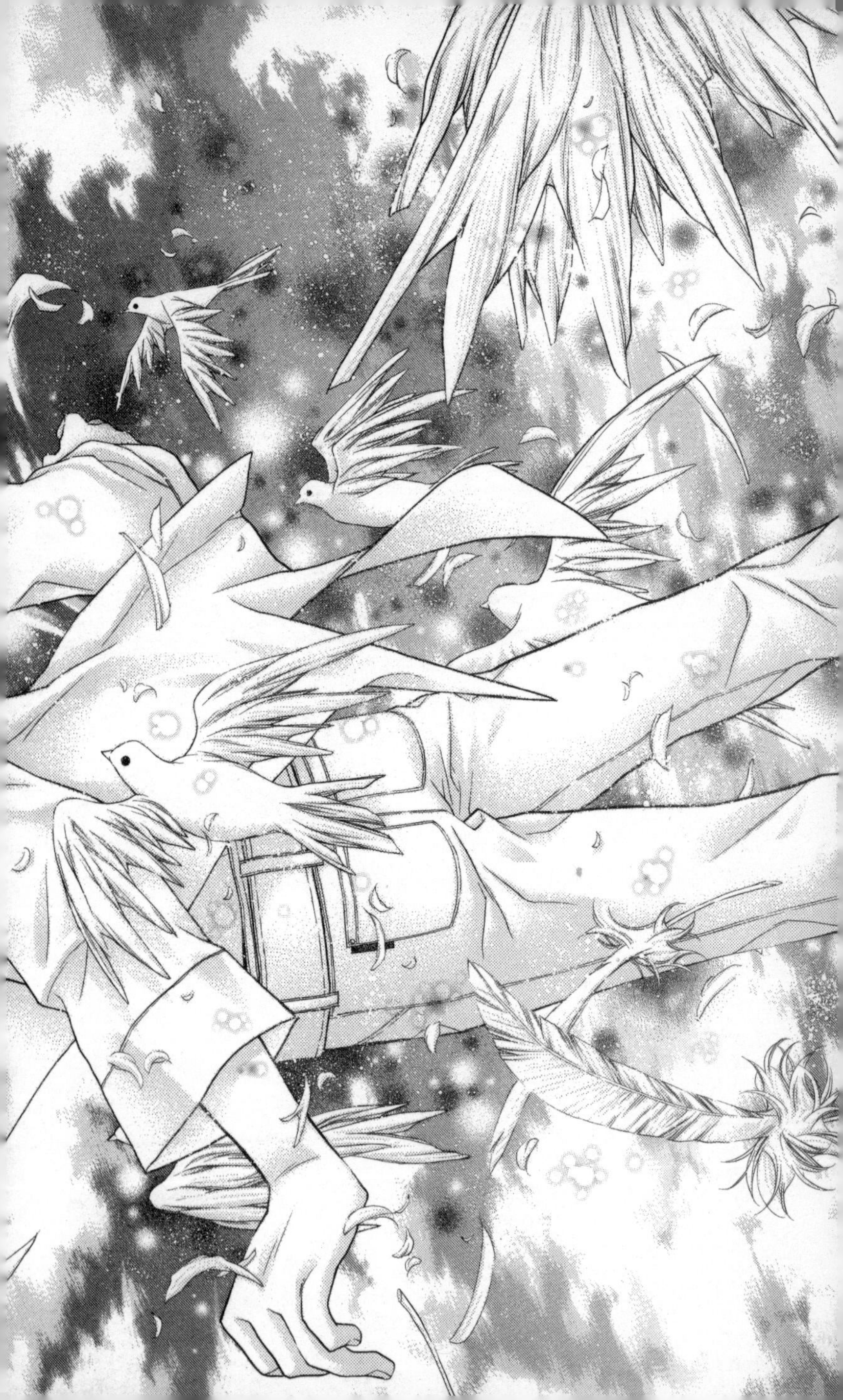

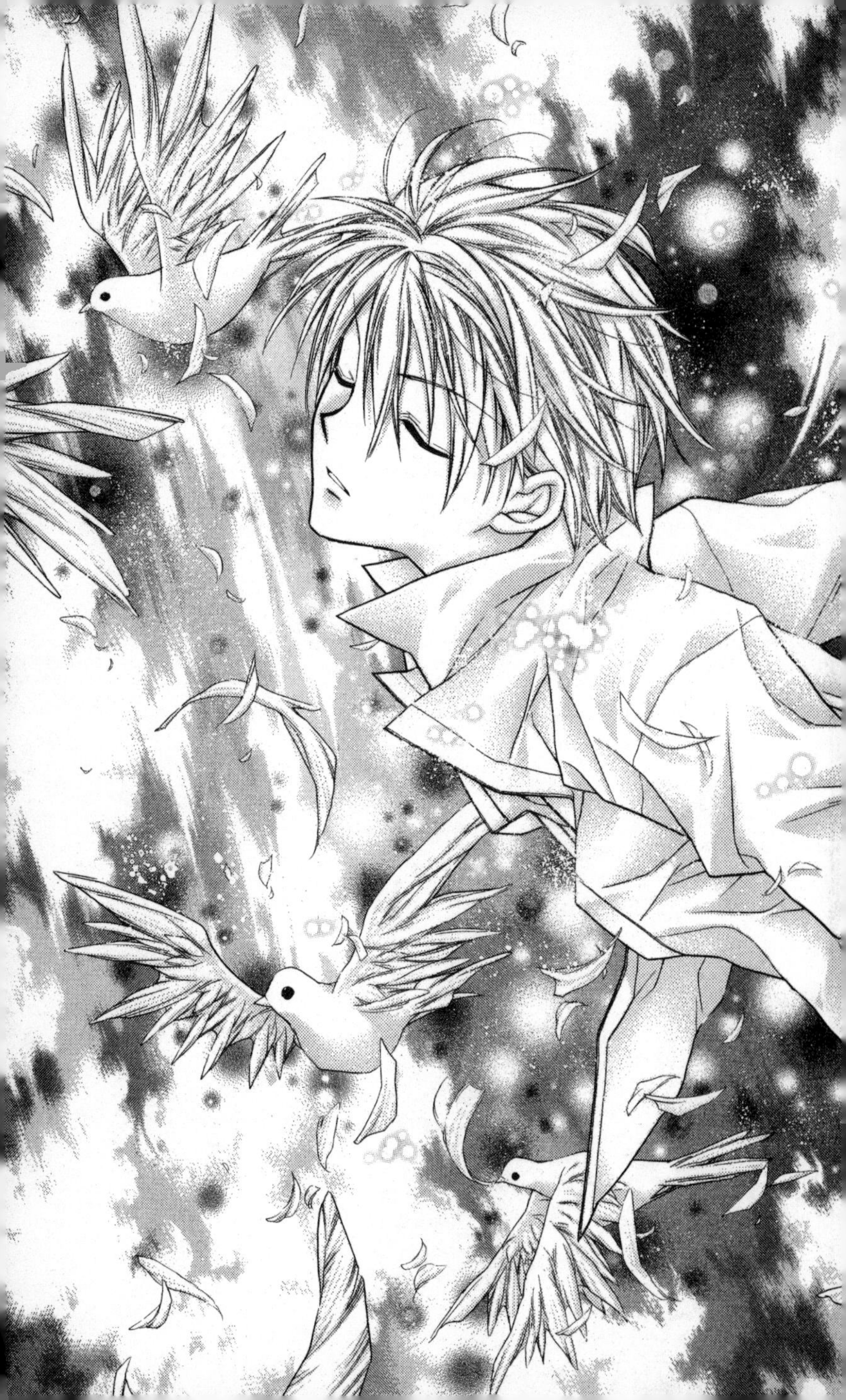

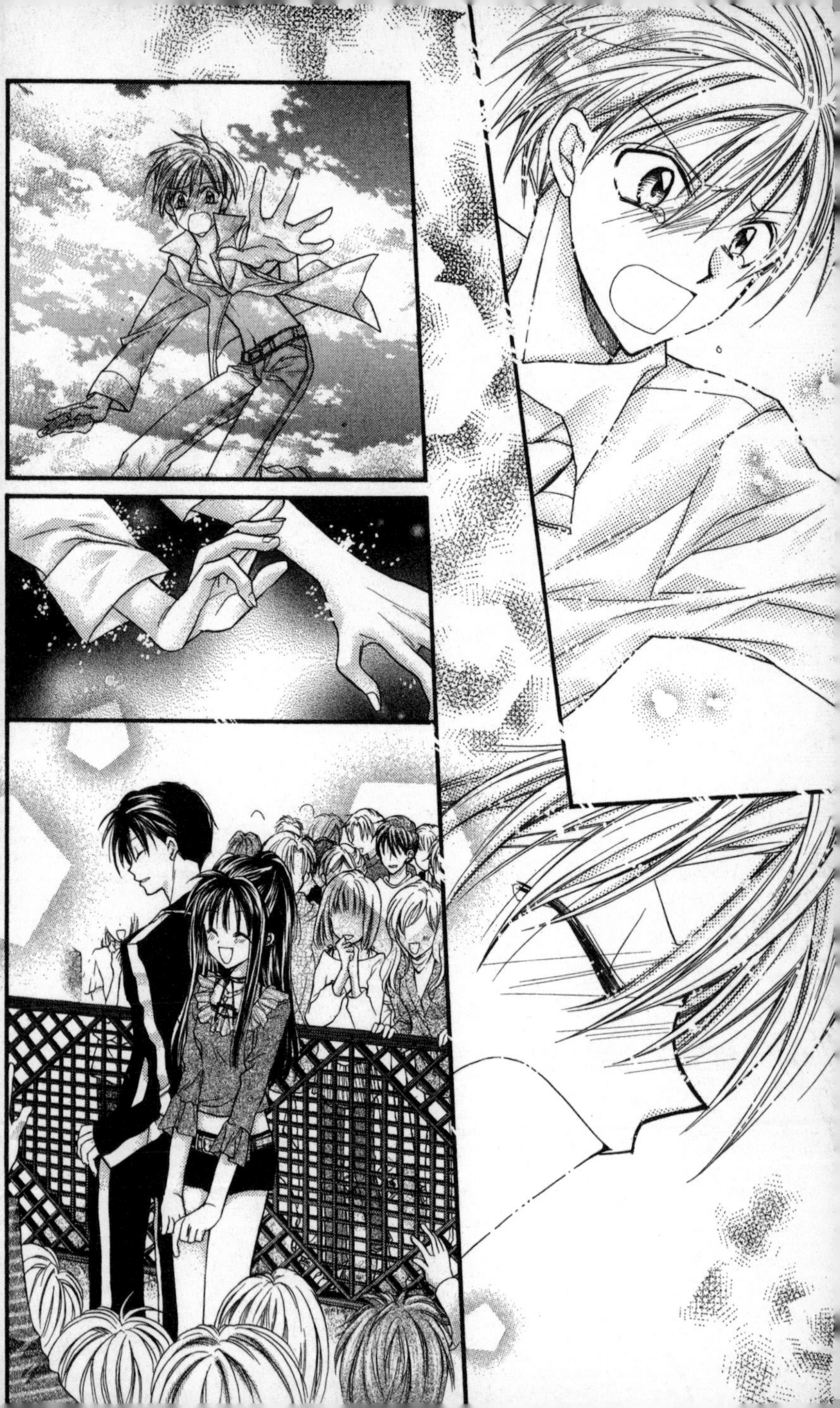

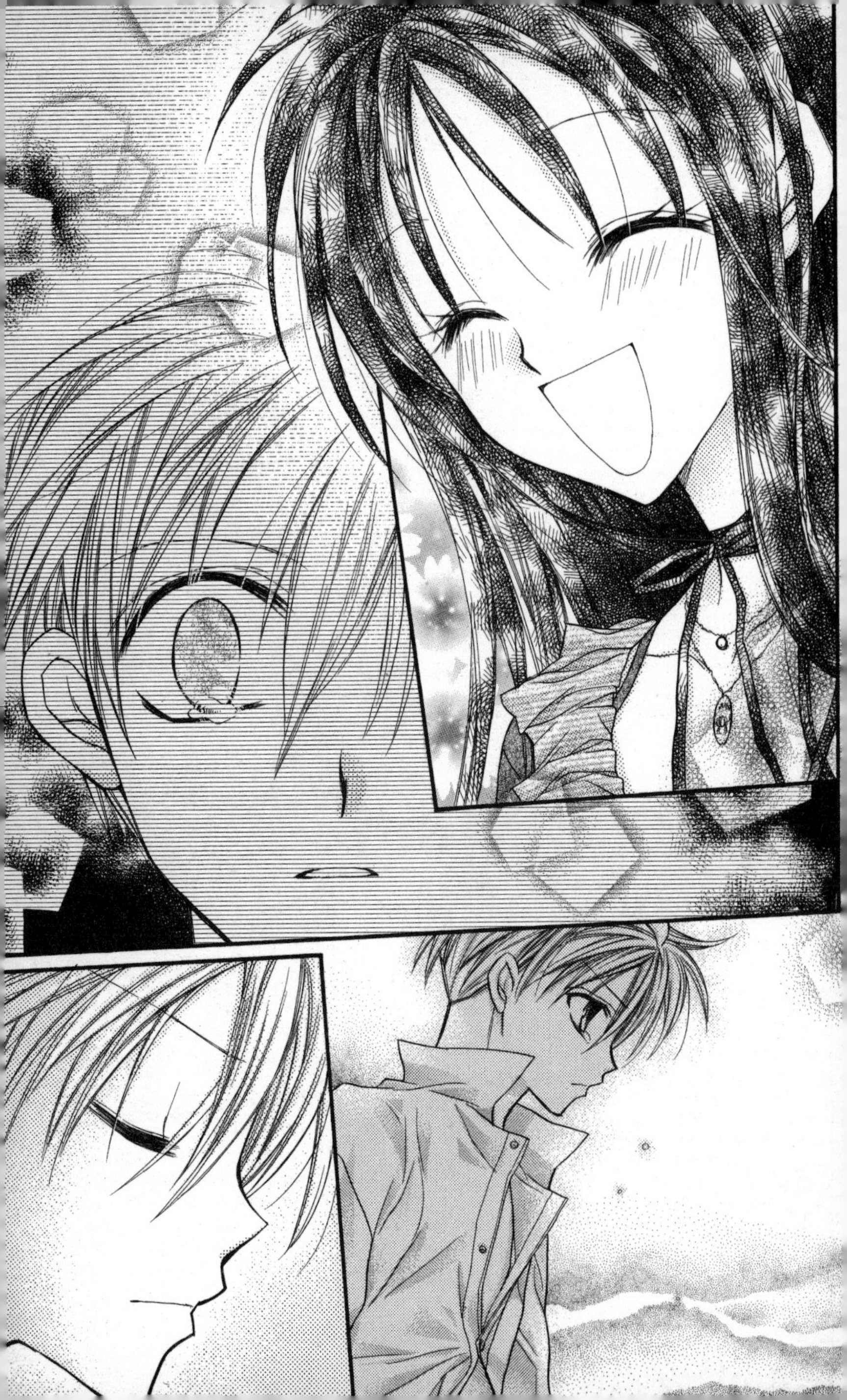

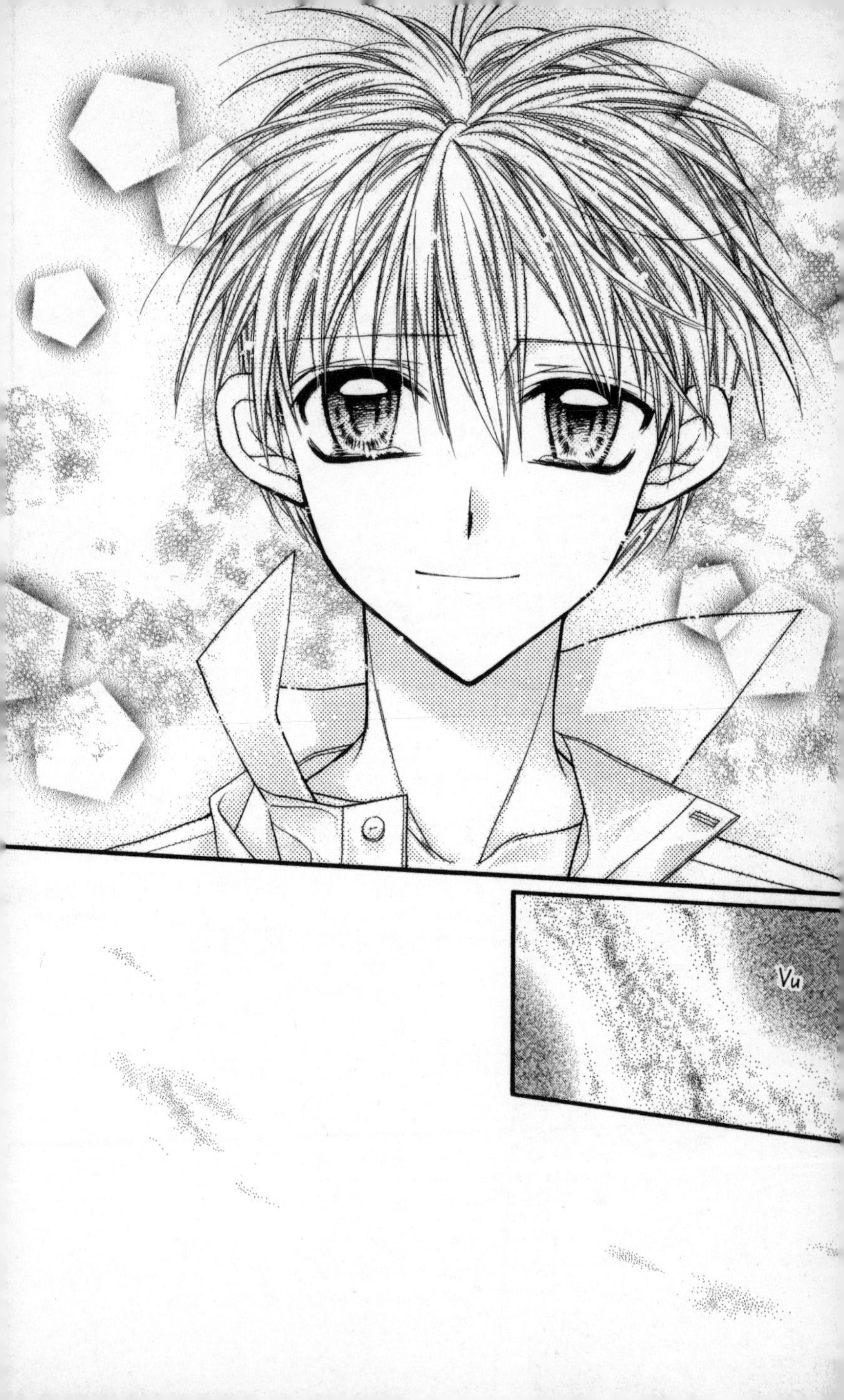
Vu

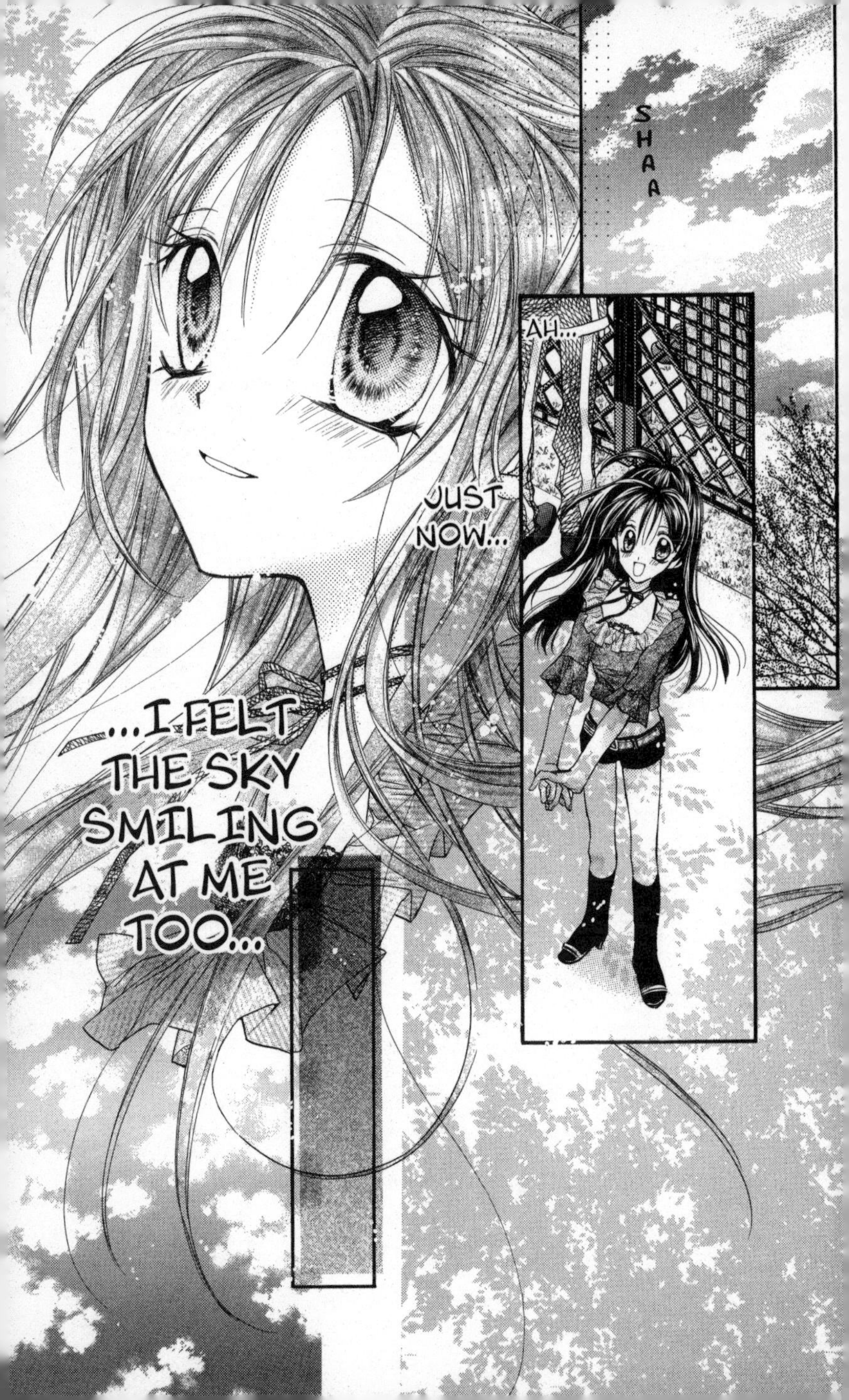
SHAA
AH...
JUST NOW...
...I FELT THE SKY SMILING AT ME TOO...

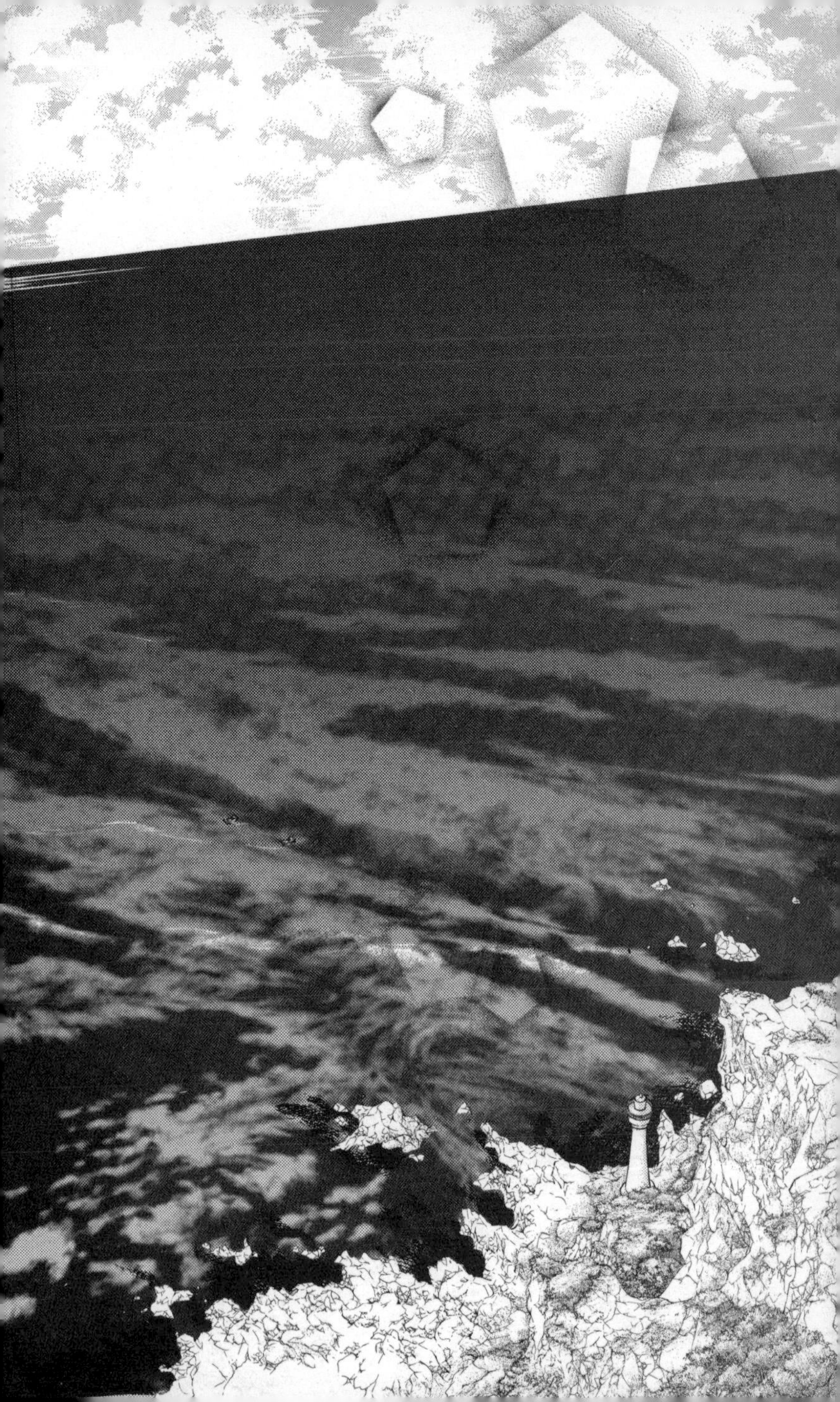

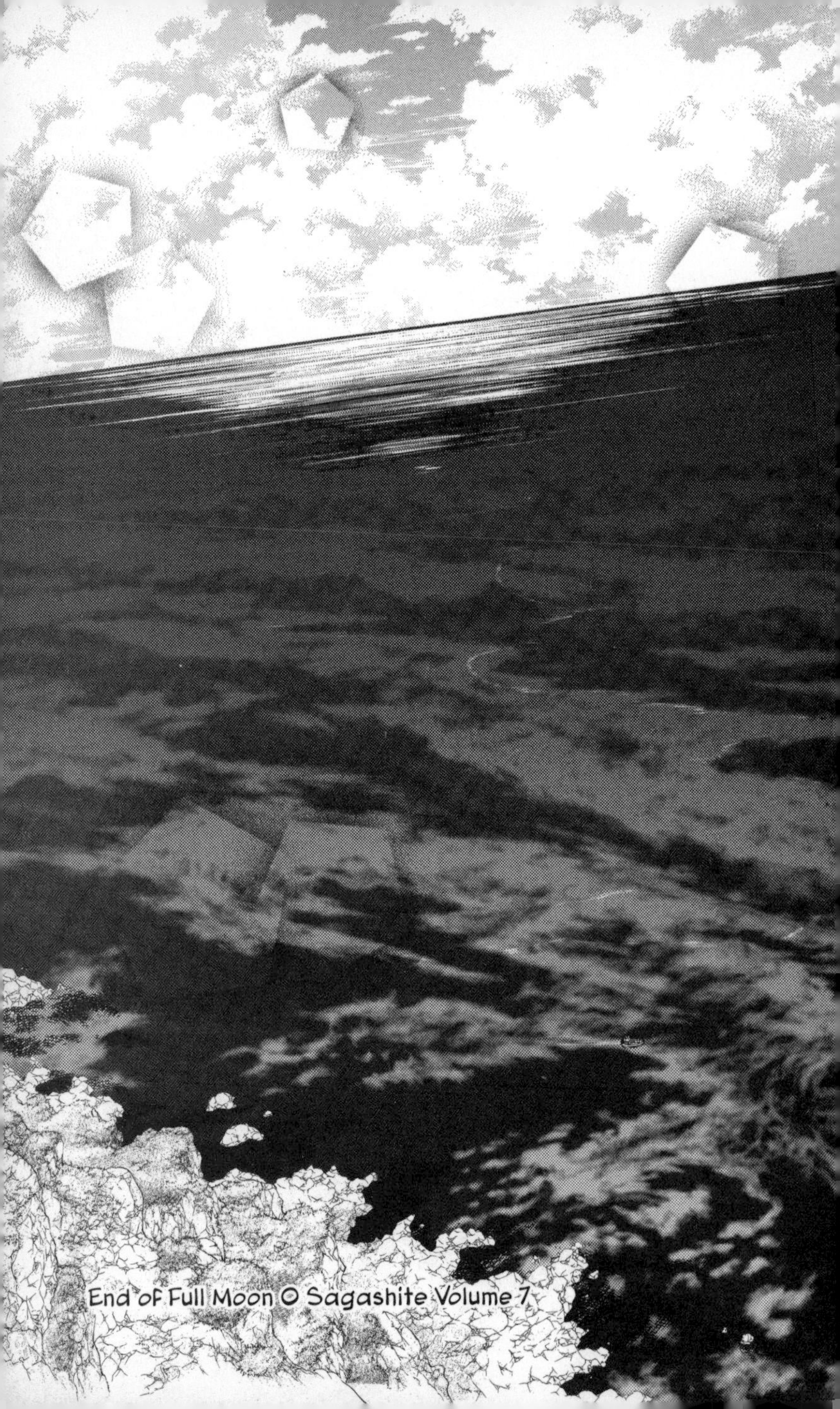
End of Full Moon O Sagashite Volume 7

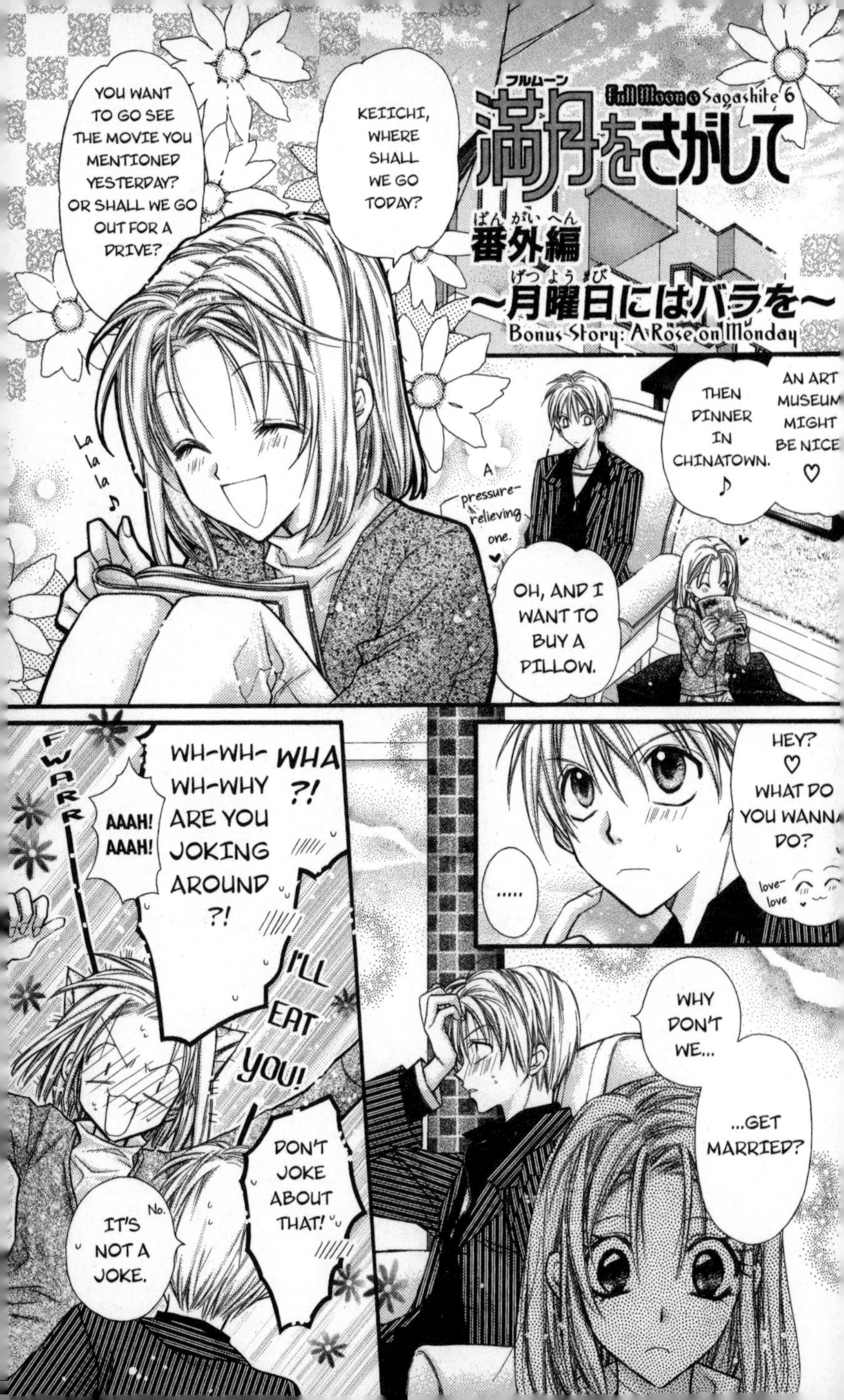
フルムーン
Full Moon o Sagashite 6
満月をさがして
ばんがいへん
番外編
げつようび
~月曜日にはバラを~
Bonus Story: A Rose on Monday
KEIICHI, WHERE SHALL WE GO TODAY?
YOU WANT TO GO SEE THE MOVIE YOU MENTIONED YESTERDAY? OR SHALL WE GO OUT FOR A DRIVE?
La la la ♪
AN ART MUSEUM MIGHT BE NICE ♡
THEN DINNER IN CHINATOWN. ♪
A pressure-relieving one. ♥
OH, AND I WANT TO BUY A PILLOW.
HEY? ♡ WHAT DO YOU WANNA DO?
love-love
.....
WHY DON'T WE...
...GET MARRIED?
WHA ?!
WH-WH-WH-WHY ARE YOU JOKING AROUND ?!
AAAH! AAAH!
FWARR
I'LL EAT YOU!
DON'T JOKE ABOUT THAT!
No.
IT'S NOT A JOKE.

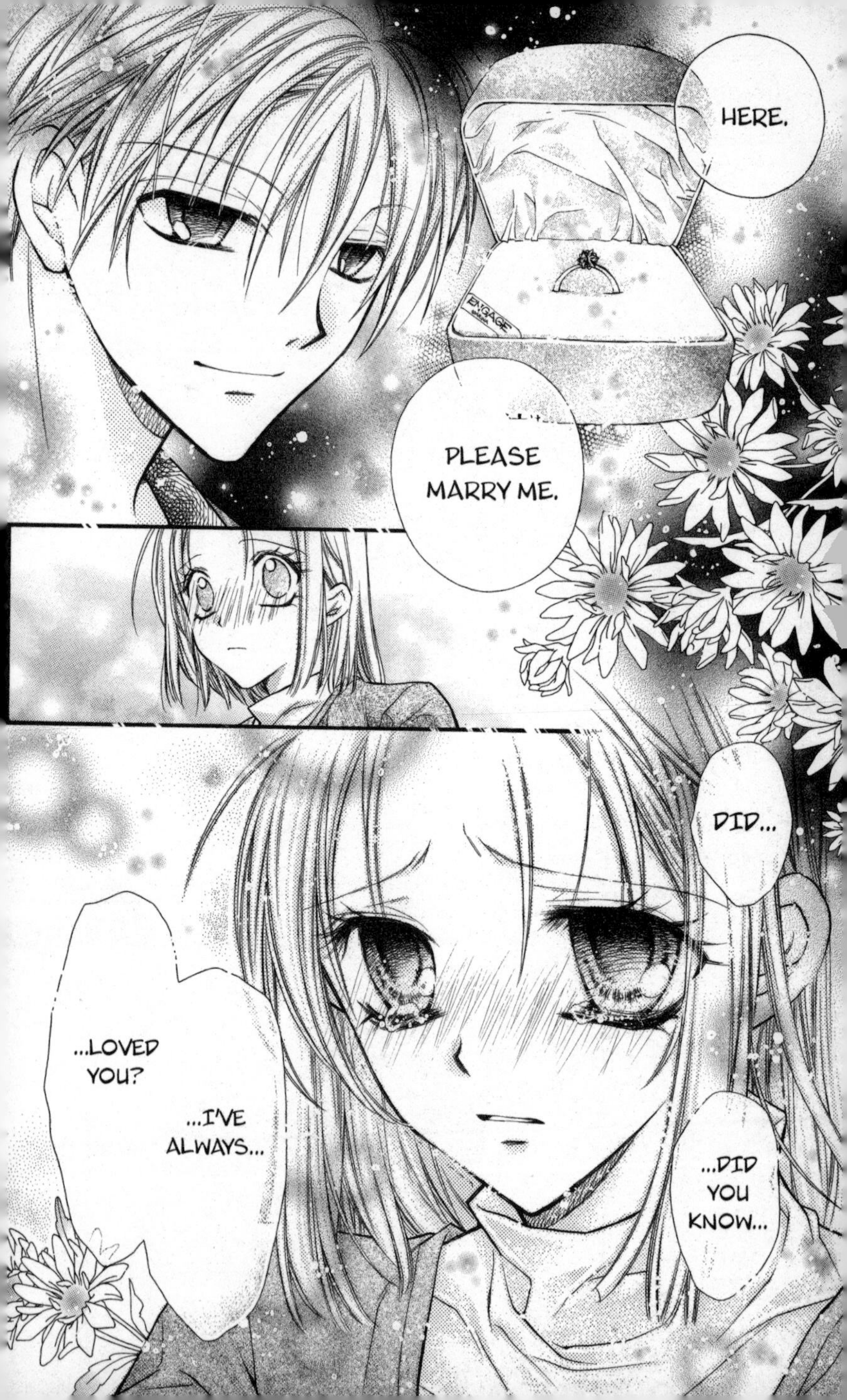
HERE.
ENGAGE
PLEASE MARRY ME.
DID...
...DID YOU KNOW...
...I'VE ALWAYS...
...LOVED YOU?

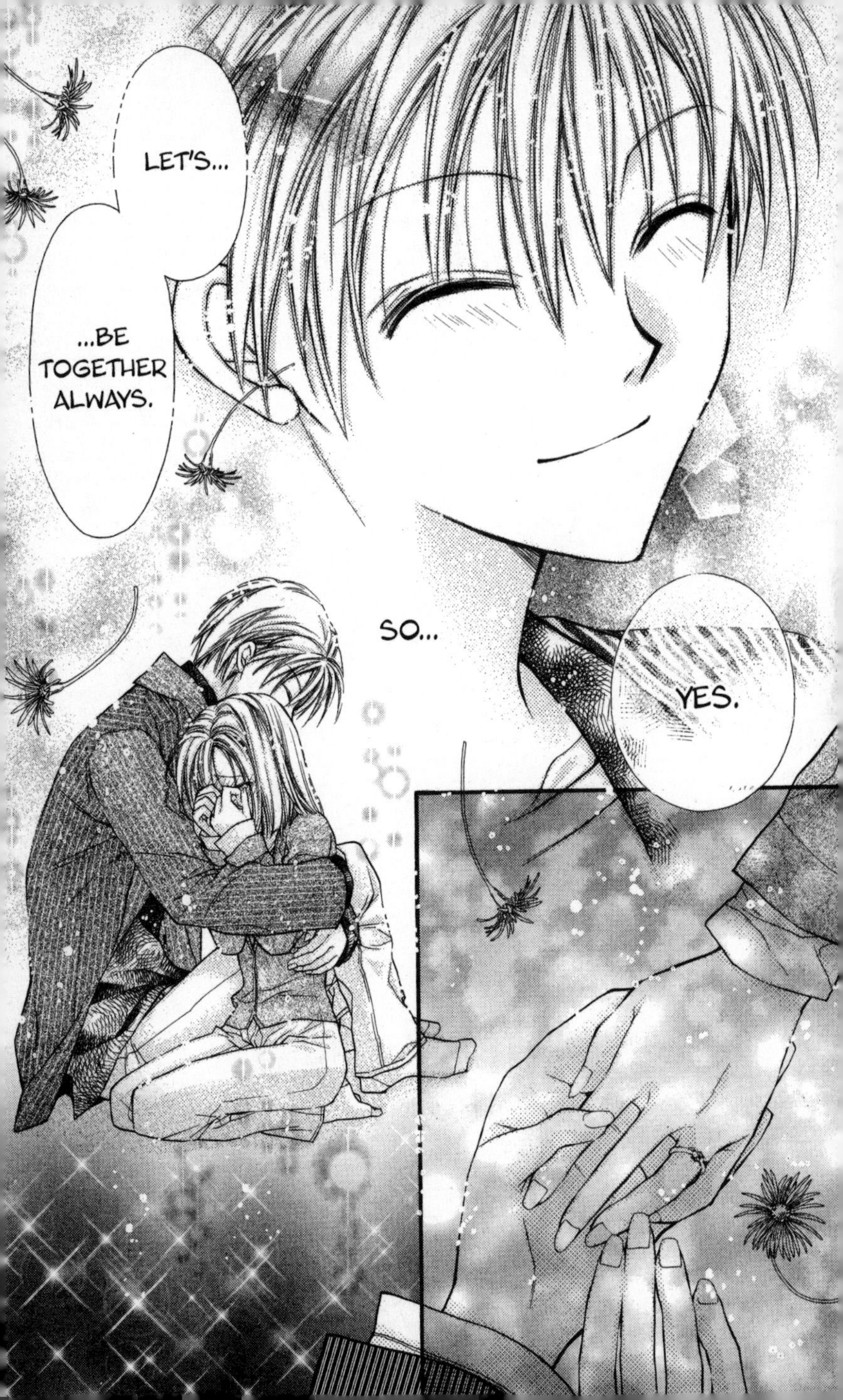
LET'S...
...BE TOGETHER ALWAYS.
SO...
YES.

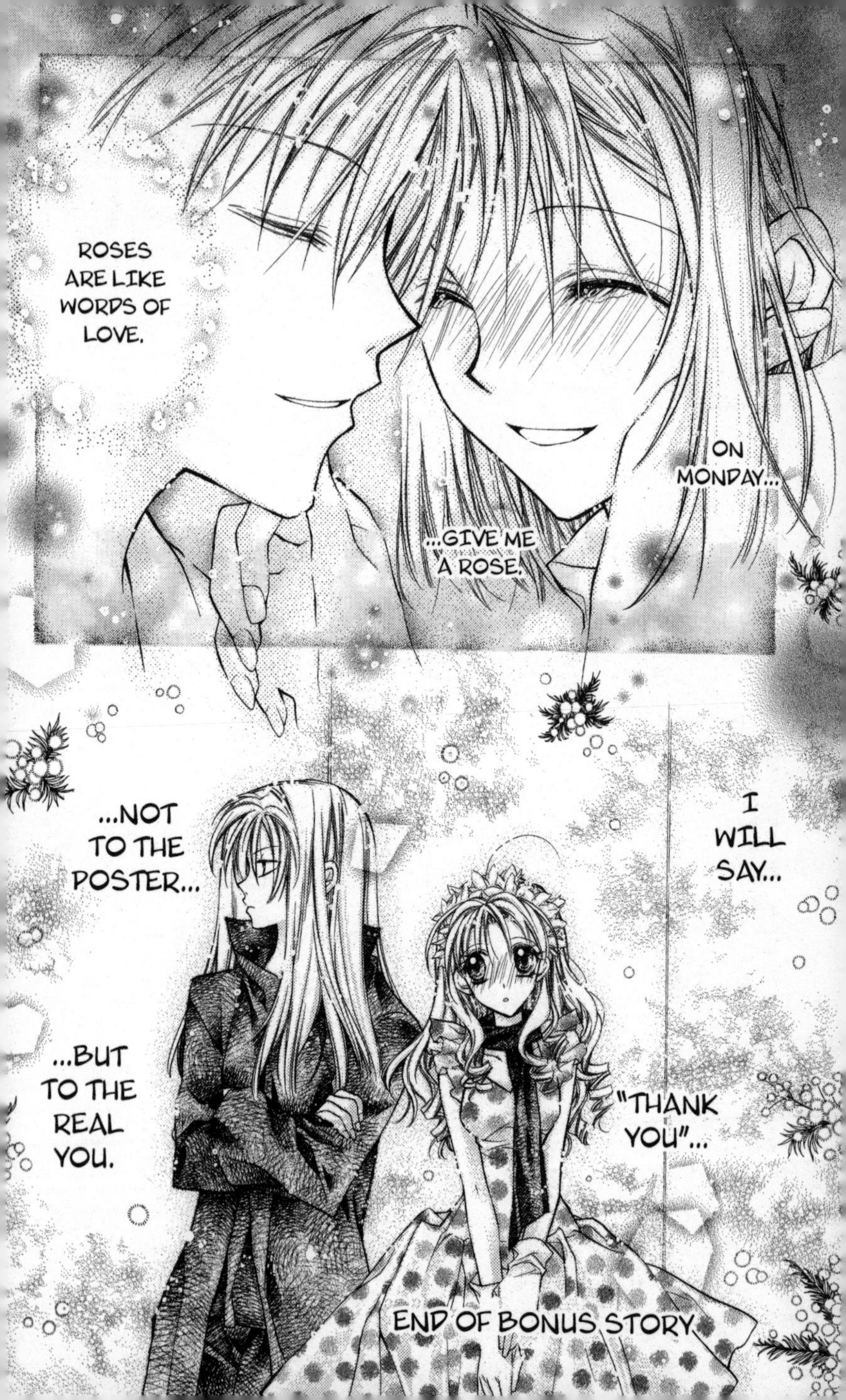
ON MONDAY...
...GIVE ME A ROSE.
ROSES ARE LIKE WORDS OF LOVE.
I WILL SAY...
"THANK YOU"...
...NOT TO THE POSTER...
...BUT TO THE REAL YOU.
END OF BONUS STORY

TOTSUGEKI! DOKODOKO ☆ FOUR-PANEL MANGA

FINAL

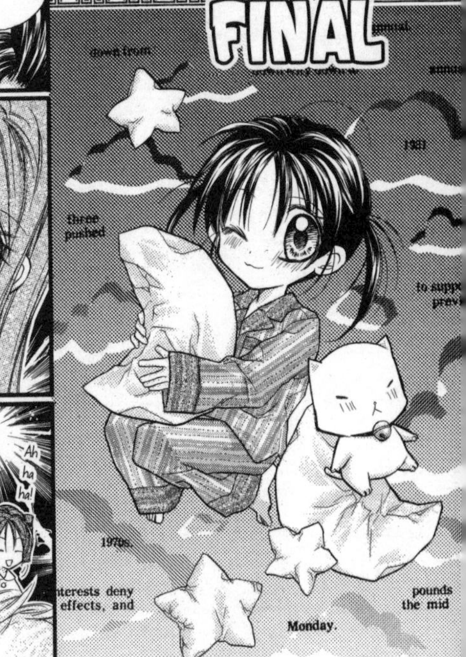

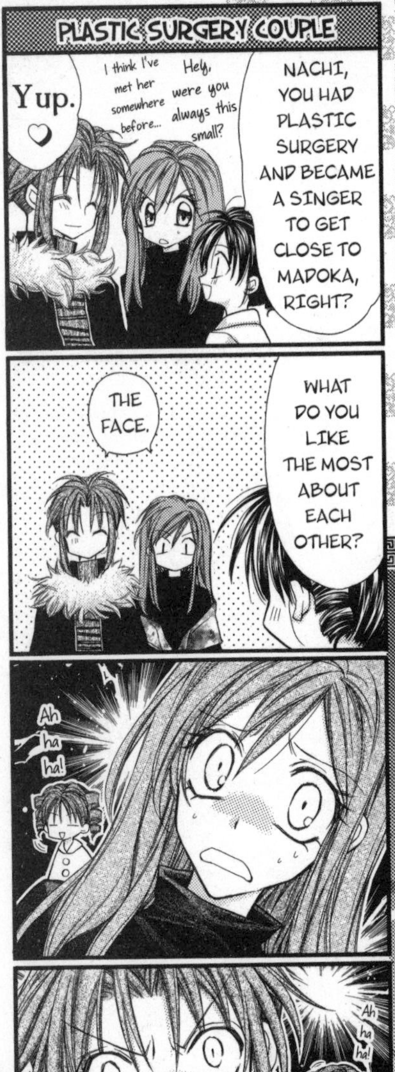
PLASTIC SURGERY COUPLE
NACHI, YOU HAD PLASTIC SURGERY AND BECAME A SINGER TO GET CLOSE TO MADOKA, RIGHT?
Hey, were you always this small?
I think I've met her somewhere before...
Yup. ♡
WHAT DO YOU LIKE THE MOST ABOUT EACH OTHER?
THE FACE.
Ah ha ha!
Ah ha ha!

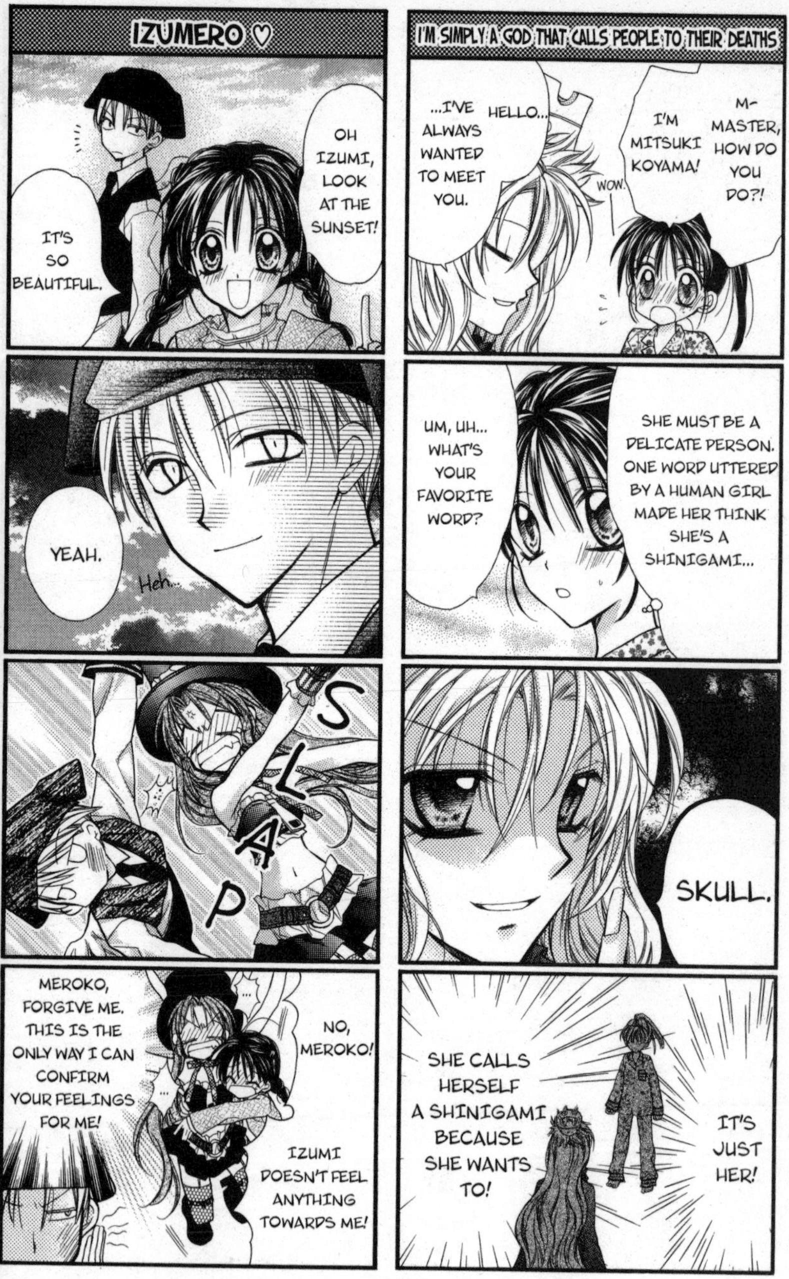
I'M SIMPLY A GOD THAT CALLS PEOPLE TO THEIR DEATHS
M-MASTER, HOW DO YOU DO?!
I'M MITSUKI KOYAMA!
WOW
HELLO...
...I'VE ALWAYS WANTED TO MEET YOU.
SHE MUST BE A DELICATE PERSON. ONE WORD UTTERED BY A HUMAN GIRL MADE HER THINK SHE'S A SHINIGAMI...
UM, UH... WHAT'S YOUR FAVORITE WORD?
SKULL.
IT'S JUST HER!
SHE CALLS HERSELF A SHINIGAMI BECAUSE SHE WANTS TO!
IZUMERO ♡
OH IZUMI, LOOK AT THE SUNSET!
IT'S SO BEAUTIFUL.
YEAH.
Heh...
SLAP
NO, MEROKO!
MEROKO, FORGIVE ME. THIS IS THE ONLY WAY I CAN CONFIRM YOUR FEELINGS FOR ME!
IZUMI DOESN'T FEEL ANYTHING TOWARDS ME!

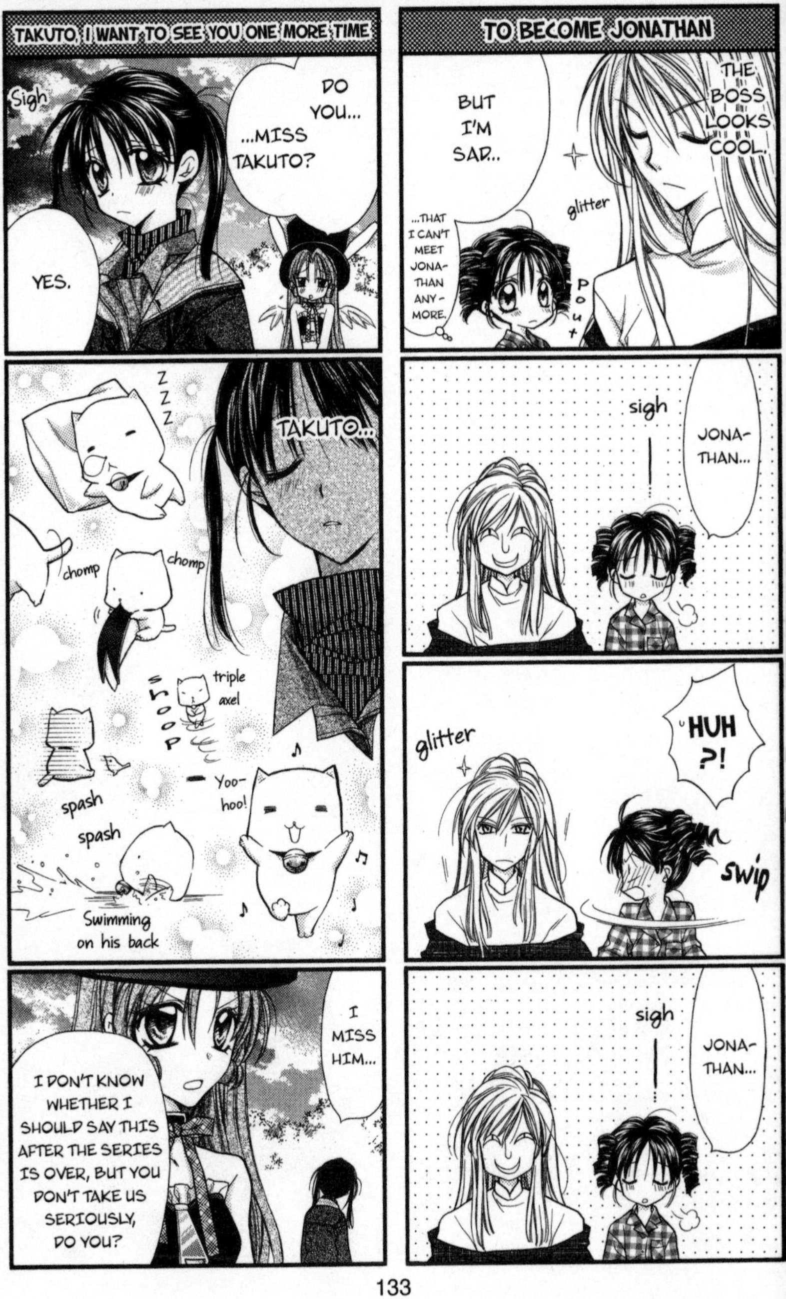
TO BECOME JONATHAN
THE BOSS LOOKS COOL.
BUT I'M SAD...
glitter
...THAT I CAN'T MEET JONA-THAN ANY-MORE.
Pout
JONA-THAN...
sigh
HUH?!
glitter
swip
JONA-THAN...
sigh
TAKUTO, I WANT TO SEE YOU ONE MORE TIME
DO YOU... ...MISS TAKUTO?
Sigh
YES.
TAKUTO...
Z Z Z
chomp
chomp
triple axel
shoop
Yoo-hoo!
spash
spash
Swimming on his back
I MISS HIM...
I DON'T KNOW WHETHER I SHOULD SAY THIS AFTER THE SERIES IS OVER, BUT YOU DON'T TAKE US SERIOUSLY, DO YOU?

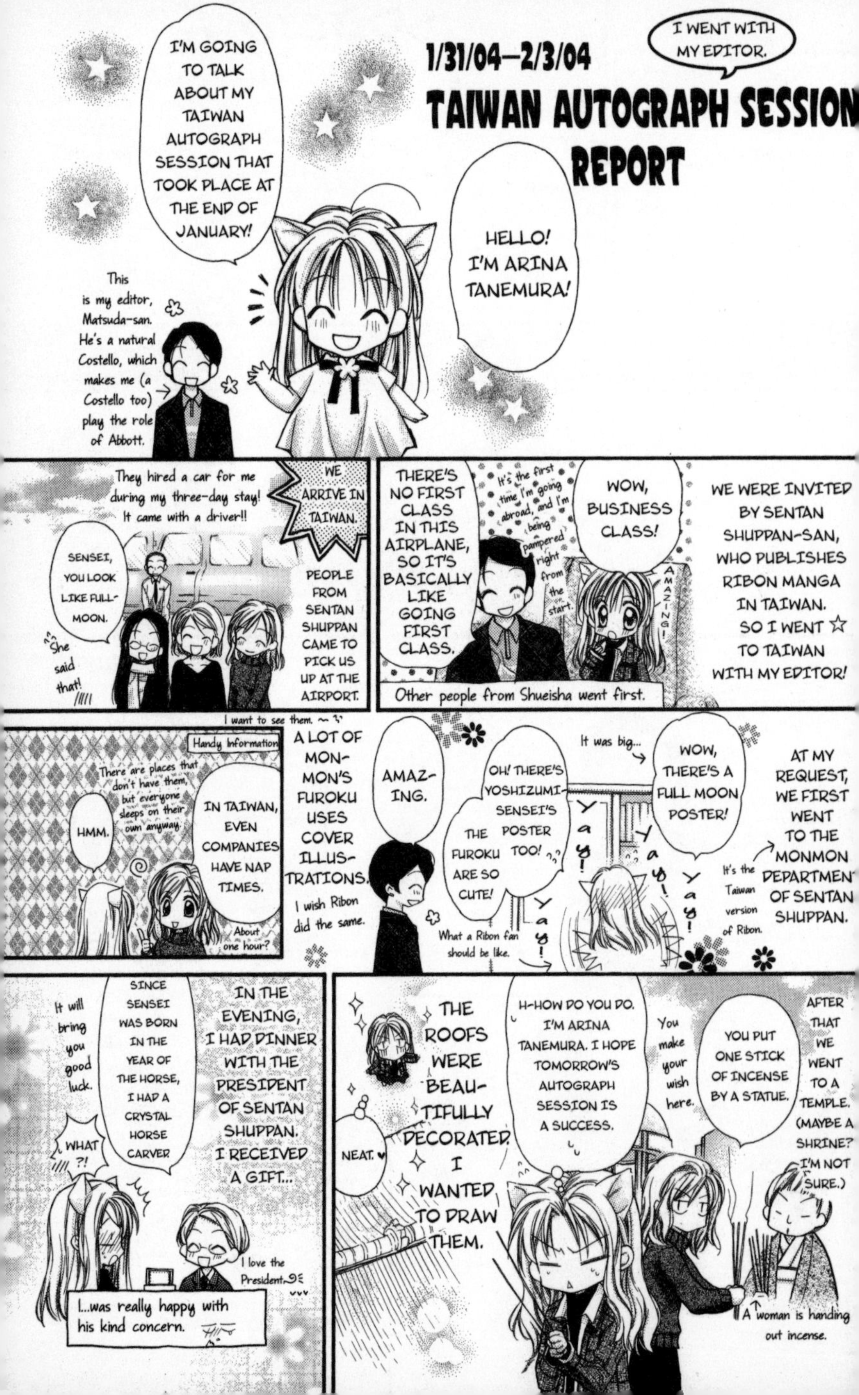
I WENT WITH MY EDITOR.
1/31/04–2/3/04
TAIWAN AUTOGRAPH SESSION REPORT
HELLO! I'M ARINA TANEMURA!
I'M GOING TO TALK ABOUT MY TAIWAN AUTOGRAPH SESSION THAT TOOK PLACE AT THE END OF JANUARY!
This is my editor, Matsuda-san. He's a natural Costello, which makes me (a Costello too) play the role of Abbott.
WE WERE INVITED BY SENTAN SHUPPAN-SAN, WHO PUBLISHES RIBON MANGA IN TAIWAN. SO I WENT ☆ TO TAIWAN WITH MY EDITOR!
WOW, BUSINESS CLASS!
AMAZING!
It's the first time I'm going abroad, and I'm being pampered right from the start.
THERE'S NO FIRST CLASS IN THIS AIRPLANE, SO IT'S BASICALLY LIKE GOING FIRST CLASS.
Other people from Shueisha went first.
WE ARRIVE IN TAIWAN.
PEOPLE FROM SENTAN SHUPPAN CAME TO PICK US UP AT THE AIRPORT.
They hired a car for me during my three-day stay! It came with a driver!!
SENSEI, YOU LOOK LIKE FULL-MOON.
She said that! ////
AT MY REQUEST, WE FIRST WENT TO THE MONMON DEPARTMENT OF SENTAN SHUPPAN.
It's the Taiwan version of Ribon.
WOW, THERE'S A FULL MOON POSTER!
It was big...
Yay! Yay! Yay! Yay!
OH! THERE'S YOSHIZUMI-SENSEI'S POSTER TOO!
THE FUROKU ARE SO CUTE!
What a Ribon fan should be like.
AMAZ-ING.
I want to see them. ~
A LOT OF MON-MON'S FUROKU USES COVER ILLUS-TRATIONS.
I wish Ribon did the same.
Handy Information
IN TAIWAN, EVEN COMPANIES HAVE NAP TIMES.
There are places that don't have them, but everyone sleeps on their own anyway.
HMM.
About one hour?
AFTER THAT WE WENT TO A TEMPLE. (MAYBE A SHRINE? I'M NOT SURE.)
YOU PUT ONE STICK OF INCENSE BY A STATUE.
You make your wish here.
H-HOW DO YOU DO. I'M ARINA TANEMURA. I HOPE TOMORROW'S AUTOGRAPH SESSION IS A SUCCESS.
THE ROOFS WERE BEAU-TIFULLY DECORATED. I WANTED TO DRAW THEM.
NEAT. ♥
A woman is handing out incense.
IN THE EVENING, I HAD DINNER WITH THE PRESIDENT OF SENTAN SHUPPAN. I RECEIVED A GIFT...
SINCE SENSEI WAS BORN IN THE YEAR OF THE HORSE, I HAD A CRYSTAL HORSE CARVED.
It will bring you good luck.
WHAT ?!
I love the President.
I...was really happy with his kind concern.

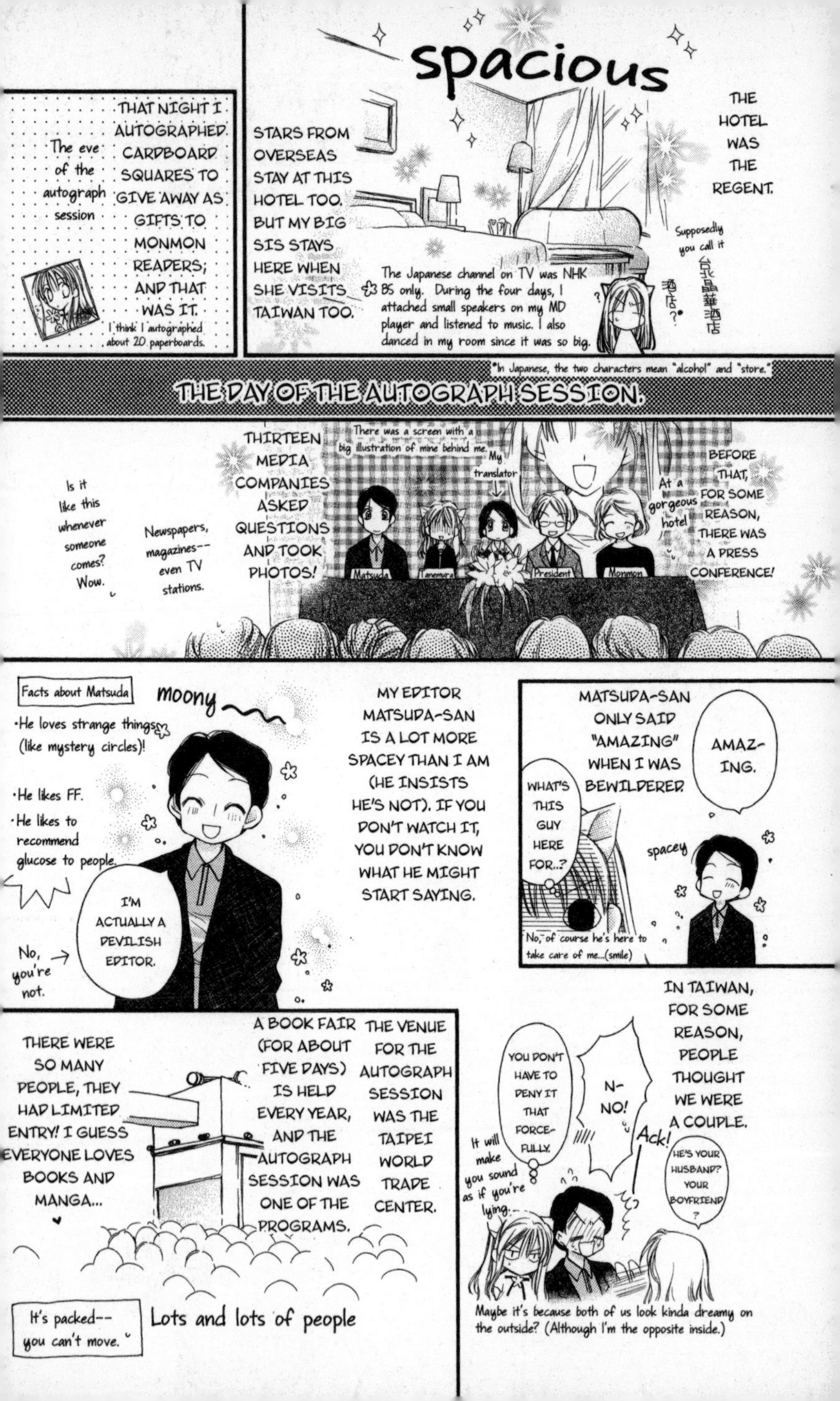
spacious
THE HOTEL WAS THE REGENT.
Supposedly you call it 台北晶華酒店
酒店?*
STARS FROM OVERSEAS STAY AT THIS HOTEL TOO. BUT MY BIG SIS STAYS HERE WHEN SHE VISITS TAIWAN TOO.
The Japanese channel on TV was NHK BS only. During the four days, I attached small speakers on my MD player and listened to music. I also danced in my room since it was so big.
THAT NIGHT I AUTOGRAPHED CARDBOARD SQUARES TO GIVE AWAY AS GIFTS TO MONMON READERS; AND THAT WAS IT.
The eve of the autograph session
I think I autographed about 20 paperboards.
*In Japanese, the two characters mean "alcohol" and "store."
THE DAY OF THE AUTOGRAPH SESSION.
BEFORE THAT, FOR SOME REASON, THERE WAS A PRESS CONFERENCE!
At a gorgeous hotel!
My translator
There was a screen with a big illustration of mine behind me.
Matsuda
Tanemura
President
Monmon
THIRTEEN MEDIA COMPANIES ASKED QUESTIONS AND TOOK PHOTOS!
Newspapers, magazines-- even TV stations.
Is it like this whenever someone comes? Wow.
MATSUDA-SAN ONLY SAID "AMAZING" WHEN I WAS BEWILDERED.
AMAZ-ING.
WHAT'S THIS GUY HERE FOR..?
spacey
No, of course he's here to take care of me...(smile)
Facts about Matsuda
•He loves strange things (like mystery circles)!
•He likes FF.
•He likes to recommend glucose to people.
moony
MY EDITOR MATSUDA-SAN IS A LOT MORE SPACEY THAN I AM (HE INSISTS HE'S NOT). IF YOU DON'T WATCH IT, YOU DON'T KNOW WHAT HE MIGHT START SAYING.
I'M ACTUALLY A DEVILISH EDITOR.
No, you're not.
IN TAIWAN, FOR SOME REASON, PEOPLE THOUGHT WE WERE A COUPLE.
HE'S YOUR HUSBAND? YOUR BOYFRIEND?
N-NO!
Ack!
YOU DON'T HAVE TO DENY IT THAT FORCE-FULLY.
It will make you sound as if you're lying.
Maybe it's because both of us look kinda dreamy on the outside? (Although I'm the opposite inside.)
THE VENUE FOR THE AUTOGRAPH SESSION WAS THE TAIPEI WORLD TRADE CENTER.
A BOOK FAIR (FOR ABOUT FIVE DAYS) IS HELD EVERY YEAR, AND THE AUTOGRAPH SESSION WAS ONE OF THE PROGRAMS.
THERE WERE SO MANY PEOPLE, THEY HAD LIMITED ENTRY! I GUESS EVERYONE LOVES BOOKS AND MANGA...
Lots and lots of people
It's packed-- you can't move.

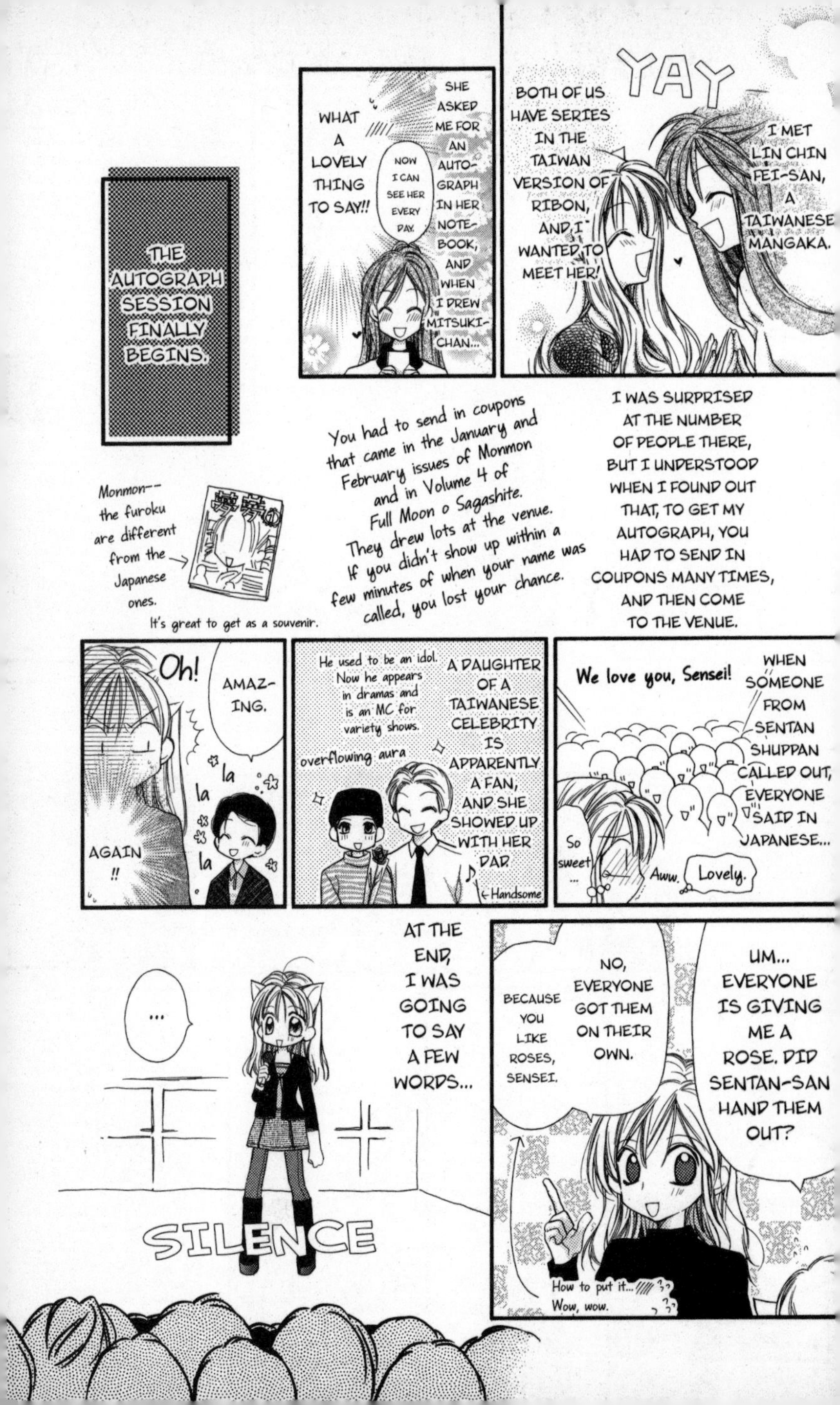
YAY
I MET LIN CHIN FEI-SAN, A TAIWANESE MANGAKA.
BOTH OF US HAVE SERIES IN THE TAIWAN VERSION OF RIBON, AND I WANTED TO MEET HER!
SHE ASKED ME FOR AN AUTOGRAPH IN HER NOTEBOOK, AND WHEN I DREW MITSUKI-CHAN...
NOW I CAN SEE HER EVERY DAY.
WHAT A LOVELY THING TO SAY!!
THE AUTOGRAPH SESSION FINALLY BEGINS.
I WAS SURPRISED AT THE NUMBER OF PEOPLE THERE, BUT I UNDERSTOOD WHEN I FOUND OUT THAT, TO GET MY AUTOGRAPH, YOU HAD TO SEND IN COUPONS MANY TIMES, AND THEN COME TO THE VENUE.
You had to send in coupons that came in the January and February issues of Monmon and in Volume 4 of Full Moon o Sagashite. They drew lots at the venue. If you didn't show up within a few minutes of when your name was called, you lost your chance.
Monmon-- the furoku are different from the Japanese ones.
It's great to get as a souvenir.
WHEN SOMEONE FROM SENTAN SHUPPAN CALLED OUT, EVERYONE SAID IN JAPANESE...
We love you, Sensei!
So sweet...
Aww.
Lovely.
A DAUGHTER OF A TAIWANESE CELEBRITY IS APPARENTLY A FAN, AND SHE SHOWED UP WITH HER DAD.
He used to be an idol. Now he appears in dramas and is an MC for variety shows.
overflowing aura
← Handsome
AMAZ-ING.
Oh!
la la la
AGAIN!!
UM... EVERYONE IS GIVING ME A ROSE. DID SENTAN-SAN HAND THEM OUT?
NO, EVERYONE GOT THEM ON THEIR OWN.
BECAUSE YOU LIKE ROSES, SENSEI.
How to put it...
Wow, wow.
AT THE END, I WAS GOING TO SAY A FEW WORDS...
...
SILENCE

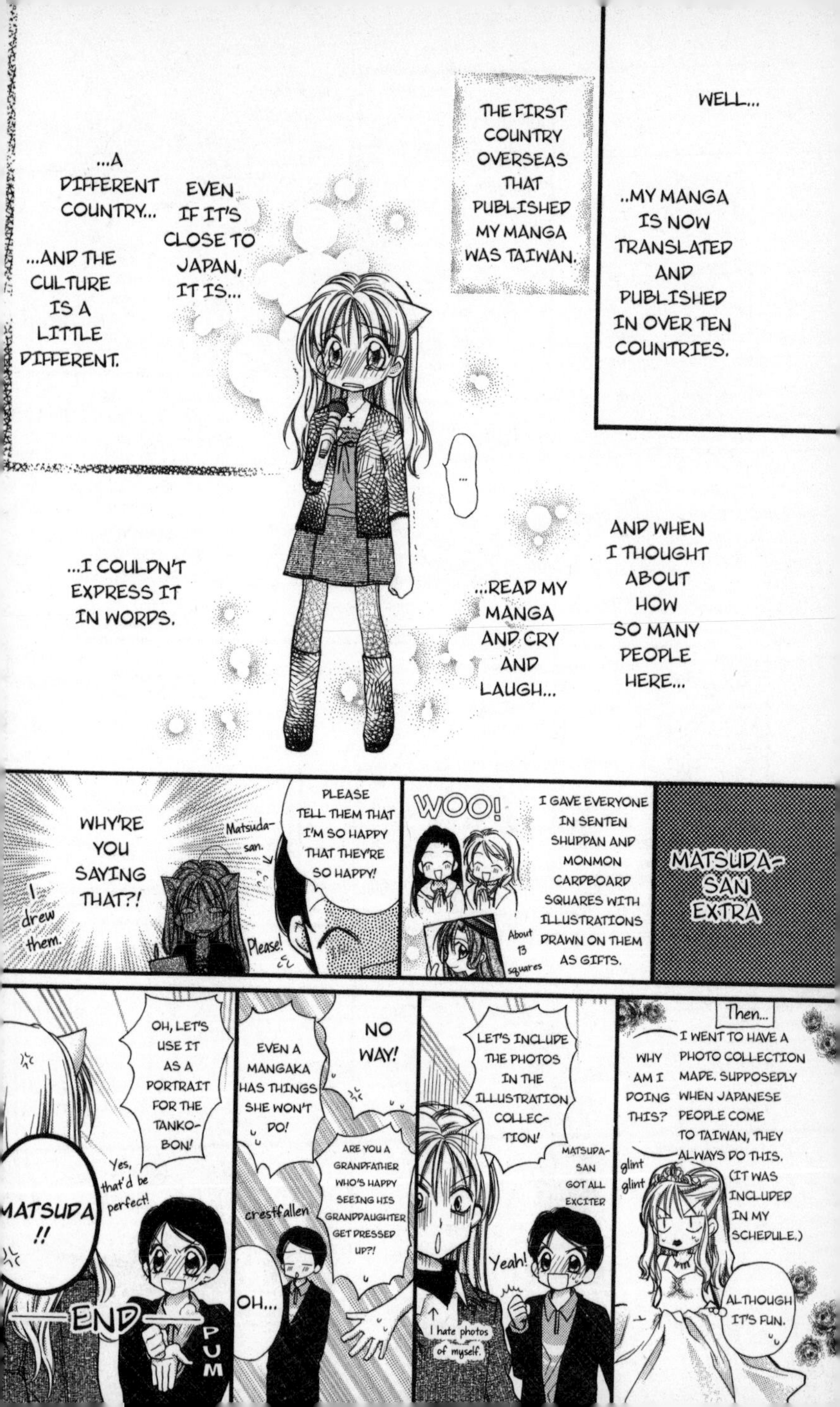

WELL...
...MY MANGA IS NOW TRANSLATED AND PUBLISHED IN OVER TEN COUNTRIES.
THE FIRST COUNTRY OVERSEAS THAT PUBLISHED MY MANGA WAS TAIWAN.
EVEN IF IT'S CLOSE TO JAPAN, IT IS...
...A DIFFERENT COUNTRY...
...AND THE CULTURE IS A LITTLE DIFFERENT.
...
AND WHEN I THOUGHT ABOUT HOW SO MANY PEOPLE HERE...
...READ MY MANGA AND CRY AND LAUGH...
...I COULDN'T EXPRESS IT IN WORDS.
MATSUDA-SAN EXTRA
I GAVE EVERYONE IN SENTEN SHUPPAN AND MONMON CARDBOARD SQUARES WITH ILLUSTRATIONS DRAWN ON THEM AS GIFTS.
WOO!
About 13 squares
PLEASE TELL THEM THAT I'M SO HAPPY THAT THEY'RE SO HAPPY!
Matsuda-san.
Please!
WHY'RE YOU SAYING THAT?!
I drew them.
Then...
I WENT TO HAVE A PHOTO COLLECTION MADE. SUPPOSEDLY WHEN JAPANESE PEOPLE COME TO TAIWAN, THEY ALWAYS DO THIS. (IT WAS INCLUDED IN MY SCHEDULE.)
WHY AM I DOING THIS?
glint glint
ALTHOUGH IT'S FUN.
LET'S INCLUDE THE PHOTOS IN THE ILLUSTRATION COLLEC-TION!
MATSUDA-SAN GOT ALL EXCITED
Yeah!
I hate photos of myself.
NO WAY!
EVEN A MANGAKA HAS THINGS SHE WON'T DO!
ARE YOU A GRANDFATHER WHO'S HAPPY SEEING HIS GRANDDAUGHTER GET DRESSED UP?!
crestfallen
OH...
OH, LET'S USE IT AS A PORTRAIT FOR THE TANKO-BON!
Yes, that'd be perfect!
MATSUDA!!
PUM
END

Extra Arinacchi: A secret page where I write what comes to mind.

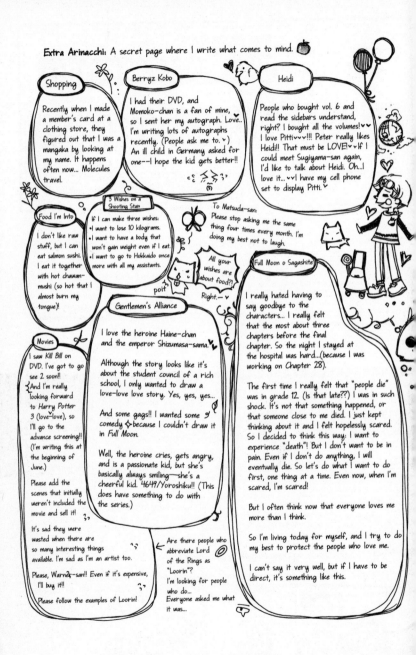

Shopping

Recently when I made a member's card at a clothing store, they figured out that I was a mangaka by looking at my name. It happens often now... Molecules travel.

Berryz Kobo

I had their DVD, and Momoko-chan is a fan of mine, so I sent her my autograph. Love.. I'm writing lots of autographs recently. (People ask me to.) An ill child in Germany asked for one--I hope the kid gets better!!

Heidi

People who bought vol. 6 and read the sidebars understand, right? I bought all the volumes! I love Pitti!!! Peter really likes Heidi!! That must be LOVE! If I could meet Sugiyama-san again, I'd like to talk about Heidi. Oh...I love it... I have my cell phone set to display Pitti.

Food I'm Into

I don't like raw stuff, but I can eat salmon sushi. I eat it together with hot chawan-mushi (so hot that I almost burn my tongue)!

3 Wishes on a Shooting Star

If I can make three wishes:

- I want to lose 10 kilograms.
- I want to have a body that won't gain weight even if I eat.
- I want to go to Hokkaido once more with all my assistants.

All your wishes are about food?!

poit

Right.—

To Matsuda-san:
Please stop asking me the same thing four times every month. I'm doing my best not to laugh.

Movies

I saw *Kill Bill* on DVD. I've got to go see 2 soon!! And I'm really looking forward to *Harry Potter 3* (love-love), so I'll go to the advance screening!! (I'm writing this at the beginning of June.)

Please add the scenes that initially weren't included the movie and sell it!

It's sad they were wasted when there are so many interesting things available. I'm sad as I'm an artist too.

Please, Warner-san!! Even if it's expensive, I'll buy it!!

Please follow the examples of Loorin!

Gentlemen's Alliance

I love the heroine Haine-chan and the emperor Shizumasa-sama.

Although the story looks like it's about the student council of a rich school, I only wanted to draw a love-love love story. Yes, yes, yes...

And some gags!! I wanted some comedy because I couldn't draw it in *Full Moon*.

Well, the heroine cries, gets angry, and is a passionate kid, but she's basically always smiling—she's a cheerful kid. 4649/Yoroshiku!! (This does have something to do with the series.)

Are there people who abbreviate Lord of the Rings as "Loorin"?
I'm looking for people who do...
Everyone asked me what it was...

Full Moon o Sagashite

I really hated having to say goodbye to the characters... I really felt that the most about three chapters before the final chapter. So the night I stayed at the hospital was hard...(because I was working on Chapter 28).

The first time I really felt that "people die" was in grade 12. (Is that late??) I was in such shock. It's not that something happened, or that someone close to me died. I just kept thinking about it and I felt hopelessly scared. So I decided to think this way: I want to experience "death"! But I don't want to be in pain. Even if I don't do anything, I will eventually die. So let's do what I want to do first, one thing at a time. Even now, when I'm scared, I'm scared!

But I often think now that everyone loves me more than I think.

So I'm living today for myself, and I try to do my best to protect the people who love me.

I can't say it very well, but if I have to be direct, it's something like this.

DEEP! INTENSE!

COMPLETE VERSION!

SECRETS AND INSIDE STORIES REVEALED (?!)

FULL MOON O SAGASHITE SUPER DICTIONARY

☆THE ULTIMATE COMPREHENSIVE DICTIONARY, NOW TOLD BY THE MANGAKA!!
BY READING IT CAREFULLY, YOU CAN BECOME A FULL MOON MASTER!!

SUPERVISED BY ARINA TANEMURA

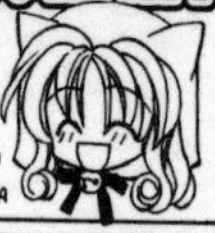

A

I ♡ U: The first opening song for the *Full Moon o Sagashite* anime. When I first saw it, I ended up crying. (The cat Takuto and rabbit Meroko are moving!) Even now, I'm moved when I watch it.

Airi: Because she's the model for Mitsuki, my editor learned her name first of all my assistants. She's a goof. What I used was that contrast in her—despite her mild-mannered looks, she's stubborn. She still puts "nya" at the end of sentences.

Kyakya Asano: A mangaka for another magazine, she's an assistant from Hiroshima. Inside myself, she's roaring as the king of omissions and errors.

Almond Jelly: Izumi-kun loves this. It goes without saying that Takuto stopped eating it after Chapter 7.

I

Kana Izumi: Lio-kun's mother. Her name never appeared in the manga. Her name is quite cute. She's a weak person... When I have someone like this appear in my manga, I always think, "If I were with her, I wouldn't let them do this." It's frustrating. She keeps the ashes from the photographs she burnt of her husband and Lio-kun inside her amulet.

Lio Izumi:* Izumi-kun when he was human. He jumped onto the railroad crossing when he was six.
[*Lio Izumi's name is spelled differently in Japanese depending on whether he's human or Shinigami, but both names are pronounced the same. –Ed.]

Lio Izumi: A sadistic Shinigami with dog ears who is in love with Meroko. He considers Jonathan to be a pet. He's actually glad that their pair name isn't "Baby Castella" or "Shio Biifun." The fact that he still wears the "Milmake" costume expresses the depth of his love for Meroko. Wonderful. ♡ I think he's traumatized by the fact that Jonathan was actually the Boss. He considers Mitsuki-chan to be like an older sister.

Dog Izumi: He's pretty cute, so I wish he took this form more often.

Suzu Imamura: I combined the names of Ribon's former Editor-in-Chief and the former-former Editor-in-Chief. She's a former idol who has a big brother that is in a (ahem) relationship with a rival. She is currently Madoka's manager.

U

Usa-Meroko: When I'm sleepy, her face sometimes turns out funny. She looked funny--not just in the manuscript, but in the furoku pen case.

E

Eternal Snow: The third ending song for the anime. I felt that I shared the same feelings as the anime staff: Eichi-kun is really special! Please create stickers from the character illustrations that are reflected in the music box!! Everyone is so cute and so cool that I'm like an overindulgent parent, getting all red when I watch it.

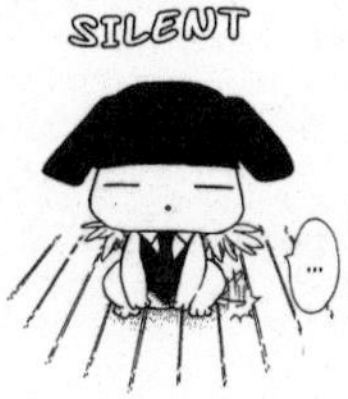
SILENT
...

O

Oh, Takuto! Takuto! Long time no see!

What Oshige-san said in Chapter 8 when she saw Takuto. It has really been a long time...this was a subtle foreshadowing. The end of the sentence is in katakana because I'm a FF fan. (If you've played 9, you understand, right?)

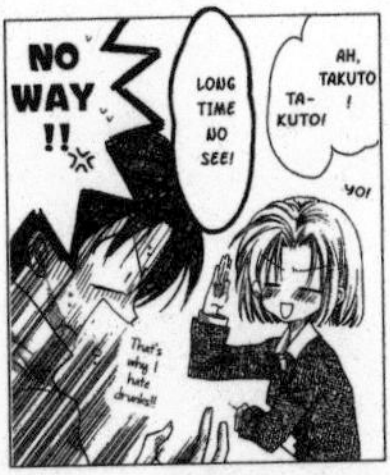
AH, TAKUTO!
TA-KUTO!
LONG TIME NO SEE!
YO!
NO WAY!!
That's why I hate dramas!!

Masami Oshige: A former idol, a Wakaoji fan, Fullmoon's manager. I love her dearly. My editor seems to love her too. Her theme song is Mariya Takeuchi-san's "Jun-ai Rhapsody." (It really suits her!!) In *Ribon* magazine, she's a person who has an (ahem) adult relationship. She actually appears a little in Chapter 1 and 2 (She had long hair.)

Search Party for Oina: Mitsuki formed this on her own with Izumi-kun. It is a group to look for the lost cat Oina-chan.

Oina-chan: The lost cat that Mitsuki found on a rainy day. She looked at the ribbon upside down, which had "LIO" written on it, so Mitsuki-chan named it Oina. I'm practicing how to draw real animals.

Megumi Ogata: The voice actor for Izumi in the *Full Moon o Sagashite* anime. When she came to record Izumi-kun's first appearance, she appeared wearing a suit and a tie like Izumi-kun. She's a real professional. (Wonderful!!) We watched that episode when working on the manuscripts. We thought we'd die from our hearts beating too fast. ♡ We watched it four times that day. ♡ (Work on your manuscripts!)

Teruaki Ogawa: The voice actor for Wakaoji-sensei in the anime. His voice matches the role so well, I'm embarrassed when I talk to him. He apparently can't say lines containing the word "operation" on the first try. And I'm rude in thinking that is a little cute.

Otanchin: My mother often used to say this. I think it's a form of the Nagoya-ben "Tawake" made a little cute. (Tawake apparently means stupid or foolish.) In Chapter 12, Takuto used it too, and I found it fun. At one point my friend Ryo Maekawa-kun emailed me saying that I was using it a lot too. ♡

Ka

Ruka Kaduki: A mangaka for *Ribon*. She still sometimes comes to help me. She's a kind person who loves birds.

Kanan-chan: She's the only assistant who doesn't give up on recommending the Wakaoji-sensei and Oshige-san couple. She's been influenced by the anime, and is a real Changin' My Life fan.

Passing through the Wall: One of the few magic things that Negi-Ramen did. It was used in Chapter 1. You supposedly mark a circle on the wall with chalk, put a spell on it, and then you can pass through. There's a ten-minute limit, so be careful when you pass through. ♡

Kayorun: A new assistant who is somewhat of a miser. She likes to say "Koreya!" ("Kore" refers to money.)

Ki

Mitsuru Kijyo: He's the president who has a wife, yet is having an affair with Oshige-san. He was actually the vocalist for a rival band of ROUTE..L.

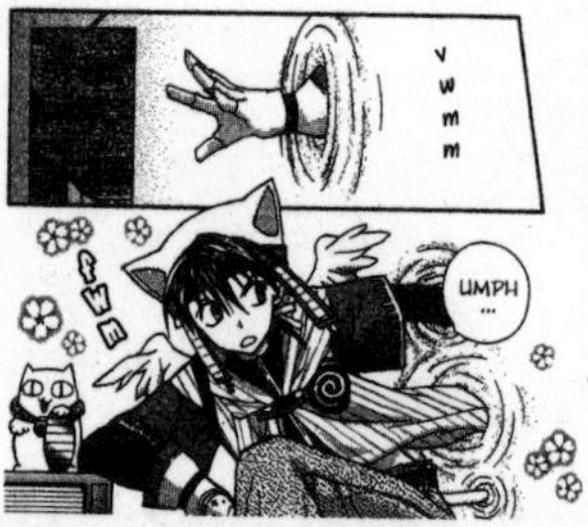
VWMM
UMPH ...

Ryohei Kimura: The voice actor for Eichi-kun in the anime. Every time I see him, he says, "I want to interact with other characters soon." He's eighteen, and studying to get into a university. I can finally say "I'm soooorry!" You won't have any chance to interact with other characters...)

Kira Takuto:* He led an intense life when he was human. The person he hated most was Aoi-san. The person he loved most was Aoi-san too.

[*Takuto's Shinigami entry is listed under "Ta," per the grouping in the tankobon. –Ed.]

Ku

Gutchan: The little pig that Madoka-chan loves. The pet that looks like it's being taken care of, but who is actually taking care of Madoka. If Gutchan slaps you, you get a bruise shaped like a cherry blossom petal. ♡ The male pig truly believed that he was Madoka-chan's boyfriend until Nachi-kun appeared. Gutchan's "Gu" is from the "g" in pig!!

Ke

KP (Kirai Points): Like HP or MP in an RPG. When you accumulate enough points, you receive a punishment that corresponds to those points. Fifty points results in a kick, 100 points results in a kiss...

100,000 Yen-a-Month Man: I received many comments that the pay is too low! But if I can just say--that's the way it is, you know??

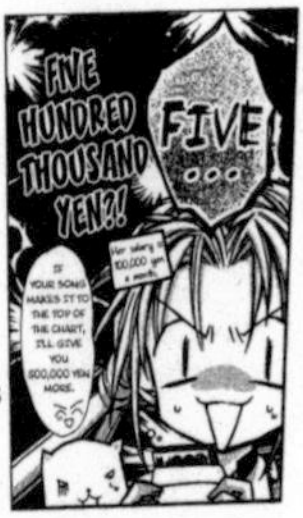
FIVE...
FIVE HUNDRED THOUSAND YEN?!
Her salary is 100,000 yen a month.
IF YOUR SONG MAKES IT TO THE TOP OF THE CHART, I'LL GIVE YOU 500,000 YEN MORE.

Ko

Hazuki Koyama: If you just read her lines, she seems to be an ill and frail girl with a strong spirit. (What does that mean?) She's Mitsuki's mom, who apparently looks exactly like Fullmoon-chan.

Fuzuki Koyama: The name of Grandma that I'd forgotten about. She almost ran away from home with a musician once but then broke up with him. I hope she appears again!! She couldn't stop falling sadly in love with Seijyuro-san, or stop Moe-san from dying, so she grew to hate music. For some reason the assistants like her. Somehow I really love Fuzuki-san too.

Mitsuki Koyama: A twelve-year-old who is friends with Shinigami. She's ill, and she is a singer. When I asked my assistants which Arina heroine they would want to be, they all replied, "I never want to be Mitsuki-chan." What a tragic heroine. When she started living by herself, buying a TV took the most courage. How many pairs of pajamas does she own?! It's really hard to draw the body of someone this age!

Aoi Koga: The leader of ROUTE..L who has a cool haircut. (smile) Mitsuki-chan's inherited her bouncy hair from her father. Even I would say that with those looks, Grandma wouldn't allow Hazuki-san to marry him. He loves wearing Buddhist priest work clothes. (Cool.♡)

May 12th: Mitsuki-chan's birthday that I'd forgotten about. Like Maron-chan (*Kamikaze Kaito Jeanne*), are Arina's heroines who transform all supposed to be born in May?

Konako: The assistant that draws a rabbit as a self-portrait, and who loves Kinki Kids. She's a supporter of Eichi♡Mitsuki!

Comics Characard: You can't open it! Even if you want it and want to take a look at it, you sorta can't open it!! It's a secret that if that's there, the tankobons are a little difficult to read.♡

Sa

Eichi Sakurai: His image is that of an angel. Mitsuki loves him. He hated the moon just because the moon saw him cry, and he was bewildered by his strong love for Mitsuki-chan. He is human after all. The orphanage of course didn't have a telescope, and he was thinking about buying one eventually by working and saving money. The last name of the couple who adopted him was "Sakurai" too, and they wanted to adopt Eichi-kun because they felt it was fate. "If you can't forget me, then answer me" is such an unfair thing to say! (Of course there's no way you can do that!) He's No. 1 on my "Self-Created Characters Love-Love Ranking" list (second is Sakataki). He was always with Mitsuki. That means he heard Takuto tell Mitsuki he loves her too...(sweat) I think he didn't show his emotions. He's never opened his heart up to anyone except Mitsuki. He is a kind person, but he acts distant. Even that is appealing to this over-indulgent parent. (I'm omitting the rest.)

Sakura no Ame, Itsuka...
A great song by Takako Matsu-san, and I based *Full Moon o Sagashite* on it.

3 years--wait--2 years!
The famous line from the drama *Shinju Fujin*. I often tell my editor "3 hours--wait--2 hours!" when my deadline is approaching, so I'll put it in this dictionary.

Yasuo Saito: The voice actor for Takuto in the anime. He's one half of the comedian pair "Abare Nunchaku." His nickname is "Yakkun" (smile). ←The same as Takkun's by coincidence. I heard that the other half of the comedian pair is also a voice actor. They're comedians with multiple talents. ♪

Shi

Zippy: It goes without saying that it's based on a music magazine that I love reading.

SEED Records: The record company Fullmoon belongs to. The agency is Village Productions. You can tell that I've taken them from my name, "seed" (*tane*) and "village" (*mura*).

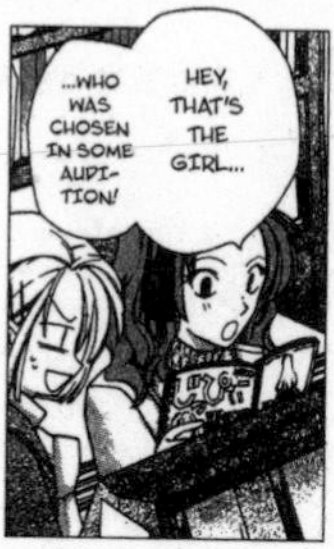
HEY, THAT'S THE GIRL...
...WHO WAS CHOSEN IN SOME AUDI-TION!

Shinigami: There are dormitories in the Underworld, where everyone lives. According to Meroko, all Shinigami outside the Pediatrics Ward are difficult and unfriendly. People who commit suicide become Shinigami. I've made it so that not everyone who commits suicide becomes a Shinigami. Only those who committed suicide because they were hurt in some way becomes Shinigami. The Underworld was set up according to the teachings of the Master. There were those who dissented, but they became silent when they heard that not being able to die is punishment for those who committed suicide.

Shingamiiz: I use this term to refer to Takuto, Meroko, Izumi, and Jonathan. I was a little particular about writing it all in katakana.

Shinigami Costumes: Pairs don't have to wear matching costumes, but there are a lot of Shinigami that wear matching costumes. Takuto's current clothes were handmade by Meroko. Even in the Underworld, Negi-Ramen were famous for being flashy.

The Kiss of Death: Izumi uses this when taking a human soul. He only does it to young girls. No, if they're young, he might do it to guys too...(sweat) Kissing Takuto was like...he could kill him...(sweat)

No. 18: Fullmoon's debut single was No. 18 the first week it appeared in the charts. By the way, Madoka's debut single made it to No. 34.

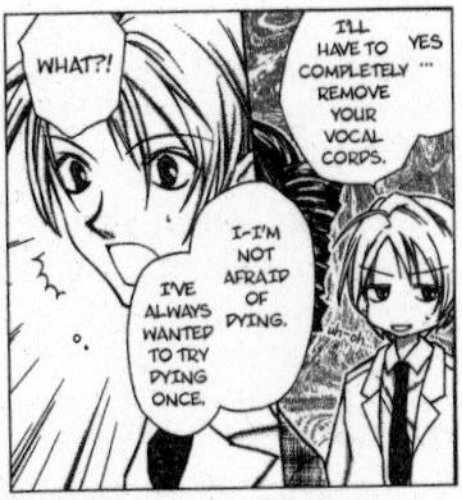
YES ...
I'LL HAVE TO COMPLETELY REMOVE YOUR VOCAL CORPS.
WHAT?!
I-I'M NOT AFRAID OF DYING.
I'VE ALWAYS WANTED TO TRY DYING ONCE.

Jonathan: Izumi-kun's current partner. There are passionate fans--maybe not. When Mitsuki-chan calls him by name, the "than" is in hiragana. ♡ He's actually the Boss. The Boss (rivers of sweat)?! I knew it from the beginning, so I watched him with a cold eye. (This guy...how can he be so nonchalant...?)

I've always wanted to try dying once: Mitsuki-chan's line in Chapter 1, which caused a stir. I revealed my wish here. The important part is "to try dying" instead of "I want to die."

Su

Super Mitsuki: Takuto transformed into Mitsuki. You can really tell that he has a complex about Eichi-kun. I've never seen Takuto smile that much.

Kazuko Sugiyama-san: The voice actor for Grandma in the anime. Heidiiii! ♡ Korosukeeee! ♡ I love them. ♡♡ I often watch *Heidi* videos when I'm working (rather, I listen to them!!). I listen to the "Kiteretsu" album too!! (So what?)

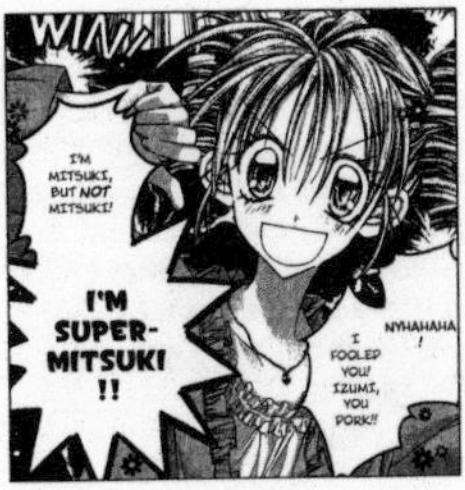
NYHAHAHA!
I FOOLED YOU! IZUMI, YOU PORK!!
I'M MITSUKI, BUT NOT MITSUKI!
I'M SUPER-MITSUKI!!

Studio Deen: The animation company that produced *Full Moon o Sagashite*. I've been a fan since *Maison Ikkoku*!! I'm overwhelmed. It's probably not just me who feels there's lots of love for Meroko. Thank you always.

Se

Seijyuro-san: Aoi-san's father and Mitsuki's grandfather. He's a sinful person who came between Fuzuki-san and Moe-san. He's the "gii goo guu" (violin noise) son of a financial group. After he met Fuzuki-san again, they got married. (His wife passed away a long time ago.)

Tomomi Seo: The voice actor for Oshige-san in the anime. She's the best voice for Oshige-san!! So I love Oshige-san even more.

Saint☆Assistants: If these people weren't there, *Full Moon o Sagashite* wouldn't exist. Our cute girls! ♡ Half of them were supposed to be trainees for replacements. With new members coming in and graduating, it was like Morning Musume... I'm sorry, that was exaggerating a bit.

Saint☆Assistants Screentone Team: The people who cut and paste screentones, which are like stickers. Before they get to work, they get in the mood by talking about which panel in *Full Moon o Sagashite* is the best. Please don't do that in front of me--it's embarrassing!

Free Character Card Set: This was available with the 2003 January issue of *Ribon*. Did you notice that the background for the ROUTE..L members are all the same?! My editor and I were a little sad that Oshige-san wasn't there.

Ta

Chapter 20, Please Call My Name When I Get Lost at the Railroad Crossing:
I chose this as the best story in *Full Moon o Sagashite*. ♪ When it first appeared in the magazine, there were a lot of comments saying that it wasn't that good, so I was sad. Later, more people said that they liked it. Good! People often tell me that they like my monologues, but when I put them in I was told that there were too many monologues. What am I supposed to do? Kids are hard to please.

Taiyaki: Mitsuki-chan likes them. She likes Japanese sweets, such as *ohagi* and *ichigo-daifuku*. I guess there are people who start eating it from the belly or the dorsal fin.

Kira Takuto: I thought he wouldn't be popular, but he was No. 1 in the character popularity poll. He's a failure as a Shinigami. But Mitsuki will always consider him as her No. 2 hero. No. 2? Mitsuki-chan!! If he hadn't met Mitsuki, he probably would've gone out with Meroko. But that's a secret for life. I think that a male character with cat ears is new. I wonder why he's calling Mitsuki-chan "shorty" and "you dork" less and less... Takkuuun. ♡ There's a theory that he couldn't take Eichi-kun's soul because Eichi-kun was too beautiful. The cat on his glove looks sad in serious scenes. I wonder how many people noticed. One time, Izumi-kun taunted him with words so much that he got a bald spot. He likes Kago-chan, so Mitsuki-chan must have been his type.

Tanaka-san: Is she a private detective or a housekeeper? ♪ I wonder why I created this character... But the anime staff seems to find her convenient, so it's okay.

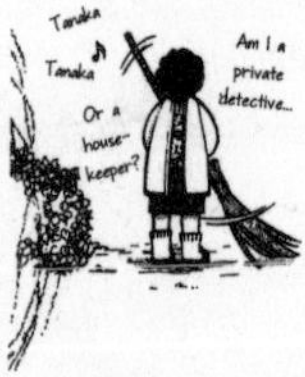
Am I a private detective...
Tanaka ♪ Tanaka
Or a house-keeper?

Arina Tanemura: The mangaka of *Full Moon o Sagashite*. If you mix up all the characters, they apparently become this person. The No. 1 question that I don't want to be asked is "How do you do the Mitsuki-chan hairstyle?" I'm a 26-year-old who uses gags that are hard for young readers to understand. 26???! (rivers of sweat) ← I realize how old I am, and fret. I'm really into drawing small cat Takuto and rabbit Meroko that almost merge in the background, so please find them. After *Jeanne*, I decided I wouldn't draw complicated costumes anymore, but I ended up designing even more complicated ones. My blood type is A, and I'm a Pisces. I'm a bit bothered by receiving fan letters that say "the clothes sensei draws are uncool." Being No. 6 in the character popularity poll (*Ribon* 2002 December issue) is a no-no! But I'm happy anyway. Thank you.♡ My cute sheepies. ♡

My editor, Matsuda-san: When I drew my Taiwan report, I wrote various things, but by the power of the editor, my poison was lessened. (But that'll make the manga less interesting!) He has a pure heart, and he soothes and heals me. I think we get along together well. I will do my best to finish my work earlier, so when *Full Moon* is over, please take me and all my assistants to eat good tempura.

🐑🐑🐑🐑🐑🐑🐑🐑🐑🐑🐑🐑🐑🐑🐑🐑🐑🐑🐑🐑🐑🐑🐑🐑🐑🐑🐑🐑🐑🐑🐑🐑🐑🐑🐑🐑🐑

Chi

Chima chima: The FX for Arina heroines walking until they are age five. By the way, Ion-chan (*I-O-N*) was the first. Because of the noise the shoes make when running, the FX was "piko piko."

I think you were given a second chance!: Mitsuki-chan's words changed something in the three Shinigami. As you can see in the side story and in Chapter 12, Meroko is the one who is most influenced by these words. Maybe it's because she's been a Shinigami for so long.

A Kiss for Meroko: This first appeared in the *Otanoshimi* supplementary issue. Meroko is the main character featured. If I knew the story was going to be so serious, I wouldn't have given it such a lighthearted title. She's wearing different clothes on the cover than in the story because I didn't like the clothes she's wearing on the cover. The sheep girl was unexpectedly popular. ♡ I had initially designed Meroko to have sheep horns, so I put them in. Izumi-kun acts differently than in the main story. You can also see his private room.

Tsu

Tsuki no Kikyu: This is a great song sung by a voice actor I love, Yui Horie-san. It suits Eiichi-kun and Mitsuki-chan so much, so please do listen to it once!

Tsubasa: Another great song sung by Yui Horie-san. It helped me when I was creating Mitsuki-chan's character. So when I listen to it, thinking that I'm Mitsuki-chan, my heart becomes weak (it sometimes becomes strong too).

Te

Death Master: The Master doesn't quite remember whether she used to be a she or a he. She likes metaphorical expressions. She was the first human soul to come to the Underworld. Her name is Mystere. When she was in utter despair, she realized that she could go take the souls of humans. She was asked, "Are you a Shinigami?" and then was convinced she was a Shinigami. She's a delicate person.

🐿🐿🐿🐿🐿🐿🐿🐿🐿🐿🐿🐿🐿🐿🐿🐿🐿🐿🐿🐿🐿🐿🐿🐿🐿🐿🐿🐿🐿🐿🐿🐿🐿🐿🐿

LONG TIME, NO SEE!

Na

Nachi: The vocalist of the male duo OZ. (I once wrote they were a band, but that's a mistake.) In the side story it was revealed that he's a rich kid from Kyoto, he's Madoka-chan's fiancé, and that he had plastic surgery to become a singer to chase Madoka-chan. Whenever he appeared, almost all the fan letters and emails to the *Ribon* website were for Nachi-kun. I was really worried about Takuto's popularity. His hair color is green. Madoka-yan's hair is purple. Oh no! It's the same as *Jeanne*'s Minazuki-kun and Miyako-chan!! And I created them! (sweat) I draw him without thinking. So he's really easy to draw. I think he has this natural aura. I nicknamed him "Natchii." When I was talking about Natchi of Morning Musume at a meeting, my editor thought I was talking about Nachi-kun. It was confusing, but even that's a good memory now.

🐿🐿🐿🐿🐿🐿🐿🐿🐿🐿🐿🐿🐿🐿🐿🐿🐿🐿🐿🐿🐿🐿🐿🐿🐿🐿🐿🐿🐿🐿🐿🐿🐿🐿🐿

Ni

Miku Niiyama: The stage name of Madoka's manager, Imamura-san, when she was an idol. Most of the readers, as well as I, had pretty much forgotten this name. She was more popular than Yuina-chan. Than...Yuina-chan.

Niki-sama: The assistant that's one of the models for Jonathan. She's a rare living being that I want to be friends with even when we're grandmas. She likes the Takuto ♡ Meroko couple.

Ne

Negi-Ramen: The Shinigami pair from the Pediatrics ward who haunt Mitsuki-chan. It's not that Meroko is "Negi" and Takuto is "Ramen." Arina is recently into nori-ramen too. Their nickname in the Underworld was "the midriff-baring stripped pair."

Neko Takuto: The other form of Takuto who is more popular than Eichi-kun. He's paunchy! In the anime he's pretty slim. (smile) But the uncool face is still there. (laugh)

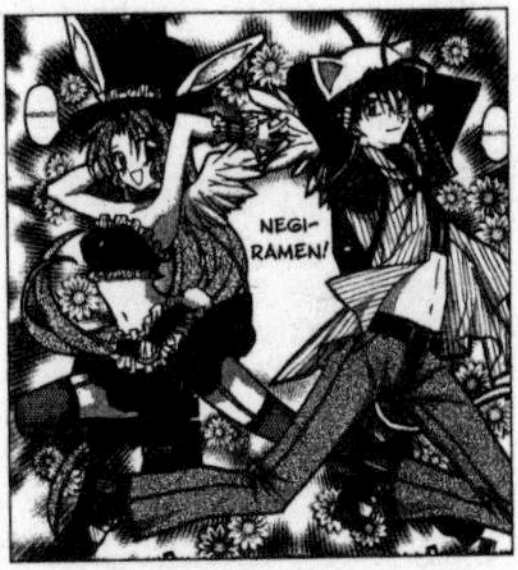
NEGI-
RAMEN!

Ha

Yuina Hanakazari: The stage name of Fullmoon's manager, Oshige-san, when she was an idol. The reason she didn't sell well was because no matter what she sung, it sounded like a Japanese folk tune. And that she's like a middle-aged man when she looks young. And that she said some risqué things on a music show that couldn't be undone. People said many things, but basically she was tone deaf. How tone deaf? As tone deaf as the big brother of Jaiko, who often holds recitals and who said these famous words: What's yours is mine. What's mine is mine." One characteristic is that she's a little bit like Fullmoon-chan.

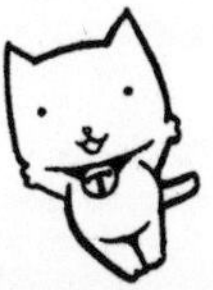

Hi

Beetlejuice: The movie that gave me hints about how Shinigami came about. It only gave me hints, so it's not that related, but I like this movie a lot, so if you're interested, please watch it. In the movie, people who committed suicide became office workers in the other world. It's an occult comedy. I really love the girl who wears mourning black!

Fu

The boss: He's cool and strict and silent and gives his underlings weird pair names. He's the boss of Takuto and company. The Shinigami don't even know when he'll appear. He uses a scythe. If he was *Medaka no Gakko*'s Kurocchi, Mori-sensei would no doubt use him as material in that space above the manga. There's a Chicchi! Just to make sure...(sweat) His real name is Sheldan. It's strange that he looks so cool, but somewhere in his heart, he's Jonathan. He tortured Izumi-kun because he wanted to make Izumi do his bidding and lure Mitsuki away. Well, it was meant as a form of punishment too. He talks even more foul than Takuto does. What sort of character is he?! (smile)

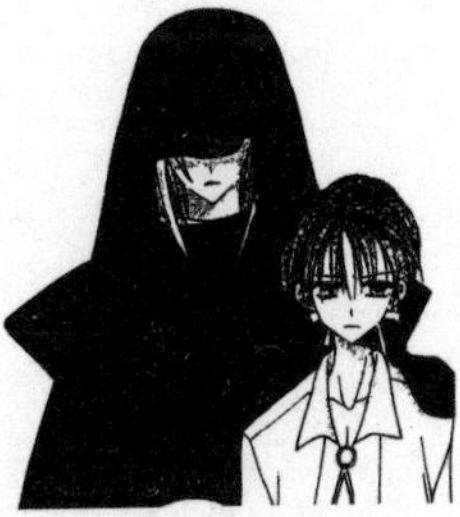

Full Moon o Sagashite: An outrageous manga in which more than half the characters are dead. Some reader said, "The mangaka who drew *Jeanne* is drawing it? Then it must be depressing." It's exactly that. The real meaning of the title hasn't been explained yet. I think it's a sober story too. I like stories where the characters transform, so someday I want to draw one more, and make an "Arina Tanemura Transformation Trilogy" together with *Jeanne*. If it's made into an anime, it'd be perfect. ♡ *Kyoko* isn't a transformation manga. Just having the hair change color doesn't do it.

Full Moon o Sagashite title: People spell it using different kanji and katakana combinations. That's wrong.

Full Moon o Sagashite Illustration Collection: The last time I worked on an illustration collection, it was a little bit easier, but as you grow older, you want to work on the details more... But, I can make my voice heard more now than when I was a newcomer, and since I have more knowledge, it's definitely better this time. ☆ There were so many color illustrations--some of them could only be printed in a small size, and there were many illustrations that couldn't be put in the book. I'm really sorry. The size of the illustrations depends on the original size, but most of it depends on how much I like them. It's just my taste that the cover illustration is Eichi-kun and Mitsuki-chan. And if it's Eichi-kun, I can color it faster...(so sad). To make excuses, there was a limit on how much I could write for the comments (because I wanted to put them near the illustrations), so the comments aren't very helpful. I'm sorry... It was a lot of work, but it was done well! I'm very satisfied!!

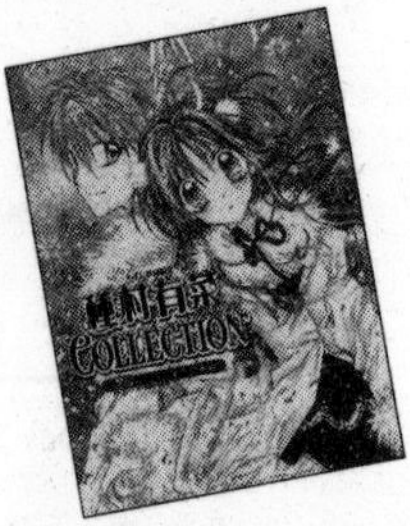
COLLECTION

Full Moon o Sagashite, Chapter 12: Near Takuto, when the Shinigami are looking in Mitsuki's apartment, there's the dress that Mitsuki-chan was wearing in Chapter 1. I drew it in my rough sketch, and the assistants drew it without my having to say anything. At times like this, I'm happy that people who love this work help me out. ♡

Full Moon o Sagashite, Chapter 14: The game Takuto's playing is *Starfox Adventures*, which I was playing back then. I'm clumsy, so I still haven't been able to complete the game.

Full Moon o Sagashite, Chapter 19: The roof of the apartment that appears in this chapter is the roof of the place where I live. Late at night and during the day, I went with my assistants to draw sketches secretly. Cell phone cameras are convenient (like when drawing hands).

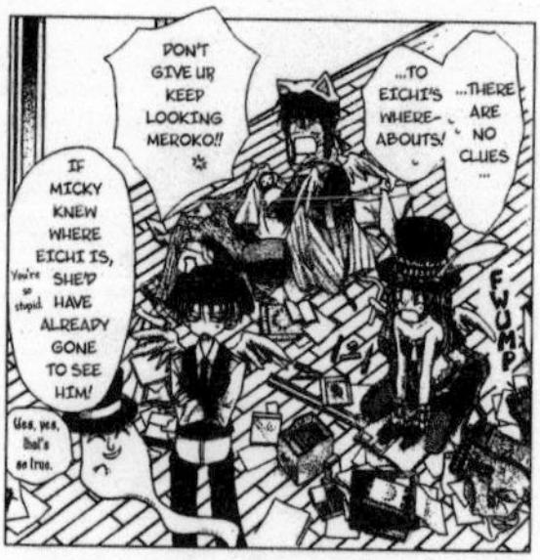
...THERE ARE NO CLUES...
...TO EICHI'S WHEREABOUTS!
DON'T GIVE UP, KEEP LOOKING MEROKO!!
FWUMP
IF MICKY KNEW WHERE EICHI IS, SHE'D HAVE ALREADY GONE TO SEE HIM!
You're so stupid.
Yes, yes, that's so true.

Buncho Buncho: The FX when Fullmoon (Mitsuki) waves her hands. When she can't wave well, it becomes "bubuncho," so be careful.

Ho

Chieko Honda: The voice actor for Meroko in the anime. Miyo-chan ♪ Miyo-chan ♪ (Kiteretsu). The anime staff use Meroko often, so she always has lots of lines. She makes it look easy. Amazing!!

Ma

myco: The voice actor for Mitsuki-chan in the anime. She can sing and act, and is the vocalist for Changin' My Life. When I saw "Eternal Snow" in episode 36, I cried. Of course I cried in episode 42 too!! I like "Smile" in episode 37. (I have a weakness for songs that are played in the anime.)

Mi

Mi-chan: The assistant who's not too well known as she doesn't appear in "Penshaki" much. She supports Takuto♡Mitsuki. (She also likes Takuto♡Meroko.) When her hair gets messed up, it means that she's sleepy.♡

Ai Minase: The regular assistant who's been helping me since *Non Fiku*. She's supposedly a member of the ROUTE..L fan club. She moves around the house, holding the *Full Moon o Sagashite* tankobons. She's a model fan (smile). She loves Neko Takuto.

Milmake: The pair name of Meroko and Izumi. Likes coffee. So, of course the name is taken from the school lunch. The pair even became a character card--I'm partial to them.

Me

Meroko Yui: I thought she'd be really popular, but she was No. 5 in the character popularity poll. She's Takuto's partner. She's a rabbit with endless worries regarding love and work and friendship. The name is because I used to say "mero mero" a lot then. I don't like always saying that... My favorite FX is "Me-ro-Kyu-Bon!!" When she's hiding something, or when she's pretending to be cute, she puts "mero" at the end of her sentences.

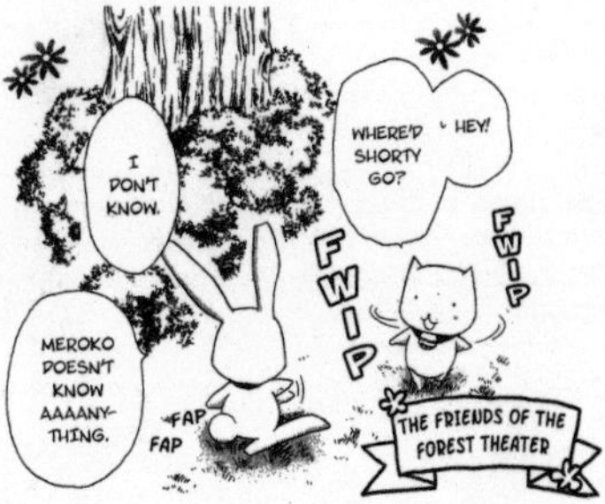
HEY!
WHERE'D SHORTY GO?
I DON'T KNOW.
FWIP
FWIP
MEROKO DOESN'T KNOW AAAANY-THING.
FAP FAP
THE FRIENDS OF THE FOREST THEATER

Moe-san: Meroko's human name, Moe Rikyou. Meroko Yui is an anagram of Moe Rikyou. She lived a little selfishly like Meroko. But fans like her... Why?

Friends of the Forest: The term Mitsuki uses to refer to the Shinigamiiz. Oh...Yami-nabe is included too...Mitsuki-chan. She speaks without using honorifics to Usa Meroko. This makes it obvious that she really believes they're friends of the forest, and that's funny.

Norihisa Mori: The voice actor for Jonathan in the anime. His face kinda looks like Jonathan... (oops.) He's really friendly with Ogata-san, who plays Izumi-kun, and that's cool.

Ya

Yami-Nabe: The contrasting pair, consisting of Izumi-kun who's cool and good-looking, and Jonathan who just can't make a serious face. Yami-Nabe is not a favorite of mine. I just used it because it felt right. Izumi-kun is competent, so even if Jonathan is like that, there are no problems. What about their job...(they're always there!!) (There is a reason for this, though.)

🦗🦗🦗🦗🦗🦗🦗🦗🦗🦗🦗🦗🦗🦗🦗🦗🦗🦗🦗🦗🦗🦗🦗🦗🦗🦗🦗🦗🦗🦗🦗🦗🦗

Yu

Ghosts: These are souls that stay in this world by their will. They are souls that even Shinigami can't see, that the Shinigami failed to retrieve. If a ghost's emotion is strong, sometimes you can see them. Eichi-kun is a ghost. By the way, this is all just in *Full Moon o Sagashite*.

Ri

Rina-chan: The assistant who loves Takuto. Her health is frail, and she often gets ill and is confined to her bed while helping out. I want to say why do you work when you're like that?! But I'm the one who asks her to help me.

Ru

ROUTE..L: The legendary band consisting of Takuto (vocals), Wakoji (keyboard), and Aoi (guitar). They're a mix of TM Network, B'z, BOOWY, and Unicorn. Old bands are included, making it sound legendary. Aoi wrote the lyrics and composed all the songs. When Takuto went solo, he wrote his own lyrics and songs. A kid, a long-haired visual-type, and a weirdo who wore Buddhist work clothes... were they really popular?! (sweat)

🦗🦗🦗🦗🦗🦗🦗🦗🦗🦗🦗🦗🦗🦗🦗🦗🦗🦗🦗🦗🦗🦗🦗🦗🦗🦗🦗🦗🦗🦗🦗🦗🦗

Re

Replicas: Takuto's ears, tail, and wings. In a word--fake. When real ones grow, you're a professional, competent Shinigami.

Wa

Madoka Wakamatsu: She's pretty stubborn, but she opened her heart up after getting slapped by a pig. She's had cosmetic surgery. After she got slapped, she took care of Gutchan lovingly. She doesn't realize she's the one being taken care of... She's the daughter of a good family. And she even had a fiancé. Someone shut me up (smile).

Keiichi Wakaoji: The woman he loved was the girlfriend of the guy he respected most. Those two died together. The boy who was left behind committed suicide because of him, and the girl who fell ill with a similar illness ran away. He's the unhappiest character in the manga. P-poor guy!! (tears) He's a doctor who jumps to conclusions. He worries too much about the future. You're just seeing things if you think he became younger when he reappeared. (sweat) Please be nicer to Oshige-san!!

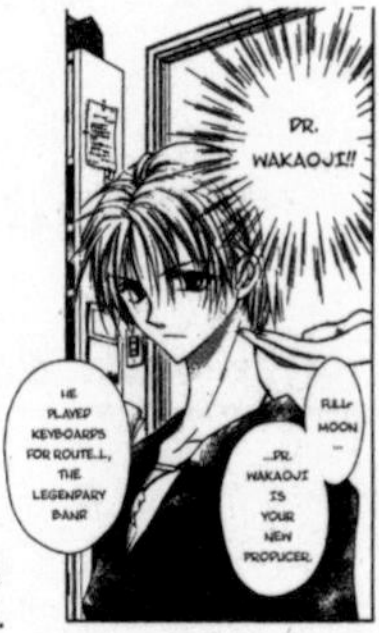
DR. WAKAOJI!!
FULL MOON —
...DR. WAKAOJI IS YOUR NEW PRODUCER.
HE PLAYED KEYBOARDS FOR ROUTE:L, THE LEGENDARY BAND

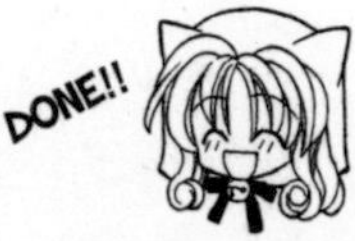
DONE!!

Super Dictionary of Full Moon

PENCHI DE SHAKIN☆ SPECIAL

BY ARINA TANEMURA

①Penchi de Shakin☆Special

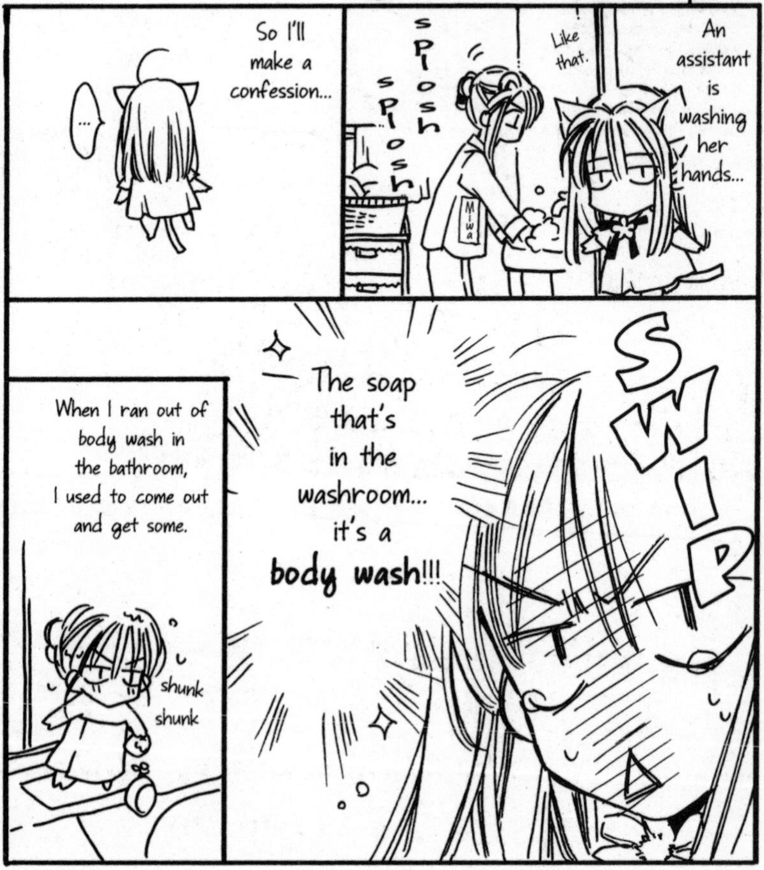
An assistant is washing her hands...
Like that.
splosh splosh
Miwa
So I'll make a confession...
...
SWIR
The soap that's in the washroom... it's a **body wash**!!!
When I ran out of body wash in the bathroom, I used to come out and get some.
shunk shunk

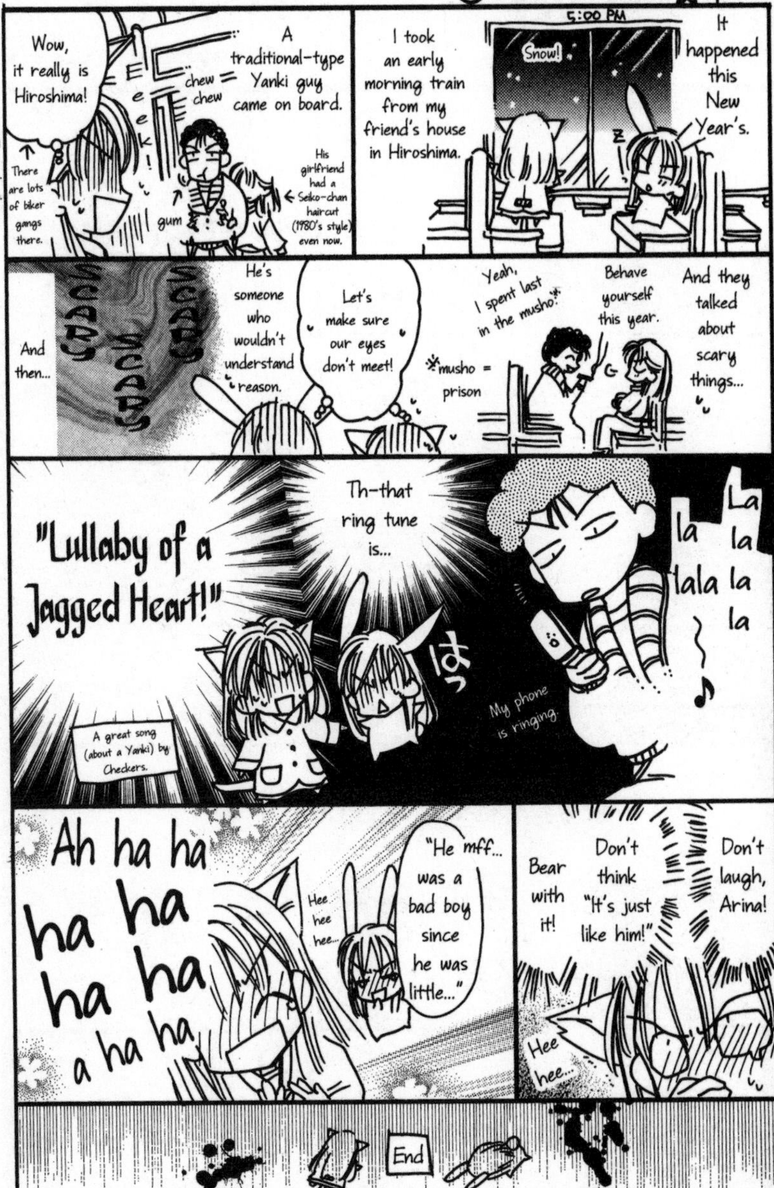

It happened this New Year's.
5:00 PM
Snow!
I took an early morning train from my friend's house in Hiroshima.
A traditional-type Yanki guy came on board.
chew chew
Eeek!
Wow, it really is Hiroshima!
His girlfriend had a Seiko-chan haircut (1980's style) even now.
gum
There are lots of biker gangs there.
But I love Hiroshima.
And they talked about scary things...
Behave yourself this year.
Yeah, I spent last in the musho.*
*musho = prison
Let's make sure our eyes don't meet!
He's someone who wouldn't understand reason.
SCARY
SCARY
SCARY
And then...
La la la lala la la la
My phone is ringing.
Th-that ring tune is...
はっ
"Lullaby of a Jagged Heart!"
A great song (about a Yanki) by Checkers.
Don't laugh, Arina!
Don't think "It's just like him!"
Bear with it!
Hee hee...
"He mff... was a bad boy since he was little..."
Hee hee hee...
Ah ha ha ha ha ha ha a ha ha
End

Penchi de Shakin 3

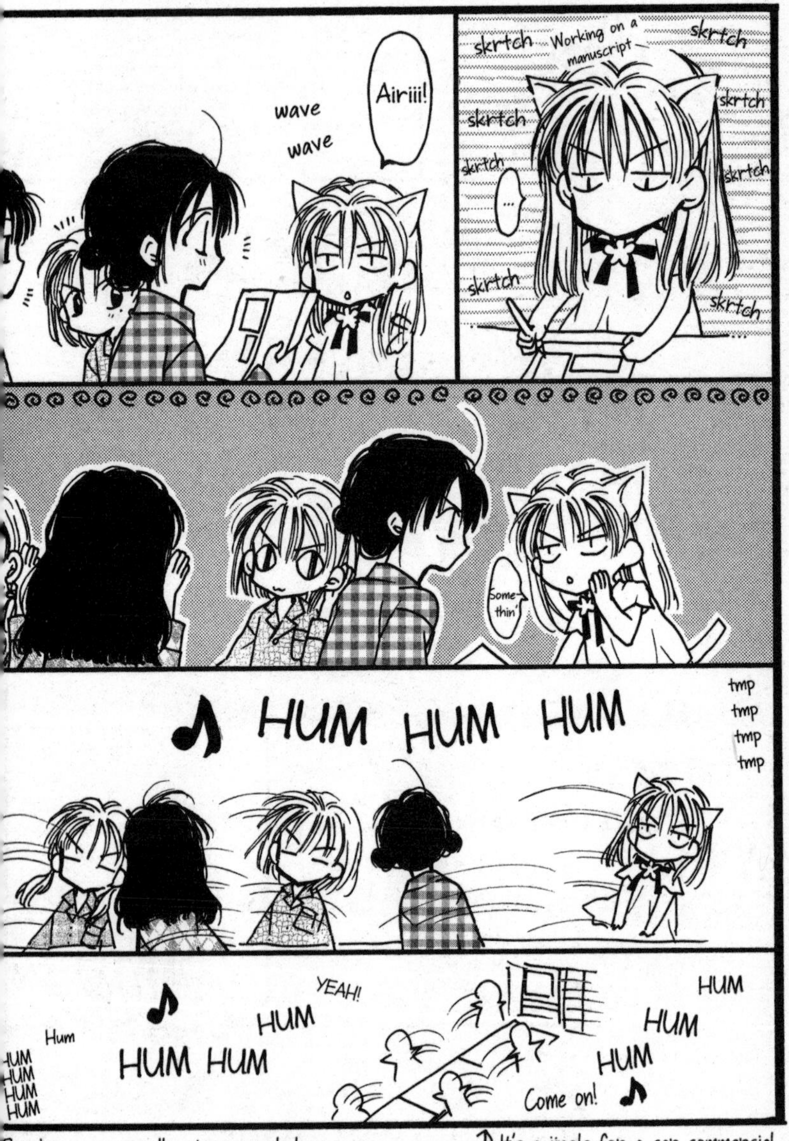
Working on a manuscript
skrtch
skrtch
skrtch
skrtch
skrtch
skrtch
skrtch
skrtch
...
Airiii!
wave
wave
Some-thin'
tmp
tmp
tmp
tmp
HUM HUM HUM
HUM
HUM
HUM
Come on!
YEAH!
HUM
HUM HUM
Hum
HUM
HUM
HUM
HUM

This happens normally at our workplace.

↑ It's a jingle for a car commercial.

Congratulations on the completion of "Full Moon o Sagashite."

I love all the Full Moon characters, so even if my head understands that it's over, my heart doesn't seem to, and it feels strange. I'm really, really happy that Mitsuki-chan is smiling.♥ It's good that she was able to become happy. (Everyone else too.)

In the end, Eichi-kun and Mitsuki-chan were able to communicate (?) and I'm personally happy about that. I'm looking forward to the new series very much too, but please let me talk about Eichi♥Mitsuki again.♥♥

I am happy that I was able to work something that I love.
Arina-sensei, thank you for giving me a wonderful job.
I love you.♥♥

2004 Airi Teito

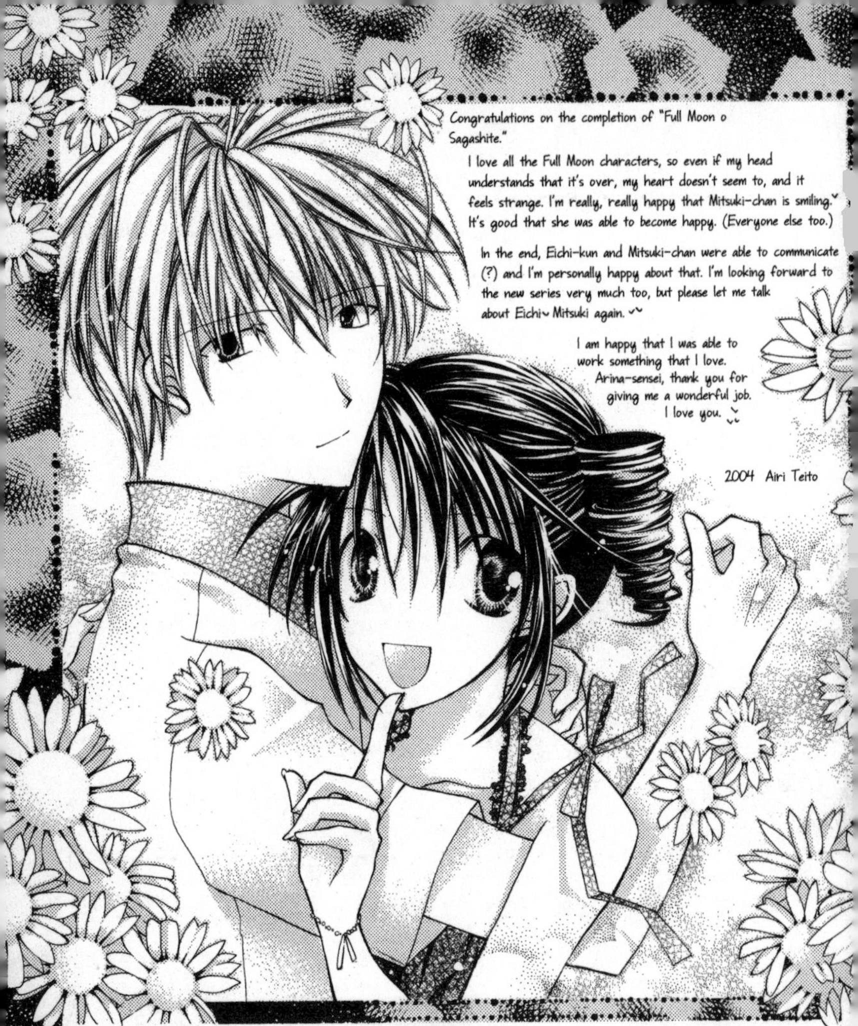

AIRI TEITO

✿ Airi and I were fellow Eichi♥Mitsuki fans, and together with Saorin we had fun talking about it at work.
Even in the new series, our favorite couple seems to be the same. Let's talk about it at night to motivate me to work!!

And the comment size is wrong (revealed!).

✿Arina✿

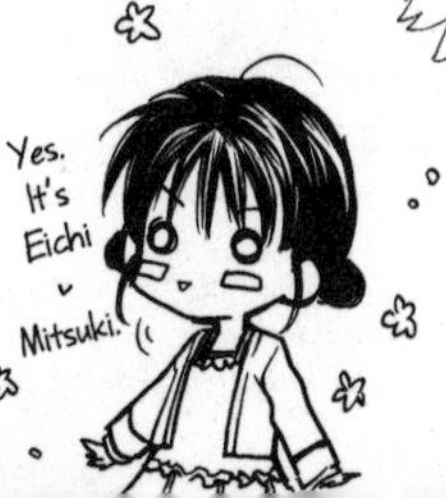
Yes. It's Eichi ♥ Mitsuki.

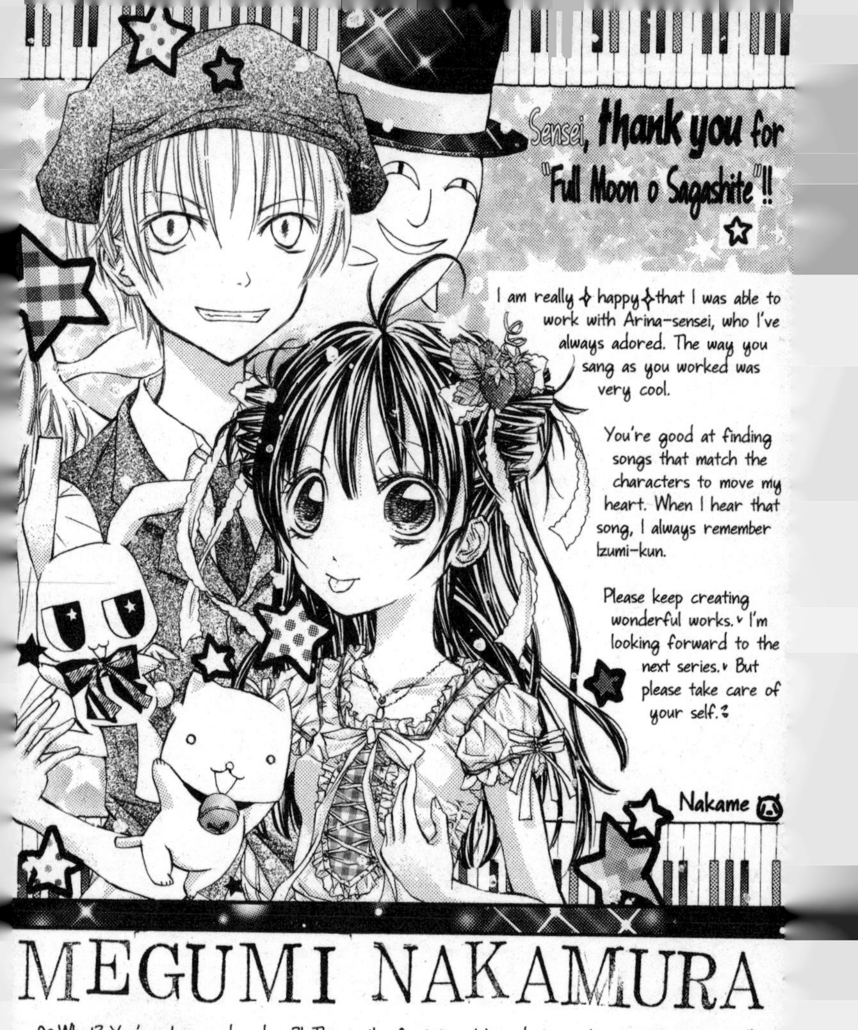
Sensei, thank you for "Full Moon o Sagashite"!! ☆
I am really ✧ happy ✧ that I was able to work with Arina-sensei, who I've always adored. The way you sang as you worked was very cool.
You're good at finding songs that match the characters to move my heart. When I hear that song, I always remember Izumi-kun.
Please keep creating wonderful works. I'm looking forward to the next series. But please take care of your self.
Nakame

MEGUMI NAKAMURA

What? You've always adored me?! This is the first time I heard about it! (smile) You were listening to me sing?! (Of course you can hear me.)

The very detailed illustration is so cute!! The piano is good! Nakame-chan is very fashionable. Her fashion is Harajuku-style—very cute! Please make me relax with your cute smile forever!

Arina

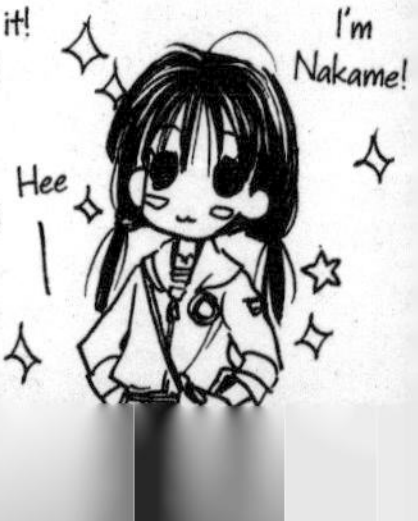
I'm Nakame!
Hee

CONGRATULATIONS ON COMPLETING FULL MOON.

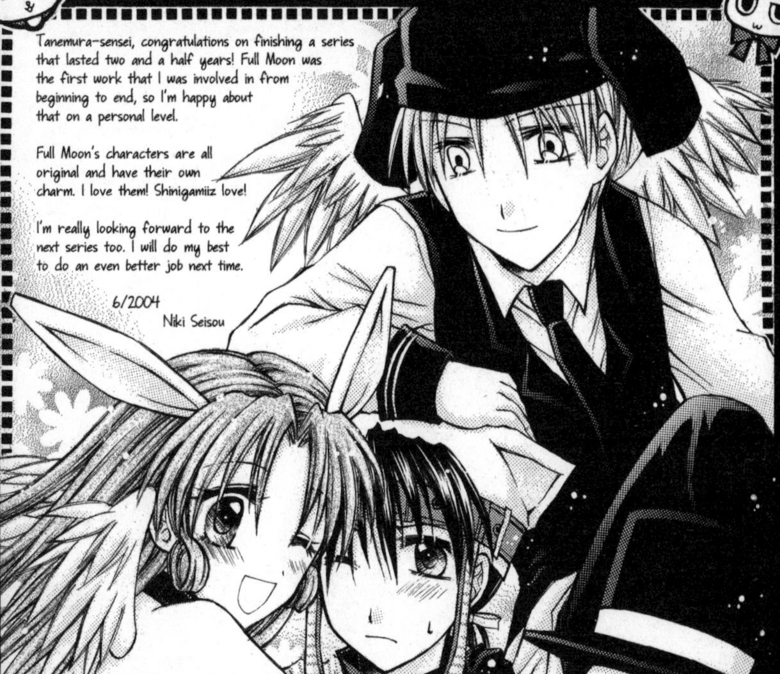
Tanemura-sensei, congratulations on finishing a series that lasted two and a half years! Full Moon was the first work that I was involved in from beginning to end, so I'm happy about that on a personal level.
Full Moon's characters are all original and have their own charm. I love them! Shinigamiiz love!
I'm really looking forward to the next series too. I will do my best to do an even better job next time.
6/2004
Niki Seisou

NIKI SEISOU

It's cool that the illustration is full of Shinigamiiz! Jona's nose is rounder than when I draw it, and this is good in its own way. Looks like he deceives people. (Is this a critique of the Manga School? You.)

Yes...I'd like you to work more on backgrounds, but if I'm having spasms, I want you to go get someone at least. (smile)

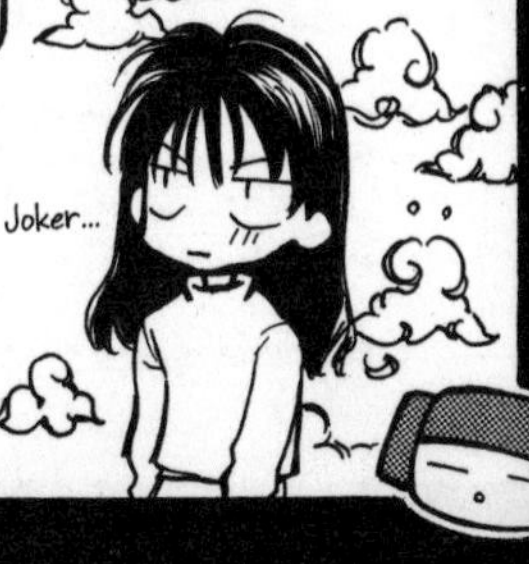
Joker...

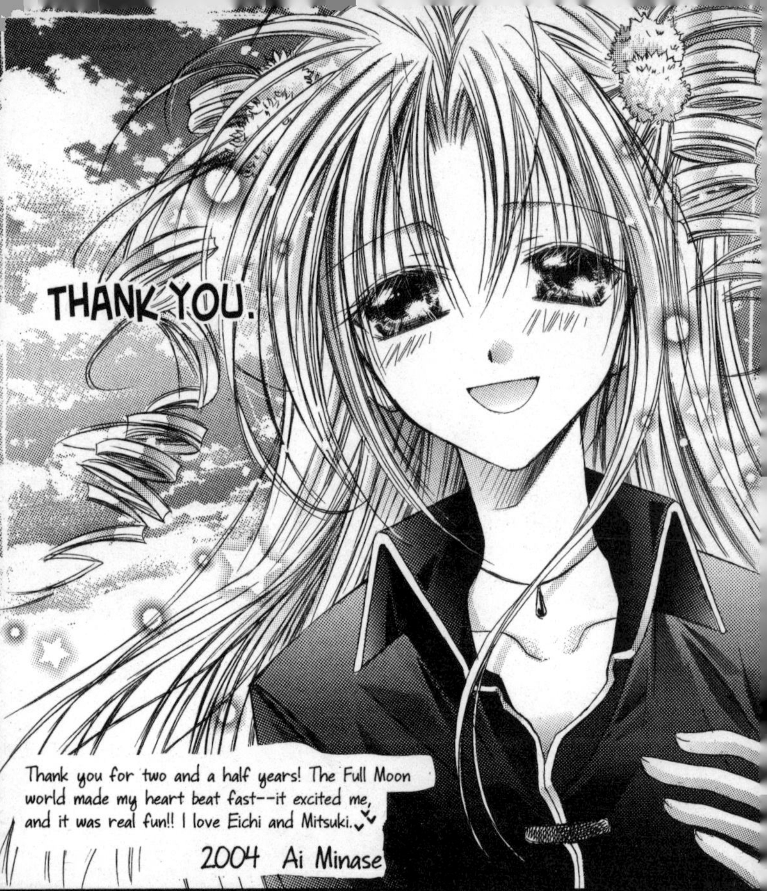
THANK YOU.
Thank you for two and a half years! The Full Moon world made my heart beat fast--it excited me, and it was real fun!! I love Eichi and Mitsuki.
2004 Ai Minase

AI MINASE (Gya Mo)

↑ Nickname

✿ Oh, a beautiful illustration! It's beautiful.
When you wake up, let's eat sushi together. Oh, you want to go too, Niki-sama? (I'm with them when I'm writing this, so it's a real-time message to them.) ...Don't do that... (smile)

✧ Eichi and Mitsuki are forever!!

✿Arina✿

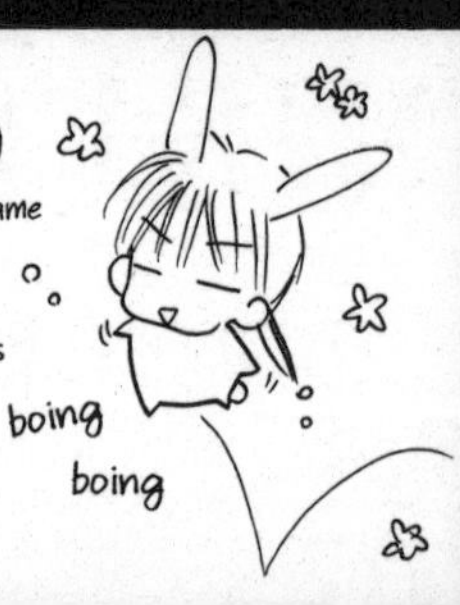
boing
boing

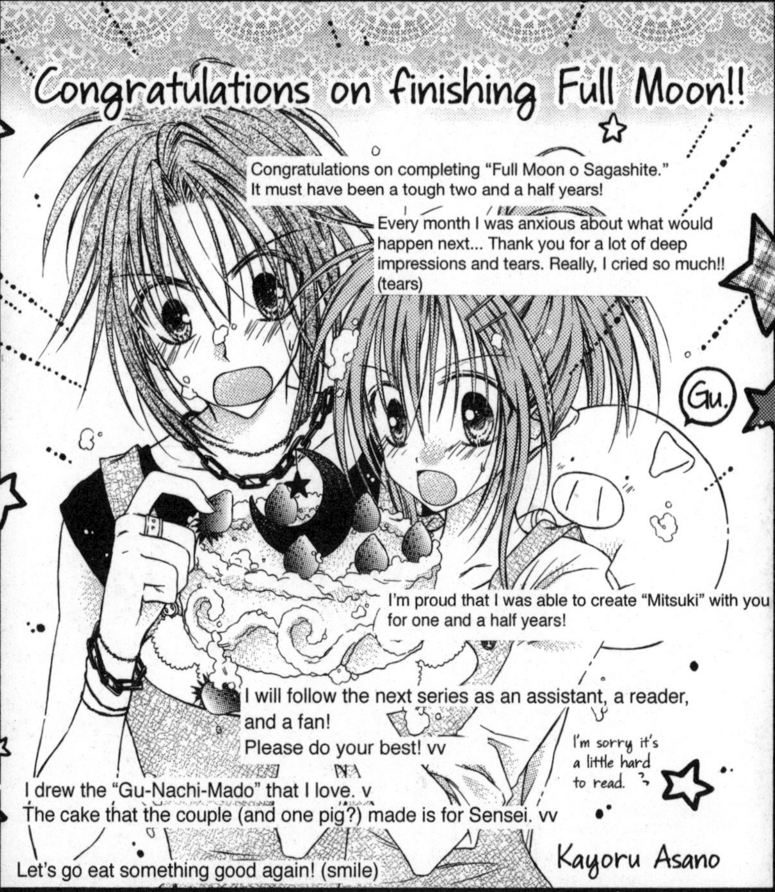
Congratulations on finishing Full Moon!!
Congratulations on completing "Full Moon o Sagashite." It must have been a tough two and a half years!
Every month I was anxious about what would happen next... Thank you for a lot of deep impressions and tears. Really, I cried so much!! (tears)
Gu.
I'm proud that I was able to create "Mitsuki" with you for one and a half years!
I will follow the next series as an assistant, a reader, and a fan!
Please do your best! vv
I'm sorry it's a little hard to read.
I drew the "Gu-Nachi-Mado" that I love. v
The cake that the couple (and one pig?) made is for Sensei. vv
Let's go eat something good again! (smile)
Kayoru Asano

KAYORU ASANO

Yay! v Yay! v It's Kayorun's Gu-Nachi-Mado. vvv
Cute! Ooooh! I love these three! Oooh! Lovely!! vv

Why is Gutchan so round? Is he a balloon?
Please find a favorite character in the next series too, and devote your affection to your screentone work.

Arina

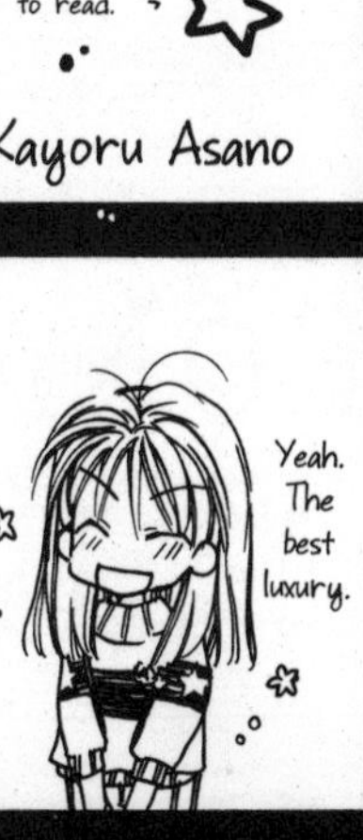
Yeah. The best luxury.

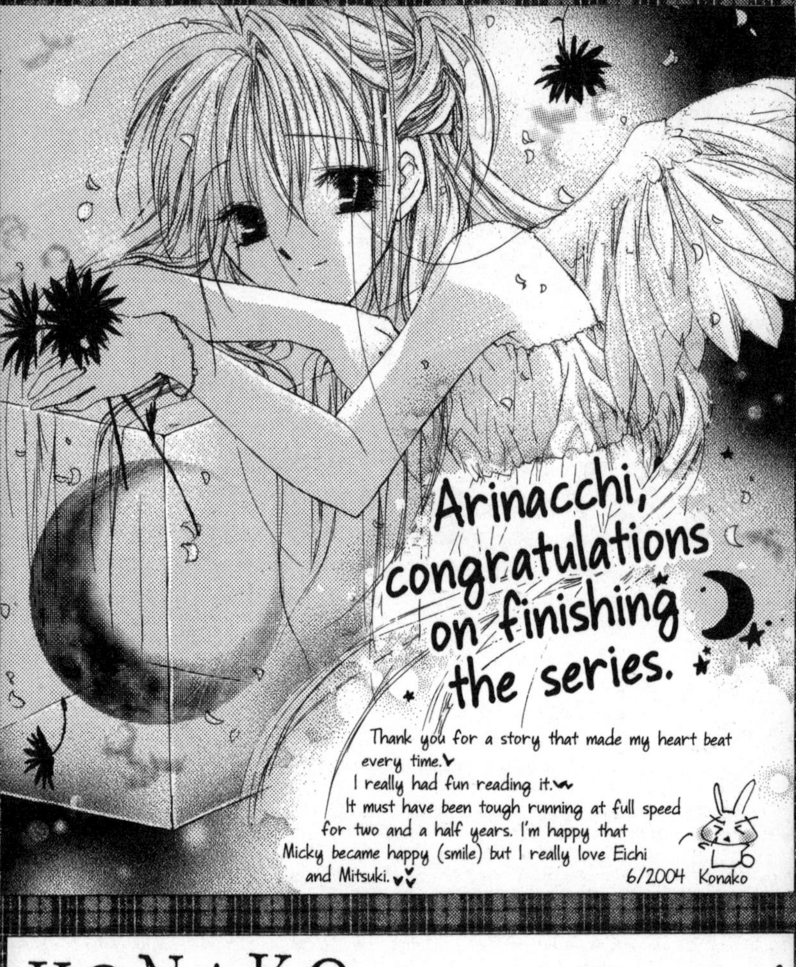
Arinacchi, congratulations on finishing the series.
Thank you for a story that made my heart beat every time.
I really had fun reading it.
It must have been tough running at full speed for two and a half years. I'm happy that Micky became happy (smile) but I really love Eichi and Mitsuki.
6/2004 Konako

KONAKO

Oh, your illustration is fantasy-like as usual!
I like Kona-chan's taste.
Eichi and Mitsuki are forever! Yes. —
Please help out with the new series too. —

Arina

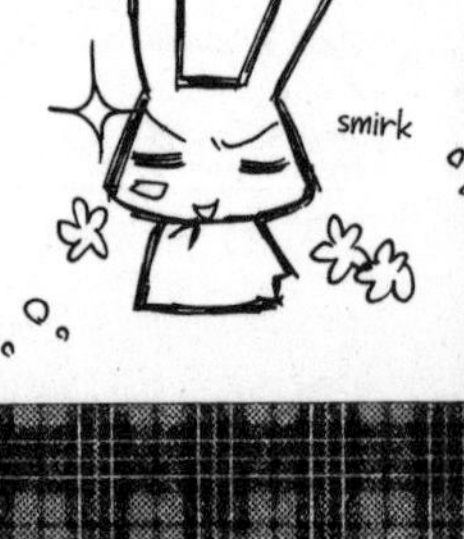
smirk

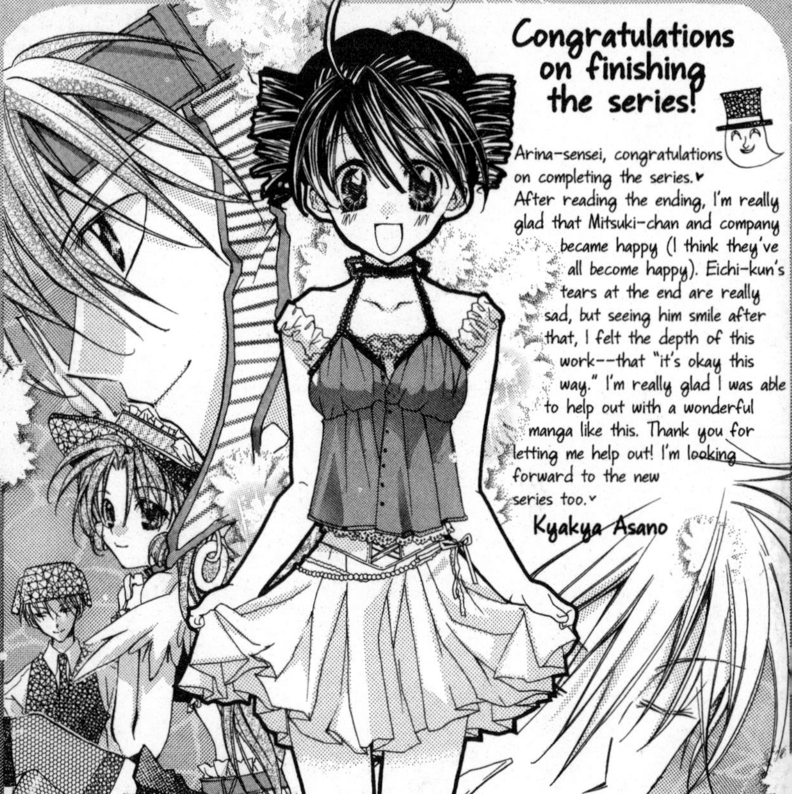
Congratulations on finishing the series!
Arina-sensei, congratulations on completing the series.♥ After reading the ending, I'm really glad that Mitsuki-chan and company became happy (I think they've all become happy). Eichi-kun's tears at the end are really sad, but seeing him smile after that, I felt the depth of this work--that "it's okay this way." I'm really glad I was able to help out with a wonderful manga like this. Thank you for letting me help out! I'm looking forward to the new series too.♥
Kyakya Asano

KYA KYA ASANO

Ainya and Niki-sama said this looks scary. To Asano-san, with my love.

✿ I really like Meroko's face in the above illustration! Cute! ~♥♥♥

I'm sad that you've made no mistakes in your spelling! What happened?? But I did find a misspelling so I was a little relieved (sorry). Yes, that's our Asa-chan!!

Let's go for karaoke again! And to game arcades!

✿Arina✿

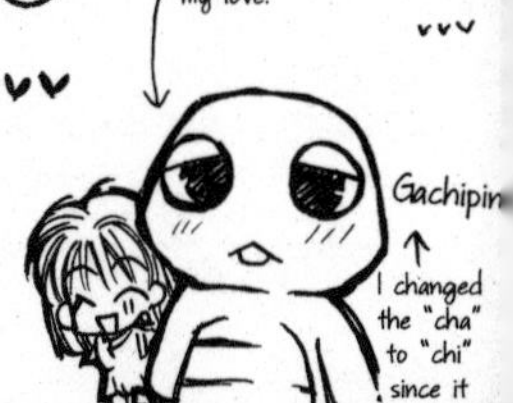
Gachipin
I changed the "cha" to "chi" since it doesn't look like Gachapin.

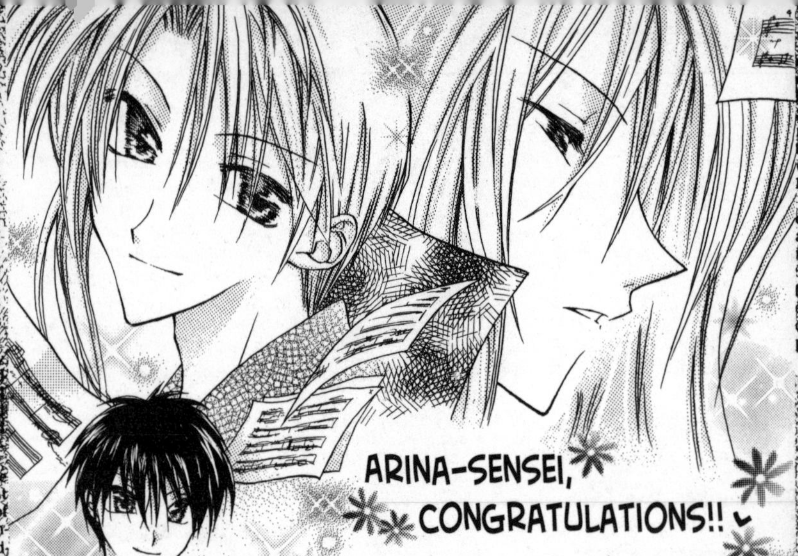

ARINA-SENSEI, CONGRATULATIONS!!

It must have been tough to do a series that lasted for two and a half years.

I helped out towards the end, watching sensei's passion up close...I came to love "Full Moon" even more. I really love it.

Thank you for creating such a wonderful work.

I'm looking forward to the next series too!!

2004 Saori Hinano

I drew ROUTE..L as you requested. (smile)

SAORI HINANO

Yay, it's ROUTE..L~~! Lookin' good!
I loved ROUTE..L too, though I like all the Full Moon characters. I like their aura.

Let's talk about the next series at night too and have fun!

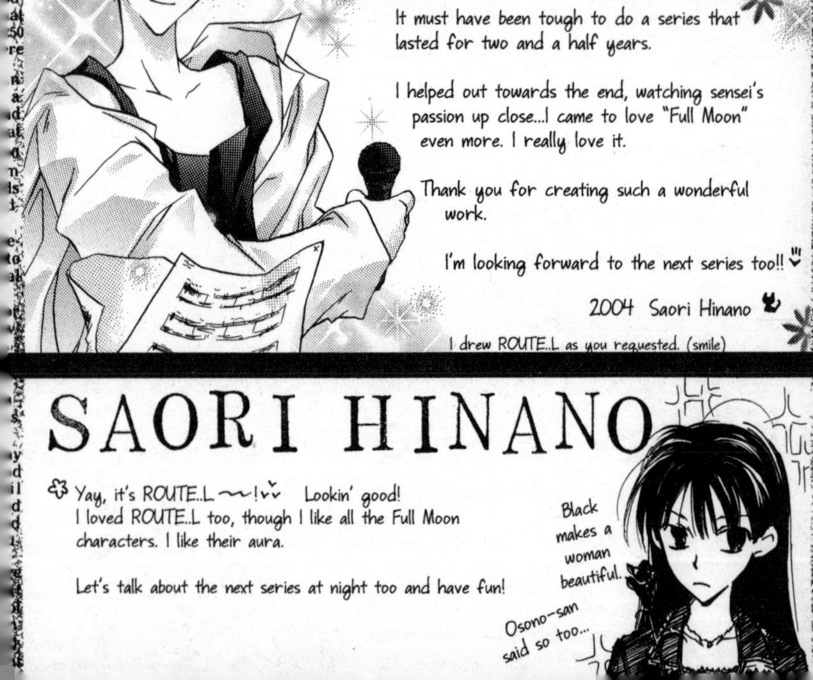
Black makes a woman beautiful.
Osono-san said so too...

CONGRATULATIONS, ARINA-SENSEI.

Congratulations on finishing "Full Moon o Sagashite"!

The Full Moon characters are all cute and cool and I love them.

I love the final chapter.

touched

Thank you for a wonderful work. I'm really looking forward to the next series too! I'll always support you!!

From Ruka Kaduki

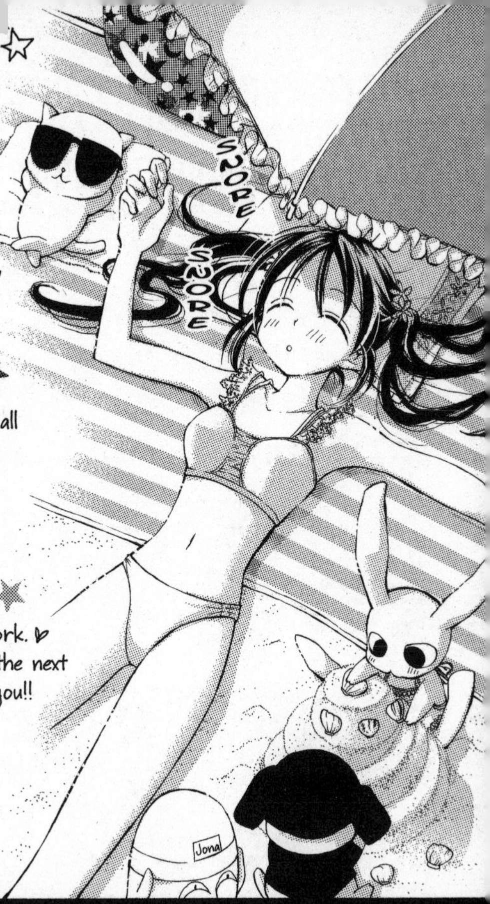
SNORE
SNORE
SNORE
Jona

RUKA KADUKI

Kyaa! Extremely pretty! Especially Meroko!
She's cute! Too cute.
Takuto's sunglasses are um...too big! (smile) (a Bud Abbott)

Rukacchi's parakeet is really cute! Please draw a manga (in Nagoya-ben dialect) where a parakeet appears.

Arina

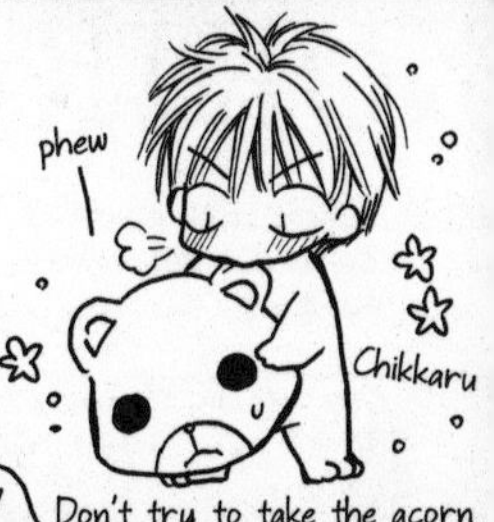
phew
Chikkaru

Don't try to take the acorn on my favorite Totoro clock.

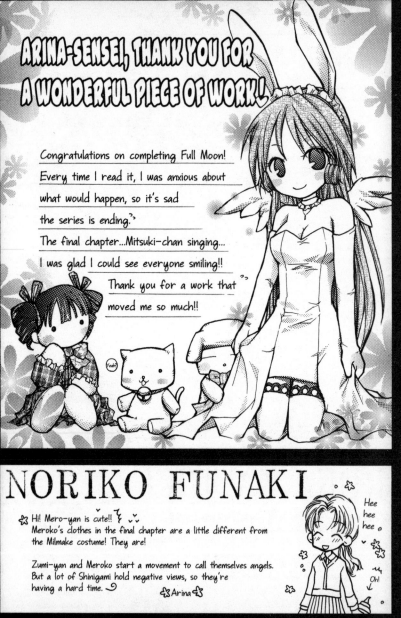

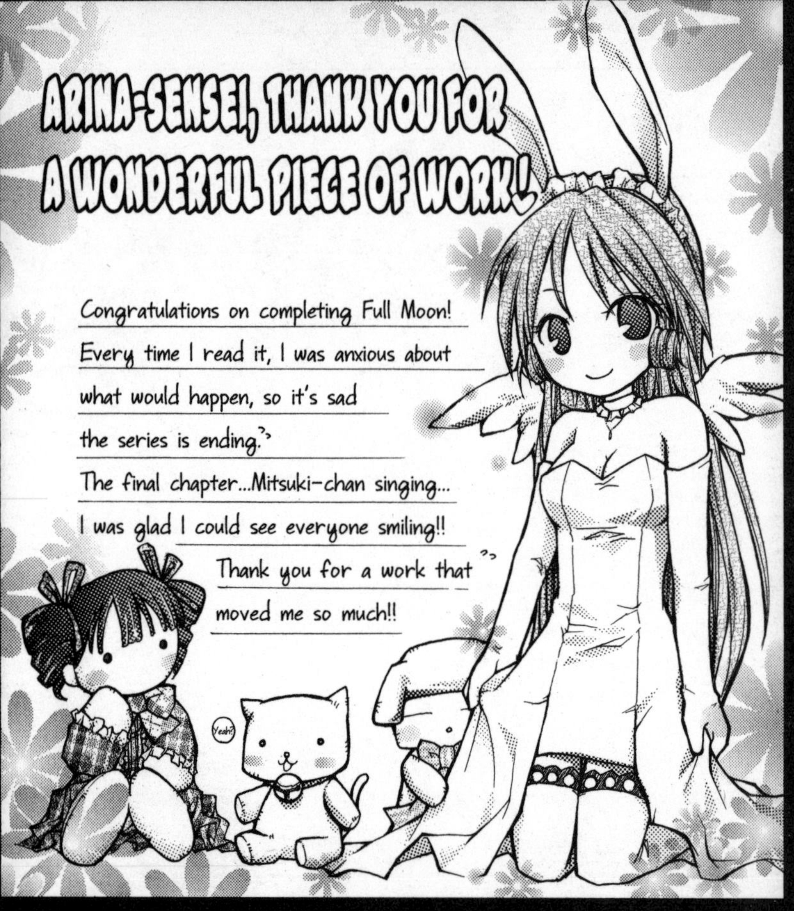
ARINA-SENSEI, THANK YOU FOR A WONDERFUL PIECE OF WORK!
Congratulations on completing Full Moon!
Every time I read it, I was anxious about
what would happen, so it's sad
the series is ending.
The final chapter...Mitsuki-chan singing...
I was glad I could see everyone smiling!!
Thank you for a work that
moved me so much!!
Yeah?

NORIKO FUNAKI

Hi! Mero-yan is cute!!
Meroko's clothes in the final chapter are a little different from the Milmake costume! They are!

Zumi-yan and Meroko start a movement to call themselves angels. But a lot of Shinigami hold negative views, so they're having a hard time.

Arina

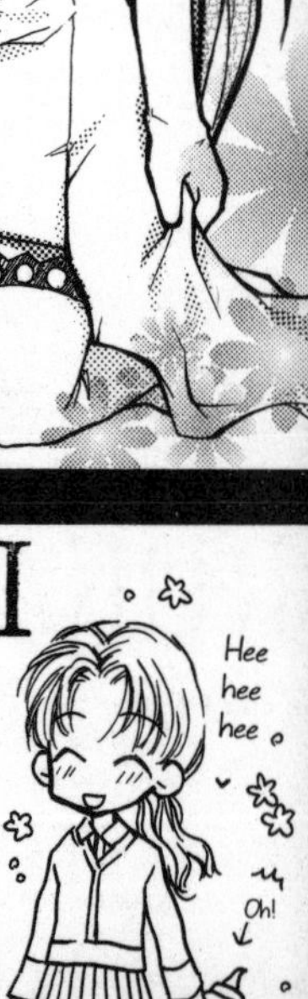
Hee
hee
hee
Oh!

It's finally over, and I feel lonely, but I was moved.

I couldn't help out in the second half, but on the other hand, I was able to really look forward to the magazine every month, as a reader and a fan, until the end (killing two birds with one stone). (smile)

I'm happy that I was able to get to know wonderful characters (especially Takuto!) in a story I could really get into.

I love "Full Moon o Sagashite." Thank you so much!

Rina Asuka

RINA ASUKA

❀ I haven't seen you at all recently. How're you doing? But when I drew Takuto, I was remembering you somewhere in my heart.

I hope you'll read my next series too. ✌✌

♪The girls that Rina-chan draws are cute. ☺ ✌✌

❀ Arina ❀

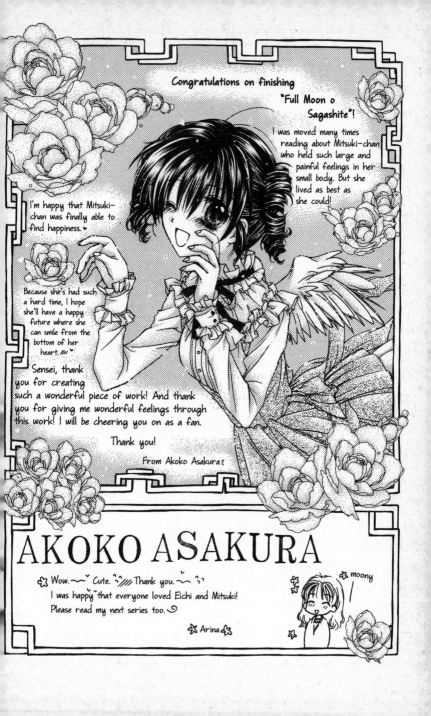

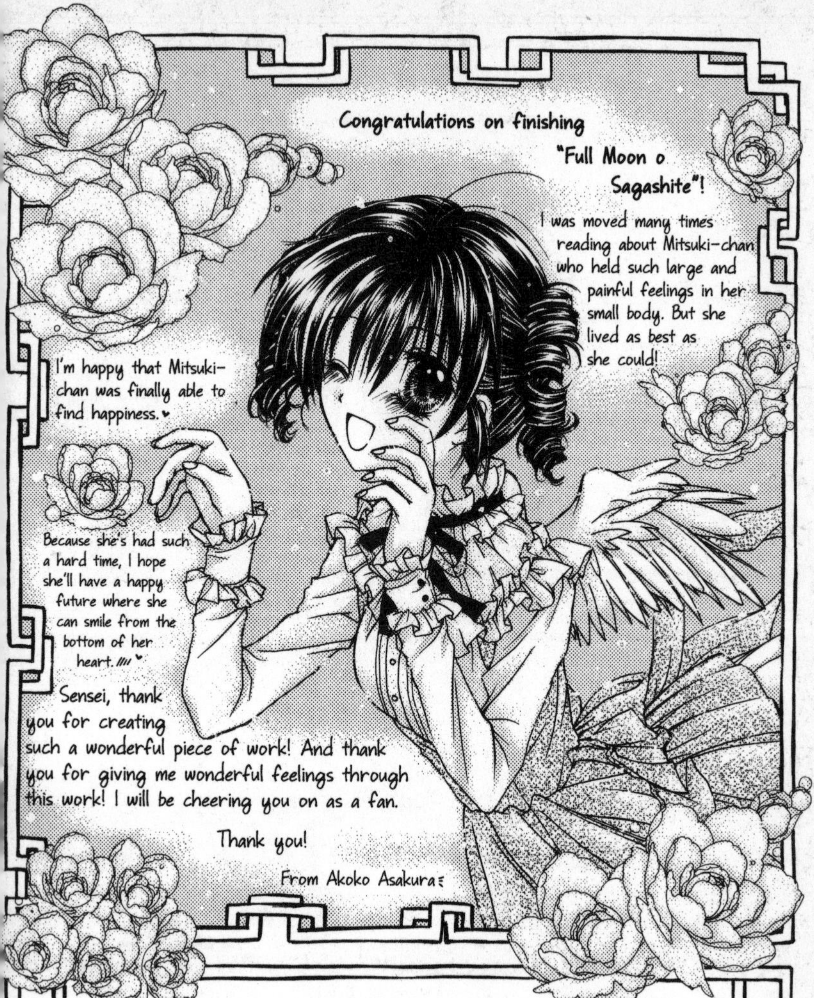
Congratulations on finishing "Full Moon o Sagashite"!
I was moved many times reading about Mitsuki-chan who held such large and painful feelings in her small body. But she lived as best as she could!
I'm happy that Mitsuki-chan was finally able to find happiness.
Because she's had such a hard time, I hope she'll have a happy future where she can smile from the bottom of her heart.
Sensei, thank you for creating such a wonderful piece of work! And thank you for giving me wonderful feelings through this work! I will be cheering you on as a fan.
Thank you!
From Akoko Asakura

AKOKO ASAKURA

Wow. Cute. Thank you.
I was happy that everyone loved Eichi and Mitsuki!
Please read my next series too.

Arina

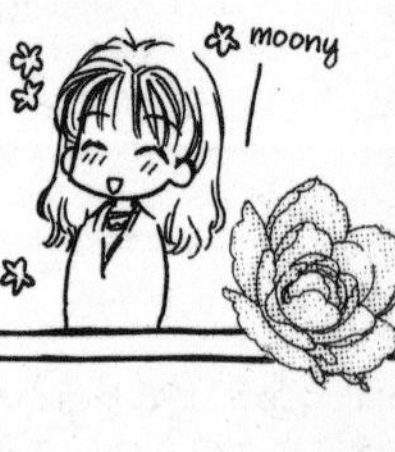
moony

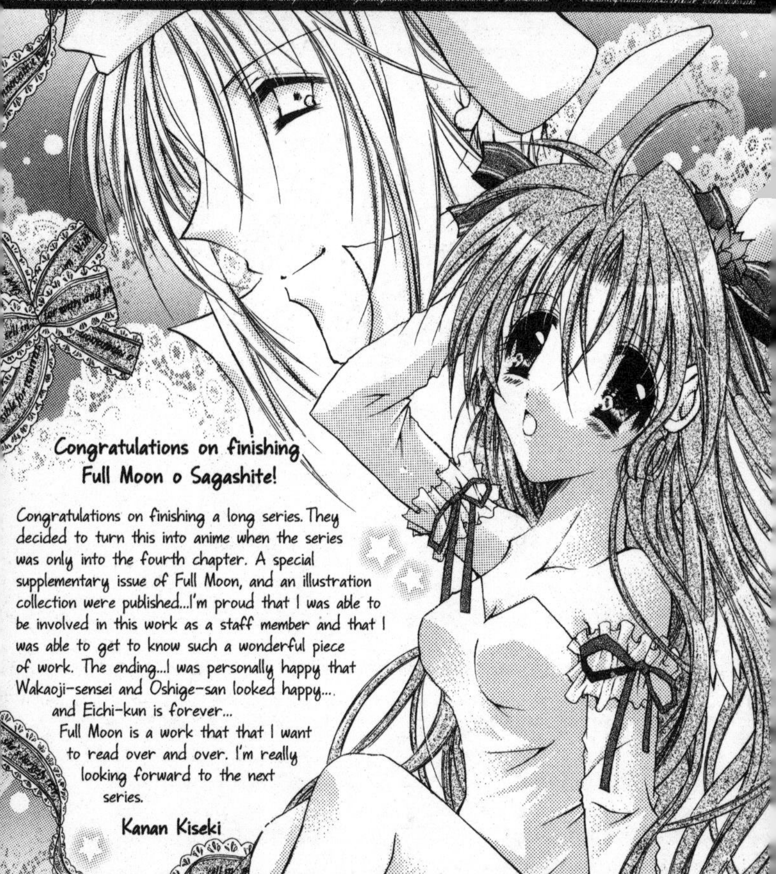

Congratulations on finishing Full Moon o Sagashite!

Congratulations on finishing a long series. They decided to turn this into anime when the series was only into the fourth chapter. A special supplementary issue of Full Moon, and an illustration collection were published...I'm proud that I was able to be involved in this work as a staff member and that I was able to get to know such a wonderful piece of work. The ending...I was personally happy that Wakaoji-sensei and Oshige-san looked happy.... and Eichi-kun is forever...
Full Moon is a work that that I want to read over and over. I'm really looking forward to the next series.

Kanan Kiseki

KANAN KISEKI

Wow! A cute Milmake!!
Yes...many things happened with Full Moon.
I'll do my next series with even more and more power, so please watch over it. (I think that the doctor might be someone Kanana might like.)
Let's go out and do something again.

Arina

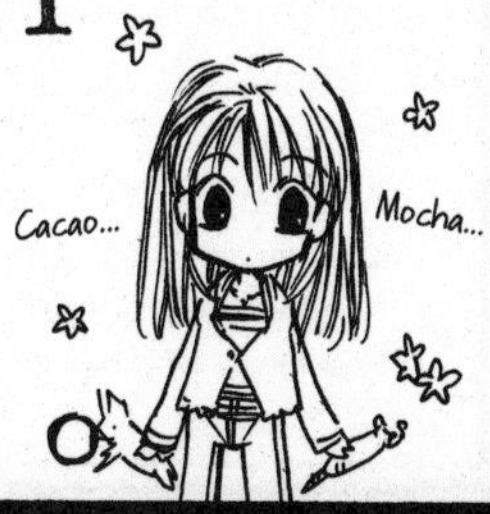
Cacao...
Mocha...

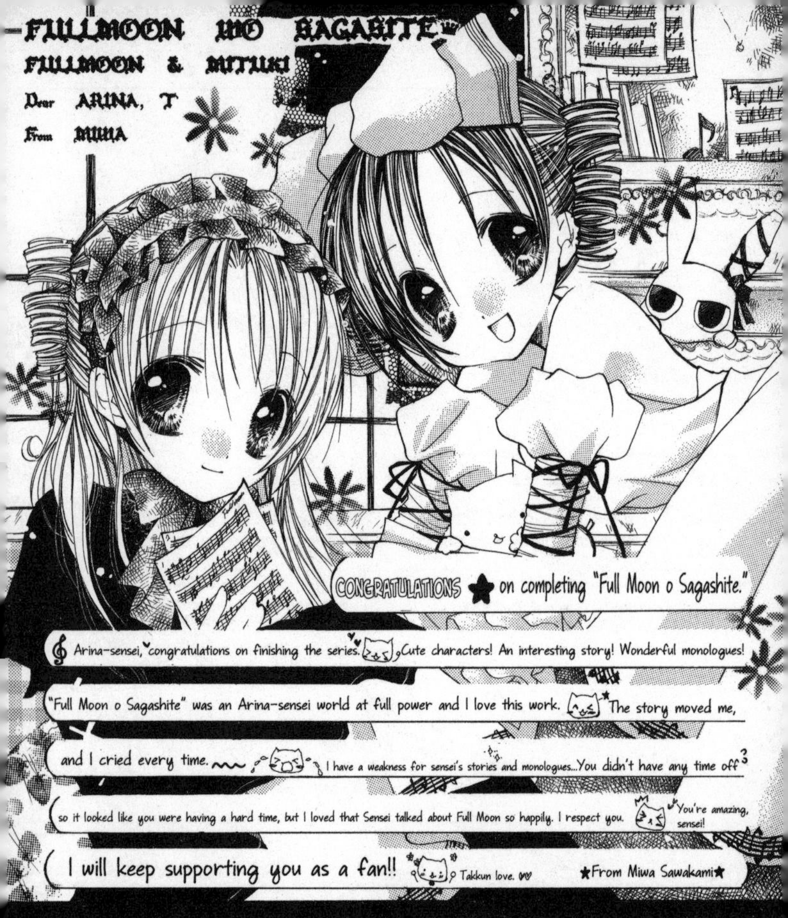
FULLMOON WO SAGASITE
FULLMOON & MITUKI
Dear ARINA, T
From MIWA
CONGRATULATIONS on completing "Full Moon o Sagashite."
Arina-sensei, congratulations on finishing the series. Cute characters! An interesting story! Wonderful monologues!
"Full Moon o Sagashite" was an Arina-sensei world at full power and I love this work. The story moved me,
and I cried every time. I have a weakness for sensei's stories and monologues...You didn't have any time off
so it looked like you were having a hard time, but I loved that Sensei talked about Full Moon so happily. I respect you. You're amazing, sensei!
I will keep supporting you as a fan!! Takkun love.
★From Miwa Sawakami★

MIWA SAWAKAMI

☆ Sawakami Mika-chan, who does backgrounds. Mitsuki-chan and Fullmoon-chan are cute. The cat Takuto that Michan draws is really cute.

Do I talk about it so happily? I don't know. The next time we meet, I want to have a lively conversation about The Gentlemen's Alliance! Thank you very much.

Arina

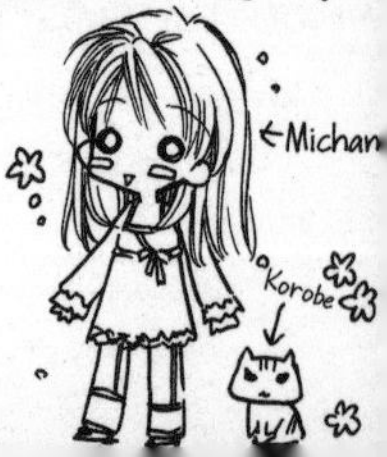
←Michan
Korobe

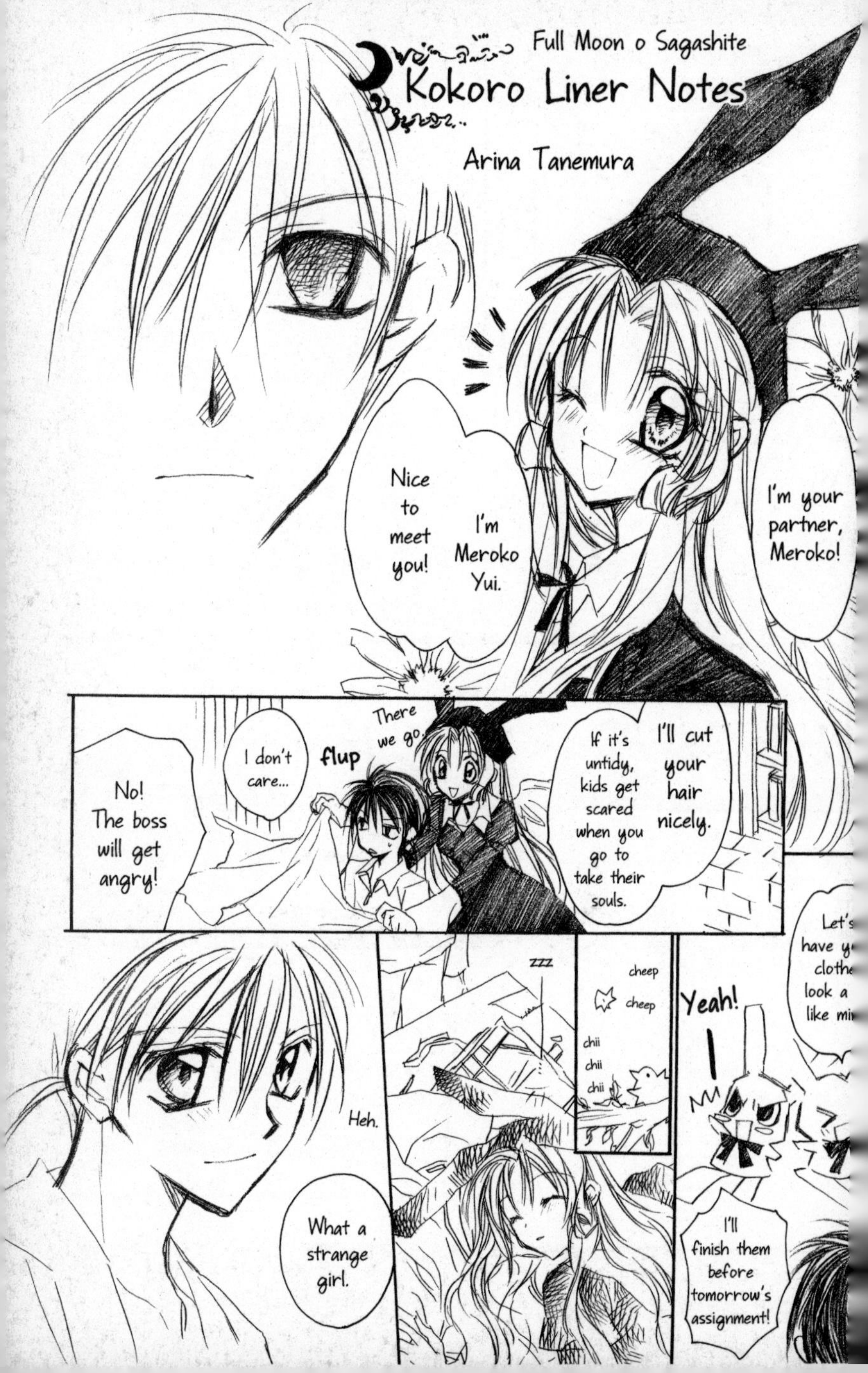
Full Moon o Sagashite
Kokoro Liner Notes
Arina Tanemura
I'm your partner, Meroko!
I'm Meroko Yui.
Nice to meet you!
I'll cut your hair nicely.
If it's untidy, kids get scared when you go to take their souls.
There we go.
flup
I don't care...
No! The boss will get angry!
Let's have y clothe look a like mi
Yeah!
I'll finish them before tomorrow's assignment!
cheep cheep
chii chii chii
zzz
Heh.
What a strange girl.

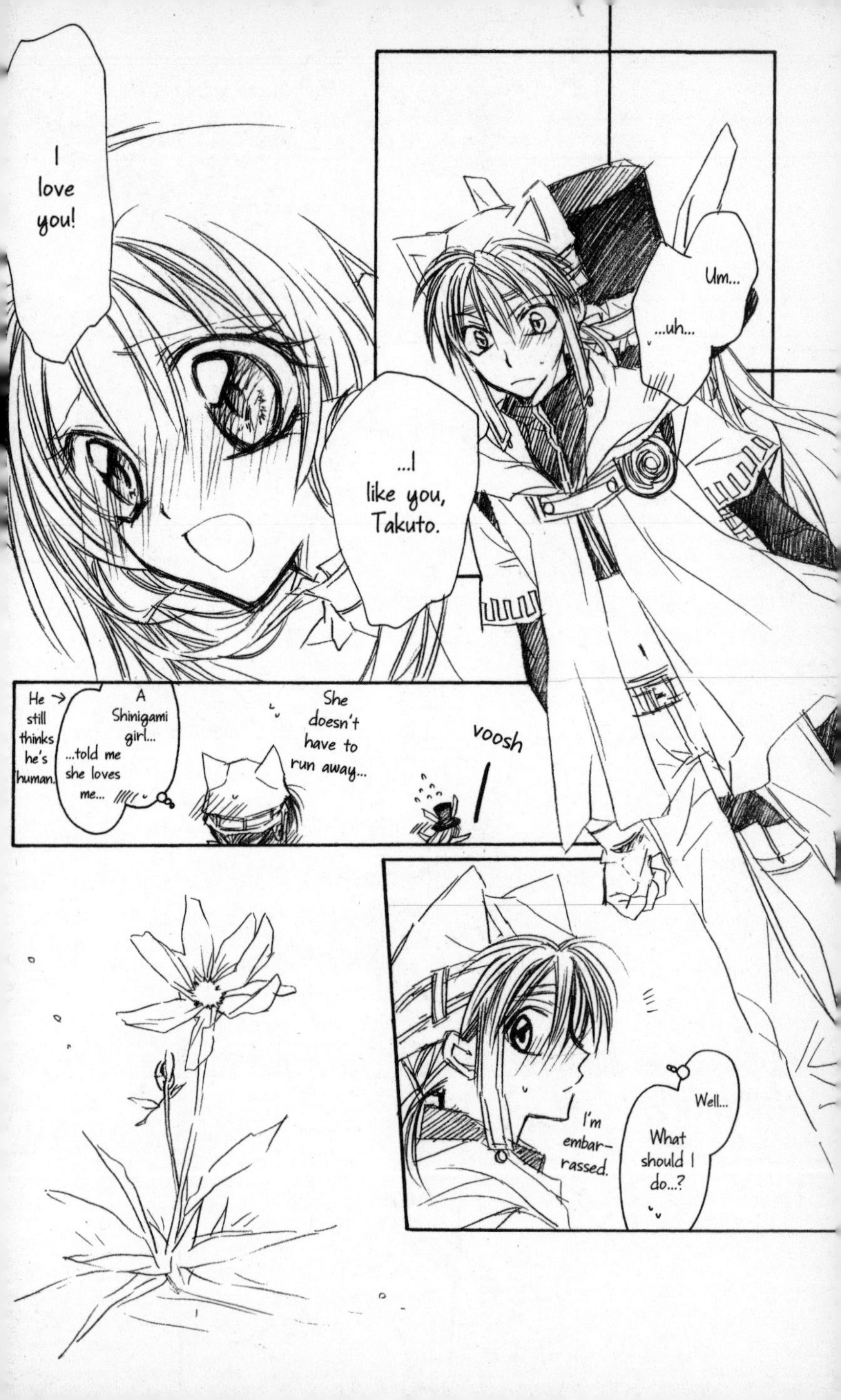
Um...
...uh...
...I like you, Takuto.
I love you!
voosh
She doesn't have to run away...
A Shinigami girl...
...told me she loves me...
He → still thinks he's human.
Well...
What should I do...?
I'm embarrassed.

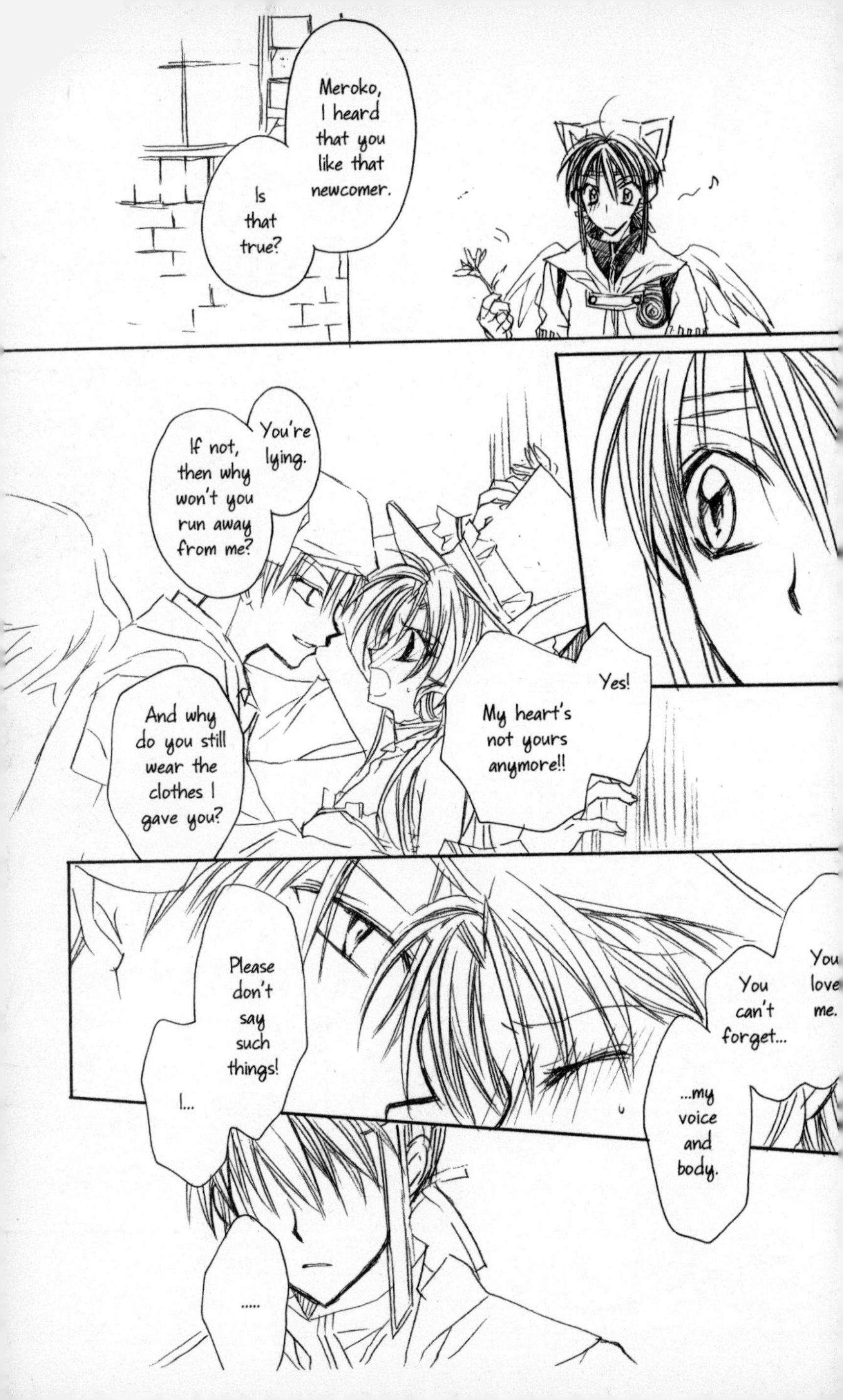
Meroko, I heard that you like that newcomer.
Is that true?
Yes!
My heart's not yours anymore!!
You're lying.
If not, then why won't you run away from me?
And why do you still wear the clothes I gave you?
You love me.
You can't forget...
...my voice and body.
Please don't say such things!
I...
.....

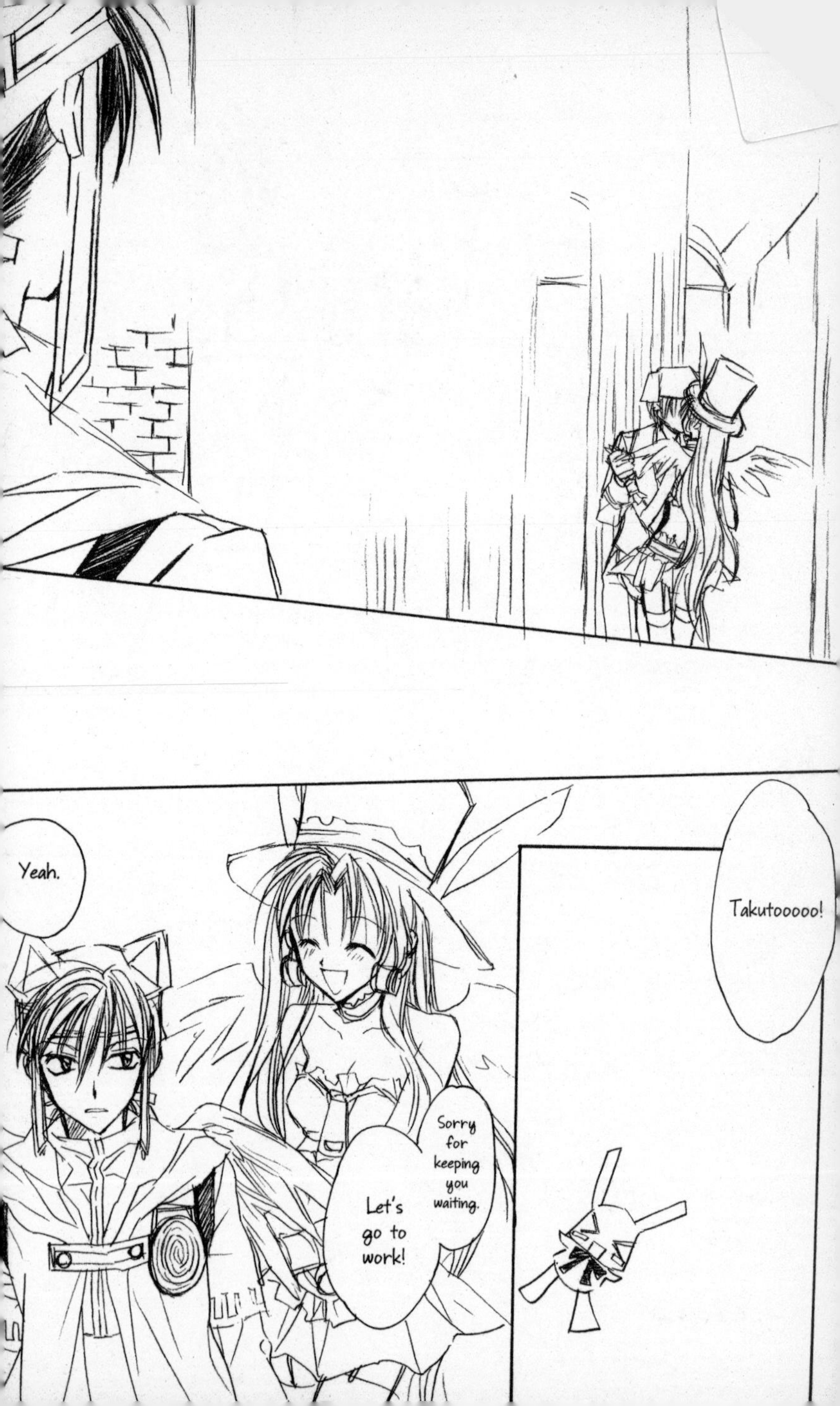
Takutooooo!
Sorry for keeping you waiting.
Let's go to work!
Yeah.

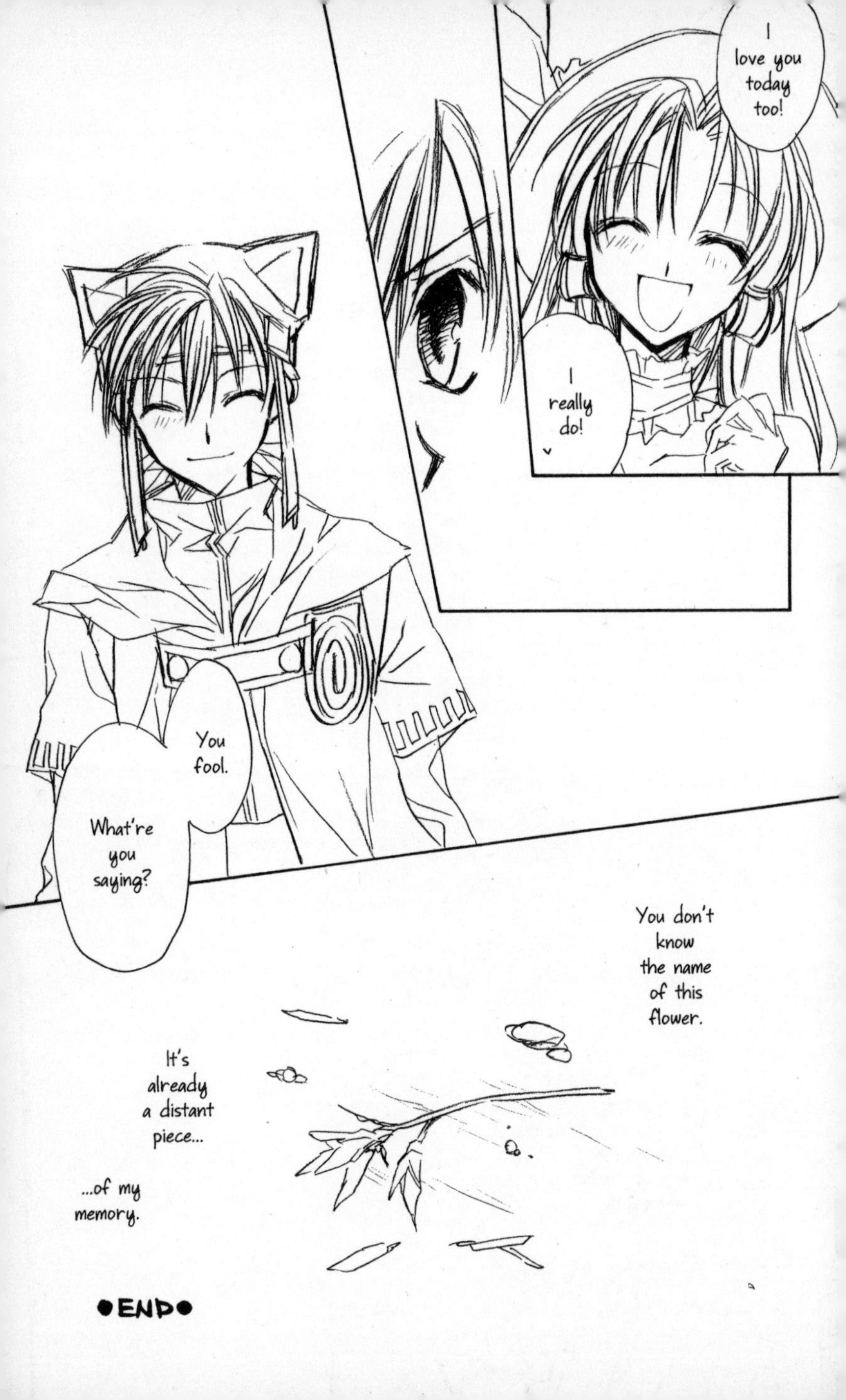
I love you today too!
I really do!
You fool.
What're you saying?
You don't know the name of this flower.
It's already a distant piece...
...of my memory.
END

Author Bio

Arina Tanemura was born in Aichi, Japan. She got her start in 1996, publishing *Nibanme no Koi no Katachi (The Style of the Second Love)* in *Ribon Original* magazine. Her early work includes a collection of short stories called *Kanshaku Dama no Yuutsu* (Short-Tempered Melancholic). Two of her titles, *Kamikaze Kaito Jeanne* and *Full Moon,* were made into popular TV series. Tanemura enjoys karaoke and is a huge *Lord of the Rings* fan.

This is the end. From the first chapter, I had decided to draw about "a girl who's lost her dear one, but still decides to live with those who are alive." But Eichi became a big presence for me too, so the story ended like this. I'd be happy if you could understand what life is, even if just a little...

Full Moon o Sagashite

Vol. 7
The Shojo Beat Manga Edition

STORY & ART BY
ARINA TANEMURA

English Translation & Adaptation/Tomo Kimura
Touch-Up & Lettering/Elena Diaz
Graphics & Cover Design/Izumi Evers
Editor/Nancy Thistlethwaite

Editor in Chief, Books/Alvin Lu
Editor in Chief, Magazines/Marc Weidenbaum
VP of Publishing Licensing/Rika Inouye
VP of Sales/Gonzalo Ferreyra
Sr. VP of Marketing/Liza Coppola
Publisher/Hyoe Narita

Title: Smile
Composer: TANABE, Shintarou
Author: MYCO
© 2002 by ROCK ON PUBLISHERS CO.,
OUR SONGS Inc.,
TV TOKYO Music, Inc.,
RIGHT SONG MUSIC PUBLISHING CO., LTD.,
& PYON ARI MUSIC PUBLISHING INC.

"New Future"
© 2002 by TV TOKYO Music, Inc.
& RIGHT SONG MUSIC PUBLISHING CO., LTD.
& OUR SONGS INC.
& ROCK ON PUBLISHERS CO., LTD.

Printed in Canada

Published by VIZ Media, LLC
P.O. Box 77064
San Francisco, CA 94107

Shojo Beat Manga Edition
10 9 8 7 6 5 4 3
First printing, October 2006
Third printing, January 2008

store.viz.com

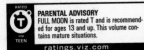

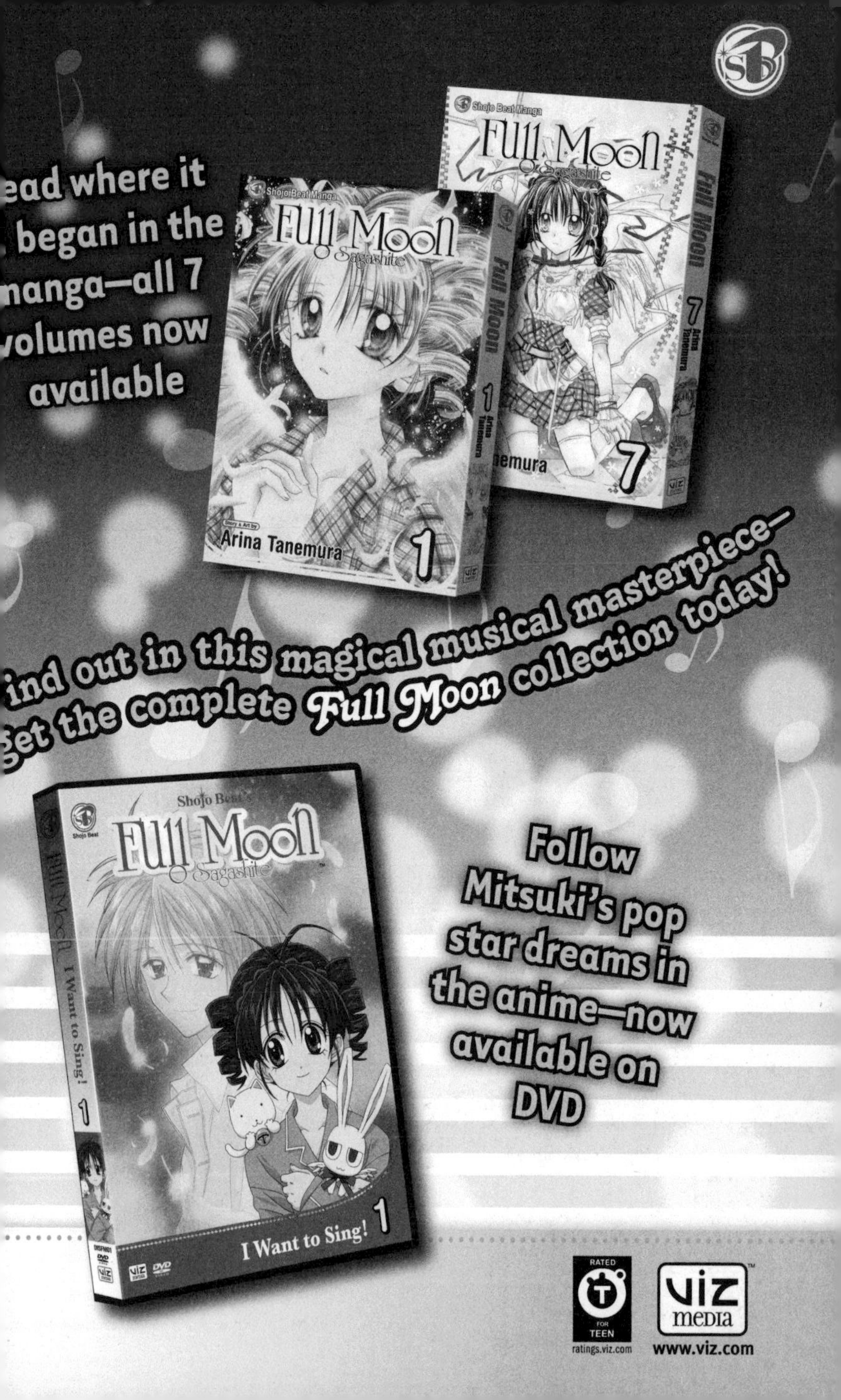
ead where it
began in the
nanga—all 7
volumes now
available
Shojo Beat Manga
Full Moon O Sagashite
Full Moon 1 Arina Tanemura
Story & Art by
Arina Tanemura
1
Full Moon 7 Arina Tanemura
7
ind out in this magical musical masterpiece—
get the complete Full Moon collection today!
Shojo Beat's
Full Moon O Sagashite
I Want to Sing! 1
Follow
Mitsuki's pop
star dreams in
the anime—now
available on
DVD
RATED T FOR TEEN
ratings.viz.com
VIZ media
www.viz.com

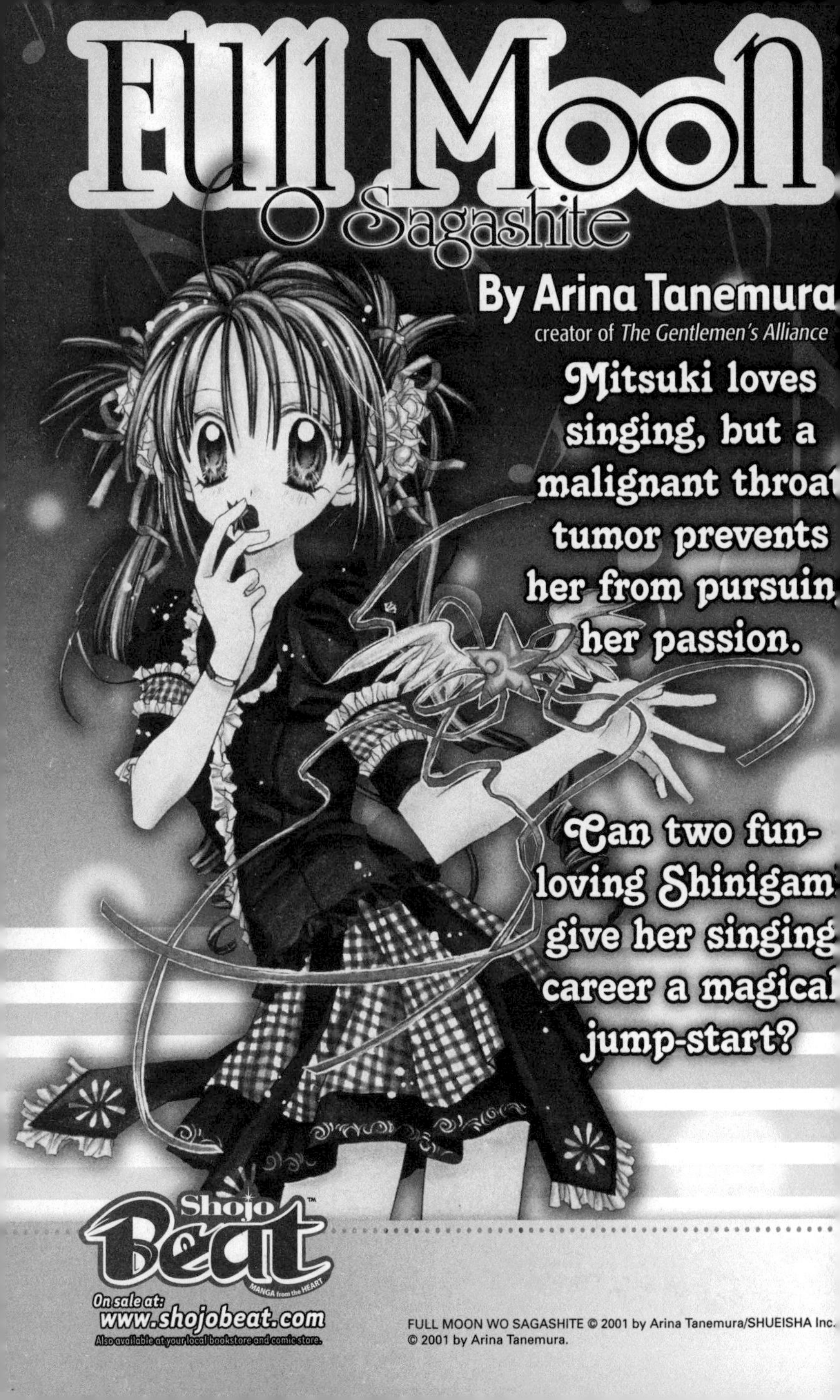
Full Moon
O Sagashite
By Arina Tanemura
creator of *The Gentlemen's Alliance*
Mitsuki loves singing, but a malignant throa tumor prevents her from pursuin her passion.
Can two fun-loving Shinigam give her singing career a magical jump-start?
Shojo Beat
MANGA from the HEART
On sale at:
www.shojobeat.com
Also available at your local bookstore and comic store.
FULL MOON WO SAGASHITE © 2001 by Arina Tanemura/SHUEISHA Inc.
© 2001 by Arina Tanemura.

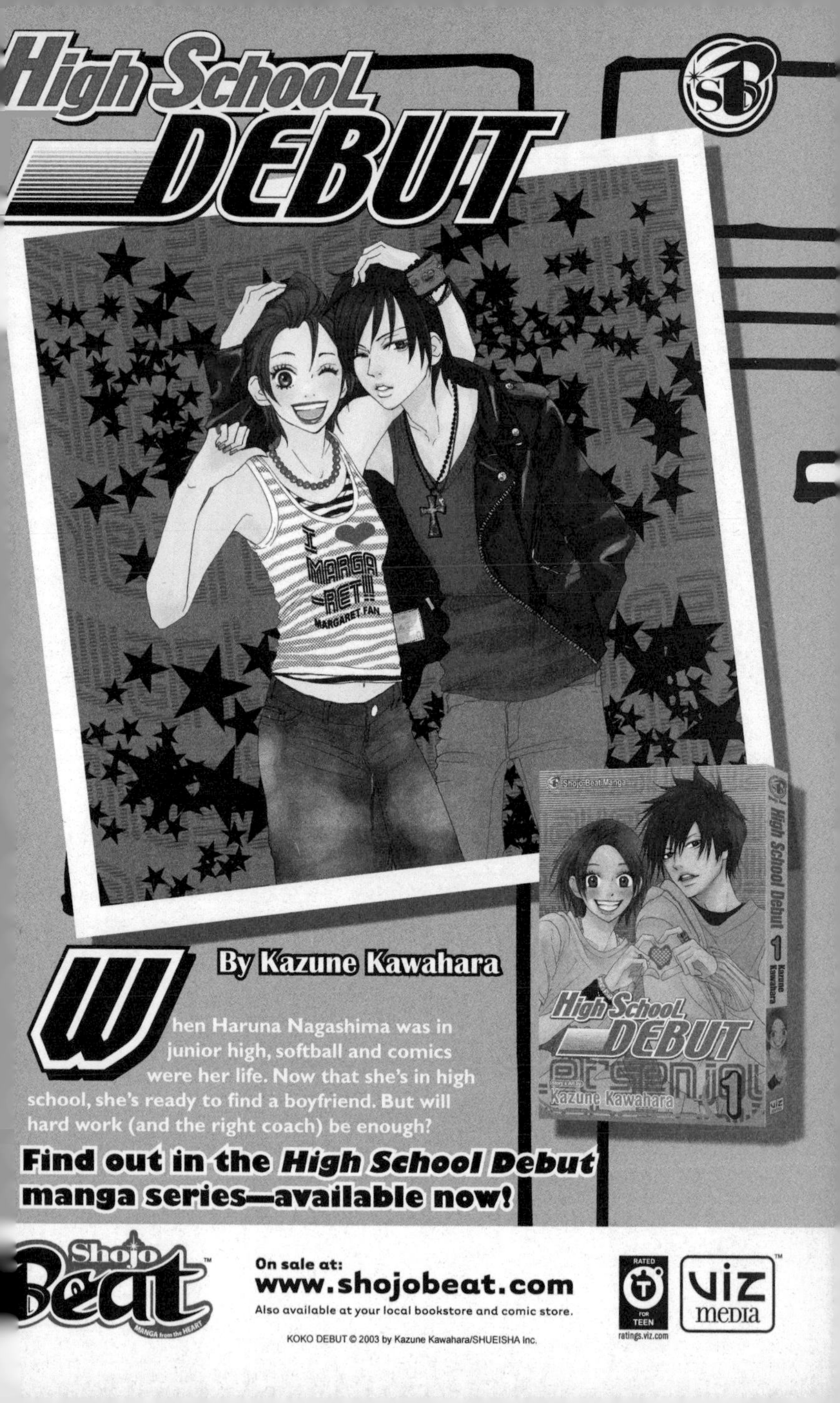
High School DEBUT
By Kazune Kawahara
When Haruna Nagashima was in junior high, softball and comics were her life. Now that she's in high school, she's ready to find a boyfriend. But will hard work (and the right coach) be enough?
Find out in the High School Debut manga series—available now!
I ♥ MARGA-RET!! MARGARET FAN
Shojo Beat Manga
High School Debut 1 Kazune Kawahara
High School DEBUT
Kazune Kawahara
Shojo Beat MANGA from the HEART
On sale at:
www.shojobeat.com
Also available at your local bookstore and comic store.
RATED T FOR TEEN
ratings.viz.com
VIZ media
KOKO DEBUT © 2003 by Kazune Kawahara/SHUEISHA Inc.

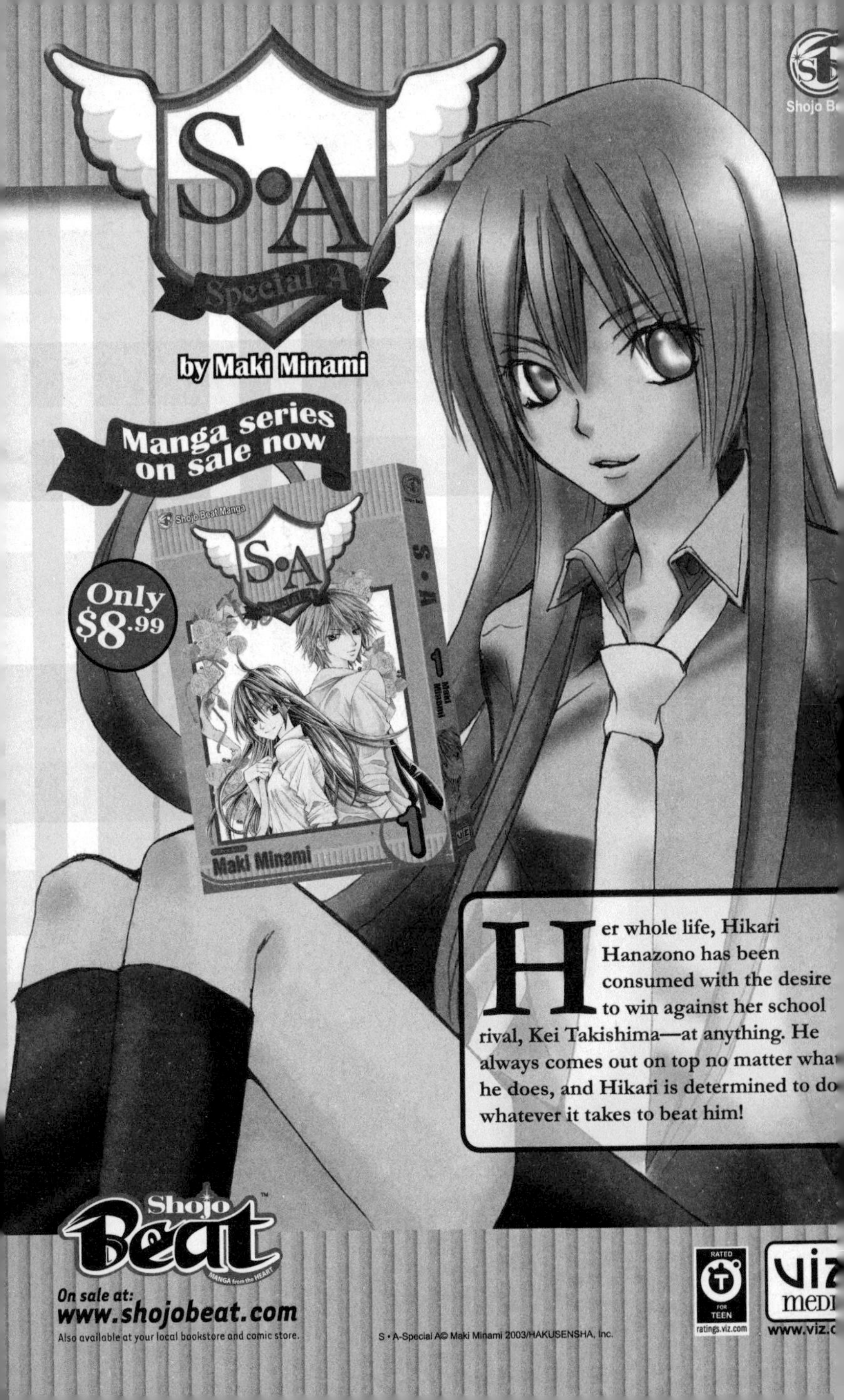
Shojo B
S•A
Special A
by Maki Minami
Manga series on sale now
Shojo Beat Manga
S•A
Only $8.99
S • A
1
Maki Minami
Maki Minami
Her whole life, Hikari Hanazono has been consumed with the desire to win against her school rival, Kei Takishima—at anything. He always comes out on top no matter wha he does, and Hikari is determined to do whatever it takes to beat him!
Shojo™ Beat
MANGA from the HEART
On sale at:
www.shojobeat.com
Also available at your local bookstore and comic store.
S • A-Special A© Maki Minami 2003/HAKUSENSHA, Inc.
RATED
T
FOR TEEN
ratings.viz.com
viz
medi
www.viz.c

Tell us what you think about Shojo Beat Manga!

Our survey is now available online. Go to:

shojobeat.com/mangasurvey

Help us make our product offerings better!

THE REAL DRAMA BEGINS IN...

Love. Laugh. Live.

In addition to hundreds of pages of manga each month, *Shojo Beat* will bring you the latest in Japan fashion, music, art, and culture—plus shopping, how-tos, industry updates, interviews, and much m

DON'T YOU WANT TO HAVE THIS MUCH FU

Only
$34.99 for
12 GIANT Issues
51% OFF
the Cover Price!

Subscribe Now!
Fill out the coupon
on the other side

Or go to:
www.shojobeat.com

Or call toll-free
800-541-787

by MITSUBA TAKANASHI   by TAEKO WATANABE   by MATSURI HINO   by MARIMO RAGAWA   by YUU WAT